The Decline of Authority

The Decline of Authority

PUBLIC ECONOMIC POLICY AND
POLITICAL DEVELOPMENT
IN NEW YORK, 1800–1860

L. RAY GUNN

Cornell University Press

ITHACA AND LONDON

Copyright © 1988 by Cornell University

All rights reserved. Except for brief quotations in a review, this book, or parts
thereof, must not be reproduced in any form without permission in writing
from the publisher. For information, address Cornell University Press,
124 Roberts Place, Ithaca, New York 14850.

First published 1988 by Cornell University Press.

International Standard Book Number 0-8014-2101-2
Library of Congress Catalog Card Number 87-47954
Printed in the United States of America
*Librarians: Library of Congress cataloging information
appears on the last page of the book.*

*The paper in this book is acid-free and meets the guidelines for
permanence and durability of the Committee on Production Guidelines
for Book Longevity of the Council on Library Resources.*

For my mother and father

Contents

Tables

Preface

THIS BOOK investigates the relationship between socioeconomic change, public economic policy, and political development in New York State in the first half of the nineteenth century. It focuses on what I perceive to be a major transformation in the structure and function of state government about mid-century. At the heart of that transformation, which was not unique to New York, was a decline of governmental authority as the state withdrew from interventionist economic policies, wrote a new constitution that prohibited most types of promotional activities, and generally relinquished its role in the allocation of resources. Accompanying this contraction of public authority were equally significant structural changes: increasing voter participation, declining legislative power, the growing significance of the judiciary, the emergence of administration, and the appearance of a form of direct democracy. Together, these developments produced a new configuration of politics and governance in New York.

My purpose here is to explain the emergence of this new political order and, in the process, to assess its significance for our understanding of political development in the nineteenth-century states generally. I have not attempted to write a comprehensive history of New York in this period; nor have I tried to describe and explain all aspects of political change. Rather, the book maps the changing patterns of governance in the state in the middle of the nineteenth century by focusing on three broad problems: the transformation of public policy as revealed in the shifting patterns of economic legislation; the evolution of political "expectations" as reflected in changing constitutional norms; and changes in the process of policy formulation and implementation as reflected in the evolution of governmental structures. I consciously chose

[*ix*]

to focus on the large question of the nature of the political system and the alterations wrought in that system in response to societal changes in the early to mid-nineteenth century. Thus, in addition to being a description of the changing structure of state government and public policy, this book may also be viewed as a speculative essay in applying a broad theoretical perspective to the analysis of American political history.

Adopting such a strategy has necessarily meant rejecting other possible approaches. For the past several decades, studies of electoral behavior and political party development have dominated the field of American political history. The emphasis on critical realignments, party systems, and the ethnocultural roots of voting behavior, the most significant contributions of the "new" political history, has fundamentally transformed our understanding of the nature of American politics. It has become increasingly clear, however, that these approaches are flawed in important respects. The starting point of research has generally been the party or electoral behavior; thus, important aspects of the political system have been neglected. This is perhaps most apparent in the inability of electoral studies to deal satisfactorily with the larger questions of public policy and governance. Even the recent outpouring of works emphasizing the social basis of politics, ideology, and political culture, while extending our knowledge and understanding of political history in exciting new ways, tends not to deal directly with the nature of governance.

The approach of this book differs from others in that I shift the focus from parties and electoral behavior to other, previously neglected aspects of the political system, particularly long-term trends in public economic policy, the state constitutional environment, and the beginnings of administration. My hope is that such a perspective will provide an added dimension to the ongoing dialogue on the character of political change in antebellum America. I might add that although I approach the issue of political development from a direction entirely different from that of much recent scholarship and focus on a different level of the political system, there is nothing inherently inconsistent between these approaches. Indeed, it is the existence of such a rich empirical and interpretive literature in political history that makes such a study possible. I have drawn on that literature wherever appropriate. The reader will note that my interpretation also owes a great deal to the work of legal-economic historians and to political scientists interested in political development and state building.

One final caveat is in order. I have deliberately adopted the terms "modernization" and "political development," despite the controversy surrounding those concepts, because of my belief that American historians need to break out of traditional modes of analysis and begin to reexamine familiar problems and events from new perspectives, ones informed by conscious comparisons with the experiences of other nations, past and present. Admittedly, attempts to construct a general theory of development or a universal sequence of political change, valid across cultures and across time, have not been notably successful. This book makes no attempt to fashion such a theory; nor does it seek to apply one of the several existing formulations slavishly to the New York experience. I have tried to use the modernization concept as a descriptive device to portray the depth and character of socioeconomic change in this period rather than as a proscriptive model of what should have happened. I believe my overall analysis implies significant revision of any notion that modernization was either inevitable or necessarily progressive, especially in the realm of politics and government. However, as a heuristic device for examining the relationship over time between a rapidly changing socioeconomic environment, political and institutional change, political culture, and public policy, the approach remains fruitful. Judiciously applied, it is a valid point of departure for historians interested in looking beyond formal institutions of government and traditional political concepts to a more functional view of the American political system. By focusing on the political response to socioeconomic modernization in New York over an extended period of time, I have sought to identify patterns of change and adaptation which have thus far eluded historians employing other interpretive models.

I HAVE accumulated many debts over the years this book has been in preparation. It is a pleasure now to acknowledge those debts and to extend my thanks and appreciation to the scholars, friends, and others who contributed in so many ways, both large and small, to the completion of this project. The Rutgers history faculty and graduate students provided an exciting intellectual environment during the early stages of my research and writing. Among the latter, I am especially grateful to Mark Connelly, Norman Katz, Harvey Green, and William B. Waits for their friendship, encouragement, and tolerance during the years of dissertation research and writing. I am also grateful to my teachers at Rutgers: Rudolph M. Bell, Gerald N. Grob, James Kirby Martin, and, for the year he was on loan from Columbia University, Stuart Bruchey. Special thanks are due to Gerald Grob and James Martin for their personal interest in my topic, continual encouragement, and professional advice.

My greatest intellectual and professional debt is to Richard P. McCormick, who first introduced me to political history in his graduate seminar at Rutgers and who infected me with his own contagious faith in the potential for a theory-oriented political history broader in scope than the traditional concerns of parties and elections. Professor McCormick first suggested the general topic from which this study grew and shepherded it and me over many difficult hurdles. Since then, his faith in the project, his constant encouragement, his critical comments on several drafts of the manuscript, and his keen insight into the American political system have been indispensable to the book's completion. His example as scholar and teacher remains a constant source of inspiration.

Several historians read and commented on portions of the book during early drafts of the manuscript. James Roger Sharp's comments on a conference paper dealing with legislative development in New York sharpened my handling of that topic in chapter 3. Richard L. McCormick and Van Beck Hall provided valuable suggestions for an early version of the material on constitutional reform in chapter 6. Portions of chapter 5 were reworked in response to editorial and substantive comments from William Pencak and Conrad Wright. At the University of Utah, Edward J. Davies read the entire manuscript and shared with me his insights into the nature of politics in the nineteenth century. His constant encouragement and reassurances are much appreciated. I am especially grateful to Ronald M. Smelser who, in countless extended conversations, forced me to consider the question of American political development in a larger, comparative framework and provided a friendly, yet rigorously critical, foil for testing ideas. I am also grateful to Lindsay Adams and Ronald Coleman, whose friendship saw me through many difficult moments. Finally, to those many friends and colleagues who listened to my speculative musings with a patience and forebearance beyond the usual demands of friendship and who contributed in so many small but indispensable ways to sharpening the focus of this book, I offer a very special thanks. Any errors of fact or interpretation are, of course, mine alone.

The courteous and professional assistance of the staffs of many libraries was essential to the completion of research for this book. Special appreciation is extended to the staffs of the Rutgers University Library, the Princeton University Library, the Economics Division of the New York Public Library, the Columbia University Library, the New York State Library, the New-York Historical Society Library, and the University of Utah Library.

Rutgers University generously provided financial support while I was a graduate student there. The University of Utah Research Committee provided a Young Faculty Summer Research Grant, which allowed me to spend a summer in New Jersey and New York at a critical juncture in the research.

Portions of chapter 3 previously appeared in *Social Science History* 4 (August 1980), and much of chapter 8 was originally published in *Mid-America* 59 (October 1977). Brief sections of several chapters have been taken from an article in *The Review of Politics* 4 (April 1979). I am grateful to the editors of these journals for their permission to use these materials.

My parents, Carl and Dorothy Frost Gunn, made all of this possible. My brother, Johnny Gunn, was there when I needed him the most. And finally, Susan Cottler shared for a time the burdens of my commitment to this project and contributed to its completion in ways only she and I can appreciate.

L. Ray Gunn

Salt Lake City, Utah

The Decline of Authority

[1]

Introduction: Public Policy and Political Development in the Nineteenth-Century States

THE MIDDLE decades of the nineteenth century witnessed an extraordinary transformation in the structure and function of American state governments. For more than a generation, from the Revolution to the Panic of 1837, Americans had accepted state intervention in the economy as a legitimate, indeed essential, function of government. Mercantilist ideals fashioned in the seventeenth and eighteenth centuries combined with the objective needs of an underdeveloped society to shape a distinctive political economy. Invoking the "public interest" as justification, the states regulated a wide variety of economic activities and consciously sought to stimulate economic growth through positive government action. They subsidized agriculture and industry, invested directly in private enterprise, constructed vast transportation systems at public expense, lent the public credit to private entrepreneurs, and granted special legal privileges to corporations. Beginning about 1840, however, public involvement in the economy began to contract. Mercantilist regulations disappeared from the statute books, and new state constitutions written in the 1830s and 1840s prohibited government promotional activities once considered legitimate. As state governments relinquished their role in the allocation of resources, the private sector expanded to fill the void.[1]

---

[1] For a general view of state economic activity in this period, see Carter Goodrich, *Government Promotion of Canals and Railroads, 1800–1890* (New York, 1960), and Harry N. Scheiber, "Government and the Economy: Studies of the 'Commonwealth' Policy in Nineteenth Century America," *Journal of Interdisciplinary History*, 3 (1972): 135–151.

Fundamental changes were occurring simultaneously in the structure and organization of state political systems. The abolition of property qualifications for voting, accomplished in most states by 1825, together with a general decline of deference and the emergence of mass-based parties broadened the opportunities for popular participation in government. By the 1830s virtually all adult males could vote. Over the next two decades, this trend toward increased participation continued as one state after another extended the elective process to more state offices, shortened terms of office, replaced multiple-member legislative districts with smaller, single-member districts, and delegated political and administrative functions previously performed at the state level to local governing boards or to the electorate.

Perhaps the most significant feature of this political transformation was a decline of legislative power. State legislatures, their authority deeply rooted in the ideology of popular sovereignty and republicanism, had emerged from the Revolution as the dominant institution in the political system. By the 1840s that dominance, and the aura of legitimacy which had sustained it, had begun to disintegrate. Constitutional conventions in this period curtailed legislative authority in a wide range of policy areas and mandated specific policy actions in others. Implicit in this erosion of legislative supremacy was the displacement of power from elected representatives to other forces in the society and political system. The judiciary, for example, became increasingly significant in the first half of the century, largely at the expense of the legislature. Similarly, by the 1850s many policy issues previously handled legislatively were being "administered," through existing departments and agencies, reinvigorated local governments, or, in some cases, private centers of power. Most extraordinary of all, the people themselves came to play a larger direct role in policy making. Certain categories of policy decisions were reserved exclusively to the electorate. A form of direct democracy, in short, began to compete with representation as the basis of government in the mid-nineteenth-century states. On the surface, changes such as these suggest a more energetic and more democratic government. But the long-term implication of these developments was the diffusion of public authority among a number of competing centers of decision making, public and private, in the society.[2]

---

[2] Constitutional developments can be traced in Francis N. Thorpe, comp., *The Federal and State Constitutions*, 7 vols. (Washington, D.C., 1909); Fletcher M. Green, *Constitutional Developments in the South Atlantic States, 1776–1860: A Study in the Evolution of Democracy* (Chapel Hill, N.C., 1930); George Parkinson, "Antebellum State Constitution-Making: Retention, Circumvention, Revision" (Ph.D. diss., University of Wisconsin, 1972); James Q. Dealey, *Growth of American State Constitutions from 1776 to the End of the Year 1914*, 2 vols. (Boston, 1915); Walter F. Dodd, *The Revision and Amendment of State Constitutions* (Baltimore, Md.,

Although the circumstances and timing of these changes varied from state to state, the tendency in the second quarter of the nineteenth century was uniformly in the direction of increasing popular participation and diminishing governmental authority. With the liberalization of suffrage requirements and the emergence of modern political parties to mobilize the electorate, more people enjoyed the opportunity to participate in the political process than ever before in American history. Election returns from the 1830s and 1840s suggest that they took advantage of that opportunity in unprecedented proportions.[3] But as government became more accessible, it also became less authoritative. The scope of public authority contracted, and the role of private decision makers expanded, even as government theoretically became more "democratic." In effect, a new political order predicated on expanded suffrage, equal political rights, government inaction, and subordination of public to private authority had appeared by mid-century. The emergence of this new configuration of politics in New York State and its significance for public policy and political development in nineteenth-century America are the subjects of this book.

SCHOLARS HAVE long recognized that the developments sketched above were central to antebellum American history. Democratization, the changing role of government in the economy, state constitutional reform, and the decline of legislative power are recurrent themes in a vast literature on the Jackson era. The manner in which historians have traditionally dealt with these familiar issues, however, leaves crucial aspects of the emergent political order unexplored. Only very recently, for example, have state legislatures begun to receive the scholarly attention they clearly deserve, and studies of administrative and judicial processes at the state level are woefully lacking. Nor have historians systematically analyzed long-term trends in the structure and content of public policy in the nineteenth century, preferring instead to treat the formulation of public policy primarily in the context of partisan politics or

---

1910); Byron R. Abernethy, *Constitutional Limitations on the Legislature* (Lawrence, Kans., 1959); Richard D. Brown, "The Ideal of the Written Constitution: A Political Legacy of the Revolution," in *Legacies of the American Revolution*, ed. Larry R. Gerlach (Logan, Utah, 1978), 8–101; and Chilton Williamson, *American Suffrage From Property to Democracy, 1760–1860* (Princeton, N.J., 1960).
    ³Richard P. McCormick, "New Perspectives on Jacksonian Politics," *American Historical Review*, 65 (1960): 288–301.

group conflict.[4] The most critical omission, however, has been the failure to develop a satisfactory explanation for the weakening of political authority after the 1830s. In general, historians in the first half of this century attributed diminished governmental power to the impact of laissez-faire ideology or saw it as the logical fulfillment of "Jacksonian Democracy." Eschewing both interpretations, historians since World War II have tended to emphasize such themes as the disintegration of an older "Commonwealth" ideal because of rapid social differentiation and fragmentation; the debilitating effects of localism and underdeveloped administrative structures; the increasing significance of private investment capital; the emergence of equal-rights arguments against state enterprise; or conflicting Whig and Jacksonian concepts of government.[5]

As illuminating as these more recent interpretations have been, they do not explain the decline of public authority in a way that adequately takes into account the restructuring of the political system *as well as* the decline of political involvement in the economy. Increasing specialization and the rise of the "new" economic and political history in the 1960s and 1970s led to the separation of politics and economics in the analysis of public policy in this period. Economic historians tended to focus upon such matters as the further elaboration of "state enterprise" and cost-benefit analysis of government aid relative to the private sector. The political history of the antebellum period moved beyond the "Jacksonian Democracy" controversy to considerations of electoral systems, political party development, and mass political behavior. Although each of these trends advanced our understanding of early-nineteenth-century political economy, neither group of historians produced

---

[4]For a more detailed discussion of these issues, see Van Beck Hall, "A Fond Farewell to Henry Adams: Ideas on Relating Political History to Social Change During the Early National Period," in *The Human Dimensions of Nation-Making: Essays on Colonial and Revolutionary America*, ed. James Kirby Martin (Madison, Wis., 1976); and Richard L. McCormick, "The Party Period and Public Policy: An Exploratory Hypothesis," *Journal of American History*, 66 (September 1979): 279–298.

[5]The list of such studies is extensive, but the following are among the most important: Oscar and Mary Handlin, *Commonwealth, A Study of the Role of Government in the American Economy: Massachusetts, 1774–1861* (Cambridge, Mass., 1947); Louis Hartz, *Economic Policy and Democratic Thought: Pennsylvania, 1776–1860* (Cambridge, Mass., 1948); Milton S. Heath, *Constructive Liberalism: The Role of the State in Economic Development in Georgia to 1860* (Cambridge, Mass., 1954); James N. Primm, *Economic Policy in the Development of a Western State: Missouri, 1820–1860* (Cambridge, Mass., 1954); Harry N. Scheiber, *Ohio Canal Era: A Case Study of Government and Economy, 1820–1861* (Athens, Ohio, 1969); James Willard Hurst, *Law and Economic Growth: The Legal History of the Lumber Industry in Wisconsin, 1836–1915* (Cambridge, Mass., 1964); and Lee Benson, *The Concept of Jacksonian Democracy: New York as a Test Case* (Princeton, N.J., 1961).

a new synthesis of economic and political development to replace the old liberal-progressive interpretation which their work did so much to destroy.[6]

Even the new political history, which a decade and a half ago seemed to promise just such a synthesis, has failed to deal satisfactorily with the larger questions of public policy and the nature of governance. Attempts to link critical realignments and long-term trends in electoral behavior to major shifts in public policy have not been notably successful. Similarly, the ethnocultural interpretation, with its emphasis on the ethnic and religious roots of popular voting behavior, works well as an explanation for certain types of social and cultural policy (temperance, education, sabbath laws, and so on), but hardly works at all as an explanation for economic policy. Recent works focusing on political culture, ideology, and the social basis of politics, while sharpening our understanding of many dimensions of nineteenth-century politics, also fail to address directly the question of the changing nature of governance.[7]

Still, there are encouraging signs that such a synthesis may yet be attainable. Especially promising has been the emergence in recent years of the field of legal-economic history. Building upon the earlier work of Oscar and Mary Handlin, Louis Hartz, and Carter Goodrich, and influenced by James Willard Hurst's view of the relationship between law and social process, scholars

---

[6] Typical of this trend in economic history are Albert Fishlow, *American Railroads and the Transformation of the Antebellum Economy* (Cambridge, Mass., 1965); Robert W. Fogel, *Railroads and American Economic Growth: Essays in Econometric History* (Baltimore, Md., 1964); Carter Goodrich, ed., *Canals and American Economic Development* (New York, 1961); and H. Jerome Cranmer, "Canal Investment in 1815–1860," in *Trends in the American Economy in the Nineteenth Century*, ed. William N. Parker (Princeton, N.J., 1960). Carter Goodrich, "Internal Improvements Reconsidered," *Journal of Economic History*, 30 (June 1970): 289–311, is a good overview of this literature. Representative of this new approach to the political history of the era are Benson, *Concept of Jacksonian Democracy*; Richard P. McCormick, *The Second American Party System: Party Formation in the Jacksonian Era* (Chapel Hill, N.C., 1966); Ronald P. Formisano, *The Birth of Mass Political Parties: Michigan, 1827–1861* (Princeton, N.J., 1971); Ronald P. Formisano, *The Transformation of Political Culture: Massachusetts Parties, 1790s–1840s* (New York, 1983); and William N. Chambers and Walter Dean Burnham, eds., *The American Party Systems: Stages of Political Development* (New York, 1967).

[7] For a perceptive analysis of recent trends in American political history with special emphasis on their implications for the question of governance, see Richard L. McCormick, *The Party Period and Public Policy: American Politics From the Age of Jackson to the Progressive Era* (New York, 1986), especially chaps. 2 and 3. Among the more important recent works treating political culture and the social basis of politics in this period are Formisano, *The Transformation of Political Culture*; Jean H. Baker, *Affairs of Party: The Political Culture of Northern Democrats in the Mid-Nineteenth Century* (Ithaca, 1983); Harry L. Watson, *Jacksonian Politics and Community Conflict: The Emergence of the Second American Party System in Cumberland County, North Carolina* (Baton Rouge, La., 1981); and Sean Wilentz, *Chants Democratic: New York City and the Rise of the American Working Class, 1788–1850* (New York, 1984).

have begun to strip away the last vestiges of the laissez-faire characterization of nineteenth-century political economy. Their many contributions need not be detailed here. It is enough to note a major shift in the focus of research away from concern with the degree of state interventionism to more systematic analysis of the policy-making process and its impact on social and economic change. This has led, among other things, to an increased awareness of the role of administrative and judicial structures in the formulation and implementation of public policy. The new focus has also stimulated a greater appreciation of the role of the private sector in allocating resources, principally through the institution of private property and the legal device of private contract. Finally, the legal system has been elevated to center stage in discussions of the nature of public economic policy. It now seems clear that law in the antebellum states, far from being abstract and static, was dynamic, pragmatic, and purposeful, a powerful instrument in the hands of emerging entrepreneurs for the establishment of a market economy and increased economic growth.[8]

An even more recent development pointing to the possibility of synthesis is the resurgence of interest in the history of American institutions and of the state. Historians seeking to revive political history and political scientists studying the problem of "state-building" are finding common ground in their shared belief that political structures and "the state" matter and that patterns of state-society relations warrant systematic inquiry. The result is a burgeoning literature devoted to "bringing the state back in."[9] Two concerns are at the core of this scholarly activity. First is the extent to which the state may be said to be autonomous, a political actor in its own right formulating and pursuing goals independently of groups and interests in society. The second focuses on "the impact of states on the content and workings of politics." States matter, according to Theda Skocpol, "not simply because of the goal-oriented activities of state officials. They matter because their organizational configurations, along with their overall patterns of activity, affect political

[8]James Willard Hurst, *Law and the Conditions of Freedom in the Nineteenth Century United States* (Madison, Wis., 1956); Harry N. Scheiber, "Federalism and the American Economic Order," *Law and Society Review*, 10 (Fall 1975): 57–100; Lawrence Friedman, *Contract Law in America: A Social and Economic Case Study* (Madison, Wis., 1965); and Morton J. Horwitz, *The Transformation of American Law, 1780–1860* (Cambridge, Mass., 1977).

[9]See especially, Peter B. Evans, Dietrich Rueschemeyer, and Theda Skocpol, eds., *Bringing the State Back In* (Cambridge, Mass., 1985); *Studies in American Political Development: An Annual*, vol. 1 (New Haven, Conn., 1986); Stephen Skowronek, *Building a New American State: The Expansion of National Administrative Capacities, 1877–1920* (Cambridge, Mass., 1982); William E. Nelson, *The Roots of American Bureaucracy, 1830–1900* (Cambridge, Mass., 1982); and William E. Leuchtenburg, "The Pertinence of Political History: Reflections on the Significance of the State in America," *Journal of American History*, 73 (December 1986): 585–600.

culture, encourage some kinds of group formation and collective political actions (but not others) and make possible the raising of certain political issues (but not others)."[10] In a similar vein, Stephen Skowronek has argued that "states change (or fail to change) through political struggles rooted in and mediated by preestablished institutional arrangements." In other words, such factors as "the structure of the preestablished regime, the struggle for political power and institutional position that it frames, and the disjunction in time between environmental changes and new governing arrangements" are crucial to an analysis of state building or institutional development. Thus, according to Skowronek, an early-nineteenth-century regime of courts and parties profoundly shaped American efforts in the late nineteenth century to develop national administrative capacities in response to the challenge of industrialism and increasing complexity.[11]

Although the concept of "the state as actor" clearly has merit in many contexts, it is this second tendency in the state-building literature that seems most relevant to the changing nature of governance in the American states in the 1840s and 1850s. Thus far, scholarly efforts to relate law, administrative developments, political attitudes, and public policy have been concerned principally (though not exclusively) with the impact of the political system upon economic policy decisions. But if it is true that government policies affected economic relations and the process of growth, a fact that can hardly be denied in light of the historiography of the last four decades, it is no less true that the transformation of the antebellum economy profoundly shaped the pace and direction of political change. This seems obvious. What has not been so obvious, however, is the equally significant fact that "preestablished institutional arrangements," to use Skowronek's phrase, and a preexisting political culture established the parameters within which responses to economic change were shaped. It follows, therefore, that efforts to study changing patterns of governance without specific and systematic reference to what we might call the structure of opportunities created by the existing regime *as well as* the socioeconomic context can at best produce only partial explanations for institutional development. We may further observe that in some historical contexts, structure may play as decisive a role in shaping process as the other way around. To put it another way, as Richard L. McCormick did in a recent assessment of the state of political history, "under many circumstances . . . the nature of governance may exert more influence upon politics

[10]Theda Skocpol, "Bringing the State Back In: Strategies of Analysis in Current Research," in *Bringing the State Back In*, ed. Evans, Rueschemeyer, and Skocpol, 8, 21.
[11]Skowronek, *Building a New American State*, ix, 24–29.

than politics does upon government."[12] Taken together, recent interpretive trends suggest that a broader perspective than has heretofore been applied is required to illuminate the nature of the political order emerging in the states in the 1840s and 1850s and, in the process, account for the decline of political authority after mid-century.

The central purpose of this book is to suggest such a perspective, one that emphasizes the nature of change in the political system and that focuses directly on the dynamic relationship between social, economic, and political development. Viewed broadly, the political order emerging in the states in the middle of the nineteenth century was a consequence of two historic necessities. The first was the need, common to all political systems, for legitimacy in the face of rapid change. Social and economic modernization in the half century preceding the Civil War fundamentally transformed the United States. Political modernization, however, proceeded unevenly: rapid in terms of participation, gradual in terms of political integration and institutional development. The combination of social and economic changes with a tremendous expansion of participation multiplied political demands and, at the same time, undermined the ability of existing political structures to satisfy those demands. The result was a crisis of legitimacy. Among the strategies political leaders devised to resolve the tensions thus created were explicit limitations on state economic activities, a restructuring of state governments through constitutional revision, further decentralization of authority, and a dramatic expansion of the opportunities for popular participation.

It is not enough, however, to suggest that the new political order emerged solely out of the tensions created by a lag in the process of political development behind social and economic change. Such an interpretation is too mechanical and endows the historical process with an unacceptable determinism and inevitability. It also begs the more important question of why, in response to a crisis of legitimacy, certain political strategies and choices were adopted and others rejected and why the modernizing process in America was so radically different from that of most other nations. Part of the answer to these questions lies in the fact that the pattern of political change in the nineteenth century was shaped by the preexisting political culture. Political leaders struggling to respond to the challenges of modernization did so within a framework of republican principles inherited from the Revolution. Particularly important in this regard were traditional American fears of power and centralized authority and a highly decentralized, locally oriented system of representation.

---

[12] McCormick, *The Party Period and Public Policy*, 17.

No less significant is the fact that the new political regime was functional in the increasingly market-oriented society of the middle to late nineteenth century. More precisely, the new configuration of politics and governance benefited those entrepreneurial elites whose interests were most closely tied to the expanding market. The separation of the political and economic spheres, the decline of legislative power, the growth of administration, and institutional decentralization provided the political stability and predictability necessary for the establishment of a self-regulating market system.[13] In the process, of course, state governments became little more than institutional frameworks for the resolution of economic issues by private rather than public authorities, and the economy was effectively insulated from democratic control.

The hypothesis sketched above admittedly poses difficult interpretive questions. First, it assumes a dramatic transformation of American society in this period under the impact of modernization. Second, it appears at first glance to contradict or ignore much of what is known about the nature and direction of political change in the antebellum period, particularly the significance historians have attached to the emergence of modern, mass-based political parties. The apparent contradiction disappears, however, upon closer analysis of the role of parties in this period. Finally, implicit in the argument is a qualified, revisionist alternative to the traditional view that the political changes occurring in the half century before the Civil War were the result simply of an "extension of democracy." As these issues are critical to the following analysis, a more detailed explanation of the assumptions underlying my approach is in order.

Scholars have not always agreed on the precise definition of the term *modernization* or its applicability to the American experience. At a minimum, however, it has come to denote a complex of societal changes including economic development (as measured by per capita output) and the differentiation, rationalization, and integration of social and political structures. Economically, this means the "enshrinement of the productive ideal," along with such structural changes as rationalization of production, specialization of economic function, and the expansion and integration of the market. Socially, the appearance of national integration, a rationalized bureaucracy, and the shift of affective attitudes from the community to the broader society are characteristic of modernization. Accompanying these changes is the

[13]Karl Polanyi, *The Great Transformation: The Political and Economic Origins of Our Time* (Boston, 1944), 71; E. E. Schattschneider, *The Semisovereign People: A Realist's View of Democracy in America* (New York, 1960), 121–122; Horwitz, *The Transformation of American Law*, 253–266.

appearance of a "modern personality type," characterized by the dominance of secular-rational values, functional rather than ascriptive status, mobility, and cosmopolitanism. Historically, these processes are evident in the form of industrialization, urbanization, "rationalized expansion of political participation," and the proliferation of mass communications and literacy.[14]

Whatever the precise chronology of socioeconomic modernization in the United States, the process was clearly under way after the middle of the eighteenth century and accelerated dramatically in the first half of the nineteenth century. Economically, the period from 1815 to 1860 witnessed the growth of commercial agriculture, the gradual integration of village economies into an expanding market system made possible by the "transportation revolution," the centralization of the capital market, the emergence of the corporation, regional specialization of economic function, the appearance of the factory system, and the beginnings of industrialization. These developments were essential preconditions for the full realization of a modern, integrated, national market economy later in the nineteenth century.[15]

The social indices of modernization are equally impressive. Not all Americans had discarded their local identifications in favor of broader loyalties and many resisted the encroachments of the new commercial society, but increasing numbers accepted or at least came to terms with the modern notion of the possibility and desirability of change. As a contemporary observer, Michael Chevalier, put it:

> If movement and the quick succession of sensations and ideas constitute life, here one lives a hundredfold more than elsewhere; here, all is circulation, motion, and boiling agitation. Experiment follows experiment; enterprise follows enterprise. Riches and poverty follow on each other's traces and each in turn occupies the place of the other. While the great men of one day dethrone

---

[14]S. N. Eisenstadt, *Modernization: Protest and Change* (Englewood Cliffs, N.J., 1966); Myron Weiner, ed., *Modernization: The Dynamics of Growth* (New York, 1966); C. E. Black, *The Dynamics of Modernization: A Study in Comparative History* (New York, 1966); Gabriel Almond and G. Bingham Powell, *Comparative Politics: A Developmental Approach* (Boston, 1966); Samuel P. Huntington, *Political Order in Changing Societies* (New Haven, Conn., 1968); and Huntington, "The Change to Change: Modernization, Development, and Politics," *Comparative Politics*, 3 (April 1971): 283–322. Richard D. Brown has applied the concept to the American experience in *Modernization: The Transformation of American Life, 1600–1865* (New York, 1976). For a particularly perceptive critique of modernization theory, see Dean Tipps, "Modernization Theory and the Comparative Study of Societies: A Critical Perspective," *Comparative Studies in Society and History*, 15 (1973): 199–266.

[15]George R. Taylor, *The Transportation Revolution, 1815–1860* (New York, 1951); Douglas North, *The Economic Growth of the United States, 1790–1860* (New York, 1966), 167–68, 175; Stuart Bruchey, *The Roots of American Economic Growth, 1607–1861: An Essay in Social Causation* (New York, 1968); and Richard D. Brown, *Modernization*, 122–158.

those of the past, they are already half overturned themselves by those of the morrow. Fortunes last for a season; reputations for the twinkling of an eye. An irresistible current sweeps everything away, grinds everything to powder and deposits it again under new forms. Men change their houses, their climate, their trade, their condition, their party, their sect; the States change their laws, their officers, their constitutions.[16]

As Chevalier's comment suggests, and as recent research confirms, America in the first half of the nineteenth century was a restless, moving society. Cities grew at an unprecedented rate, and individual Americans were more mobile than ever before. Recent studies of geographical mobility are replacing the image of relatively isolated, stable communities with an image of a "restless and footloose" society in which attachment to community was becoming less and less important. Indeed, two close students of the subject have characterized American society in the middle of the century as "more like a procession than a stable social order."[17] Underlying this surface movement, furthermore, were deep-seated demographic trends, including a steady decline of fertility after 1800 and changing patterns of family structure.[18]

Rapid social, economic, and demographic change undermined traditional social relationships, altered the nature of work, transformed the role of primary social institutions such as the family, and stimulated the appearance of new forms of association. With the decline of the village community and the specialization of production, for example, specialized interest groups began to emerge, replacing traditionally informal and personal social groupings. As old identities and loyalties were eroded, voluntary associations created to perform specific economic, reform, educational, and cultural functions became more important. Viewed from hindsight, this social differentiation may appear to have been an inevitable prerequisite for the creation of a modern, integrated social system. For those who lived through such wrenching changes and whose lives were directly shaped by them, however, "moderni-

---

[16]Michael Chevalier, *Society, Manners, and Politics in the United States*, ed. John W. Ward (Garden City, N.Y., 1961), 299.

[17]Stephen Thernstrom and Peter Knights, "Men in Motion: Some Data and Speculations about Urban Population Mobility in Nineteenth Century America," in *Anonymous Americans: Explorations in Nineteenth Century Social History*, ed. Tamara Hareven (Englewood Cliffs, N.J., 1971), 40; see also George R. Taylor, "American Urban Growth Preceding the Railway Age," *Journal of Economic History*, 27 (September 1967): 309–339, and Peter Knights, *The Plain People of Boston, 1830–1860: A Study in City Growth* (New York, 1971).

[18]J. Potter, "The Growth of Population in America, 1700–1860," in *Population in History: Essays in Historical Demography*, ed. D. V. Glass and D. E. C. Eversley (London, 1965), 666–679; Nancy F. Cott, *The Bonds of Womanhood: "Woman's Sphere" in New England, 1780–1835* (New Haven, Conn., 1977).

zation" probably seemed neither inevitable nor, in many instances, even desirable. For many Americans it meant instability, a loss of status, a confusion of values, cultural tension, class conflict, political turmoil, and an increasingly atomized society.[19]

Even as traditional patterns of life were disintegrating, however, the process of social integration was proceeding at several different levels. As Walter Glazer has pointed out, for example, voluntary associations represented functional substitutes for the traditional relationships of the organic community, which was breaking down. In effect, such associations "formed a loose network within the community that served as the institutional framework for citizen participation and power in local affairs."[20] Moreover, though the period is notable for the emergence of an extreme form of individualism and the "diffuseness" of its culture, it is equally notable for the growing impact of public opinion on values and behavior and, at one level of consciousness, for an intellectually powerful search for community. More tangibly, social ties extending beyond the local, community level increased with the expansion of the market and the development of a transportation and communications network that brought all parts of the Union closer together, in terms of both trade and the flow of information. Improved roads, the canal system, the beginnings of the railroad network, the expansion of the postal service, and the increasing significance and circulation of newspapers stimulated the diffusion of information and laid the foundations for the gradual development of a cosmopolitan outlook once limited to a relatively few commercial centers. At the same time, the appearance of mass-based political parties structurally linked local political action to events and contests at the national level. Complementing this informal diffusion of information, the expansion of state common school systems and the establishment of the principle of "free schools" facilitated the formal dissemination of knowledge and contributed to an overall increase in the literacy of antebellum Americans.[21]

---

[19]Richard D. Brown, "Modernization and the Modern Personality in Early America, 1600–1865: A Sketch of a Synthesis," *Journal of Interdisciplinary History*, 3 (1972): 220–222; Rowland Berthoff, *An Unsettled People: Social Order and Disorder in American History* (New York, 1971), 127–298; Oscar and Mary Handlin, *The Dimensions of Liberty* (Cambridge, Mass., 1961), 91–102.

[20]Walter Glazer, "Participation and Power: Voluntary Associations and the Functional Organization of Cincinnati in 1840," *Historical Methods Newsletter*, 5, NO. 4 (September 1972): 153.

[21]John Higham, *From Boundlessness to Consolidation: The Transformation of American Culture, 1848–1860* (Ann Arbor, Mich., 1969); Alexis de Tocqueville, *Democracy in America*, ed. J. P. Mayer (Garden City, N.Y., 1966), 433–436; Yehoshua Arieli, *Individualism and Nationalism in American Ideology* (Baltimore, Md., 1964); Taylor, *Transportation Revolution*, 15–152;

Industrialization, urbanization, economic growth, mobility, declining fertility, and a general fragmentation of society, all frequently mentioned features of the 1830s and 1840s, are specific facets of the broader phenomenon of modernization. The depth and rapidity of these changes suggest a profound transformation of the social and economic systems. This is not to suggest that the process was complete before 1860. The great period of industrial growth came after the Civil War. The United States, furthermore, remained predominantly rural long after this period. Moreover, the degree of social and economic integration in the antebellum years is much more impressive when compared with the seventeenth and eighteenth centuries than with the late nineteenth and twentieth centuries, when economic consolidation and mass communications created a highly centralized, complex, integrated society. Finally, even though historians such as Richard D. Brown have argued that the "modern personality 'syndrome' had been substantially realized among white Americans" by the early national period,[22] it seems more likely that the United States was still in a transitional stage. A deep-seated ambivalence toward progress, the pervasiveness of violence, the religious and cultural conflicts generated by massive immigration, and a general deterioration of respect for law and authority suggest that although Americans were clearly experiencing social and economic modernization in this period, they had by no means resolved the fundamental value conflicts thrust upon them by such change.[23] Indeed, many of the conflicts of the era arose directly from the forces of change, as groups affected by modernization clashed over the nature and direction of social and economic development. In the final analysis, however, the fact that many Americans were adversely affected by this process or resisted it does not alter the reality of such change over the course of the nineteenth century.

The extent of political modernization in the United States in the antebellum period is a more complicated problem. Unquestionably, an explosion of participation in America began in the middle of the eighteenth century and

---

Allan R. Pred, *Urban Growth and the Circulation of Information: The United States System of Cities, 1790–1840* (Cambridge, Mass., 1973); Richard P. McCormick, "Political Development and the Second Party System," in *American Party Systems*, ed. Chambers and Burnham, 90–116; Rush Welter, *Popular Education and Democratic Thought* (New York, 1962).

[22] Brown, "Modernization and Modern Personality," 219.

[23] Marvin Meyers, *The Jacksonian Persuasion* (Stanford, Calif., 1957); Leonard Richards, *"Gentlemen of Property and Standing": Anti-Abolition Mobs in Jacksonian America* (New York, 1970); Ray Allen Billington, *The Protestant Crusade, 1800–1860* (Chicago, 1964); David B. Davis, "Some Ideological Functions of Prejudice in Antebellum America," *American Quarterly*, 15 (1963): 115–125; and the same author's "Some Themes of Counter-subversion: An Analysis of Anti-Masonic, Anti-Catholic, and Anti-Mormon Literature," *Mississippi Valley Historical Review*, 47 (1960): 205–224.

reached its peak in the 1840s. The debate over English colonial policy in the 1760s and 1770s, the practical experience of writing state constitutions in the 1770s, the conflict over the federal Constitution in the 1780s, and the polarization of the nationalist leadership and the appearance of political parties in the 1790s all contributed to the emergence of "participant attitudes." The early nineteenth century, furthermore, brought a gradual decline of deference, a broadening of representation, and a general relaxation of suffrage and office-holding requirements. At the same time, presidential elections were given a popular dimension as a result of the appearance of the nominating convention and the shift to the popular election of presidential electors. Finally, the emergence of the second party system in the 1830s — highly organized, national in scope, and competitive at all levels of government — drew Americans to the polls as never before or since.[24]

Apart from this dramatic expansion of participation and the emergence of political parties, however, the political system of the United States operated much as it had in the late eighteenth century. Most nations experiencing modernization have rationalized and centralized authority and created functionally differentiated and hierarchical administrative structures.[25] In America, a dynamic socioeconomic system combined with traditional fears of centralized authority to produce a different result. National political integration, usually considered an essential aspect of modernization, was not achieved until at least the Civil War, if indeed that early. Even within the individual states, there was little attachment to a statewide political community. Towns, cities, and entire regions competed with one another for state economic assistance with little regard for any abstract "public interest" or for the consequences of unplanned and uncoordinated growth. It is equally difficult to discern any significant progress at the national and state levels toward the creation of a rationalized bureaucracy, another commonly mentioned attribute of political modernization. Administration was essentially personal, informal, and decentralized in nature. Indeed, according to the most recent assessment of the national government, the principal integrative feature of an otherwise "radically deconcentrated governmental scheme" was the rules and procedures of courts and parties.[26] Some states did develop elaborate admin-

---

[24]Gordon Wood, *The Creation of the American Republic, 1776–1787* (Chapel Hill, N.C., 1969); William N. Chambers, *Political Parties in a New Nation: The American Experience, 1776–1809* (New York, 1963); Williamson, *American Suffrage*; McCormick, "New Perspectives on Jacksonian Politics;" Ronald P. Formisano, "Deferential-Participant Politics: The Early Republic's Political Culture, 1789–1840," *American Political Science Review*, 68 (1974): 473–487.

[25]Huntington, *Political Order in Changing Societies*, 34.

[26]Skowronek, *Building the New American State*, 24.

istrative structures to build and operate internal improvements and experimented with regulatory agencies, but these structures typically deteriorated during the 1830s and 1840s before the impact of localism, a democratic ethic that insisted upon popularly elected administrative officials, and a deeply ingrained fear of centralization. Indeed, most studies of state economic policy in this period stress the debilitating effect of the absence of effective administration on promotional and regulatory policies.[27]

It is true, of course, that the emergence of modern, mass-based political parties and a dramatic expansion of political rights profoundly transformed the nature of American politics in the Jackson era. Nothing I have said is meant to challenge this. However, the impact of these changes on the operation of the political system is less clear than is commonly believed. Antebellum political parties were marvelous creations: intricately organized, sensitive to the nuances of participatory politics, and skilled in the modern techniques of electioneering. Most historians have assumed that they were equally effective as policy-making and governing institutions. Recent research, however, casts doubt upon this assumption. Specifically, the connection between voting and public policy, long taken for granted, appears to have been more complex than historians imbued with the "responsible-party-government" model of politics have believed. Indeed, it is possible to argue, following Theodore J. Lowi's categorization of party functions, that early-nineteenth-century parties were essentially "constituent" rather than policy-oriented institutions.[28] That is to say, they were more effective in electing party candidates than in structuring political participation so as to link voters with the activities of government and the formulation of broad policies. As Richard L. McCormick has shown, however, they *were* uniquely suited for a political universe dominated by distributive economic policies.[29] Furthermore, as Ronald Formisano and Kathleen Kutolowski have pointed out, the process by which parties were "modernized" was much more gradual than

[27] Carter Goodrich, "American Development Policy: The Case of Internal Improvements," *Journal of Economic History*, 16 (December 1956): 449–460; Friedman, *Contract Law in America*, 146–154; Scheiber, *Ohio Canal Era*, 355–358. For a different view of the extent of bureaucratization in this period, see Matthew A. Crenson, *The Federal Machine: Beginnings of Bureaucracy in Jacksonian America* (Baltimore, Md., 1975).

[28] For an imaginative discussion of the relationship between voting and public policy in this period, see McCormick, "The Party Period and Public Policy"; see also Theodore J. Lowi, "Party, Policy, and Constitution in America," in *American Party Systems*, ed. Chambers and Burnham, 238–276.

[29] McCormick, "The Party Period and Public Policy."

most historians have assumed.[30] At the very least, such interpretations compel us to confront the difficult question of whether or not political parties were in fact capable of operationalizing "democracy" in policy terms.

An even more fundamental question concerns the significance of the extension of formal political rights. American historians have tended to assume that the broadening of the suffrage, the growth of the number of popularly elected officials, political decentralization, and frequent elections—all characteristic political changes of the antebellum period—were synonymous with democratization. In doing so, they have rarely made explicit the definition of democracy upon which they were basing their judgment. Indeed, there has been surprisingly little theorizing about democracy, even as historians have made it the central theme in the national experience. Another tendency has been to ignore certain paradoxes associated with the growth of democratic institutions. In the period under investigation here, for example, the opportunity to participate in political decisions was indisputably broadened. But the substantive meaning of such participation was effectively diluted at precisely the historical moment when that right was achieved because of the new limitations on governmental activities. The differentiation of society into distinct political and economic spheres, a major consequence of modernization and an expanding market system, assured that the American version of democracy would be exclusively political and procedural, and that much of social and economic life would be outside the boundaries of politics. What I am suggesting is that historians who attribute the political changes in the antebellum states simply to an extension of democracy may be accepting uncritically the definition of democracy that emerged to explain and legitimate those very changes. Equal participation in formal political processes is indeed an essential prerequisite in a democratic system. But it is less certain whether equal participation constitutes a sufficient, objective definition of democracy or, more likely, one profoundly rooted in the milieu that produced it. It is itself, in other words, an integral part of the emerging political order which must be explained rather than simply assumed.[31]

---

[30]Formisano, "Deferential-Participant Politics" and Kathleen Smith Kutolowski, "The Janus Face of New York's Local Parties: Genesee County, 1821–1827," *New York History*, 59 (April 1978): 145–172; see also Formisano's *The Transformation of Political Culture*, which questions, among other things, the existence of a First Party "system" in the 1790s.

[31]My thinking on this difficult issue has been influenced by a number of scholars. Chief among these are the following: C. B. McPherson, *The Life and Times of Liberal Democracy* (New York, 1977); Jack Lively, *Democracy* (New York, 1977); Carole Pateman, *Participation and Democratic Theory* (New York, 1970); Schattschneider, *The Semisovereign People*; Polanyi, *The Great Transformation*, 225–226; Henry S. Kariel, *The Decline of American Pluralism* (Stanford,

As the preceding discussion suggests, I share many of the insights of those scholars who argue that the American political system has been peculiarly resistant to developmental change even as Americans were creating the most dynamic society and economy in the world. In brief, antebellum America was characterized by rapid social and economic modernization, but, as Samuel P. Huntington, Walter Dean Burnham, and others have suggested, it remained politically "Tudor."[32] Although participation in the political system increased dramatically, the process of political integration and institutional development lagged significantly behind. Such differential rates of change in the socioeconomic system on the one hand and the political system on the other had important consequences for the nature of public policy and governance. Some students of political development in the twentieth century have suggested that broadened participation in a modernizing society may initially undermine traditional authority structures and frustrate attempts to create new political institutions. When traditional authority is already weak, the result can be political instability. Therefore, unless the rate of political institutionalization corresponds to the rate of the expansion of participation, the appearance of differentiated and integrated political structures may well be delayed.[33]

One does not have to accept the determinism and institutional bias implicit in this model of political development to recognize its potential as a vantage point from which to survey and assess the nature and direction of political change in America. I have in mind an argument along the following lines. The continuance of a highly decentralized, locally based political system in the context of an increasingly market-oriented economy that was organized on a regional or even national basis shaped both the particular kinds of demands made on government and the policy responses to such demands. I would also suggest that structures of representation and of policy making that were created before the onset of rapid social and economic modernization hindered efforts to control those forces and to regulate new economic interests in the name of democracy or some concept of the public interest.

Although major elements of this argument are drawn from recent theoretical and interpretive developments, it also has much deeper roots. A number of historians have identified similar kinds of tension between participation and institutional development in the nineteenth century. David Donald, for

Calif., 1961); Darryl Baskin, *American Pluralist Democracy: A Critique* (New York, 1971); and Theodore J. Lowi, *The End of Liberalism: Ideology, Policy, and the Crisis of Public Authority* (New York, 1969).

[32] Huntington, *Political Order in Changing Societies*, 93–139; Walter Dean Burnham, *Critical Elections and the Mainsprings of American Politics* (New York, 1970), 176–187.

[33] Huntington, *Political Order in Changing Societies*, 5.

example, suggested that the inability of the nation to withstand the crisis of expansion at mid-century resulted from a general rejection of authority, social disorganization, the erosion of "recognized values of orderly civilization," and "an excess of democracy." Similarly, Stanley Elkins attributed American ineffectiveness in solving the problem of slavery to institutional breakdown and a general American insensitivity to the need for institutions. Seymour Mandelbaum, furthermore, has written that the "cruelty of slavery, the terror of the Civil War, the denuded forests and the exciting but also hellish cities"—what he called the "faults of the nineteenth century"—were "intrinsic parts of the democratization of American society." James Sterling Young, in his brilliant study of the Washington Community, has pointed out the debilitating effect of "government by separate and rival interests" on the national political system between 1800 and 1828. Finally, James Willard Hurst, Lawrence Friedman, Gerald Nash, and Harry N. Scheiber have identified similar tensions at the state level.[34]

By focusing on nineteenth-century assumptions regarding authority and the structure of society, these scholars have pointed out that part of the responsibility for the nation's inability to resolve many of the important issues confronting it in this period lay in the nature of the political culture itself. American attitudes toward authority were deeply rooted in the revolutionary solution to the problem of government. Confronted by what they perceived as a conflict between power and liberty during the 1760s and 1770s, Americans created governments predicated upon the dispersal and decentralization of authority. Later, when the Constitution was written, this principle was wedded to Madison's theory of social pluralism to resolve the problem of interests in society. Assuming, with Madison, that a variety of interests "grow up of necessity in civilized nations, and divide them into different classes, actuated by different sentiments and views," Americans accepted his solution of regulating these interests by balancing them against one another.[35] Implicit in this remedy was the belief, again Madison's, that the more interests there are in society, the less likely that any one of them could seize control and exercise power, even in the name of the majority. The

[34]David Donald, *Lincoln Reconsidered: Essays on the Civil War* (New York, 1968), 209–235; Stanley Elkins, *Slavery: A Problem in American Institutional and Intellectual Life* (Chicago, 1968), 27–37; Seymour Mandelbaum, *Boss Tweed's New York* (New York, 1965), v; James Sterling Young, *The Washington Community, 1800–1828* (New York, 1966); Hurst, *Law and the Conditions of Freedom*; Friedman, *Contract Law in America*; Gerald D. Nash, *State Government and Economic Development: A History of Administrative Policies in California, 1849–1933* (Berkeley, 1964); and Scheiber, *Ohio Canal Era*.

[35]Clinton Rossiter, ed., *The Federalist Papers* (New York, 1961), 71–84; the quotation is from page 79; see also Bernard Bailyn, *The Ideological Origins of the American Revolution* (Cambridge, Mass., 1967); and Wood, *Creation of the American Republic*.

result of this scheme of politics was a general diffusion of authority and the rejection, implicitly at least, of the concept of a "general will" or absolute standard by which to judge the public good. The public interest came to be defined simply as the end product of the political process. Government's role was limited to ensuring the procedural right of all groups to participate in that process. This, of course, is the essence of modern pluralism.

The Madisonian vision of government was a brilliant solution to the political problems of the Revolutionary era. If government was made somewhat less efficient by the dispersal and fragmentation of authority, that was simply the price Americans had to pay for liberty. Indeed, thoughtful Americans pointed to the absence of mediating institutions as the peculiar genius of the American system. But as some modern critics of pluralism have pointed out, many questions were left unanswered: What if the interests kept multiplying? Was there no point at which pluralism ceased to provide even the necessities of organized society? Was there no conceivable situation in which the inefficiency of a government so constrained and so incapable of articulating a majority view overbalanced the benefits of fragmented power? Did the pluralist solution adequately safeguard society against potential abuses of private power or, for that matter, even recognize the existence of private power? Finally, what were the consequences for democracy of such a system of politics?[36]

Such questions, only dimly perceived in the still relatively homogeneous, undifferentiated society of the late eighteenth century, took on new significance in the altered circumstances of the nineteenth century. In the fifty years after Madison wrote *Federalist Number 10*, rapid economic change and social differentiation profoundly transformed the social context within which the pluralist vision had emerged. The spread of market relationships, the increasing division of labor and complexity of society, the emergence of quasi-public institutions such as corporations, the proliferation of voluntary associations, and the extension of individual political rights placed new stresses on the pluralistic model of politics. Madison's genius, of course, had been in foreseeing this splintering of society and in trying to construct a constitutional order at the federal level to contain and divert these tendencies into productive channels. Leaving aside the question of whether or not the Madisonian design has proven successful in the long run, the adoption of the new federal Constitution left state political systems less resilient in the face of rapid social and economic modernization. The ways in which Americans sought to resolve this dilemma in the context of the existing political culture help to

---

[36]In general, see Lowi, *The End of Liberalism*; Kariel, *The Decline of American Pluralism*; and Baskin, *American Pluralist Democracy*.

explain the political order beginning to take shape in the states at mid-century.

THIS BOOK tests these general propositions by examining political development in New York State between the Revolution and the Civil War. The application of such a broad model of social, economic, and political change to a single state in the American system is advantageous in several ways. First, it is practical because it provides a manageable body of data. More important, the nature of American federalism and the localistic organization of society before the Civil War necessitate that the approach be tested first at the state level. John Marshall's familiar assertions of national power notwithstanding, the state was the most important arena for the formulation of social and economic policy in this period. State economic activities were, of course, shaped by the broad constraints of the national legal and constitutional environment, as well as by spatial limitations on their jurisdiction and by the necessity to compete with other states for economic advantage. But, as Harry N. Scheiber points out, "real power" was diffused among the several states. The result was a "decentralized federalism," within which "each state had its own particular 'mix' of public policy, with preferences for one interest or another, and with its own set of rules in the establishment of priorities for economic development."[37]

It should be clear from the outset that I do not assume that New York was typical. On the contrary, not its typicality, but the fact that it experienced the problems associated with rapid social and economic modernization so early, before the existence of models that it could emulate, makes the Empire State an ideal test case. As a result of this fact, plus the scale of its involvement in the economy and the innovative character of its political system, New York became an example for other states grappling with similar problems. It is also worth noting that although New York clearly enjoyed certain locational and other advantages that hastened its economic ascendancy after 1815, the state was sufficiently diverse that its experience was not completely unique.

With these considerations in mind, the analysis proceeds as follows. Chapter 2 examines the transformation of New York's economy and society from 1800 to 1860 when rapid socioeconomic modernization produced an increasingly complex, differentiated, interdependent, and cosmopolitan society. Chapter 3 explores the process of political development from the Revo-

---

[37] Scheiber, "Federalism and the American Economic Order," 97; see also Daniel Elazar, *The American Partnership: Intergovernmental Cooperation in the Nineteenth Century United States* (Chicago, 1962).

lution to the 1830s and argues that political and economic development were proceeding in opposite directions. A highly fragmented, decentralized political system emerged at the very moment when economic relationships were becoming more impersonal and market relationships increasingly centralized. This disjunction between economic and political development shaped the character of public policy and had profound implications for the new political order that would emerge at mid-century. Chapter 4 provides an in-depth examination of the character and quality of public economic policy in antebellum New York. It describes a highly pragmatic, nonideological, distributive policy system, which became increasingly disfunctional as the economy surged into a period of unprecedented growth and structural transformation.

The seeds of crisis embedded in this "political economy of distribution" bore fruit after the Panic of 1837. Faced with mounting debts, charges of legislative corruption and inefficiency, and urgent decisions on the future of the state's development policy, New Yorkers began to reevaluate the role of government in society and to question some of the basic premises of their system of politics. Chapter 5 analyzes this debate, focusing on contrasting Whig and Democratic positions, the "People's Resolutions" of 1841, and the "Stop and Tax" policy of 1842. Two competing responses to the crisis of distributive politics emerged. One stressed democratization; the other, administrative rationality and predictability. Chapter 6 examines the democratic strategy as it is revealed in the constitutional revision movement in the 1840s and analyzes the work of the Convention of 1846. The central thrust of the new constitution was to further democratize the state's political system and to involve the people more directly in governmental processes. Chapter 7 traces the administrative strategy of legitimacy by focusing on the growth of local government, the creation of functionally specific state agencies and departments, early experiments with regulatory commissions, and the resurgence of judicial power. Together, these developments suggest the beginnings of an administrative approach to governance in the two decades before the Civil War. The democratic and administrative strategies of legitimacy converged in the arena of corporation policy. Chapter 8 explores the changing relationship between government and the corporation as the state began to adopt general laws establishing the principle of incorporation by administrative procedure. The result was the legitimation of the private business corporation and a concomitant weakening of political control over substantive economic policy decisions.

The last chapter draws together the underlying themes of the preceding analysis of political change and infers from that analysis some of the characteristic features of the emerging political order. Decades of political development in the context of rapid socioeconomic change and the expansion of the market had produced in New York a liberal order of politics in which democratic and administrative values coexisted in delicate balance, but with administrative values increasingly shaping the day-to-day workings of government. A form of procedural democracy had emerged which was uniquely functional in a market economy, but vast areas of social and economic life were effectively insulated from democratic power.

In the final analysis, political development in antebellum New York must be seen as a creative process of interaction and adaptation. New institutional arrangements and distributions of power evolved through interaction with a rapidly changing socioeconomic environment. If the particular type of economic system appears to have been relatively more determining than other forces—and a case can be made for the transforming power of the market in the nineteenth century—it is nevertheless true that important features of the new political order can be understood only in the context of the political culture. That political culture, in turn, can be understood only by reference to the particular circumstances and conditions that produced it in the late eighteenth and early nineteenth centuries. In short, neither economic forces nor the inexorable progress of American democracy explain sufficiently the political order that emerged in the middle of the last century. The truth, as is so often the case in history, is more complicated. In this instance, the search for that truth must begin with the realization that nineteenth-century Americans were confronted with a unique challenge: how to reconcile a constitutional order designed specifically not to govern with the new forces of industrialization and political democracy.

[2]

Society and Economy

FROM THE vantage point of 1837, before the onset of one of the most severe depressions of the nineteenth century, New Yorkers could look back on a half century of unparalleled development. By whatever measurement of growth—population, wealth, agricultural production, manufacturing output, transportation facilities, or commerce—the state had earned the renown increasingly accorded it at home and abroad. By the 1830s, New York had already outdistanced its rivals Massachusetts and Pennsylvania in the quest for economic supremacy in the nation. Indeed, to many New Yorkers the economic horizon must have seemed as limitless as the steady stream of barges plying the 363-mile canal route between Lake Erie and the Hudson River. Two decades later, on the eve of the Civil War, the state's preeminence in the national economy was so secure that few could dispute its claims to be the "Empire State." Thoughtful observers may also have pondered the consequences of this economic transition. Rapid population growth, urbanization, improved communications, the expansion and integration of the market, and the growth of manufacturing fundamentally altered traditional patterns of social and economic behavior in the state and laid the foundations for a modern social order.

NEW YORK'S spectacular growth was part of the broader transformation of American society and economy in the first half of the nineteenth century. From a predominantly agricultural and commercial society of about four million, concentrated principally along the narrow Atlantic seaboard, the United States had become, by 1860, a nation of over thirty million people at the threshold of the industrial age. Rapid population growth, fueled by the influx of some five and one half million immigrants between 1815 and 1860, combined with an equally dramatic expansion of cities and towns to alter forever the American landscape.[1] These developments, in turn, were symptomatic of a general quickening of economic activity. At some point between 1810 and 1840 — historians continue to debate the appropriate date for the "takeoff" of the American economy — the United States began to experience significantly higher rates of economic growth, rates that would be sustained for the remainder of the century. Although the precise dynamics of this process are complex and defy simple description, increased demand owing to an expansion of the domestic market was almost certainly a central factor. The construction of turnpikes in the early decades of the century, the introduction of steamboats on western rivers after 1815, and the penetration of the Appalachian mountain barrier by the Erie Canal in the 1820s lowered the cost of transportation and opened new areas to commercial farming. Declining freight rates resulting from transportation improvements made possible the regional specialization and enlarged market that economic historians believe lay at the heart of accelerated growth in the antebellum period.[2]

The extension of the market into previously subsistence or semi-subsistence areas increased agricultural productivity and freed a steadily expanding proportion of the population for nonagricultural pursuits centered in the newly emerging towns. At the same time, as the portion of farm products entering the market grew, cities and towns began to compete for control of the trade in agricultural goods. Existing urban centers such as New York City, Philadelphia, and Baltimore tightened their control over the surrounding hinterland and began reaching out to absorb ever more distant areas into their economic orbits. New towns and cities emerged along key transportation routes to dominate regional markets and to serve as intermediaries in the wider, interregional distribution system. As a result, the quantity of western agricultural goods reaching the Atlantic increased dramatically, as did the value of merchandise traveling in the opposite direction.[3]

---

[1] Potter, "The Growth of Population in America," 666, 668, 686; Douglas T. Miller, *Jacksonian Aristocracy: Class and Democracy in New York, 1830–1860* (New York, 1967), 82–83. U.S. Bureau of the Census, *Historical Statistics of the United States, Colonial Times to 1957* (Washington, D.C., 1960), 14; Taylor, *Transportation Revolution*, 388; Taylor, "American Urban Growth," 309; Bruchey, *Roots of American Economic Growth*, 74–78.

[2] North, *Economic Growth of the United States*, 167–68; Bruchey, *Roots of American Economic Growth*, 74–91, 159–160; and Harvey H. Segal, "Canals and Economic Development," in *Canals and American Economic Development*, ed. Carter Goodrich (New York, 1961), 247.

[3] Clarence Danhof, *Change in Agriculture: The Northern United States, 1820–1870* (Cambridge, Mass., 1969), 2–7, 9–12, 13–21; Segal, "Canals and Economic Development," 229–230; Bruchey, *Roots of American Economic Growth*, 159.

The expansion and integration of spatially separated markets and the consequent regional specialization of labor set the stage for the beginnings of industrialization. Increased agricultural productivity resulting from the spread of commercial farming indirectly boosted industrial production by providing a wider market for eastern manufactured goods. Total manufacturing capital in the United States increased from $50 million in 1820 to $1 billion in 1860, doubling every decade after 1826. The value of manufacturing output increased ten times in the fifty years from 1810 to 1860, reaching the $2-billion mark at the end of that period.[4] By 1860, only Great Britain surpassed the United States as a manufacturing nation. Most of this growth in the American economy occurred in the Northeast, which accounted for three-fourths of the nation's manufacturing employment in 1850 and for 71 percent in 1860.[5]

The growth of commerce and manufacturing produced equally significant changes in the marketing and distribution of goods. At the end of the eighteenth century, the American economy was dominated by the general or all-purpose merchant. Operating out of the principal port cities, these merchant capitalists dealt in generic goods and performed the complete range of commercial functions. They were equal parts importer and exporter, wholesaler and retailer, banker and insurer, shipper and forwarder. Goods moved slowly and irregularly, always subject to the uncertainties of nature along the shipping routes. Economic relationships were highly personal, and business was conducted much as it had been for centuries. After 1815, however, the rising volume of trade and the growth of the number of commercial transactions placed a premium on specialization. New enterprises concentrating on a particular product or function began to appear. With the emergence and proliferation of specialized firms in commerce, finance, and transportation, the traditional sedentary merchant declined in significance and the nature of commercial transactions was profoundly altered. Specialization necessitated greater reliance on impersonal, market mechanisms for coordinating commercial activities. As more enterprises engaged in a multiplicity of transactions over greater and greater distances, personal business networks and the informal style of an earlier age were no longer adequate. New institutions, such as banks, corporations, and insurance companies, emerged to facilitate the accumulation of risk capital and to manage the efficient flow of goods and services through the rapidly expanding market economy. Similarly, contract law, rules governing the negotiability of commercial paper, and the law

---

[4] Victor S. Clark, *History of Manufactures in the United States*, 3 vols. (New York, 1929), 1: 369; Taylor, *Transportation Revolution*, 248–249.
[5] North, *Economic Growth of the United States*, 204, 159.

of private property were transformed in response to the needs of entrepreneurs for a stable, predictable legal environment for continued growth and development.[6]

The ordinary American in the 1830s was probably unaware, at least in any systematic way, of these broad structural changes in the economy. He or she could not have avoided their consequences, however, in the changed circumstances of everyday life. Economic growth caused per capita income to rise steadily in this period, making life easier and more comfortable for some Americans—particularly middle-class whites. The spread of commercial agriculture broadened the social and economic horizons of countless farm families whose lives had been severely circumscribed by their harsh existence on the margins of subsistence. These changes, and the increased availability of a greater variety of manufactured goods, undoubtedly enhanced the quality of American life generally.[7]

But the very same forces that propelled the United States toward industrialization, economic growth, and prosperity also disrupted the lives of thousands, possibly millions, of Americans. For one thing, the consequences of market expansion varied with an individual's relationship to the market. It could be an enormously liberating experience for those integrated into the market for the first time, opening new opportunities for enterprise and new avenues for social and economic advancement. But it could also result in a devastating loss of opportunity, position, and status for those in older areas who, with the extension of the market, confronted new sources of competition. Furthermore, the decline of household production after 1815, the rise of the factory system, the decline of skilled craftsmen and artisans, and the emergence of an industrial labor force sent shock waves throughout American society and culture. Traditional concepts of family, home, work, leisure, time, and morality were transformed by the forces of industrialization and

---

[6]Glenn Porter and Harold C. Livesay, *Merchants and Manufacturers: Studies in the Changing Structure of Nineteenth-Century Marketing* (Baltimore, 1971), 1–35; Alfred D. Chandler, Jr., *The Visible Hand: The Managerial Revolution in American Business* (Cambridge, Mass., 1977), 15–48; Tony Allen Freyer, *Forums of Order: The Federal Courts and Business in American History* (Greenwich, Conn., 1979); Horwitz, *Transformation of American Law*, 160–252.

[7]Bruchey, *Roots of American Economic Growth*, 74–88; George R. Taylor, "The National Economy Before and After the Civil War," in *Economic Change in the Civil War Era*, ed. David T. Gilchrist and W. David Lewis (Greenwich, Del., 1965), 1–22; Robert E. Gallman, "Commodity Output, 1839–1899," in *Trends in the American Economy in the Nineteenth Century*, ed. William N. Parker (Princeton, N.J., 1960), 13–71; Danhof, *Change in Agriculture*, 18–19.

the growth of a market mentality.[8] Nor were the benefits that did come from economic growth distributed equally throughout society. Recent research suggests that, far from being the "Age of the Common Man," the pre–Civil-War years witnessed a widening of the gap between the rich and the poor, a hardening of class lines, and a decline in the reality, if not the myth, of social mobility. Class conflict, increasing poverty and unemployment, city slums and tenement houses, crime and prostitution revealed the darker side of American economic growth.[9]

The texture of American life was transformed in other, more subtle, ways as well. The spread of market relationships and the increasing division of labor in society undermined traditional modes of social intercourse and forged new patterns of interaction. Under the impact of social differentiation, specialization, and the advance of the cash nexus, traditional community values declined and were replaced by those of the marketplace. Informal, face-to-face relationships gave way to more formal and impersonal modes of human interaction. Particularism and localism, though never completely absent in American society, confronted a competing value system oriented toward universalism and cosmopolitanism. At the same time, the very structure of American society was being reshaped along more pluralistic lines by the rapid proliferation of functional and supralocal organizations.

Perhaps the most important consequence of market expansion in the first half of the nineteenth century, and certainly the most relevant to the present discussion, was the increasing interdependence of all elements in the social order and the creation of a new web of dependencies unlike any that had existed in traditional society. The experience of the newly emerging, specialized merchant is typical. The individual merchant focusing all of his attention and business acumen on a single product or function was economically

---

[8]Thomas L. Haskell, *The Emergence of Professional Social Science: The American Social Science Association and the Nineteenth Century Crisis of Authority* (Urbana, Ill., 1977), 35–36; Danhof, *Change in Agriculture*, 1–26; Christopher Clark, "Household Economy, Market Exchange and the Rise of Capitalism in the Connecticut Valley, 1800–1850," *Journal of Social History*, 13 (Winter 1979): 169–189; Paul E. Johnson, *A Shopkeeper's Millennium: Society and Revivals in Rochester, New York, 1815–1837* (New York, 1978), 15–61; Cott, *Bonds of Womanhood*; Mary P. Ryan, *Cradle of the Middle Class: The Family in Oneida County, New York, 1790–1865* (Cambridge, 1981). For an exhaustive investigation of the impact of economic change on labor in New York City in these years, see Wilentz, *Chants Democratic*.

[9]Chapter 5 of Edward Pessen's *Jacksonian America: Society, Personality, and Politics* (Homewood, Ill., 1978) is an excellent summation of the relevant literature on the issue of social mobility in the "Age of Jackson." See also Pessen's "The Egalitarian Myth and the American Social Reality: Wealth, Mobility, and Equality in the 'Era of the Common Man,'" *American Historical Review*, 76 (October 1971): 986–1034; and *Riches, Class, and Power Before the Civil War* (Lexington, Mass., 1973) by the same author. A more impressionistic study which makes essentially the same point is Miller, *Jacksonian Aristocracy*.

more efficient than his more diversified predecessor. For precisely the same reason, however, he was also more vulnerable to adverse business conditions. In short, the other side of the coin of specialization was diminished autonomy and interdependence. To a greater extent than ever before, businessmen of all kinds found themselves enmeshed in a regional, national, and even international system of commerce and exchange and subject to economic forces beyond their immediate control. The same may be said for farmers who sold their products in increasingly distant markets at prices determined by international supply and demand and for workers compelled by the forces of economic change to sell their labor in a highly competitive market system. In the broadest sense, a new society was in the process of emerging, a society founded on functional rather than communal values and bound together by a rapidly expanding network of supralocal dependencies.[10]

NEW YORK STATE reflected the structural changes occurring in the larger society and economy and, because of its strategic location and the prominence of New York City, it also acted as a catalyst that set those very changes into motion. At the conclusion of the revolutionary war, a disproportionate share of which had been fought within New York's boundaries, the state's population stood at roughly one quarter of a million, fully three-fourths of which was clustered in the southern part of the state and along the banks of the Hudson River. Despite the physical devastation of the war, the socioeconomic dislocations engendered by British occupation, and the departure of thousands of its citizens who had been loyalists, the state recovered quickly and grew rapidly. By 1820 its population had quadrupled, and New York ranked first in the nation in number of inhabitants. Equally significant, settlement had shifted northward and westward into the interior. Four decades after the Revolution, a majority of New Yorkers resided in the newly settled regions west of Rome and the Mohawk Valley. The rate of population growth was highest in the 1790s (73 percent) and declined steadily in the seven decades down to 1860, as it did for the nation as a whole. Still, New York continued to grow at an average rate of 29 percent each decade between 1820 and 1860. On the eve of the Civil War, the state boasted a population of nearly four million, an elevenfold increase since the first federal census in 1790.[11]

---

[10]Haskell, *Emergence of Professional Social Science*, 28–40, 78–79; Porter and Livesay, *Merchants and Manufacturers*, 9; Stuart M. Blumin, *The Urban Threshold: Growth and Change in a Nineteenth Century American Community* (Chicago, 1976), 3–4; Robert H. Wiebe, *The Segmented Society: An Introduction to the Meaning of America* (New York, 1975), 28–29, 44–45.

[11]New York State *Census*, 1855, xxxiii; David Maldwyn Ellis, "Rise of the Empire State, 1790–1820," *New York History*, 56 (January 1975): 5–6.

The population explosion was nowhere more apparent than in the rapid expansion of the cities. Throughout the colonial and revolutionary eras and for at least two decades in the nineteenth century, virtually the only "urban" centers in the state were New York City and Albany, situated at opposite ends of the commercial axis formed by the Hudson River. Albany, in addition to being the state capital, served as the commercial center of upstate New York. Through it passed the agricultural products, lumber, potash, and furs of western and northern New York on their way to the markets of New York City and merchandise destined ultimately for distribution among the scattered farms and settlements of the interior counties. Never as large or as important economically as its neighbor to the south, Albany nonetheless prospered and grew rapidly during the years from the Revolution to the Civil War. Between 1790 and 1820 its population increased fourfold, from 3,498 to 12,630, and doubled again during the next decade. After the 1820s the rate of growth slowed somewhat, but by 1855 Albany's population had reached 57,333.[12]

One of every ten New Yorkers in 1790 resided in the great seaport at the mouth of the Hudson. With more than 33,000 residents, New York City was not only the largest urban center in the state, but also second in the nation, just behind Philadelphia. More important, the city was poised on the threshold of a period of extraordinary growth and development which would propel it to a position of preeminence by the second decade of the nineteenth century. With a growth rate of 83 percent in the 1790s and 50 percent in the first decade of the nineteenth century, New York quickly overtook Philadelphia to become the most populous city in America by 1810. The rate of increase dropped sharply in the next decade, but by 1820 the city's population had reached 130,000. Two decades later, in 1840, the total stood at 348,943, and by 1860, New York City, including Brooklyn, had passed 1,000,000.[13]

It was also during this period that New York's commercial supremacy was assured. Centrally located on the Atlantic seaboard, linked to the interior by one of the greatest navigable rivers on the North American continent, and possessing one of the finest natural harbors anywhere in the world, the city was uniquely endowed by nature to play a leading role in the commerce of the new nation. To these geographical advantages were added a large measure of luck and the entrepreneurial initiative and foresight to take advantage of favorable circumstances. Although the volume of trade passing through

---

[12]New York State *Census*, 1855, 1; Taylor, "American Urban Growth," 312; David M. Ellis, *Landlords and Farmers in the Hudson–Mohawk Region, 1790–1850* (New York, 1967), 80–81.

[13]Taylor, "American Urban Growth," 311, 325; Taylor, *Transportation Revolution*, 388; and Wilentz, *Chants Democratic*, 109–110.

New York grew steadily at the end of the eighteenth and the beginning of the nineteenth century—owing largely to the city's dominance of the re-export trade between 1793 and 1807—the greatest expansion occurred during the decade between 1815 and the completion of the Erie Canal in 1825. During these years, a series of fortuitous developments converged to widen the gap between New York and its commercial rivals. Great Britain, eager to undermine American domestic manufactures that had grown up during the war, began to dump British goods on the American market in 1815, focusing their efforts at the port of New York. This ensured that New York had a disproportionate share of the total imports coming into the country and gave it an advantage over its commercial rivals. That advantage was strengthened by the adoption of the auction system in 1817; the establishment of the first packet line in 1818, with New York as the American terminus for the Atlantic crossing; and the development of the "cotton triangle," whereby Southern cotton, exported through New York, provided profitable cargoes for packets on their return voyage to England. Thus, by 1825 New York's preeminent role in American commerce was undisputed. The official opening of the Erie Canal in November of that year laid to rest any lingering doubts by extending the city's economic sphere of influence into western New York beyond the Mohawk River and, via the Great Lakes, into the new states of the Ohio Valley. Over the course of the succeeding quarter of a century, furthermore, New York City emerged as the leading manufacturing center in the country.[14]

The growth of Albany and New York City only partially explains the rapid increase in the urban population in this period. Equally significant was the expansion of the number and size of smaller towns and cities in the state. It is not surprising that, given their location on the state's major commercial artery and the accessibility of markets, settlements along the Hudson expanded first. In the two decades following the Revolution, existing river communities such as Catskill and Poughkeepsie grew rapidly, and new towns like Hudson and Troy began to appear. After 1800, the center of urban growth shifted westward, first to the villages and towns on the Mohawk and then into the westernmost counties opened up by the Erie Canal. Thus, while the rate of urbanization leveled off in the southern and eastern sections of New York, western cities grew spectacularly. Troy experienced a 267-percent increase between 1820 and 1840. Utica grew by 330 percent in the same period; Rochester, 1,244 percent; and Buffalo, 769 percent. This extraordinary growth of cities in western New York, representing the highest rate of urbanization of any region in the country in this period, and the rapid expansion

[14]Robert G. Albion, *The Rise of New York Port, 1815–1860* (New York, 1939), vi, 1, 12–15, 28; Wilentz, *Chants Democratic*, 107–142; Ellis, *Landlords and Farmers*, 78.

of New York City propelled the state toward an increasingly urban society. Between 1820 and 1860 the proportion of city dwellers to the total population rose from 11.7 to 39.3 percent.[15]

As the state's population grew and became more urban, it also became more diverse. In the eighteenth century, the predominantly Dutch and English makeup of New York society was leavened by the presence of Palatine Germans and smaller numbers of Scots, Scots-Irish, Irish, French, and, of course, blacks. Adding to the increasingly heterogeneous and cosmopolitan character of the state, furthermore, was the great influx of Yankees from New England, first into eastern and southern New York and later, by the end of the century, spreading outward from the Hudson and Mohawk valleys into the west. As important as these trends were, however, they pale in comparison with the great waves of foreign immigrants passing through or settling in the state in the first half of the nineteenth century. Most immigrants entering the United States between 1815 and 1860 disembarked at the port of New York. At first a mere trickle, the number of arrivals jumped from fewer than eight thousand in 1817 to thirty thousand by 1830 and would continue to rise at an even higher rate over the course of the next three decades. In 1854 alone, some 327,000 German, Irish, English, Scottish, and Welsh immigrants made the transatlantic crossing to New York City. Many immigrants continued up the Hudson and across western New York via the Erie Canal to Buffalo and points west. Others chose to remain in the city. By 1855, 26 percent of the state's total population was foreign-born, with the heaviest concentrations of immigrants in the rapidly expanding cities. Indeed, by 1860, persons born outside the United States made up 48 percent of the total population of New York City.[16]

Rural New York, which still accounted for 60 percent of the total population in 1860, was also transformed in these years. Indeed, urbanization could not have proceeded at the rate that it did without a dramatic increase in the productivity of the agricultural sector of the state's economy. In the broadest sense, the half century or so before the Civil War witnessed the expansion of the cash market into all regions of the state and the general commerciali-

---

[15]U.S. Bureau of the Census, *The Statistical History of the United States, from Colonial Times to the Present* (New York, 1976), 33; Taylor, "American Urban Growth," 311–315; Ellis, *Landlords and Farmers*, 79–82; Ronald Shaw, *Erie Water West* (Lexington, Ky., 1966), 263.

[16]New York State *Census*, 1855, xl; David Maldwyn Ellis, "The Yankee Invasion of New York, 1783–1850," *New York History*, 32 (January, 1951): 3–17; Ellis, *Landlords and Farmers*, 4–5; Albion, *Rise of New York Port*, 336–338; Robert Ernst, *Immigrant Life in New York City, 1825–1863* (Port Washington, N.Y., 1949), 184; Miller, *Jacksonian Aristocracy*, 88–89; Shaw, *Erie Water West*, 274–275. The extent and impact of immigration, as well as the state's response to it, between 1847 and 1860 can be followed in the *Annual Reports of the Commissioners of Emigration of the State of New York . . . 1847 to 1860* (New York, 1861).

zation of agriculture. It was, of course, an uneven process, with the pace of change in a given region dependent on such factors as what crops were being grown, the receptivity of farmers to new ideas and techniques, accessibility to roads and waterways, and the economic impact of new modes of transportation. Commercialization was also, initially, a mixed blessing, often requiring a fundamental readjustment of farming practices in response to the price fluctuations created by an enlarged market and the competition that older, more mature agricultural regions began to experience from the newer lands of the West.[17]

We must be wary of making too sharp a distinction between self-sufficient and market farming. A more accurate picture of agriculture in New York in this period would be one that placed farmers on a continuum between subsistence and commercial farming, depending on the degree to which they were involved in local, regional, or national and international market patterns. At the end of the eighteenth century, most farmers of New York combined elements of both extremes of the continuum. Clearing the land and providing the family with the basic necessities of life still absorbed much of the time of the typical farmer. Agricultural methods were primitive, and since little was known of the importance of crop rotation and fertilizers, most New Yorkers engaged in extensive farming, exploiting the land until soil exhaustion produced declining yields. For those living closest to the subsistence level of the scale, it was a difficult and harsh existence. Money was scarce, often necessitating an economy of barter. Farm products, livestock, or the farmer's labor were traded with neighbors or used at the country store in lieu of cash. The farmer, furthermore, was his own carpenter, mason, toolmaker, and harness mender. The standard of living on such farms, needless to say, was low.[18]

Even in the early years, however, relatively few farmers were completely isolated or beyond the influence of market forces. Only those in the most remote regions, far from the line of settlement and well away from rivers and streams, approached total self-sufficiency. Most were close enough to the Hudson or Mohawk rivers to have access to the markets of Albany and New York City or one of the several smaller, river towns—such as Catskill—whose wharves served as transshipment points. Indeed, farmers in eastern New York were better situated, possessed superior transport facilities, and experienced

---

[17]Danhof, *Change in Agriculture*, 1–21; Ellis, *Landlords and Farmers*, vii–viii. An older, but still valuable, study is Ulysses Prentiss Hedrick, *A History of Agriculture in the State of New York* (1933; reprint, New York, 1966).

[18]Ellis, *Landlords and Farmers*, 76–77, 88–90, 116; Percy W. Bidwell and John I. Falconer, *History of Agriculture in the Northern United States, 1620–1860* (Washington, D.C., 1925), 164–165.

commercialization earlier than those in other parts of the country. Most were well within the hinterland of New York City and had long since begun to produce wheat, potash, corn, or lumber for shipment down the Hudson to New York for eventual sale in the national and international market. Farther north and west, farmers experienced greater difficulties in getting surplus agricultural products to market, but still managed to do so in significant quantities. By 1800 wheat was being grown for export as far as 100 miles up the Mohawk River. In the winter, wheat, flour, and other products were shipped by sleigh to Schenectady, down the Mohawk to Albany, and on to New York City via the Hudson. Other frontier farmers found an outlet for their surplus beef, flour, or potash in Quebec, which could be reached by way of Lake Ontario and the St. Lawrence River. Still others shipped farm products down the Susquehanna to Baltimore. Although transportation difficulties severely limited the volume of this interregional trade, the cash produced was a welcome addition to what was still predominantly a self-sufficient agricultural economy.[19] Local and interregional trade was even more significant in this regard. In many areas, local residents bartered farm products for merchandise at a country store, whereupon the storekeeper either sold these goods to other residents or sold them in eastern markets. In either case, the merchant required capital, was very much a part of a supralocal market system, and was responsible for bringing money into the local economy. Often, the first settlers in the region were themselves businessmen, laborers, or real estate developers as well as farmers, thus adding still another dimension to the early rural economy.[20]

That few farms were completely isolated and that many farmers participated in local, regional, and even limited national markets in no way contradicts the larger point that agriculture in New York assumed an increasingly modern and commercial character between the end of the eighteenth century and the Civil War. Horatio Seymour, speaking before the New York State Agricultural Society in 1852, summed up what must have been the experience of countless New York farmers in these years:

> At an early period "production for self consumption" was the leading purpose; now no farmer would find it profitable "to do everything within himself." He now sells for money and it is his interest to buy for money, every article that

[19] Ellis, *Landlords and Farmers*, 78–79, 84–85, 115; Bidwell and Falconer, *History of Agriculture*, 140, 171; Caroline E. McGill et al., *History of Transportation in the United States before 1860* (Washington, D.C., 1917), 165; Ellis, "Rise of the Empire State," 7–21.

[20] Roberta Balstad Miller, *City and Hinterland: A Case Study of Urban and Regional Development* (Westport, Conn., 1979), 33; Philip L. White, *Beekmantown, New York: Forest Frontier to Farm Community* (Austin, Tex., 1979), 54, 70, 83.

he cannot produce cheaper than he can buy. He cannot afford to make at home his clothing, the furniture or his farming utensils; he buys many articles for consumption for his table. He produces that which he can raise and sell to the best advantage, and he is in a situation to buy all that he can purchase, cheaper than he can produce. Time and labor have become cash articles, and he neither lends or barters them. His farm does not merely afford him a subsistence; it produces capital, and therefore demands the expenditure of capital for its improvement. An extended cash market also enables him to simplify his processes. He can now take advantage of the principle which lies at the foundation of success in commercial and manufacturing pursuits, of "doing one thing; doing it extensively and well."[21]

In short, as David M. Ellis has put it, "farming as a way of life was yielding place to the concept of farming as a means of profit."[22]

The modernization of New York agriculture did not come easily. Traditional values of self-sufficiency, no longer adequate in the increasingly market-oriented economy of the first half of the nineteenth century, died hard. Commercialization, as Horatio Seymour so shrewdly observed, generated new problems requiring new skills, not the least of which was a greater appreciation of the impersonality and interdependence of the new system. As individual farmers struggled to adjust to new conditions, furthermore, commercialization also brought rural decline to some areas of the state owing to the impact of western competition, the outmigration of population in search of cheaper land, and the flight of farmers' sons to the new, exciting cities appearing throughout New York.[23]

By far the most dramatic response to commercialization, however, was the emergence of the antirent movement. The leasehold system of land tenure, a remnant of the semifeudalism of the colonial period, had survived into the nineteenth century in a number of counties in the Hudson River Valley and, to a lesser extent, along the Mohawk. Opposition to this system dated back at least to the land riots of 1751 and 1766, when tenants on the Livingston, Van Rensselaer, and Van Cortlandt estates refused to pay rent and demanded recognition of their land titles in fee simple. Although the tenants failed to overturn the system in these early uprisings, antirent sentiment reappeared sporadically for the next century. After the death of Stephen Van Rensselaer in 1839, and partially in response to the demands of commercialization, the

---

[21] Quoted in Danhof, *Change in Agriculture*, 21–22.

[22] Ellis, *Landlords and Farmers*, viii.

[23] Bidwell and Falconer, *History of Agriculture*, 252; Ellis, *Landlords and Farmers*, 184–185, 218–224.

antirent movement erupted into a full-scale revolt against the leasehold system and spread to virtually all the counties of eastern New York.[24]

For most New York farmers, the pattern of adjustment was difficult but peaceful. At the beginning of the century, for example, wheat was the major source of farm income in eastern New York. Indeed, the Hudson–Mohawk Valley was the chief wheat-producing region in the nation. By the 1820s and 1830s, however, the production of wheat was declining, the result of soil exhaustion and the increasing competition of the more fertile farmlands in the western part of the state. As the center of the wheat culture moved westward into the Genesee country, where it had become firmly established by 1840, the farmers of eastern New York were forced to seek alternative sources of income. Gradually, after much experimentation, the older counties along the Hudson and Mohawk began to specialize in other agricultural products. Some turned to cattle and sheep grazing, others to a variety of dairy products. By 1850, the production of wool was also in decline, again owing to western competition. But the profitability of cattle grazing had been demonstrated by this time, and the region was rapidly becoming the nation's leading producer of dairy products. This continuing process of adjustment, necessitated by the changing fortunes of the various regions as they sought competitive advantages in the context of constantly shifting market patterns, had produced, by 1860, a modern, diversified, and specialized system of agriculture.[25]

THE COMMERCIALIZATION of agriculture, and the complex of social and economic changes associated with it, was the direct result of the development of more extensive and efficient transportation facilities. New York's "transportation revolution" began in the late eighteenth and early nineteenth centuries with the construction of turnpikes to link towns and cities on the Hudson and Mohawk rivers with their agricultural hinterlands. Before the turnpike era, travel and trade followed the river courses and a few primitive roads literally hacked out of the forest. Passage over these early roads was arduous at best and virtually impossible during certain seasons of the year.[26]

[24]Ellis, *Landlords and Farmers*, 225–283; E. P. Cheyney, "The Anti-Rent Movement and the Constitution of 1846," in *The Age of Reform*, vol. 6 of *History of the State of New York*, ed. Alexander C. Flick (10 vols., New York, 1933–37), 283–321; and Henry Christman, *Tin Horns and Calico: A Decisive Episode in the Emergence of Democracy* (New York, 1945).

[25]Ellis, *Landlords and Farmers*, 118, 158, 184–188, 197–198, 201; Bidwell and Falconer, *History of Agriculture*, 260.

[26]Joseph A. Durrenberger, *Turnpikes: A Study of the Toll Road Movement in the Middle Atlantic States and Maryland* (reprint, CusCob, Conn., 1968), 58–59; Oliver Wendell Holmes, "The Turnpike Era," in *Conquering the Wilderness*, vol. 5 of *History of the State of New York*, ed. Alexander C. Flick, 257–262.

As Congressman Peter Porter of western New York pointed out in 1810, such conditions retarded settlement and the extension of market farming:

> The great evil, and it is a serious one indeed, under which the inhabitants of the western country labor arises from the want of a market. There is no place where the great staple articles for the use of civilized life can be produced in greater abundance or with greater ease, and yet as respects most of the luxuries and many of the conveniences of life the people are poor. They have no vent for their produce at home, and, being all agriculturists, they produce alike the same articles with the same facility; and such is the present difficulty and expense of transporting their produce to an Atlantic port that little benefit is realized from that quarter. The single circumstance of want of a market is already beginning to produce the most disastrous effects, not only on the industry, but on the morals of the inhabitants.[27]

Efforts to improve transportation were already under way when Congressman Porter described the plight of western farmers to his colleagues in Washington. The first turnpike company, the Albany and Schenectady Turnpike Company, was chartered by the state legislature in 1797. It was followed in 1800 by the Mohawk Turnpike and Bridge Company, linking Schenectady and Utica, and the Seneca Turnpike Company, which was to connect Utica and Canandaigua. Rivaling the Mohawk route into western New York was the Great Western or Cherry Valley Turnpike, originally incorporated in 1798, which had reached Sherburne on the Chenango River by 1807. Farther south, the Susquehanna Turnpike, chartered in 1800, connected Catskill with Wattle's Ferry on the Susquehanna River. The Newburgh and Cochecton Turnpike, incorporated the following year, linked Newburgh and, eventually, Ithaca by way of northeastern Pennsylvania. Turnpikes were also extended eastward from Albany, Hudson, and Poughkeepsie to link with Massachusetts and Connecticut roads, and northward toward Vermont. A rapidly expanding network of shorter, feeder turnpikes ultimately connected the whole system. By 1821, 278 turnpike companies had been incorporated and the number of bridge companies had grown to 58; the turnpike system covered four thousand miles. New companies would be chartered and additional roads constructed over the course of succeeding decades, but the early 1820s marked the peak of the turnpike era in New York. A cheaper and more efficient mode of transportation had already made its appearance.[28]

---

[27] *Annals of Congress*, 2nd Cong., 2nd sess. (Washington, D.C., 1853), 1388.
[28] Durrenberger, *Turnpikes*, 59–65; Holmes, "The Turnpike Era," 262–270; Ellis, *Landlords and Farmers*, 85–86, 132–133; McGill, *Transportation in the United States*, 170.

The opening of the Erie Canal on November 4, 1825, has been called "the most decisive single event in the history of American transportation."[29] The story of its inception, construction, and remarkable success has been told many times. Suffice to say, proposals for a canal linking the Hudson River and the Great Lakes had been made as early as the 1790s. It was not until 1817, however, after the failure of several private ventures and the rejection of New York's request for federal assistance, that the state legislature authorized building such a canal at state expense. Construction began on the first section of the canal between Rome and Utica in July 1817. Two years later, work began at each end of this middle section and pushed westward toward Lake Erie at Buffalo and eastward toward the Hudson River at Albany. By the end of 1823, the canal was completed from the Genesee to the Hudson. Two years later, the first boats made the 363-mile journey from Buffalo to Albany, then down the Hudson to New York City.

The completion of the Erie Canal stimulated demands for additional public works, particularly in sections of the state which had been bypassed by the Erie. The Champlain Canal, to link the Hudson and Lake Champlain in northern New York, had been authorized at the same time as the Erie and was completed in 1823. Two years later, in the enthusiasm and excitement following the opening of the Erie, the legislature authorized surveys for seventeen additional canals. Not all were built, of course, but between 1825 and 1840, New York subsidized construction of nine major canal projects, along with several feeder and river-improvement projects. These included the Oswego Canal, linking Lake Ontario to the Erie System at Syracuse; the Cayuga and Seneca, connecting those lakes to the Erie at Montezuma; the Chemung and Chenango canals, connecting the Pennsylvania and New York systems via the Susquehanna River; the Genesee Valley Canal from Rochester to Olean in the south; and the Black River Canal from Rome to High Falls in the north. In addition, in 1836 the legislature authorized a massive enlargement of the Erie.[30] By 1841 New York had constructed more than six hundred miles of canals; another three hundred miles were already in progress.[31]

The final link in New York's developing transportation system was the railroad. The first in the state, and the third in the nation, was the Mohawk

[29] Goodrich, *Government Promotion of American Canals and Railroads*, 55.

[30] The most comprehensive modern account of the construction of the Erie Canal is Shaw, *Erie Water West*. Reliable short summaries include Goodrich, *Government Promotion of American Canals and Railroads*, 51–61; Noble E. Whitford, "The Canal System and Its Influence," in *Conquering the Wilderness*, vol. 5 of *History of the State of New York*, ed. Alexander C. Flick, 297–336; and Ellis, *Landlords and Farmers*, 159–175.

[31] J. Disturnell, *Gazetteer of the State of New York* (Albany, N.Y., 1842), 48.

and Hudson, incorporated in 1826, to provide a direct, overland route between Albany and Schenectady. Completion of the 16-mile route between these two cities in 1831 set off a railroad mania, which, before it subsided more than two decades later, would produce a rail network linking eastern and western New York and the principal cities of the state. Throughout the 1830s, railroad entrepreneurs and communities eager for rail connections to stimulate economic development deluged the state legislature with requests for corporate charters. Railroads with a total capitalization of $22 million were proposed in 1831 alone. Each succeeding legislative session saw similar requests. The majority of applications were denied, and many of the approved projects never materialized.[32]

Those which survived and were ultimately built formed the core of New York's modern rail system. The Hudson and Mohawk line was extended northward with the completion of the Saratoga and Schenectady in 1832, but most of the early construction was directed toward providing a rail route into western New York between Albany and Buffalo. This process occurred piecemeal as a number of independent companies provided rail service between major western cities over the next decade. The Utica and Schenectady, which paralleled the Erie Canal, was completed in 1836; the Tonawanda Railroad had been extended from Rochester to Batavia by 1837 and would reach Attica in 1842; the Syracuse and Utica and the Auburn and Syracuse were opened in 1839; and the Auburn and Rochester was completed in 1841. With the opening of the Attica and Buffalo on November 24, 1842, the first through railroad from Albany to Buffalo became a reality. The first through train service began the following year as a result of an agreement among the eight separate companies that controlled the route. In 1853 these roads were combined to form the New York Central under the leadership of Erastus Corning.

Meanwhile, efforts were under way to provide rail connections in other regions. As early as 1832, residents of southwestern New York, allied with New York City promoters, successfully petitioned the legislature for a charter creating the New York and Erie to connect the Hudson River and Lake Erie by a direct route through the southern tier. After numerous financial difficulties and frustrating delays, the Erie Railroad was finally completed between Piermont on the Hudson and Dunkirk on Lake Erie in 1851. The Hudson River Railroad, which ran up the east side of the Hudson through Poughkeepsie to Greenbush across the river from Albany, was completed the same year. In 1852, the New York and Harlem Railroad, originally incorpo-

---

[32] MacGill, *History of Transportation*, 356–357; Thomas F. Gordon, *A Gazetteer of the State of New York* (Philadelphia, 1836), 108.

rated in 1831, was extended all the way to Albany. Meanwhile, the Northern Railroad, between Ogdensburgh and Lake Champlain, had opened in 1850. Altogether, including branches and connecting lines, some thirty railroads were operating in the state in 1850 with a total of 1,649 miles of track completed by 1851 and more than 1,000 miles in progress.[33]

Railroads were destined, in the long run, to displace canals as the leading carrier of passengers and freight in the state. But it was not until the 1850s and after that the tremendous potential inherent in railroad technology began to be felt. Initially, railroads were conceived and constructed to supplement the canal system. Indeed, where projected railroads paralleled canals, early corporate charters specifically prohibited them from carrying freight in competition with the state-owned canals. This restriction to passenger service was eased somewhat in 1836 when the first railroad company won the right to carry freight on the condition that it pay the regular canal tolls on such freight. In 1844 the legislature extended this privilege to all railroads, and seven years later, in 1851, the state abolished all such restrictions, thus assuring the future domination of New York's inland commerce by the new technology.[34]

FEW DEVELOPMENTS contributed more to the modernization of New York's society and economy in the first half of the nineteenth century than the extension of the transportation network. Wherever its influence was felt, the transportation revolution literally remade society. Improved transportation, particularly the canal system, reoriented traditional trade patterns; stimulated major shifts of population; undermined and replaced customary modes of production; altered forever the rural-urban population mix and the ratio of agricultural to other forms of employment; and, in the broadest sense, spurred the process of economic diversification and social differentiation. It is not possible to describe in detail the many local and regional variations of this transformation. But we can highlight broad structural changes in the society and economy induced by transportation developments and identify somewhat more precisely the nature of the transformation wrought by canal development in several representative localities.

More than any other single event, the coming of the Erie Canal dictated the character of the society that emerged in the western counties of New York between 1820 and 1860. In addition to expanding the cash market, link-

---

[33] MacGill, *History of Transportation*, 358–381; Gordon, *Gazetteer*, 105–108; Disturnell, *Gazetteer*, 48.

[34] Ellis, *Landlords and Farmers*, 180; Donald C. Sowers, *The Financial History of New York State from 1789 to 1912* (New York, 1914), 85–90; Shaw, *Erie Water West*, 287.

ing western New York and the Ohio Valley to the Atlantic, and increasing the volume of commerce flowing through New York City, the canal played a developmental role in the local economy. Construction activity provided a source of nonagricultural employment and money income, encouraged new extractive industries such as lumbering and quarrying, attracted contractors and other entrepreneurs to the region, and increased local bank reserves as a consequence of the transfer of construction funds to the area. Once built, the canal necessitated transshipment, warehousing, financial, and distribution facilities at terminal points and fostered an expansion of commercial farming, increased population, and the appearance of manufacturing centers along the canal route.[35]

An examination of key economic indicators in the Erie Canal counties from 1820 to 1840 reveals even more clearly the structural changes produced by improved transport facilities. Land values in the counties bordering the canal increased by 91 percent between 1820 and 1846, while the rate of increase for noncanal counties and for the state as a whole was 52 and 65 percent, respectively.[36] The influx of new settlers to the region produced the highest rate of population growth in the country, owing largely to the expansion of Albany, Utica, Syracuse, Buffalo, and Rochester. Indeed, the five counties bordering the western half of the Erie experienced a 135-percent increase during the 1820s.[37] Construction of the canal also hastened the decline of household textile manufactures in western New York. Between 1820 and 1845, household production of woolen goods dropped sharply in every county along the canal line.[38] Finally, the percentage of persons employed in manufacturing and commerce in the fourteen canal counties grew from 4.2 percent in 1820 to 8 percent in 1840, a more rapid rate of change than for the state as a whole. During the same period, agricultural employment remained stable at about 20 percent of the total.[39]

[35]Segal, "Canals and Economic Development," 224–225.

[36]Ibid., 235; see also Dixon Ryan Fox, *The Decline of Aristocracy in the Politics of New York* (New York, 1919), 303.

[37]Whitney R. Cross, *The Burned-Over District: The Social and Intellectual History of Enthusiastic Religion in Western New York, 1800–1850* (New York, 1965), 56.

[38]Arthur H. Cole, *The American Wool Manufacture*, 2 vols. (reprint, New York, 1969), 1: 281–282.

[39]Segal, "Canals and Economic Development," 235–236; Shaw, *Erie Water West*, 264. See also Albert W. Niemi, Jr., "A Further Look at Interregional Canals and Economic Specialization: 1820–1840," *Explorations in Economic History*, 7 (Summer 1970): 499–520, and Roger L. Ransom, "A Closer Look at Canals and Western Manufacturing," *Explorations in Economic History*, 8 (Summer 1971): 501–508. These two articles are important because they provide additional data on employment in agriculture, commerce, and manufacturing in the canal counties.

New modes of transportation affected individual localities differently, depending on preexisting conditions and the nature of an area's prior relationship to the market. Onondaga County, which lay astride the middle section of the canal, is a case in point. Originally settled in the 1790s, the county grew slowly but steadily in the early decades of the nineteenth century before the Erie opened. Through Onondaga's borders ran several major interregional turnpikes—most notably the Seneca Turnpike—which linked the area socially and economically to eastern New York and southern New England and assured the county at least limited access to the national market. These transportation routes also conditioned social and economic patterns *within* the county. Townships and villages on the turnpikes grew more rapidly than those located away from major roads; the county's commercial activities, agricultural processing facilities, and industry tended to be concentrated in areas with interregional transportation connections.[40]

Completion of the interregional canal network altered established trade patterns with the East Coast and, in the process, disrupted social and economic relationships within the county. The most obvious change was a wholesale shift of social and economic activities away from areas of the county serviced by the turnpike to those through which the Erie and Oswego canals passed. The center of population shifted northward as outmigration from established communities began to take its toll and as settlements along the canal route flourished in response to new migration and trade patterns. Settlements along the turnpike declined economically as the canal garnered an ever-increasing share of the interregional traffic. This process was hastened by the migration of entrepreneurial talent and development capital out of the older communities where opportunity was becoming more constricted and into the suddenly prosperous villages and towns on the canal.[41]

Agricultural and industrial patterns were similarly disrupted. Initially, increased accessibility to national markets and declining transport costs led to higher profits and an expansion of the amount of land under cultivation. By the late 1830s, however, as the long-term consequences of these new marketing patterns became clearer, the prospect of agricultural crisis had replaced the initial optimism felt by Onondaga farmers. Local transportation facilities deteriorated as the bulk of interregional trade shifted to the canal, thereby undermining the efficiency and increasing the cost of moving goods within the region. Onondaga farmers also began to feel the adverse effects of competition from wheat and wool produced in the states farther west and shipped across New York via the Erie Canal. Thus, instead of the widespread pros-

[40] Miller, *City and Hinterland*, 7, 23–30, 34–36.
[41] Ibid., 43–53, 152.

perity that many anticipated in the wake of canal development, rural Onondaga was confronted with a highly unstable agricultural economy as the residents of the county sought to adjust to new marketing patterns. Comparable shifts occurred in the nature and location of industrial activity. Small, rural processing industries declined, either because the growth of interregional transportation made them obsolete—as in the case of distilleries—or because such activities were increasingly concentrated in larger facilities located along the canal. As a result of this reorientation of agriculture and industry, the economy of Onondaga County became increasingly differentiated between a rural hinterland and the new urban centers made possible by the Erie.[42]

These new marketing patterns transformed Syracuse from a sleepy village some distance from the principal turnpike routes into a major commercial, industrial, and interregional distribution center. Ideally situated at the weighlock of the Erie Canal and the southern terminus of the Oswego Canal, Syracuse rapidly came to dominate the county and the region. Population, businesses, and investment capital flowed out of declining turnpike villages and into Syracuse. At the same time, the city's economy was stimulated by the establishment of new industries and new canal-related transportation facilities and services and by the influx of immigrants coming up the Erie Canal in search of jobs. The population of Syracuse grew by more than 900 percent in the 1820s and exceeded six thousand by 1840. Increased political power accompanied the concentration of commercial and industrial activities in the city. In 1829 Syracuse replaced Onondaga West Hill as county seat. This brought a predictable influx of lawyers and public officials and made the city the political as well as economic center of Onondaga County.[43]

Similar transformations occurred across New York in the wake of canal and other transportation developments. Completion of the Erie Canal was directly responsible for the rise of major cities such as Rochester and Buffalo as well as second-rank urban centers such as Lockport. Located at the center of the wheat-producing Genesee country, Rochester rose rapidly to dominate the grain trade and, by 1840, had become a major manufacturing center and the nation's leading producer of flour. Buffalo's growth, on the other hand, was a function of having been chosen as the western terminus of the Erie Canal. Across its wharves passed not only much of the commerce of western New York, but also, and in the long run more important, agricultural goods from northern Ohio shipped eastward via Lake Erie. Although one was principally a processing and manufacturing center and the other was

---

[42] Ibid., 60–71, 130–153.
[43] Ibid., 50, 68–72, 112.

a commercial center, both Rochester and Buffalo grew spectacularly during the 1830s. By 1840 each possessed some twenty thousand inhabitants and a prosperous and diversified economy.[44]

The Champlain Canal, completed in 1822, wrought similar changes in northern New York. The opening of an all-water route from Lake Champlain to Albany and New York City reduced that region's dependence on Quebec as a market for its agricultural and forest products. Before the construction of the Champlain Canal, the difficulty of overland transportation discouraged the shipment of lumber and other products downstate. After 1822, however, both the time and the cost of shipping goods southward to New York City were dramatically reduced, with predictable results. Goods that had previously flowed northward to Canada were diverted to the more convenient market at New York City. At the same time, the cost of imports coming into the north country from New York declined, with a consequent increase in the relative purchasing power of upstate residents. Perhaps even more important, northern New York, while still the most underdeveloped region of the state, was effectively integrated into a statewide marketing system increasingly centered in the metropolis at the mouth of the Hudson.[45]

The transportation revolution also transformed older, more established communites. Stuart Blumin has described what happened to Kingston in the wake of the construction of the Delaware and Hudson Canal in the 1820s. Situated on the west bank of the Hudson River roughly midway between New York City and Albany, Kingston was a rural, predominantly agricultural town of about three thousand inhabitants at the beginning of the decade. For all of its rural character, however, the town was neither isolated nor underdeveloped, having already achieved the status of an important link in the trading networks of both New York City and New England ports. Kingston was also integrated into a variety of extralocal social, political, religious, and communications networks. Even so, the Delaware and Hudson profoundly altered the social order of this stable agricultural community. Within one generation of the completion of the canal connecting the Pennsylvania anthracite coalfields and the Hudson River, the town was transformed into a commercial city. Its population grew from three thousand in 1820 to more than sixteen thousand in 1860. More important, the anthracite trade touched off an economic boom. Although not directly involved in the ownership and operation of the canal, Kingstonians participated fully in this economic

---

[44]Shaw, *Erie Water West*, 131–136, 263, 265–273; Albion, *Rise of New York Port*, 88–90; Johnson, *Shopkeeper's Millennium*, 16–20; see also Blake McKelvey, *Rochester: The Water Power City, 1812–1854* (Cambridge, Mass., 1945).

[45]White, *Beekmantown*, 44–45, 71–73, 75–76, 92.

growth by providing such ancillary services as banking and insurance and as wholesalers, forwarders, innkeepers, grocers, manufacturers, and laborers. The canal also led to increased trade between Kingston and its agricultural hinterland. As its economy grew, the town also became more modern. By 1860 the practice of bartering grain or other agricultural goods at Kingston's retail stores had given way almost entirely to the cash or cash-based credit system. Home manufacturing was no longer a significant factor in the town's economy, and specialization of economic function had become the rule rather than the exception.[46]

THE ESTABLISHMENT of a modern transportation network and the new marketing patterns that it created also stimulated the growth of manufacturing and the beginnings of industrialization in the state. New York had been one of the leading manufacturing states in the nation even before the opening of the Erie Canal, ranking third in the nation in the value of manufacturing output in 1810 and second, behind Pennsylvania, in 1814.[47] The state led in the household production of textiles, including cotton, flax, and woolen goods valued at $50,222 in 1810.[48] Between 1800 and 1823, furthermore, New York led the nation in total number of incorporations and was second only to Massachusetts in total capitalization.[49]

Much of this early manufacturing activity represented the culmination of trends established in the colonial period or reflected the growth of industries—such as grist and flour milling—typically found in rural, frontier areas. But the foreign policies of Jefferson and Madison also contributed to the state's burgeoning industrial output. The Embargo and Non-Intercourse acts and the war with England disrupted trade and forced New Yorkers and other Americans to manufacture for themselves goods that had previously been imported. Simultaneously, the decline of American trade freed commercial capital for reinvestment in new manufacturing ventures. State laws offering premiums and bounties for the production of household fabrics provided an additional stimulus.[50]

The most important period of manufacturing development, however, came after 1825. The completion of the Erie Canal opened up the new lands of the

[46]Blumin, *The Urban Threshold*, 2–3, 9, 14–18, 44–49, 52–65, 75.

[47]*A Statement of the Arts and Manufactures of the United States of America, for the Year 1810: Digested and Prepared by Tench Coxe* (Philadelphia, 1814), 36.

[48]Harry J. Carman, "The Beginnings of the Industrial Revolution," in *Conquering the Wilderness*, vol. 5 of *History of the State of New York*, ed. Alexander C. Flick, 344–345.

[49]Clark, *History of Manufactures*, 266.

[50]Richard L. Ehrlich, "The Development of Manufacturing in Selected Counties in the Erie Canal Corridor, 1815–1860" (Ph.D. diss., State University of New York, 1972), 18; Ellis, *Landlords and Farmers*, 127–128; Miller, *City and Hinterland*, 23–24.

West, thereby creating a huge new market for existing and future manufacturers and, at the same time, making western agriculture sufficiently profitable to allow farmers to purchase eastern manufactured goods. Primary and extractive industries based on locally supplied raw materials and servicing a regional market also grew in the areas through which the canal passed. The result was a boom in the manufacturing sector of the state's economy in the second quarter of the nineteenth century.[51]

Although statistical data on manufacturing in the early nineteenth century is imprecise, information available in federal and state censuses and a few supplemental sources allows us to map the general contours of industrial growth. The limited and incomplete state census of 1835, for example, reported 13,667 manufacturing establishments and estimated the value of manufacturing output at $59 million, a 58-percent increase since 1814. The U.S. Census of 1840, more complete than its predecessors, but still fragmentary, put the total value of New York's manufacturing output at slightly less than $96 million, with New York City alone contributing more than $23 million. Capital investments in manufacturing totaled more than $55 million. A decade later, in 1850, New York could boast 23,555 individuals and establishments engaged in manufacturing, total capital investments of nearly $100 million, and an annual industrial product valued at more than $237 million.[52]

Growth of industry is also reflected in the changing ratio of agricultural to nonagricultural employment, the decline of household industries, and the spread of factory production. As late as 1840, 18.8 percent of the total population of New York was engaged in agriculture.[53] By 1850 that figure had declined to 10.2 percent. During the same period, nonagricultural employment nearly doubled. At mid-century 17.2 percent of New Yorkers were engaged in commerce, manufacturing, mining, navigation, professional, or other nonagricultural employment, with the shift being most dramatic in the Erie Canal counties and in New York and Kings counties.[54]

Equally significant was the decline of household production as the market expanded to encompass new areas of the state. In the textile industry, for

[51] Albion, *Rise of New York Port*, 91; Miller, *Jacksonian Aristocracy*, 110–111; Segal, "Canals and Economic Development," 224–225; Miller, *City and Hinterland*, 63, 68–69.

[52] New York State *Census*, 1855, lviii–lx; J. D. B. DeBow, *Statistical View of the United States . . . Being a Compendium of the Seventh Census* (reprint, New York, 1970), 179; Adna F. Weber, *The Growth of Industry in New York* (Albany, 1904), 25; Harry J. Carman and August B. Gold, "The Rise of the Factory System," in *The Age of Reform*, vol. 6 of *History of New York State*, ed. Alexander C. Flick, 193.

[53] Segal, "Canals and Economic Development," 236.

[54] DeBow, *Statistical View*, 125, 128–129; New York State *Census*, 1855, xli.

example, household manufactures dropped off by nearly 50 percent between 1825 and 1835, from 16.5 to 8.8 million yards. Twenty years later the total stood at less than 1 million yards.[55] The most dramatic decline was in the production of woolen goods. After the introduction of transportation facilities into areas where family production had been predominant earlier, household manufacturing of wool cloth dropped precipitously, from 6.5 million yards in 1825 to .6 million yards in 1855.[56]

The decline of household industry was accompanied by the emergence of the factory system of production. The process was gradual and was by no means complete in the first half of the nineteenth century. But by the 1840s and 1850s, the factory had come to play an increasingly significant role in most industries in New York and would, of course, become the dominant mode of production after mid-century.[57] Once again, the textile industry best illustrates this economic transformation. The first cotton mill in New York, established in 1789 under the auspices of the New York Manufacturing Society, was shortlived, failing in 1793 after a brief four-year existence. Other early efforts to establish cotton mills met a similar fate. By 1809, however, five mills were operating in the state, and some 36 companies devoted to cotton manufactures had been incorporated by 1823.[58] In 1831 New York possessed 112 mills, capitalized at $3.6 million, with 5,510 employees.[59] Twenty years later, the 1850 census reported 86 such establishments, capitalized at $4.1 million.[60] The growth of factories similarly transformed the woolen industry. In 1831 New Yorkers had some $900,000 invested in woolen mills employing more than 1,200 workers. By 1840 the number of mills had grown to 323 with a total capitalization of $3.4 million and with 4,636 employees. At mid-century 249 woolen mills, capitalized at more than $4.4 million, operated in the state.[61] By this time, factories had begun to replace household manufacturing in virtually every field of industrial activity.

With a highly diversified manufacturing sector, New York was indisputably the leading industrial state in the nation by mid-century. It led the nation

---

[55] Taylor, *Transportation Revolution*, 213.

[56] Cole, *American Wool Manufactures*, 1: 184–185, 279n; New York State *Census*, 1855, lv.

[57] Ehrlich, "Development of Manufacturing," 31, 34; Miller, *Jacksonian Aristocracy*, 111–113.

[58] Carman, "The Beginnings of the Industrial Revolution," 340–342, 347; Carman and Gold, "The Rise of the Factory System," 195.

[59] Timothy Pitkin, *A Statistical View of the Commerce of the United States of America* (reprint, New York, 1967), 526.

[60] U.S. Bureau of the Census, *Abstract of the 7th Census, 1850* (Washington, D.C., 1853), 154; Carman and Gold, "The Rise of the Factory System," 193.

[61] U.S. Bureau of the Census, *Abstract of the 7th Census*, 155; Carman and Gold, "The Rise of the Factory System," 198.

in iron casting, was second in the production of woolen goods and wrought iron and in distilleries and breweries, fifth in cotton manufacturers, and seventh in the production of pig iron. Metal goods from the Albany-Troy region, wood products manufactured from the lumber of northern New York, flour from Rochester and Buffalo, and leather goods tanned in the Catskills and finished in New York City dominated regional and national markets in these products. The linchpin of this burgeoning industrial economy was New York City, which produced manufactured goods valued at $159 million in 1860, making it the principal manufacturing center in the country.[62]

EVIDENCE THAT New York was experiencing a dramatic transformation in the first half of the nineteenth century is not limited to the economy. Among other things, the emergence and increasing significance of organizations transformed the very structure of society. These changes did not reflect an organizational revolution of the same magnitude as that which transformed late-nineteenth-century America. Nor would it be correct to assert that society in general was becoming significantly more bureaucratic, though bureaucratic structures were beginning to emerge in some sectors of society. Clearly, though, the proliferation of voluntary associations and the appearance of new organizational forms in the economy, society, and polity reflect the evolution of an increasingly complex, differentiated, and pluralistic social order and the emergence of new attitudes toward participation. As was the case throughout the United States, New Yorkers created societies to encourage manufacturing; associations to promote internal improvements; trade unions; local agricultural societies; medical and bar associations; and societies for the advancement of the arts and sciences. Reformers organized to eradicate a wide variety of social ills, including slavery, war, alcohol, prostitution, and poverty. A host of Bible, missionary, and other religious societies appeared, seeking to spread the gospel and to safeguard the moral values of a predominantly Protestant culture against the onslaught of Catholic immigrants. There were also charitable and benevolent societies, young men's associa-

---

[62]U.S. Bureau of the Census, *Abstract of the 7th Census*, 154–158; DeBow, *Statistical View*, 179–183; Miller, *Jacksonian Aristocracy*, 116–118; North, *Economic Growth of the United States*, 168. For a sophisticated analysis of the process of metropolitan industrialization in New York City, see Wilentz, *Chants Democratic*, 107–142.

tions, fraternal orders, lyceums, library societies, and volunteer fire associations.[63]

A complete rendering of the extent of this associational activity would require intensive research into the local records and newspapers of virtually every locality in the state, and is beyond the scope of this study.[64] But one measure of the pace at which voluntary associations multiplied in this period is the early date at which general laws were passed providing for the administrative incorporation of various categories of such associations. Initially all incorporations, whether of a business or nonbusiness nature, were by special act of the legislature. As the demand for corporate privileges grew, however, and as a larger and larger proportion of the legislature's time was consumed in granting special charters, the benefits of general incorporation became increasingly apparent. Thus, between 1784 and 1811, the New York legislature passed general laws for the incorporation of religious congregations (1784), colleges and academies (1787), library companies (1796), county medical societies (1806), and Bible societies (1811).[65] Other such laws followed later in the century. Most voluntary associations, of course, were either unincorporated or continued to be created by special act until the 1840s and 1850s. But the trend is clear. In the early nineteenth century, New Yorkers, like Americans generally, turned with increasing frequency to specialized associations of one kind or another to accomplish a wide variety of political, economic, social, and cultural goals. These associations represented new, often extralocal, forms of participation. In the pursuit of specialized goals, they helped to create and shape a social order increasingly inhabited by a multiplicity of formal institutions extending upward and outward from the locality.

[63]Although historians make frequent reference to the emergence of voluntary associations as a characteristic of this period, there has been surprisingly little systematic analysis of the social significance of this phenomenon. A good starting point, however, is Alexis de Tocqueville, *Democracy in America*, ed. J. P. Mayer (Garden City, N.Y., 1966), 189–195, 513–524; Richard D. Brown, "The Emergence of Voluntary Associations in Massachusetts, 1760–1830," *Journal of Voluntary Action Research*, 2 (1973): 64–73; Robert F. Berkhofer, Jr., "The Organizational Interpretation of American History: A New Synthesis," *Prospects*, 4 (1979): 611–629; Donald G. Matthews, "The Second Great Awakening as an Organizing Process, 1780–1830," *American Quarterly*, 21 (Spring 1969): 23–43; and Walter S. Glazer, "Participation and Power: Voluntary Associations and the Functional Organization of Cincinnati in 1840," *Historical Methods Newsletter*, 5 (September 1972): 151–168.

[64]For a sampling of the literature on the extent and significance of associational activity within specific localities in New York, see Blumin, *Urban Threshold*, 150, 160–165; White, *Beekmantown*, 147–170; and Ryan, *Cradle of the Middle Class*, 105–144. Sean Wilentz's analysis of the emergence of trade unions and other labor organizations in New York City is the best account of such activity in any locality in this period; see *Chants Democratic*, 172–254.

[65]*Laws of New York*, chap. 18, 1784; chap. 82, 1787; chap. 43, 1796; chap. 38, 1806; chap. 190, 1811.

Not the least significant aspect of this process was the virtually complete reorganization of the economic system as a result of the increasing differentiation and specialization of economic functions and the emergence of the private business corporation. These two developments went hand in hand as banks, insurance companies, and other specialized economic activities, a large proportion of which were incorporated, increased dramatically in the early nineteenth century. For the present discussion, it is enough to point out that during the half century or so between the end of the American Revolution and the third decade of the nineteenth century, the corporation evolved from a device used infrequently and principally for public purposes into a modern, essentially private, instrument of economic organization. Legal advantages such as unlimited life and limited liability, as well as the ease with which large amounts of capital from a number of different sources could be pooled for a single enterprise, assured that the corporation would quickly become the preferred form of business organization.[66]

The rapid growth of corporations in New York is well documented. Before 1800 New York had chartered a total of only 28 business corporations, including 13 turnpike companies, 4 banks, 3 canal companies, 3 insurance companies, 2 manufacturing companies, 2 water companies, and 1 toll-bridge company. In contrast, the state incorporated 179 businesses in the first decade of the nineteenth century! The expansion of the business corporation over the next three decades was even more striking, with the creation of 1,352 such "bodies corporate" during the period 1810 to 1840. The decade of the 1830s alone witnessed the creation of 573 businesses. Nearly half were public utilities (for example, transportation, communications); mining and manufacturing corporations accounted for 28 percent, banks for 10 percent, and all other categories for 11 percent.[67] These figures illustrate the revolution in business organization wrought by the emergence of the corporation. They also reflect the decline of the traditional sedentary merchant and the proliferation of specialized firms in commerce, finance, transportation, and manufacturing. The process of specialization, furthermore, is indicative of the growth and maturity of the New York economy in the first third of the nineteenth century.

---

[66]L. Ray Gunn, "The Political Implications of General Incorporation Laws in New York to 1860," *Mid-America*, 59 (October 1977): 171–191; Ronald E. Seavoy, "The Origins of the American Business Corporation, 1784–1855: New York, the National Model" (Ph.D. diss., University of Michigan, 1969).

[67]Joseph S. Davis, *Essays in the Earlier History of American Corporations*, 2 vols. (Cambridge, Mass., 1917), 2: 22–23. George H. Evans, Jr., *Business Incorporation in the United States, 1800–1943* (New York, 1948), 17; and Gunn, "Political Implications of General Incorporation Laws in New York to 1860," 173.

The expansion of the banking system was particularly dramatic. The first banking institution in the state, the Bank of New York, opened in June 1784, though it had to wait seven years for a corporate charter. Between 1791 and 1800, three additional banks were created: the Bank of Albany (1792); the Bank of Columbia, located in Hudson (1793); and the Manhattan Bank (1799). Excluding the operations of the Bank of the United States, these four banks, with a total capitalization of $3,370,000, represented the entire banking industry in New York in 1800.[68] After the turn of the century, however, the number of banks increased spectacularly. Six more were incorporated in the decade 1801 to 1810, and twenty-three received corporate charters in the second decade of the century.[69] Although by this time banking had become enmeshed in state politics, the partisanship surrounding the granting of charters did little to stem the diffusion of banking facilities. By 1835 there were eighty-six banks in New York with an aggregate capital of $31,481,460, a total circulation of $16,732,014, and specie reserves totaling $7,345,195.[70] The demand for even more banks to meet the capital needs of a dynamic, speculative economy was so great that in 1838 the state legislature passed the Free Banking Act, throwing open the banking industry to virtually all comers. Eight years later, according to a report of the state comptroller, New York could boast eighty-one incorporated banks (created under the Safety Fund System) with a total capitalization of $30,491,460, and seventy-one banks, capitalized at $12,437,654, created under the Free Banking Act.[71]

The pattern of growth and diffusion in the insurance industry was similar to that in banking. During most of the eighteenth century, such insurance as was available was provided by individual underwriters in the manner common in Europe since the fifteenth and sixteenth centuries.[72] As in other forms of enterprise, however, the emergence of the corporation transformed the business of insurance by stimulating the pooling of capital with a minimum of risk. The transformation was gradual at first, with only three insurance companies receiving corporate charters before 1800. After that, however, the expansion was dramatic. Between 1800 and 1835, according to one compilation, ninety-four insurance companies were incorporated in New York State. Most were for fire and marine insurance, though a few life insurance companies had by this time appeared. Not all survived, of course, but in 1835, sixty insurance companies operated in the state, with a total capitalization of

---

[68] Davis, *Essays in the Earlier History of American Corporations*, 2: 80–95, 97, 100, 332–333.
[69] Evans, *Business Incorporation*, 17.
[70] Gordon, *Gazetteer*, 276.
[71] New York State, *Documents of the Constitutional Convention of 1846*, vol. 1, no. 34.
[72] New York State Insurance Department, *First Annual Report of the Superintendent of the Insurance Department* (Albany, N.Y., 1860), 3–5.

$17,301,731. Thirty more had been incorporated by 1845.[73] The state responded to the increased demand for such financial devices by enacting general laws for the incorporation of insurance companies in 1849 and 1853. In 1859, furthermore, responsibility for regulating the insurance industry was transferred from the state comptroller to an independent Insurance Department.[74]

Banks and insurance companies were both a consequence of, and agents for, modernization. Banks were the principal mechanism for pooling capital for investment in transportation, commerce, and manufacturing. To the extent that bank notes circulated as currency, the proliferation of banks contributed to the monetization of economic relationships and the establishment of a market economy. The extension of credit and the rational management of money also made possible the emergence of a cash-based credit system. It was precisely because banks performed these critical functions in the modernizing economy of the period that the state sought ways to regulate and rationalize the activities of banks, first through the Banking Commission established in 1829, then through the regulatory provisions of the Free Banking Act, and finally through the creation of the Bank Department in 1851. The significance of insurance companies to the process of social and economic change also went beyond their strictly financial role. The emergence of the concept of "insurance" typifies modern attitudes in that it involves the calculation and rationalization of risk. Fatalism, or the conviction that "whatever will be, will be," is replaced by a desire to predict and control the consequences of future events, whether they be fire, natural disaster, or death. The growth of insurance companies is also symptomatic of the rise of private administration consequent on the establishment of the market economy. In modern, highly interdependent societies, insurance companies perform a critical function by administering conflicts and, in effect, socializing risk.[75]

The growth of a more complex, differentiated, and interdependent social order was accompanied by the emergence of modern systems of communication. Of course, in comparison with the technological advances in communications in the twentieth century, the changes in this period seem modest. But in comparison with preceding centuries, communications became significantly faster, more efficient, and more cosmopolitan. To a large extent, these changes were a function of the transportation revolution. But

[73] Davis, *Essays in the Earlier History of American Corporations*, 2: 235, 334–335; Evans, *Business Incorporation*, 17; Gordon, *Gazetteer*, 271–272.

[74] *Laws of New York*, chap. 308, 1849; chap. 463, 1853; chap. 366, 1859.

[75] Brown, *Modernization*, 111–112; Lowi, *End of Liberalism*, 30–39.

the modernization of communications was most graphically reflected in a dramatic expansion of the postal system and in an equally dramatic revolution in newspaper publishing. In 1789, for example, there were only seven post offices in the state and 160 miles of post road—the distance from New York City to Albany. By 1793 the number of post offices had risen to twenty. Three decades later, there were 876 post offices, reflecting the rapid settlement of western and northern New York in the late eighteenth and early nineteenth centuries.[76]

The number of newspapers grew equally rapidly. At the close of the Revolution, only three newspapers were actually being printed in the state. By 1810 there were 66. These included seven dailies, one semiweekly, and five weeklies published in New York City, and three semiweeklies published in Albany. All other newspapers were weeklies. As might be expected, newspapers were still concentrated in the more settled areas of southern and eastern New York and along the Mohawk, with only four newspapers west of Onondaga. Over the next four decades, however, the number of newspapers and periodicals grew spectacularly, with 161 being published in 1828, more than 200 in 1840, 428 at mid-century, and 671 by 1855.[77]

Concomitant with this growth in numbers, newspapers also changed in character. Early-nineteenth-century newspapers were small, limited in content to commercial and political subjects, expensive, and, usually, highly personal enterprises. By the 1830s newspapers had begun to take on more modern characteristics. The introduction of steam presses and other mechanical improvements revolutionized the printing process and made larger circulations possible. More important, the emergence of the "penny press" wrought a revolution in newspaper publishing and in journalism. Penny papers, such as the *New York Sun* and James Gordon Bennett's *New York Herald*, consciously sought large circulations through lower prices, street vending rather than subscription sales, a more open and market-oriented advertising policy, political independence, and a shift in content from commercial and political news of interest primarily to an elite to greater emphasis on news reflecting social life generally. These developments, themselves the product of democratization and the expansion of the market, signaled the birth of modern journalism.[78]

[76] Horatio Gates Spafford, *A Gazetteer of the State of New York*, (Albany, N.Y. 1824), 619; Brown, *Modernization*, 117.

[77] William H. Seward, "Notes on New York," in *The Works of William H. Seward*, ed. George E. Baker, 3 vols. (New York, 1853), 2: 30–36; DeBow, *Statistical View*, 155–156; New York State *Census*, 1855, 480–496.

[78] Michael Schudson, *Discovering the News: A Social History of American Newspapers* (New York, 1978), 12–60.

The period also witnessed the proliferation of newspapers and periodicals serving specialized clienteles. In addition to those devoted principally to politics, which themselves reflected the cacophony of political views and factions in the state, were papers devoted exclusively to commercial, religious, agricultural, and literary affairs. Foreign-language newspapers served a variety of immigrant groups, and many reform and professional associations had their own press organs. Of the more than 670 periodicals published in New York in 1855, 274 dealt with political subjects, 67 religion, 35 literary, 19 medicine, 15 temperance, 13 juvenile, 13 agriculture, 10 education, 9 science and the arts, and 219 miscellaneous.[79]

The new role of the press was best summarized by William H. Seward in his "Notes on New York":

> The press *was* dependent on European facts, sentiments, opinions, tastes, and customs; *now*, it is in all things independent, and purely American. It was metropolitan; *now* it is universal. The newspaper in each important town conveys intelligence of all interesting incidents which occur within its vicinity, to the central press, and receives in return and diffuses information gathered from all portions of the world.
>
> The press studies carefully the condition of all classes, and yields its reports with such a nice adaption of prices as to leave no portion of the community without information concerning all that can engage their curiosity or concern their welfare. It no longer fears the odious *information*, or the frowns of power; but dictates with boldness to the government, and combines and not unfrequently forms the public opinion which controls everything. . . . It is at once the chief agent of intellectual improvement and the palladium of civil and religious liberty.[80]

Not only were communications within the state changing in decidedly modern ways, but New York City emerged during the first four decades of the century to a position of dominance in an increasingly integrated national communications system. Before the War of 1812, domestic communications remained largely unintegrated owing to the underdeveloped state of transportation. Information moved slowly and irregularly, keeping distant cities relatively isolated from one another. After the war, the flow of information increased dramatically in response to the transportation revolution. New York City, which by this time had begun its drive to commercial supremacy, was uniquely positioned to capitalize on this development. Indeed, the city's

[79]Seward, "Notes on New York," 30–36; New York State *Census*, 1855, 497; Brown, *Modernization*, 109, 117–118.

[80]Seward, "Notes on New York," 37–38.

role in the communications network was a function of its increasing significance as a port. Foreign information of an economic, political, or social nature arrived at the port of New York via ships engaged in the Atlantic trade, then followed the established trade routes up and down the coast and into the interior. The increased volume of commerce at New York City after 1815, the establishment of packet lines, the city's dominance of the southern cotton trade, and its link with the West via the Erie Canal assured that the port of New York would dominate not only the distribution of imported goods but also the dissemination of information. According to Allan Pred in *Urban Growth and the Circulation of Information*, "by 1817 New York had clearly outdistanced Philadelphia and all other competitors and had established an information hegemony." The combination of economic expansion and the explosion of the publishing industry, moreover, had increased this lead even further by 1841, on the eve of a still more dramatic revolution in communications resulting from the invention of the telegraph.[81]

The connection between these social and economic processes is nowhere better illustrated than in the centralization of the capital market and credit system in New York City. After 1836, when the charter of the Second Bank of the United States expired, New York City began to emerge as the leading money market in the country, gradually displacing Philadelphia and Boston in that role. As was the case with the flow of information, New York City occupied a strategic position in the increasingly interdependent national and international credit system. The city's bankers and merchant princes extended credit to southern planters, western farmers, country storekeepers, and merchants in lesser cities throughout the country. They themselves were linked to the international money market, concentrated principally in London, through such commercial banking houses as Prime, Ward and King in New York and the Baring Brothers of London. The result, as Robert Albion has pointed out, "was a steady chain of credit [which] extended from the London bankers, and behind them the Bank of England, down to the country store-keeper of the United States, who allowed his customer to build up a debt account."[82] This pyramiding of credit provided the capital needs of a dynamic, expanding economy. But there were also risks involved. Each level of the pyramid became increasingly sensitive to business fluctuations anywhere in the Atlantic economy and, with greater and greater frequency, in the rapidly

---

[81] Alan Pred, *Urban Growth and the Circulation of Information: The United States System of Cities, 1790–1840* (Cambridge, Mass., 1973), 22, 28, 32, 43, 48–49; the quote is from page 43.

[82] Albion, *Rise of New York Port*, 284–285; see also Ralph W. Hidy, *The House of Baring in American Trade and Finance, 1763–1861* (Cambridge, Mass., 1949); and Margaret Myers, *Origins and Development of the New York Money Market* (New York, 1931).

expanding, worldwide capitalist system. The Panic of 1837 and the ensuing depression, as we shall see, brought this fact home with a vengeance.

The already considerable role of New York City in meeting the country's capital needs was enhanced still further by the boom in railroad construction in the 1840s and 1850s. Railroad financing, more than any other single factor, solidified New York's dominance of the money and credit system and made possible the emergence of a modern, centralized, and institutionalized capital market. Here again, New York's ascendance was accomplished at others' expense, in this case Boston. By the end of the 1840s, railroad entrepreneurs gravitated increasingly to New York City, where investment capital was more plentiful and, as a consequence, cheaper. With the rapid growth of trading in railroad securities, the New York Stock Exchange, relatively insignificant in the 1830s, became the focal point of the nation's financial activities. Hundreds of thousands of shares in not only railroads, but also banks, insurance companies, public bonds and securities, and other business enterprises, were traded in a typical week by the decade of the 1850s. Indeed, by 1860 New York City had established itself, in the words of Alfred D. Chandler, "as one of the largest and most sophisticated capital markets in the world."[83]

BY MID-CENTURY, the forces of modernization had transformed the society and economy of the state. As traditional social and economic relations broke down under the impact of rapid change, a new social order gradually emerged. The transportation and communications revolutions, the expansion and integration of the market, population growth and urbanization, and the growth of manufacturing produced an increasingly complex, differentiated, interdependent, and cosmopolitan society. The emergence of this new social order made obsolete the traditional forms of coordination and control. Impersonal market mechanisms assumed a greater and greater role in the coordination of commercial activities, and newly emergent, specialized economic institutions managed the flow of goods and services through an ever-widening network of transactions.

Not everyone in New York applauded these developments. The process of social and economic change had costs as well as benefits, losers as well as winners. Localities and regions bypassed by the expanding network of transportation facilities withered economically. Farmers caught up in shifting market patterns faced new, often distant competitors. The changing relations of production destroyed the traditional world of the artisan and gave birth to a working class. Inequalities of wealth, class conflict, and cultural tensions

---

[83] Chandler, *Visible Hand*, 91–93; the quote is from page 92.

accompanied economic growth and social transformation. In short, the process of development itself generated new and intense societal conflicts as some New Yorkers questioned the desirability and direction of social and economic change.[84]

Not the least significant consequence of these deep-seated changes was their impact on the political system. The transformation of the socioeconomic environment within which politics and political decision-making were conducted brought about the disruption of the traditional political order and stimulated the search for new political relationships to match those of the increasingly modern society. We turn next, therefore, to a consideration of political development in New York, for the disjunction between the processes of economic and political development in the first half of the nineteenth century and New Yorkers' response to it help to account for the new political order emerging at mid-century.

[84]These are central themes in much of the recent work on the social history of antebellum New York. See, for example, Wilentz, *Chants Democratic*; Johnson, *A Shopkeeper's Millennium*; and Ryan, *Cradle of the Middle Class*.

[3]

The Political System

"Nothing strikes a European traveller in the United States," Alexis de Tocqueville wrote in the 1830s, "more than the absence of what we would call government or administration. One knows that there are written laws there and sees them put into execution every day; everything is in motion around you, but the motive force is nowhere apparent. The hand directing the social machine constantly slips from notice."[1] Tocqueville's fellow countryman Michael Chevalier echoed these sentiments during his visit to America. "The fundamental maxim of the Federal and State constitutions," he wrote, "is that the supreme authority is null and void; there is no government here in the true sense of the word; that is, no directing power. Each one is his own master; it is self-government in all its purity."[2]

From our twentieth-century perspective, the suggestion that Americans were an "ungoverned" people strikes a discordant note. Yet Tocqueville and Chevalier were correct in seizing on the relative weakness of political authority as one of the most important legacies of the American Revolution and as one of the principal characteristics distinguishing the American system of government from those in Europe. This key insight into the character of political authority in America provides a valuable clue to the essential nature of governance in the early nineteenth century and serves as a useful point of departure for an examination of the process of political development in New York State in the half century after 1776.

---

[1] Tocqueville, *Democracy in America*, 72.
[2] Chevalier, *Society, Manners, and Politics*, 43.

The term "political development" requires brief explanation. Most students of politics in the early republic have tended to focus on the emergence and development of political parties and the determinants of electoral behavior. Although these are obviously legitimate and, indeed, critical concerns, the approach here is somewhat broader. It sees parties as subsystems of a larger political system and popular voting behavior as only one of the political phenomena that must be investigated if we hope to understand the performance of that political system. Specifically, this approach proceeds from, but is not limited to, the vast literature on political development which has emerged in the last three decades, the purpose of which has been to elucidate, comparatively and theoretically, the nature of political change and its relationship to stability and change in the society at large. The strength of the developmental approach against alternative modes of analysis lies in its emphasis on the ways in which the various elements of the political system interact and the relationship between the political and socioeconomic systems over time.[3]

The problem, of course, is in applying such broad models of political change, often derived from other cultures and eras, to a specific historical context without violating the historian's first duty to be faithful to the historical evidence. This task is complicated by a plethora of competing theories of development and by the realization that no theoretical construct, by definition, is likely to correspond exactly to all the particulars of a given historical reality. Nor should it be expected to. The objective is to discover relationships not readily discernible through more traditional methods of historical reconstruction and, in the process, to illuminate the dynamics of the political system over an extended period of time. In pursuing this objective, I have sought to resolve some of the difficulties of a theoretical approach by adopting certain key insights from the developmental perspective rather than by simply accepting one of the several existing, and possibly too rigid, developmental theories. I have also deliberately returned to some of the earliest formulations of the developmental perspective in the belief that the initial insights of social scientists searching for a more integrated approach to the study of political systems are more relevant to historical analysis than the

---

[3]For an introduction to this literature, see Almond and Powell, *Comparative Politics*; Lucian Pye, *Aspects of Political Development: An Analytical Study* (Boston, 1966); Huntington, *Political Order in Changing Societies*; Lucian Pye and Sidney Verba, *Political Culture and Political Development* (Princeton, N.J., 1965); Raymond Grew, ed., *Crises of Political Development in Europe and the United States* (Princeton, N.J., 1978); and Charles Tilly, ed., *The Formation of Nation States in Western Europe* (Princeton, N.J., 1975). See also Huntington, "The Change to Change"; Bogue, Clubb, and Flanigan, "The New Political History"; and Grew, "Modernization and Its Discontents."

more complex and abstract theories that have appeared since. This compromise obviously involves certain risks, not the least of which is the possibility of criticism from *both* the social scientists *and* the traditional historians. The risk is acceptable, however, if the endeavor contributes in some small way to moving students of American politics beyond an eighteenth-century vision and language of politics and an equally limiting ethnocentrism.

As it is used here, the term "political development" is deliberately less precise than is commonly the case among social scientists. In general, it refers to the adaptation of the political system, over time, to changes in the socioeconomic environment of politics. An important theme in the literature of political development has been the idea, first put forth by Gabriel Almond and G. Bingham Powell, that development occurs "when the existing structure and culture of the political system is unable to cope with the problem or challenge which confronts it without further structural differentiation and cultural secularization."[4] This implies that central to the process of development is the relationship between demands and inputs on the one hand and the ability of the existing political system to meet the problems and challenges confronting it on the other. But the response of any given political system is not automatic. It depends, rather, on the types of problems it faces, the resources it can draw on in times of stress, developments in other social systems, the total "functioning pattern" or political culture, and the choices and responses of political elites.[5] To make matters more complicated, these ingredients in the calculus of development are interrelated. Social and economic developments, for example, may contribute to rising demands for broadened political participation which, if granted, may conceivably limit the effectiveness of the political system in controlling and channeling such developments in the interest of a broad public. The classic conflict, furthermore, and one particularly relevant to the problem of government in the nineteenth century, is that between a consent-based legitimacy on the one hand and the desire for rational administration and efficiency on the other. Nor should we forget that political elites can, and often do, shape the political system's response to challenges through control of critical access points and the political agenda.

Although some developmental theories seem to assume a continuous evolution toward higher levels of participation, increased capacity to manage problems, and greater organizational complexity, nothing is foreordained or inevitable about the extent and direction of political change. Indeed, development in the "regressive" sense is possible if there is a decline in the scope

---

[4] Almond and Powell, *Comparative Politics*, 34; see also Pye, *Aspects of Development*, 45–57.
[5] Ibid., 39–40.

or content of inputs or if the volume of demands overloads the capacity of the system.[6] In modernizing situations, furthermore, the political system tends to reach peak effectiveness quickly. Thus, the more intense the process of modernization, the greater the challenge to the policy-making process. That is to say, in periods of especially intense and rapid change, with increasing volumes of demands being made on government (often entirely new kinds of demands), existing structures and decision-making procedures can be quickly overwhelmed, in which case control and management of the policy-making process itself becomes a problem. This is related to Theodore Lowi's suggestion of "an inverse relation between the need and the availability of informal and automatic social controls. Those societies most in need of automatic social controls have fewer of them to bank on." The result, normally, is the emergence of administration, defined as "rationality applied to social control."[7] It has also been suggested, however, that since political development involves broadened participation and popular involvement in political activities, a period of "political decay" may well be the initial response to a developmental crisis. In other words, social mobilization not only raises the level of demands placed on the political system, but it also has the potential to undermine the ability of existing political structures to satisfy those demands.[8] From still another perspective, terms such as "regression," "decay," and "arrested development," which focus attention on what is presumed to be the pathology of the political system, have no relevance at all. In this view, the political changes that these phrases describe are in reality symptomatic of a profound transformation, brought on by the emergence of the market, in which the public and political component of society is subordinated to the private and economic.[9]

With these theoretical considerations in mind, this chapter considers the nature of political change in New York from the Revolution to the Panic of 1837. The underlying assumption is that if we are to explain the new political

[6]Ibid., 34.

[7]Lowi, *The End of Liberalism*, 27; David Apter, "Political Systems and Developmental Change," in *Some Conceptual Approaches to the Study of Modernization*, ed. David Apter (Englewood Cliffs, N.J., 1968), 333–336.

[8]Huntington, *Political Order in Changing Societies*, 5, 85. For a general discussion of social mobilization, see Karl Deutsch, "Social Mobilization and Political Development," *American Political Science Review*, 55 (September 1961): 493–514.

[9]Although rarely argued explicitly, this view is implicit in such works as Polanyi, *The Great Transformation*; Lowi, *The End of Liberalism*; Kariel, *The Decline of American Pluralism*; Baskin, *American Pluralist Democracy*; Grant McConnell, *Private Power and American Democracy*; Hurst, *Law and the Conditions of Freedom*; Horwitz, *Transformation of American Law*; and Alan Wolfe, *The Limits of Legitimacy: Political Contradictions of Contemporary Capitalism* (New York, 1977).

order emerging in the middle of the century, we must first clearly define the policy-making process, the character of the demands being made on the political system, and the interaction of the two. We must also identify the elements in that process which helped to produce a "crisis of legitimacy" in the 1830s and those elements which ultimately conditioned the political system's response to that crisis. Briefly stated, a half century of development after independence produced a political system that, when combined with the disruption of society occasioned by social and economic change and the expansion of participation in the first third of the nineteenth century, was fundamentally incapable of the formulation and implementation of sustained, coordinated policy.

THE FIRST state constitution in New York was drawn up in 1777, one year after the Declaration of Independence, in the midst of war, revolution, and the most intense consideration of political principles in American history. New Yorkers, and Americans generally, were actively engaged in the deliberate creation of governments. In those original constituent assemblies, Americans sought to translate a revolutionary ideology into tangible governmental structures, to balance aspirations for liberty against the necessities of authority, and to resolve the problem of legitimacy in the context of an unstable pluralism. The absence of a consensus on revolutionary goals and the best method to achieve them, in a society desperately in search of consensus, exacerbated an already near-impossible task.[10] Furthermore, the fact that the revolutionary conception of politics itself was not static, but an ever-shifting compound of radical English libertarian ideas which constantly changed in response to circumstances and newly emerged social forces, probably guaranteed that the new state constitutions would be neither unanimously accepted nor final. What does seem clear is that revolutionary assumptions about politics and the governmental structures those assumptions produced profoundly affected the course of political development and the nature of public policy in the nineteenth century.

Bernard Bailyn and Gordon Wood have provided historians with a brilliant analysis of the political debate that wracked the Anglo-American world from the mid-eighteenth century to 1787. In the broadest sense, Americans

---

[10]For a discussion of the colonial period in terms of the problems of legitimacy and "unstable pluralism," see Michael Kammen, *People of Paradox: An Inquiry Concerning the Origins of American Civilization* (New York, 1972), 31–78. The quest for consensus is a major theme of Michael Zukerman, *Peaceable Kingdoms: New England Towns in the Eighteenth Century* (New York, 1970), and, more important for my purpose, Gordon Wood's discussion of "Republicanism" in *The Creation of the American Republic, 1776–1787*, especially chaps. 2 and 3.

totally reconceptualized the science of politics during these years in response to fundamentally disruptive changes in the social fabric, efforts by British authorities to impose administrative centralization on the colonies, and a predisposition on the part of Americans to link the two together as incontrovertible evidence of a conspiratorial design against liberty.[11] From the rapid escalation of colonial opposition after 1765 through the 1770s, when most of the states wrote constitutions, British and American understandings on such key political principles as representation, sovereignty, constitutionalism, and authority diverged to the point of irreconciliation. Independence resolved the problem of imperial relations, but in the process it created a new challenge that proved both more difficult and more lastingly significant: how to recreate authority in the midst of an ongoing revolution the very thrust of which is to question authority itself. The challenge is common to all revolutions. The American response, however, is probably unique: disperse power, decentralize authority, and institutionalize revolution.

New York's experience graphically illustrates the difficulty of converting this solution into institutional reality. On July 10, 1776, the Fourth Provincial Congress, which had convened the previous day, was transformed into a convention for the purpose of creating a permanent government. It was not until August 1, however, that the convention appointed a committee of thirteen to draft a constitution, and even then, the process proceeded slowly. Differences between conservative and radical members of the committee and frequent interruptions to deal with the more pressing problems of the war delayed the committee's final report until March 12, 1777.[12]

The internal divisions on the committee, and in the convention generally, were reflected in the final plan of government. The conflicting claims of different social groups, the logic of revolutionary ideology, and conservative fears of disorder created in New York what one historian has called "a constitution in tension."[13] On the one hand, the new constitution characteristically restrained the power and authority of the governor by denying him a veto or exclusive control over appointments and by generally limiting the executive influence in lawmaking.[14] On the other hand, New Yorkers refrained from the total emasculation of the magistracy, so characteristic of

[11]Bernard Bailyn, *The Ideological Origins of the American Revolution* (Cambridge, Mass., 1967); Wood, *Creation of the American Republic*; see also Bailyn's *The Origins of American Politics* (New York, 1970) and Kenneth Lockridge, "Social Change and the Meaning of the American Revolution," *Journal of Social History*, 6 (Summer 1973): 403–439.

[12]Bernard Mason, *The Road to Independence: The Revolutionary Movement in New York, 1773–1777* (Lexington, Ky., 1966), 213–249.

[13]Wood, *The Creation of the American Republic*, 433.

[14]*New York Constitution of 1777*, Articles 18 and 19.

most revolutionary state constitutions, by providing for a three-year term, by giving the governor a role in the unique institutions established for the purpose of making appointments and overseeing the legislature, and by creating a special category of the electorate for his selection.[15] The governor also retained many of the traditional functions of that office, some of which were not inconsequential. He was to be general and commander in chief of the militia and admiral of the state's navy; he was given the power to convene the legislature on extraordinary occasions and even to prorogue the legislature, although this was limited to sixty days in any year; he could grant reprieves and pardons; and he was directed to inform the legislature, at every session, of the condition of the state, make recommendations, faithfully execute the laws, and expedite all measures passed by the legislature.[16] In short, though severely restricted in comparison with colonial governors, the magistrate in New York was relatively more independent than those in most other states.

New York's first constitution had surprisingly little to say on the subject of judicial power. The concept of a tripartite separation of powers had not yet emerged in American constitutional thought when the former colonies began the task of constructing new governments. Thus, as Gordon Wood has made clear, the emphasis was less on establishing three separate and equal branches of government than on ensuring that the executive could not manipulate or control the legislature and the judiciary. This, combined with the perception that colonial judges had been instruments of the crown, initially focused attention on questions of appointment and tenure rather than on the larger role of the judiciary vis-à-vis the executive and legislative branches.[17]

In practice, New York retained its colonial court system virtually intact. Under a 1691 law the judiciary consisted of a Court of Chancery, a Supreme Court, a Court of Common Pleas, Courts of Sessions, and Justices' courts. This basic structure was continued with some modifications designed to remedy abuses in the appointment of judges. Henceforth, judges would be appointed by the Council of Appointment. The chancellor, judges of the supreme court, and the first judge of the county court would serve during good behavior or until the age of sixty. Judges of the county court and justices of the peace had to be reappointed every three years. In addition, some judicial officials were given new responsibilities. The chancellor and the supreme court justices were to join with the governor to constitute the

[15] Ibid., Articles 17, 3.
[16] Ibid., Articles 8, 19.
[17] Wood, *Creation of the American Republic*, 156–161.

Council of Revision to review legislation. With the senate, they were also to make up two new courts: the Court for the Trial of Impeachments and the Court for the Correction of Errors. The upshot of these changes was to reduce executive influence over the judiciary, but given the extent to which courts continued to be intermingled with both the executive and the legislative branches of government, they hardly represented the emergence of an independent judiciary. That would come later.[18]

The principal beneficiary of the Revolution was unquestionably the legislature. Out of a complex mixture of fear and distrust of the executive and the courts, both of which embodied royal authority in the colonies, and the deliberate effort to apply the new science of politics to practical politics, the legislatures achieved an ascendancy in the political systems of the new states which remained virtually undiminished until well into the nineteenth century.[19] Throughout the eighteenth century, the lower houses of the colonial legislatures had been engaged in an extended contest with royally controlled governors and courts. This "quest for power"[20] was, of course, an important factor in the coming of the American Revolution. But it also contributed to the emergence of a peculiarly American conception of the role of the legislature. As colonial assemblies gradually accumulated more and more initiative in the lawmaking process, they assumed many executive and judicial responsibilities, thereby obscuring functional distinctions among the various departments. To bolster claims of independence, furthermore, the colonists contended that their assemblies were exact replicas of the English Parliament. Paradoxically, however, Americans patterned their colonial assemblies after a conception of the House of Commons which was already becoming archaic by the middle of the eighteenth century. Parliament had originally developed as a judicial body, but over a period of several centuries, legislative and judicial functions became distinct. Although a similar trend appears to have been gaining ground in the colonies by about 1750, the assemblies continued to perform what were essentially judicial duties. In effect, they saw themselves, in the older parliamentary tradition, "as a kind of medieval court, making private judgments as well as public law."[21]

---

[18]Charles Z. Lincoln, *Constitutional History of New York,* 5 vols. (Rochester, N.Y., 1906), 1: 162–188, 461–462.

[19]Wood, *Creation of the American Republic,* 141; James Willard Hurst, *The Growth of American Law: The Law Makers* (Boston, 1950), 86.

[20]Jack P. Greene, "The Role of the Lower Houses of Assembly in Eighteenth Century Politics," *Journal of Southern History,* 27 (November 1961): 451–474.

[21]Wood, *Creation of the American Republic,* 154–155; see Max Rheinstein, ed., *Max Weber on Law in Economy and Society* (Cambridge, Mass., 1954), 47, for Weber's analysis of the relationship between judicial and legislative functions in the development of Parliament.

The Revolution accelerated the drive for legislative hegemony, and reversed the trend toward functional differentiation. More than any other political institution, the legislature embodied the essence of revolutionary ideology. The transformation of the concepts of sovereignty and representation in colonial minds and the practical role of assemblies, conventions, and extralegal committees during the Revolution had combined by the 1770s to lift the legislature to a symbolic status. Out of the debate over the limits of parliamentary authority in the colonies, Americans fashioned a conception of sovereignty that was radically different from that held in England and Europe. In contrast to the traditional view, the colonists came to argue that supreme authority resided in the people and that sovereignty could and often should be divided.[22]

Revolutionary ideas concerning the nature and function of representation gave added force to this view of sovereignty and assured the dominant role of the legislature. It is one of the greatest ironies of American history that local conditions in the seventeenth and eighteenth centuries and colonial haste to reproduce English institutions brought about in America an essentially medieval conception of representation. Even as England moved toward a system of virtual representation in which Parliament, as Edmund Burke put it, was "a *deliberative* assembly of *one* nation, with *one* interest, that of the whole,"[23] the colonies adhered to the older notion of "attorneyship in representation." Direct or actual representation meant that members of the legislature acted as agents or attorneys for the constituencies or local interests that elected them, for the purpose of voting supplies to the rulers and presenting local grievances. There was little regard for any common good. In order to ensure that representation reflected the interests of their constituencies and to check independent action, furthermore, Americans developed a system of residence requirements, short terms, dynamic apportionment, instruction, and property qualifications. The Revolution continued this pattern of representation and added a broadened suffrage.

Legislative supremacy, in short, existed in fact and theory. It was the linchpin of the American position, not because of blind attachment to a particular institution or distrust of alternative ones, but because the legislature was the only structure through which the implications of popular sovereignty and continuous participation of the people in government could be fulfilled. A major consequence of this development was that the distinction between government and those governed virtually disappeared. If representative insti-

---

[22] This paragraph and the two that follow are based broadly on Bailyn's *The Ideological Origins of the American Revolution* and Wood's *Creation of the American Republic*.
[23] Quoted in Bailyn, *The Ideological Origins of the American Revolution*, 163.

tutions exactly mirrored society, as they theoretically should, then representation, in effect, became a substitute for direct popular action.[24] Government
by consent of the governed, therefore, meant far more than simply the right
of the people to act in extraordinary circumstances; it meant that the people
had continuous responsibility in the public life of the community. "No longer
merely an ultimate check on government," as Bailyn puts it, "they *were* in
some sense the government."[25] As the most representative structure in the
political system and the very embodiment of the doctrine of consent, the legislature, it is not surprising, quickly took on a sacred aura of legitimacy.

Following this logic, New Yorkers assigned the major responsibility for
lawmaking or governing to the legislature. This can be inferred from the stark
contrast between the executive and legislative sections of the constitution.
The powers and duties of the former were explicitly delegated in clear and
concise language; those of the latter depend on the simple statement that the
"supreme legislative power within this State shall be vested" in the legislature.[26] The inference is that legislative power rests on custom, precedent, and
its peculiar identification with the "people," and executive power comprised
specific grants of authority. New York also followed current practice[27] in creating a bicameral legislature, providing for frequent sessions, and establishing
a system of direct and dynamic representation. The legislature was to consist
of a senate made up of twenty-four freeholders, chosen from four districts
in the state for four-year terms, and an assembly of at least seventy members
chosen annually from the several counties. Direct representation was insured
by a six-month residency requirement for persons voting for members of the
assembly. In addition, New York provided for a sliding scale of representation which, through periodic adjustments of apportionment, prevented the
recurrence of a system of "rotten boroughs" such as had existed in England
or the appearance of divisive apportionment struggles such as those which
characterized many of the American states in the first half of the nineteenth
century.[28]

In three very crucial areas, however, New Yorkers rejected the more radical tendencies of the Revolution. One of the least democratic features of the
new constitution, for example, related to suffrage requirements. New York
not only kept its property qualification for voting, but also created a system

---

[24]Ibid., 174.
[25]Ibid., 173.
[26]*New York Constitution of 1777*; compare Articles 17–19 with Article 2.
[27]Pennsylvania's unicameral legislature, of course, was the exception.
[28]*New York Constitution of 1777*; only four other states—New Jersey, Pennsylvania, Vermont, and South Carolina—provided for periodic adjustments of representation in their original constitutions.

of dual voting whereby the governor and state senate were chosen by wealthier constituents than were the state assembly and representatives to the U.S. House of Representatives. Thus, the property qualification for voting for assemblymen and U.S. congressmen was a £20 freehold or rented tenement with a yearly value of 40 shillings; a £100 freehold was required to vote for governor, lieutenant governor, or state senator.[29] Under this system, only about 40 percent of adult white males could vote for governor and another 30 percent for assemblymen.[30]

Popular participation in the government was further limited by the creation of a Council of Appointment with the power to select most state, county, and municipal officials. Since the appointment power had been a major source of contention between royal governors and colonial assemblies, it is not surprising that New Yorkers wished to restrict executive control over subordinate offices. But conservatives were unwilling to grant complete legislative control over appointment; nor were they willing to make such offices elective. Instead, New York created an entirely unique institution to consist of the governor and one senator from each of the four senatorial districts, chosen annually by the assembly. The governor was to be president of the council, and senators were prohibited from serving two terms successively. By 1821 this five-man council sitting in Albany controlled nearly fifteen thousand civil and military offices including sheriffs, county clerks, mayors, city recorders, justices of the peace, chancellor, and all the state officers except treasurer, who was appointed by the legislature. The council became so omnipotent and so partisan that Jabez Hammond, historian and member of the council in 1818, exclaimed that its "power entered the log hut of the lieutenant or ensign of a militia company, or that of the county justice of the peace, as well as the mansion of the mayor of New York, the Secretary of State, or the Comptroller, and hurled them from their places at its own sovereign will and pleasure."[31]

In an effort to check the radical implications of revolutionary ideology even further, the convention also established a Council of Revision. Distrust of the magistracy precluded granting the governor an exclusive veto over legislation. But conservatives, fearful of popular disorder flowing from an unchecked legislature, insisted on some device to insure against "laws incon-

[29] *New York Constitution of 1777*, Articles 7 and 10.
[30] McCormick, *The Second American Party System*, 105–106.
[31] Jabez D. Hammond, *The History of Political Parties in the State of New York*, 3 vols. (Syracuse, N.Y., 1852), 3: 670; *New York Constitution of 1777*, Articles 22, 23, 24, 26; Hugh M. Flick, "The Council of Appointment of New York State: The First Attempt to Regulate Political Patronage, 1777–1822," *New York History*, 15 (1934): 253–280; J. M. Gitterman, "The Council of Appointments in New York," *Political Science Quarterly*, 7 (1890): 80–115.

sistent with the spirit of this constitution, or with the public good, which may be hastily and unadvisedly passed." The result was a council, to be composed of the governor, chancellor, and judges of the supreme court, to "revise all bills about to be passed by the legislature." Council vetoes could be overridden by a two-thirds majority of the legislature, and a bill would become law automatically if not returned within ten days.[32] Of a total of 6,590 bills passed between 1777 and 1821, the Council of Revision vetoed 128, while the legislature overrode 17 of these.[33]

The Constitution of 1777, one of the most conservative to come out of the Revolutionary era, remained essentially unchanged for more than forty years. The fluidity of the last decades of the eighteenth century inevitably produced some changes in the relative positions of various institutions, but the trend was toward definition and consolidation rather than major alterations of patterns established by the Revolution. When the full potential of the power residing in the Council of Appointment was recognized, for example, a dispute developed between succeeding governors and senatorial members of the council over who should rightfully control nominations for office. The dispute was clearly engendered by patronage politics, but its resolution was achieved only through a constitutional amendment in 1801 affirming the council's concurrent power with the governor in making nominations.[34] The same convention more explicitly defined the makeup of the legislature by establishing numerical limits on membership and creating the mechanism for continuing adjustments of apportionment. Future assemblies were to consist of a minimum of 100 and a maximum of 150 members. Two members were to be added to the assembly each year, furthermore, until the figure of 150 was reached, at which time assemblymen and senators were to be apportioned according to periodic censuses. The number of senators was permanently set at 32.[35]

More important than these structural changes, at least in regard to implications for the nineteenth century, was the attempt during the 1780s to define and limit legislative power, especially in relation to the judiciary. Colonial conditions, principally the lack of adequate courts and lawyers, had tended to encourage the fusion of legislative and judicial powers in legislative bodies. Practical necessity was given philosophical justification by Coke's celebration of such a fusion in England's "High Court of Parliament." The collapse of

[32] *New York Constitution of 1777*, Article 3.
[33] Thorpe, *Federal and State Constitutions*, 5: 2629n.
[34] Flick, "The Council of Appointment in New York," 260–269; Thorpe, *Federal and State Constitutions*, 5: 2639.
[35] Thorpe, *Federal and State Constitutions*, 5: 2368–2369.

royal courts during the Revolution, the eagerness of patriots to proscribe British sympathizers, and the substitution of special remedial legislation for equity jurisdiction in some states (New York and Massachusetts, for example) reversed the trend toward differentiation which was evident by 1750.[36] Blackstone's categorical denial of any restraint on legislative omnipotence, fashioned in the 1760s to support parliamentary supremacy, was incorporated into revolutionary ideology along with American ideas about representation to give further underpinning for the legislature's position.

During the 1780s, however, some elements of society, chiefly conservatives and those who would advocate a new national constitution in 1787, attributed the social, economic, and political instability of the period to the abuse of legislative power. Legislatures, it was charged, encroached on the powers of other branches of government by performing all sorts of judicial and administrative functions. Implicit in such charges, furthermore, was the belief that legislative supremacy combined with lowered suffrage requirements and expanded participation had produced a new class of men ill-prepared by social standing or political experience to govern. Such concerns, combined with the instability of legislation resulting from rapid turnover and frequent sessions, stimulated a two-pronged assault on the legislatures. In the first instance, state courts sought to define the limits of legislative authority. The result of this process, which involved a redefinition of the doctrine of separation of powers, the nature of law, and the role of the judiciary too complex to engage us here, was the birth of the doctrine of judicial review. In a series of cases such as *Holmes* v. *Walton* in New Jersey, *Trevett* v. *Weeden* in Rhode Island, and *Rutgers* v. *Waddington* in New York, state courts challenged the notion that legislative enactment was the exclusive foundation of law and argued that the courts had the duty and responsibility to judge legislation against the standards of the law of nations, equity, and most important, written constitutions.[37]

But the trend toward judicial review proved inconclusive in most of the states because the second prong of the attack on legislative supremacy removed the debate to the federal level. As those disillusioned with politics and government in the states grew impatient with reform efforts, they increasingly turned to the task of restructuring the central government as a means of alleviating the problems of state politics. This goal was achieved with the ratification of the national Constitution in 1788. But even though

---

[36] Edward S. Corwin, "The Progress of Constitutional Theory between the Declaration of Independence and the Meeting of the Philadelphia Convention," *American Historical Review*, 30 (1925): 511–536.

[37] Ibid., passim; Wood, *Creation of the American Republic*, 453–463.

the new Constitution restrained the power of state legislatures, it left unresolved the problem of defining legislative and judicial power within the states. The pressure to clarify the authority of the legislature and judiciary relative to one another was largely relieved by the creation of a stronger central government.[38] In short, the new conception of politics embodied in the United States Constitution did not remove the tensions and contradictions in state political systems; it simply diverted attention from them and ensured that they would resurface under the pressure of social and economic change in the nineteenth century.

The final bit of background for our discussion of government and the policy-making process in the second quarter of the nineteenth century is the Constitution of 1821. Popular dissatisfaction with the conservative features of New York's government had produced, by 1821, a rising chorus of demands for constitutional revision. The convention of that year, called in response to such pressure, reopened many issues of the revolutionary era by drastically altering the structural solutions to the problems of appointment, review of legislation, and suffrage. No one, not even conservatives, defended the Council of Appointment, which had centralized the distribution of patronage into the hands of a tiny minority in Albany and which had given New York politics a reputation for personalism and corruption unsurpassed in any other state. The convention unanimously abolished the council and dispersed the appointing power to different political subdivisions within the state, further dividing and checking it at each level. All but the highest-ranking militia officers were to be elected by their subordinates. The principal state officers—secretary of state, comptroller, treasurer, attorney general, surveyor general, and commissary general—would be appointed by joint ballot of the assembly and senate. All were to serve three-year terms except the treasurer, who was to be elected annually. At the local level, sheriffs and county clerks were made elective, mayors were to be appointed annually by common councils, and justices of the peace were to be selected by county boards of supervisors and the judges of county courts. All other appoint-

---

[38]Corwin first and Wood more recently have advanced the idea that much of the movement for the federal Constitution was in response to state politics. "In the end it was not pressure from above, from the manifest debility of the Confederation," Wood writes, "that provided the main impulse for the Federalist movement of 1787; it was rather pressure from below, from the problems of politics within the separate states themselves, that eventually made constitutional reform of the central government possible." (Wood, *Creation of the American Republic*, 465).

ments, including judges, were to be made by the governor, with the consent of the senate.[39]

The convention also abolished the Council of Revision and transferred its legislative veto to the governor. Although this clearly enhanced the independence and power of the executive to some extent, his position remained circumscribed by legislative checks on his appointing power, the independence of the major state officers, and a shortened term of office. (The new constitution reduced the governor's term of office from three to two years.)[40]

The most important consequence of the convention, however, and certainly the most discussed, was the broadening of participation in the political system which resulted from the abolition of property qualifications for suffrage. The franchise was extended to every white male twenty-one years old who had been a resident of the state for one year and the county or town for six months and who paid state or county taxes, served in the militia, or worked on public highways.[41] As a result, the number of eligible voters increased to more than four-fifths of the adult white-male population, a fact reflected in the dramatic rise in voter participation after 1821.[42]

In his classic study of New York politics in this period, Dixon Ryan Fox concluded that "the eighteenth century closed in 1821; its problems, most of them, had been settled."[43] The overflow of unresolved political problems from the eighteenth century had indeed necessitated the modifications brought about in that year. The questions discussed in convention were essentially the same as those considered in 1777, and the solutions were even more in the revolutionary tradition than they had been earlier. But there is a finality to Fox's statement which seems to ignore the legacy of the eighteenth century. For if it is true that the issues of the previous century had been settled, it is equally true that the problems of the nineteenth century had scarcely been envisioned. New Yorkers were compelled to confront the demands of

---

[39]*New York Constitution of 1821*, Article 4; Hammond, *History of Political Parties in New York*, 2: 64–81; Fox, *The Decline of Aristocracy*, 246–247. For a discussion of the political impact of the Council of Appointment and its abolition, see McCormick, *Second American Party System*, 109, 113–114. In 1826 an amendment to the Constitution provided for the election of justices of the peace; similarly, the office of mayor was made elective in New York in 1833 and in all the cities in 1839; see Thorpe, *Federal and State Constitutions*, 5: 2651, 2652.

[40]*New York Constitution of 1821*; Thorpe, *Federal and State Constitutions*, 5: 2641, 2643.

[41]Ibid., Art. 2, Section 1; An amendment in 1826 removed the tax or militia requirement; Thorpe, *Federal and State Constitutions*, 5: 2652. Blacks residing in the state for three years and possessing a $250 freehold for at least one year and who actually paid a tax on that property were allowed to vote.

[42]McCormick, *Second American Party System*, 113–114.

[43]Fox, *Decline of Aristocracy*, 300.

a rapidly modernizing society and economy with eighteenth-century conceptions of politics and a distrust of power bred in the agony of revolution.

As IN any society experiencing the transition to modernity, traditional habits and attitudes coexisted with more modern orientations in the political culture of New York in the early nineteenth century. Political structures and philosophical concepts rooted in medieval English experience blended with concepts of representation and popular sovereignty formed in the revolutionary era. Ironically, those elements of the polity which emerged from the late eighteenth century reinforced an earlier trend toward decentralization, diffusion of power, and undifferentiated structures, all of which, at the beginning of the century at least, were superimposed on a society essentially local in char..cter. In fact, the Revolution propelled that process forward to its logical extremity in the 1830s. It remained to be seen, however, whether a political system predicated on the negation of authority could govern effectively in an increasingly modern and market-oriented society.

At the center of that political system stood the legislature, endowed by tradition and ideology with primary responsibility for policy formulation. Any attempt to assess the effectiveness of New York's political system in this period, therefore, must begin with an analysis of this central institution. The concept of "institutionalization," as developed by Nelson W. Polsby, is a useful point of departure for such an investigation. According to Polsby, a legislature is "institutionalized" to the extent that it is "bounded" or differentiated from its environment, structurally complex, and universalistic in conducting its internal business. The establishment of boundaries is a function of the relative stability of membership, the difficulty in becoming a member, and the degree to which leaders are recruited from within. The development of functionally specific roles and the growth of standing committees are indicators of the relative complexity of internal structures. Increasing reliance upon precedent, standardization of procedures, and development of the seniority system are evidence of a shift from particularistic and discretionary to automatic procedures for the conduct of internal business.[44]

These criteria provide a rough measure of the dimensions of legislative development in New York in the first half of the nineteenth century. A key indicator of the extent to which a legislature is differentiated from its environment is the rate of turnover among its members. The higher the rate, the more permeable that institutional boundaries are presumed to be. A more stable membership implies a higher level of differentiation and the existence

---

[44]Nelson W. Polsby, "The Institutionalization of the House of Representatives," *The American Political Science Review*, 62 (March 1968): 144–168.

Table 1. Years' service of members in the New York Assembly 1777–1867: decadal means

Decade	% 1st term	1 year	2 years	3 years	4 or more years
1777–1787	32.4	18.0	13.8	11.7	24.2
1788–1797	40.4	21.1	14.1	8.6	16.0
1798–1807	49.1	23.2	10.8	6.0	11.0
1808–1817	54.6	23.3	10.4	5.1	7.5
1818–1827	63.3	18.8	8.2	4.2	5.4
1828–1837	68.2	21.1	6.9	1.9	2.1
1838–1847	75.5	16.8	4.5	1.6	1.5
1848–1857	83.3	14.5	1.8	.5	.05
1858–1867	72.6	21.6	4.5	1.0	.35

Sources: S. C. Hutchins, comp., *Civil List and Forms of Government of the Colony and State of New York* (Albany, N.Y., 1869) and Franklin B. Hough, comp., *The New York Civil List* (Albany, N.Y., 1855). The above figures include service in the four Provincial Congresses from 1775 to 1777. Thus, the percentage of first-term members down to the 1790s is slightly lower than if the data had included only the assembly after adoption of the first constitution. Inclusion of the Provincial Congresses is justified, however, on the grounds that the object here is to measure relative legislative experience rather than simply the turnover rate.

of significant roadblocks to becoming a member. Legislative turnover is usually conceived as the proportion of new or first-term members to the total membership in a given session, with a "new" legislator defined as one who had not served in the previous session.[45] But a preferable index of institutional development is the relative experience or inexperience of legislators. For our purposes, a first-term assemblyman or senator is one with no prior experience in the house in which he presently sits, though he may have been a member of the other house previously. Since a legislator may have served discontinuously, legislative inexperience should normally be lower than simple turnover.

An analysis of legislative experience from 1777 to 1870 reveals not only that membership in the New York legislature was extremely unstable in the early nineteenth century but also that it was becoming increasingly so toward mid-century. In the average legislative session during this period, 60 percent of the members of the assembly had no previous experience. Even more revealing, however, is the long-term trend. The proportion of first-term members in the assembly increased steadily in these years, peaking in the 1850s, then beginning to drop off slightly in the 1860s (see table 1). A comparison of two decades at the beginning and end of this period illustrates the dimensions of the trend. The average number of first-term members in the assembly in the first decade of the legislature's existence (1777–1787) was 32.4 percent; 18 per-

[45] Alan Rosenthal, "Turnover in State Legislatures," *American Journal of Political Science*, 18 (August 1974): 670.

cent had at least one year of experience; 49.7 percent had previously served two or more terms.[46] In contrast, the average number of first termers in the decade 1848–1857 was 83.3 percent; 14.5 percent had at least one year of prior experience; but only 2.2 percent had previously served two or more terms. Even more significant is the fact that every decade from 1777 to 1857 registered an increase in the average number of first-term members and a corresponding decrease in the number of experienced legislators in the assembly. The peak year was 1845, when 89 percent of the members of the assembly were first termers. Less than 4 percent had sat in the previous session; another 7 percent had served one or two terms at some time in the past. No one had been in the assembly for more than two terms. In fact, only three Democratic members in 1845 had had any previous legislative experience.[47]

Membership in the senate was more stable because of the four-year, staggered term that prevailed until 1846. But the pattern of increasing turnover and decreasing experience was essentially the same (see table 2). In studies of fifteen sessions between 1777 and 1847, the percentage of first-term members averaged slightly more than 22 percent. The turnover of senators in any given year was thus much lower than in the assembly. But allowing for deaths and resignations, an overwhelming majority of senators served a single four-year term. (If all senators served exactly one term in a staggered system, the percentage of first termers should always be 25.) After 1847, when senators were elected for two-year, nonstaggered terms, the percentage of first-term members increased dramatically—to 75 percent in 1852–1853 and 65.5 percent in the 1856–1857 sessions.

Prior senatorial experience and length of total service in the senate also declined significantly in the eighty years after the Revolution. In the five legislative sessions examined before 1800, the average senator had 3.91 years experience and served a total of 8.89 years. The average senator in the last five sessions studied before the mode of senatorial election was changed, between 1827 and 1847, had 1.86 years of experience and could expect to serve only 4.25 years total. The change is even more dramatic after the adoption of the two-year term. The average senator in the 1852–1853 and 1856–1857 legis-

---

[46]These figures are somewhat misleading since legislators from the Southern District were appointed by the legislature, rather than elected, during the British occupation of that area from 1777 to 1783. Thus, the figure given for first-term members in the assembly is low, and the percentage of members with one or more years experience is artificially high. However, an examination of the decade from 1784 to 1793, when all members were elected, indicates that the comparison made in this paragraph is not significantly affected. The average number of first termers in this period was 36.6 percent; 19.2 percent had at least one year of experience; and 44.2 percent had served two or more years.

[47]Hammond, *History of Political Parties in New York*, 3: 513.

Table 2. Tenure of members in the New York Senate, 1777–1857 (every five sessions)

Session	Year	% New members	Mean years prior experience	Mean number sessions served
1	1777–1778	32.00	1.64	7.08
5	1781–1782	4.76	4.66	9.71
10	1787	9.09	5.36	10.90
15	1792	8.30	5.16	9.87
20	1796–1797	43.90	2.73	6.92
25	1802	11.40	4.20	7.22
30	1807	18.70	2.96	6.21
35	1812	18.75	2.50	5.43
40	1816–1817	25.80	1.81	5.51
45	1822	25.00	1.90	3.46
50	1827	31.30	1.68	4.00
55	1832	25.00	1.50	4.65
60	1837	21.80	2.09	5.00
65	1842	31.25	1.96	4.50
70	1847	25.00	2.08	3.18
75/76	1852–1853	75.00	.53	2.78
79/80	1856–1857	65.60	.38	2.81

Source: S. C. Hutchins, comp., *Civil List and Forms of Government of the Colony and State of New York* (Albany, N.Y., 1869).

latures had only .44 year prior experience and could expect a total career of only 2.79 years.

This extraordinary rate of turnover suggests that the boundaries between the legislature and society were fluid and indistinct in the first half of the nineteenth century. Procedures for recruiting leaders confirm this conclusion. As an organization institutionalizes, leadership becomes more stable and professional, and recruitment is more likely to come from within the organization and only after an initial period of apprenticeship. In undifferentiated organizations, on the other hand, leaders tend to emerge rapidly and are frequently recruited from outside.[48] Such was the case in New York. Prolonged service in the assembly was not a prerequisite for being chosen speaker in this period. Between 1777 and 1867, for example, a total of sixty-one men held the speakership. The average length of prior legislative service for speakers during this period was 2.37 years (see table 3). Eleven men achieved the office in their first term, and thirteen had served only one term before becoming speaker. Previous experience declined slightly toward the middle of the century, with those who served during the decade between 1848 and 1867 having the least amount of experience. The tenure of speakers was also

[48] Polsby, "Institutionalization of the House of Representatives," 145–146.

Table 3. Mean years served by speaker in the Assembly before first selection, by decades

Decade	Years
1777–1787	2.83
1788–1797	1.25
1798–1807	3.00
1808–1817	2.00
1818–1827	4.37
1828–1837	2.16
1838–1847	3.22
1848–1857	.90
1858–1867	1.20

Source: S. C. Hutchins, comp., *Civil List and Forms of Government of the Colony and State of New York* (Albany, N.Y., 1869).

Table 4. Mean years' tenure as speaker, by decades

Decade	Years
1777–1787	2.00
1788–1797	2.00
1798–1807	2.20
1808–1817	1.42
1818–1827	1.25
1838–1847	1.11
1848–1857	1.42
1858–1867	2.00

Source: S. C. Hutchins, comp., *Civil List and Forms of Government of the Colony and State of New York* (Albany, N.Y., 1869).

extremely brief, averaging only 1.48 years for the entire period (see table 4). The decadal mean never exceeded 2.2 years, with the lowest point being in the period 1838–1847, when the average time of service was 1.11 years. In short, the leadership role clearly was not yet institutionalized to any significant degree and, indeed, may have experienced substantial deterioration around mid-century.

The simplicity and fluidity of internal structures is further evidence that the New York legislature was not highly institutionalized. The committee system became more differentiated and complex in this period, but the process was slow and erratic. The first standing committees had appeared as early as the 1780s, but most of the work of the assembly in the early nineteenth century occurred in the committee of the whole, which consisted of the entire house operating under informal rules of procedure. As late as 1812 there were only six standing committees: privileges and elections, claims, ways and means, rules, grievances, and expiration of laws. Select committees occasionally handled issues for which no standing committee existed.[49] As the state assumed new social and economic responsibilities after 1815, reliance on select committees became more frequent. In 1818 the assembly created thirteen select committees on subjects ranging from agriculture, manufacturing, turnpikes, and canals to prisons, poor relief, and Indian affairs. As these and similar issues reappeared in succeeding legislative sessions, they gradually became part of the standing committee system. By 1850 the assembly appointed thirty-one standing committees and the subjects for which select committees were required had become more narrow and specialized.[50]

The brief tenure of legislators severely limited the impact of this evolving committee system on the legislative process. Given the high turnover of members, there could be little continuity of service on committees from session to session. Nor does it appear that committee service was weighted in favor of those who had prior legislative experience. In the 1825 session, for example, 82 of the 129 members of the assembly sat on one or more standing committees. Of these, 61 percent were first-term members. In 1845 the figure was even higher, with 92.5 percent of the members of standing committees having no prior experience in the assembly. Most assemblymen, furthermore, received only one committee assignment. Only 18 members of the 1825 session and 22 members in 1845 sat on more than one committee.[51] Standing committees thus were unable to provide the advantages of continuous existence and expertise which lengthened tenure and seniority would make possible later. In practice, they were little more than select committees that were automatically appointed year after year. They gathered information for the house but did not challenge the dominant role of the committee of the whole in the legislative process in the first half of the nineteenth century.

Policy did not ordinarily originate in committees in any case. Frequent sessions, annual elections for members of the assembly, and rapid turnover made legislators, after 1821, remarkably effective conduits for the concerns of local publics and/or special interests. In addition, legislative structures and the norm of direct representation facilitated maximum input from nonlegislative sources. Direct petitions, for example, accounted for much, if not most, legislation. Indeed, it was the need for a time-saving procedure for processing petitions that led to the establishment of the first standing committees.[52] A major consequence of the predominance of the petition and memorial in the legislative process, furthermore, was the reinforcement of

---

[49] Ralph V. Harlow, *The History of Legislative Methods in the Period Before 1825* (New Haven, Conn., 1927), 7–9, 64, 70, 75–77, 81n; New York State, *Journal of the Assembly*, 1812, 11.

[50] New York State, *Journal of the Assembly*, 1818, 47; *The Red Book*, 368–373.

[51] New York State, *Journal of the Assembly*, 1825, 34–35; 1845, 82–83.

[52] Harlow, *History of Legislative Methods*, 64.

Table 5. Legislative expenses (in thousands of dollars), 1798–1896: decadal means

Decade	Amount
1798–1807	46.6
1808–1817	72.7
1818–1827	85.2
1828–1837	93.1
1838–1847	96.4
1848–1857	115.0
1858–1867	154.5
1868–1877	343.0
1878–1887	469.7
1888–1897	860.1

Source: Donald C. Sowers, *Financial History of New York State, 1789–1912* (New York, 1914), 295–339. The above figures do not include the cost of printing laws. No claim is made here that these figures are precise. Given the number of separate funds making up the state's financial system, attempts to arrive at exact expenditures for any part of the government in this period are hazardous at best. Even as approximations, however, they reflect a meaningful trend.

an already fragmented decision-making apparatus. There was little incentive for the development of structures and processes capable of "generalizing" policy because the demands being made on the legislative system were themselves typically fragmentary, representing private, local, or sectional interests. No one was in a position to view the needs of the whole political system as distinct from its parts.

An additional factor shaping the legislative process in this period was the level of financial and staff support. Legislative expenses rose gradually between 1798 (the first year in which they were a separate category) and 1862, but the average yearly expenditure for the entire period was only about $88,000. Not until the decade of the 1860s did legislative expenditures begin to increase dramatically (see table 5). The legislature also operated with minimal staff. As late as 1852, for example, the senate employed only fifteen people in addition to its members, and the assembly employed only thirty-six. Almost all performed routine clerical and housekeeping chores and had no discernible impact on public policy.[53]

The foregoing description of legislative development raises significant questions about the role of the legislature in the early nineteenth century. What, for example, did the legislature actually do when it met? What was the impact of rapid turnover and poorly developed internal structures on the character of public policy? What was the nature of the relationship between the legislature and the social environment within which it was sited? To what

[53] New York State, *Senate Document*, no. 42, 1852, vol. 1.

extent did the legislature contribute to the stability and/or instability of the larger political system? Finally, what part did the legislature play in the process of political development? The answers to these questions are not as obvious or as simple as they may appear. Historians have tended to assume that representation operated as the theory held that it should and that policymaking was the primary function of legislatures. A large body of research on modern legislatures, however, suggests that the standard policy–demand–input model of representation will not stand close scrutiny.[54]

How, then, are we to answer these critical questions? One way, suggested by some students of recent legislative behavior, is to locate the New York legislature of the early nineteenth century on a continuum of legislative power based on the extent to which the legislature was independent from or dependent upon outside forces. This mode of analysis posits two basic legislative models arrayed at opposite ends of a continuum: the "transformative" and the "arena." Transformative legislatures are those sufficiently independent of external influences and with a sufficiently differentiated internal structure to be able to "transform" proposals for legislation as they progress through the legislative process. At the other end of the continuum are legislatures that can be likened to arenas, so-called because they are essentially formalized settings for political interaction and because external rather than internal forces are decisive in determining the final product of the legislative process. This image of the legislature as arena becomes even sharper if we conceive of an arena, as Nelson Polsby has, as "'a continuous performance' or an institutionalized 'occasion.'"[55]

As unconventional as it may seem, New York's early-nineteenth-century legislatures resembled nothing so much as "institutionalized occasions." Legislative sessions were not lengthy, and though the process of electing and convening the legislature was regularized, there was little carryover of structures and business between sessions. More important, the annual sessions of the legislature were essentially convocations of strangers. The same sort of transiency which James Sterling Young noted for the American Congress in the period from 1800 to 1828 prevailed in Albany during the Jackson era and with similar consequences for legislative behavior. Only one assemblyman in four served more than one term in the three decades between 1830 and 1860; only one in sixteen served more than two years. Most assemblymen, furthermore, were relatively obscure men, with little or no previous office-

---

[54] The clearest statement of this view is in John C. Wahlke, "Policy Demands and System Support: The Role of the Represented," *British Journal of Political Science*, 1 (July 1971): 271–290.

[55] Nelson W. Polsby, "Legislatures," in *Governmental Institutions and Processes*, ed. Fred I. Greenstein and Nelson W. Polsby, vol. 5, *Handbook of Political Science* (Reading, Mass., 1975), 277–292, 308.

holding experience and with little prospect for subsequent political careers.[56] Given such instability of membership, the lack of legislative experience, and the absence of institutionalized leadership roles, the wonder is that the legislature could manage its own internal affairs, much less govern an increasingly complex and differentiated society.

If the selection and tenure of legislators and internal organization were not conducive to effective governance, the types of demands being made on the legislature only accentuated the difficulty. A major inheritance from the Revolution, as we have already seen, was the belief that legislatures should mirror society as accurately as possible—thus the emphasis on direct representation, annual elections, yearly sessions, and residence requirements. After 1815, however, rapid social and economic change shattered the relatively stable world of the eighteenth century and fundamentally altered the social context within which this legislative system had evolved. The legislature mirrored an increasingly fragmented, mobile, individualistic society, which seemed to derive its very energy from the competitiveness of local communities. As a consequence, policy demands were themselves highly fragmentary, representing local or sectional interests and only rarely expressing the possibility of a "general" interest. Thus, the legislature more nearly approximated a public market in which the agents (legislators) of local and special interests bargained and traded for considerations favorable to their clients (constituents) than a deliberative assembly making public policy for the common good. In part, this situation resulted from the absence of well-defined institutional boundaries separating the legislature from society. But it should also be noted that this was a wholly acceptable, indeed desirable, condition in the context of American ideas about representation.

The "product" of this legislative process is equally revealing of the legislature's larger role in the political system. The New York State legislature performed an extraordinary range of functions in the early nineteenth century. But modern notions of what constitutes policy-making or appropriate legislative behavior are inadequate to describe the breadth and character of legislative activities in this period. In 1830, for example, the legislature passed 337 "laws." More than one-third (36.4 percent) dealt with such purely routine matters as the construction of local jails or poorhouses, or authorizing local governments to perform certain specific tasks. "Laws" in the second largest category (with 32.3 percent) were those granting or amending special incorporation charters for businesses, towns, villages, and benevolent associations.

---

[56]Based on the data presented in Table 1.

Only 19 percent of all legislative enactments were general or statewide in scope, and private relief laws made up 12 percent.[57]

The essential point is the disaggregative character of policy outputs. To the extent that the session laws are an accurate reflection of legislative activities, the legislature was not primarily involved in formulating or implementing sustained, coordinated policy for some abstract general interest or abstract category of interest. Rather, its primary function was to allocate resources, privileges, and favors to individuals, localities, and narrow special interests. This is precisely the type of political outcome that Theodore Lowi sought to describe with his concept of "distributive outputs." According to Lowi, it is possible to construct a typology of public policy built around three categories of output: distributive policies, which are easily disaggregated and dispensed unit by unit in isolation from each other; regulative policies, which cannot be disaggregated to the level of individual units; and redistributive policies, in which the impact of policy decisions approaches the level of social class. Each category, furthermore, is associated with a characteristic "arena of policy" or decision-making process. Indeed, the underlying assumption of Lowi's conceptualization, and an important insight, is that policy and structure are somehow dynamically related. "Policy" in the distributive arena, if it is accurate to use the term at all, is incremental and consists of the accumulation of a number of highly individualized decisions. Bargaining or logrolling is the distinctive mode of policy formulation.[58] There is no more apt characterization of legislative behavior in New York in the first half of the nineteenth century.

By modern standards many of the activities described were judicial or administrative in character. Because of the preeminence of the legislature in the political system and revolutionary ideas justifying its supremacy, there was as yet little division of labor within government. Legislative, judicial, and administrative functions remained essentially undifferentiated. The mass of relief laws, for example, by which the legislature processed claims against the state or changed the names of individuals, were clearly judicial in nature. Moreover, the senate, along with the chancellor and the judges of the supreme court, formed the Court for the Correction of Errors, which exercised final appellate jurisdiction in the state until 1847.[59] Similarly, the legislature acted in an administrative capacity when it became mired in the minutia of local government or when it created a corporation through a spe-

---

[57] New York State, *Laws of the State of New York, 1830.*

[58] Theodore H. Lowi, "Business, Public Policy, Case Studies, and Political Theories," *World Politics*, 16 (July 1964): 677–715.

[59] *New York State Constitution of 1821*, Article 5, Section 1; Hurst, *Growth of American Law*, 101.

cial act.[60] It was also the principal regulatory agency in state government, since regulation depended, in all industries except banking, upon self-enforcing corporate charters issued by the legislature. Even when making policy of a general nature, such as establishing a prison or constructing a canal, the legislature frequently assumed direct administrative control.

The legislature also performed certain electoral functions. Under the state's first constitution, the assembly chose the four senators who sat with the governor on the Council of Appointment to select most state and local officials. After 1821, as we have seen, many of these positions became elective or their appointment was vested in local government agencies. But the legislature continued to have sole responsibility for choosing the principal state officers: secretary of state, comptroller, treasurer, attorney general, and commissary general. It also selected the state's presidential electors until 1828, and most gubernatorial appointments required the consent of the senate.[61]

The fusion of legislative, judicial, and administrative functions involved more than simply a breakdown of the principle of separation of powers. The enormously disproportionate number of special and local laws passed by the legislature betrays an inability to distinguish procedurally and substantively between the realms of public and private policy. Private bills, which were clearly the lion's share of legislative activity, were handled exactly the same as public bills. There was no conscious effort to distinguish between the two; indeed, it is unclear that anyone appreciated a need for such a distinction. This is symptomatic, it seems, of a society in which political and social life were still fundamentally undifferentiated. The legislature in early-nineteenth-century New York was not a representative forum for the discussion and resolution of public policy for the common good. It was not making "law" in any modern sense of the term. The legislature was essentially an arena where local and private interests contended for privileges and influence in a society in which public and private roles were virtually indistinguishable.[62]

---

[60]For a detailed account of the history of corporations in New York, see Seavoy, "The Origins of the American Business Corporation."

[61]*New York State Constitution of 1821*; Flick, "The Council of Appointment in New York State," and Hammond, *History of Political Parties*, 3: 670.

[62]The problem of private versus public policy is a complex one involving fundamental social and psychological identifications; but I am convinced that the process by which public and private spheres became differentiated is a crucial one in the nineteenth century. There has been relatively little effort among historians to grapple with this issue, although Max Weber hinted at its significance in the broader process of social, economic, and political development many years ago (see Rheinstein, *Max Weber on Law in Economy and Society*, 47). More recently, Lucian Pye has suggested that the problem of distinguishing between the realms of private and public policy is "precisely the problem of identity which often plagues people in transitional societies" (Pye, *Aspects of Development*, 80–81). An important clue to the meaning of this

If this characterization of legislative behavior is even partially correct, it raises serious questions about the nature of government in this period. The legislature appears to have been more responsive to "the people" in the middle decades of the nineteenth century than in any previous or subsequent era. The commitment to direct representation, annual elections of assemblymen, and yearly sessions guaranteed frequent opportunities for the voters to express their support for or opposition to the activities of their representatives. The extraordinary rate of legislative turnover suggests either that voters exercised their constituent power with great effect by regularly turning out incumbent legislators or that extended service in the legislature, for whatever reason, was not a normal expectation. It is also arguable, of course, that the legislature was not really representative of "the people" but that it reflected the political aspirations of local communities, sections, and regions, and more important, those who were most influential at those levels. Leaving aside for the moment the question of who was being represented, the legislative system in New York State appears, on the surface at least, to have been a close approximation of the ideal of republican representation.

But even republics must ultimately govern. As James Sterling Young perceptively noted in his analysis of Congress, the attributes of a political system which make it representative are not necessarily those most conducive to effective government.[63] The same distinction is valid here. Although there is no denying that the New York legislature, for reasons already mentioned, was remarkably sensitive to its constituencies, it does not follow that it was an equally effective instrument of government. Indeed, the reverse may well have been the case. Its very representativeness produced a bargaining style of politics and political outcomes so disaggregated as to virtually defy, except in a few instances, the rational consideration of policy alternatives.

---

transition has been provided by Michael H. Frisch in *Town Into City: Springfield, Massachusetts and the Meaning of Community, 1840–1888* (Cambridge, Mass., 1972). According to Frisch, Springfield developed during the four decades of his study from a community in which "people tended to think, act, and view their community in direct, personal, informal, and non-abstract terms. Community institutions, even formal ones, were strongest where they were rooted in this immediate sense of contact, in the traditional culture of cohesion . . . and the sense of community had the least meaning and reality where people were asked to think in indirect, formal, abstract, and projective terms about the nature of the general welfare or even about their own self-interest." This conceptual situation was reversed between 1840 and 1880 with "the divergence of public and private, the decline of community as a cultural reality and its emergence as an abstracted concept." (See pages 48–49.) In short, the differentiation of public and private spheres seems to involve a redefinition of the nature of the "political community."

[63] Young, *The Washington Community*, 108–109.

THE SAME structural and ideological factors that prevented the development of a legislative system capable of the rational formulation of policy also impeded the emergence of an administrative apparatus capable of controlling the forces unleashed by social and economic change. In comparison with other states, New York did make significant progress toward administrative development in this period. Both Tocqueville and Chevalier, the two most perceptive foreign visitors to the United States in this period, characterized New York as an exception to the extraordinary decentralization of American administration. Tocqueville, for example, remarked that New York had gone farthest along the road toward centralization, pointing to the fact that state officials seemed to exercise some control and supervision over secondary authorities.[64] Michael Chevalier, on the other hand, celebrated the "grandeur, unity, and centralization" of the state's administration, emphasizing the extent to which New York "in its imperial humor, has laid hands on public instruction, banks, and the means of communication with the purpose of centralizing them."[65] Although it is true that by the 1830s New York had begun to perceive the necessity for administrative and regulative structures to "manage" the state's social and economic responsibilities, a close examination of the evolution of administrative structures reveals that the process was not as advanced as the two foreigners assumed and that administration in New York, as in other states, was more apparent than real.

The legislature, as already noted, was itself heavily involved in performing what were essentially administrative duties. It consumed countless hours and days overseeing the day-to-day affairs of counties, cities, and towns, administering the construction and maintenance of roads and highways, and supervising the collection of taxes. The session laws, for example, are filled with statutes prescribing detailed provisions for the assessment or collection of taxes in some county or village, all of which was accomplished through special acts on an ad hoc basis. In addition to the reasons already mentioned, this legislative involvement in local administrative details resulted partly from the slow evolution of local government. Although the first counties were established in New York as early as 1683, they were not meant to perform legislative and administrative functions. In fact, the county board evolved into a local governing body only gradually, a process that spanned the last quarter of the eighteenth century and most of the nineteenth century. Up to 1838, special legislative acts periodically conferred powers and duties upon individual county boards. But until that date, which marked the beginning

---

[64]Tocqueville, *Democracy in America*, 83–84.
[65]Chevalier, *Society, Manners, and Politics in America*, 358, 364.

of a series of general laws delegating ever-increasing responsibilities to county government, many local administrative tasks were of necessity performed by the legislature.[66] Needless to say, the deeper the legislature became involved in the administrative process, the more that administration became subject to the same debilitating factors that prevented rational policy formulation in the legislative setting.

The executive branch, furthermore, was ill-suited because of the nature of its organization to take up the slack in administration. The state's first constitution had invested the governor with the responsibility for "faithfully executing the law" and generally created a more powerful and independent executive than was the case in most of the states. But even in New York, the governor's ability to act as an independent force in state government was severely constrained. He was required to keep the legislature apprised of the "state of the state" and to make recommendations at each session, but he was given few of the resources necessary to push through a legislative program to fruition. Until 1822 he shared the veto power with the other members of the Council of Revision. After 1822 the governor's arsenal of powers included the suspensive veto, but it is interesting that this power was exercised only twenty-nine times between 1823 and 1850, with four of these being overturned by the legislature and ten coming in the year 1850 alone.[67]

One of the greatest potential powers of a chief executive is control over subordinate administrative officials, either through formal constitutional authority or through the distribution of patronage. In both cases, there were sharp limits on the governor's effective power. Under the Constitution of 1777, the governor's role in making appointments depended on his ability to influence the senatorial members of the Council of Appointment, a body not especially noted for its pliability. Indeed, the early history of the council is one of almost constant discord between the governor and senators. Under the Constitution of 1821, the governor appointed, with the consent of the senate, many of the lesser state functionaries, but he still possessed little formal control over the administrative machinery of the state. The most important limitation in this regard was that the great state officers were chosen not by the governor but by joint ballot of the two houses of the legislature and were, in a very real sense, extensions of the legislature. They thus existed

[66]William C. Morey, *The Government of New York: Its History and Administration* (New York, 1902), 97–103, particularly 99–100n.

[67]*New York State Constitutions of 1777, 1821*; Margaret C. Alexander, *The Development of the Powers of the State Executive, with Special Reference to the State of New York* (Northampton, Mass., 1917), 177–194, 230.

independently of the governor and constituted, in effect, autonomous centers of power within the administration.[68]

The principal state officers—comptroller, secretary of state, treasurer, surveyor general, and attorney general—made up the core of New York's administrative structure. All these offices had been created during or soon after the Revolution to perform the limited duties of an eighteenth-century state government. The secretary of state was the chief custodian of state records; the treasurer was the principal financial officer; the surveyor general was responsible for superintending the surveys and sales of state lands; and the attorney general was the chief legal officer. The office of comptroller was not even created until 1797. In the half century after the Revolution, however, the state confronted new and unforeseen tasks as a result of the expansion of settlement, population growth, and economic development. To meet the challenge of new responsibilities in such social and economic areas as internal improvements, regulation of banks and corporations, and public education, New York gradually enlarged the responsibilities of its administrative officers, piling new duties onto what was already a fragile structure. As a group the officers became commissioners of the Land Office, commissioners of the Canal Fund (with the lieutenant governor), members of the Canal Board (with the canal commissioners), and members of the Board of State Canvassers.[69] In addition to these general accretions of power, the duties of each were enlarged from time to time by special acts of the legislature. In the early years, the various officers were relatively equal in their duties. But by the 1840s, the secretary of state and the comptroller had achieved an ascendancy not only over the other state officers but also, critics charged, over the entire government. A closer look at the development of these two offices will provide additional insight into the administrative process and help to explain the growing criticism of the power and influence of the state officers in the middle 1840s.

The duties of the secretary of state, the lesser of the two officers, grew steadily in the first half of the nineteenth century. In addition to responsibilities regarding the collection, preservation, and distribution of state documents and laws, he was clerk of the Council of Appointment until its abolition; commissioner of the Land Office with power to convene that body; commissioner of the Canal Fund and member of the Canal Board; state canvasser; superintendent of common schools after 1821; superintendent of

---

[68] Alexander, *Development of the Powers of the State Executive*, 181–188; Gittleman, "The Council of Appointment."

[69] *New York State Constitutions of 1777, 1821*; S. C. Hutchins, comp., *Civil List and Constitutional History of the Colony and State of New York* (Albany, N.Y., 1882), 80–82, 244–249.

weights and measures; trustee of the State Library, Capital, and State Hall; and regent of the University of New York after 1842.[70] The secretary of state, moreover, received reports from various state and local officers as to their activities and transmitted such information to the legislature. In this connection, for example, the legislature in 1839 required that he annually collect, arrange, and report the criminal statistics of the state. In 1842 the overseers and superintendents of the poor were required to report to the secretary of state, and in 1847 the legislature required annual reports on the number of births, marriages, and deaths in the state.[71] With the passage of general incorporation laws, furthermore, the secretary of state was usually designated to receive articles of incorporation. Finally, almost every legislature directed some special action on the part of the secretary of state, whether it involved the publication and distribution of laws or documents, the performance of some duty relative to elections, or the disposition of unsold state lands.[72]

The most important single addition to the power of the secretary of state in this period, however, and the most illustrative of the fusion of administrative duties, was his assumption in 1821 of responsibility for the common schools in New York. The Office of Superintendent of Common Schools had been created as a separate and distinct department in 1813; it was abolished in 1821, however, reportedly for political reasons growing out of the appointment of a successor to the then superintendent, Gideon Hawley. His duties were merged with those of the secretary of state, who became ex officio superintendent. As such, he was charged with the annual visitation and inspection of several literary and charitable institutions in New York City; general supervision of the State Normal School; and the preparation of forms, instructions, and blanks for distribution to subordinate officials. In addition, he was required to submit an annual report to the legislature containing a statement of the conditions of the common schools; estimates and accounts of expenditures of school money; plans for the improvement of the school system; and other matters relating to his office. Finally, and most important, the secretary of state was responsible for the apportionment of school funds among the various counties. The duties of superintendent remained with the secretary until 1854.[73]

[70]*Laws of New York*, 50th Session, 1827, vol. 2, 34–36; chap. 249, 1830; chap. 66, 1834; chap. 173, 1842.

[71]Ibid., chap. 240, 1821; chap. 259, 1839; chap. 258, 1842; chap. 152, 1847; *Senate Document*, no. 39, 1854.

[72]New York State Assembly, *General Index of the Laws*.

[73]*Laws of New York*, chap. 240, 1821; *Revised Statutes*, vol. 2: 303–305; *Senate Document*, no. 39, 1854.

Although it was not created until 1797, the office of state comptroller paralleled and soon surpassed the growth of the secretary of state's office. Under the terms of the original act, the comptroller assumed all the responsibilities of the auditor general, whose office was abolished. He possessed the power to audit; to draw warrants authorizing the payment of funds from the treasury; to maintain a record of financial transactions; to invest surplus state funds; and to borrow money, whenever existing funds were inadequate to meet the lawful obligation of the state.[74]

The comptroller's office was reestablished every three years until 1812 when it was made permanent. In 1799 the legislature prohibited the payment of any money from the treasury except under the warrant of the comptroller. In 1800 he became custodian of the general fund, which was the principal source of money for maintenance of the government until it dried up in 1834. In 1801 the comptroller was made a member of the State Board of Canvassers and a commissioner of the Land Office. He played an active role, moreover, in the inception, construction, and management of the Erie Canal as commissioner of the Canal Fund and later as a member of the Canal Board. Indeed, the influence and power of the comptroller in these early years was principally a function of his domination of canal administration and public financing of internal improvements, as Nathan Miller's study of the role of the Canal Fund Commission in the New York economy during the 1830s makes clear.[75] In 1827 the comptroller was given the general power "to superintend the fiscal concerns of the state."[76]

Nor did the flow of power to the comptroller stop here. In 1837 he became the custodian of the United States Deposit Fund.[77] The following year, his responsibilities were augmented even further by the Free Banking Act, which granted to the comptroller supervisory powers over the state's free banks. He was to manage the security deposit system by which free banks deposited public stocks with his office in return for an equal amount of circulating notes, which were engraved, printed, and certified by the comptroller. In addition, the law required banking associations to report semiannually to the comptroller on their transactions.[78] In 1843 incorporated banks also came under the comptroller's jurisdiction when the Bank Commission was abol-

[74]*Laws of New York*, chap. 21, 1797; J. A. Roberts, *A Century in the Comptroller's Office* (Albany, N.Y., 1897).

[75]Roberts, *A Century in the Comptroller's Office*, 10–15; Nathan Miller, *The Enterprise of a Free People: Aspects of Economic Development of New York During the Canal Period, 1792–1838* (Ithaca, N.Y., 1962), passim.

[76]*Revised Statutes*, vol. 2, 9–41.

[77]*Laws of New York*, chaps. 2 and 150, 1837.

[78]Ibid., chap. 260, 1838.

ished and its duties transferred to that officer. The comptroller was required to register and countersign the notes of chartered banks. Both kinds of banks, moreover, had to submit quarterly reports to the comptroller, and he possessed the power to require banks to redeem their circulation if capital was reduced below the minimum specie reserve. In addition, he could appoint a special agent to investigate any bank whose condition was suspect.[79] The legislature granted the comptroller similar powers over insurance companies in 1849.[80] Little wonder that many New Yorkers came to believe that the comptroller, because of his command of the state's finances during this period, was more powerful than the governor.

A clear pattern emerges from this overview of the development of state administration in the early nineteenth century. Until the 1840s, New York responded to the necessity for action in new areas primarily by assigning responsibility to existing agencies.[81] The result was that vast potential powers accrued to some state officers. But a note of caution is perhaps warranted at this point. The word *administration* carries a distinctly modern connotation, perhaps too much so to be an accurate description of what was happening in this period. For one thing, there was little in the way of formal administrative integration. Each state officer possessed a separate, and theoretically equal, jurisdiction, and all were responsible directly to the appointing authority—the legislature between 1821 and 1846 and the people after 1846. This meant that there was no institutionalized central direction; effectiveness almost certainly suffered, therefore, as a result of a fusion of functions and overlapping of roles.

The operations of these state officers, furthermore, remained small, personal, and highly political affairs. The role of the legislature in the appointing process and the peculiar control of the Albany Regency during the 1820s and 1830s virtually assured that the administration would be highly politicized. Politics also permeated the selection of departmental personnel. Indeed, the control of patronage was a major incentive to officeholding, and state officers made ample use of that power in choosing their subordinates. A further limitation on the administrative effectiveness of these state departments was their size. Staffs were small, and they did not increase significantly toward mid-century. As late as 1854, for example, the offices of the treasurer, attorney general, and state engineer–surveyor employed only two clerks

---

[79] Ibid., chap. 218, 1843.

[80] Ibid., chap. 308, 1849.

[81] An exception, of course, was canal administration. The Canal Fund Commission and the Canal Board were separate agencies created to deal with financing, constructing, and managing the state's internal improvements. The state officers, however, were ex officio members of these two bodies and wielded considerable influence in their deliberations.

each. The secretary of state had three clerks and the comptroller had ten. The greatest growth occurred in the comptroller's office. In 1834 that department hired a total of twelve clerks, nine for the "Comptroller's Office proper," and three for the "canal room." In 1845 it employed twenty persons, divided into the comptroller's office (nine), the canal department (five), the free banking department (three), and the incorporated bank department (three). That figure was reduced, however, with the creation of a separate Bank Department and transferral of canal responsibilities to the auditor of the canal department.[82] For all the accumulation of power by state officers, therefore, administration, as Tocqueville correctly observed, was hardly imposing.

Further complicating the exercise of the administrative function was the existence of boards and commissions created to deal with specific problems. Chevalier apparently had such institutions in mind when he praised New York for its administrative centralization. But the reality is that this solution to the problem of administration applied only to canals and banks before the 1840s, and in each instance the specific structures created exhibited characteristics directly contrary to modern notions of effective administration. Canal administration, for example, was entrusted to two separate institutions, the Canal Fund Commission and the Canal Commission, which met together to form a third, the Canal Board. The Canal Fund Commission, which consisted of the elective state officers, was responsible for financing the canals and managing canal revenues. The Canal Commission, appointed by the legislature until 1844 when its members became elective, had actual administrative responsibility for the system.[83]

Although this arrangement was remarkably successful in constructing, financing, and operating the state's canals, these agencies fell far short of being modern, bureaucratic structures. Management of the canals, particularly in the first two decades, was characterized by personalism, inadequate record-keeping procedures, the absence of accountability for the disbursement of funds, and outright fraud in the letting of contracts for construction and repairs. Not least among the maladies afflicting canal administration was rampant political favoritism. From canal commissioner down to the lowliest weigh master or lock tender, party affiliation was the primary qualification for canal personnel. Whigs and Democrats alike accepted and capitalized on the patronage potential of the canal department.[84] Thus, stability and con-

---

[82] New York State, Audit and Control Department, *Annual Report*, 1854; *Senate Document*, no. 21, 1834, vol. 1; *Senate Document*, no. 45, 1845, vol. 1.

[83] Sowers, *Financial History of New York State*, 74–75; Chevalier, *Society, Manners, and Politics*, 323–324.

[84] Shaw, *Erie Water West*, 250–254.

tinuity in the management of the state's waterways depended almost entirely on stability and continuity in partisan control of state government.

No less significant, from an administrative point of view, were two additional characteristics of the agencies charged with administering New York's canals. From the very beginning, the line between public and private interest in the formulation and implementation of canal-related policies was poorly drawn. The first Canal Commission, established in 1816, was made up of internal-improvement enthusiasts who had been active earlier in lobbying for the canal. Indeed, some of the members had a direct economic interest in the construction of a waterway from Lake Erie to the Hudson. Joseph Ellicott, for example, was an agent for the Holland Land Company, which stood to gain from increased land values along the canal route.[85] More important, many activities of the Canal Commission and the Canal Fund Commission went beyond administration. In practice, both bodies wielded immense influence in the policy-making process. The financial manipulations of the Canal Fund Commission, as Nathan Miller has shown, reverberated throughout the state's economy during the 1830s. The Canal Commission, charged by the statute that created it with responsibility for determining and recommending to the legislature the best routes for canals, also exercised great influence in the policy-making arena. In effect, the commission acted as a sieve through which political and sectional considerations were sifted to produce politically acceptable proposals for presentation to the legislature. In the planning stages of the Erie Canal, for example, the commission sought to allay the fears of those who were hesitant about the project by proposing that only two small canals be constructed at first—one between the Mohawk and Seneca rivers and one between the Hudson River and Lake Champlain. It was a shrewd political decision. The quick commercial success of the middle section (Mohawk and Seneca) would create a strong political bond between western farmers and New York City businessmen, and simultaneous construction of the Champlain Canal would ensure the support of northern New York for the entire project.[86] The point is that these were policy decisions, made not by the duly elected representatives of the people, but by a subordinate agency to whom such authority was delegated by the legislature.

It would be shortsighted, therefore, to view the establishment of commissions as nothing more than a device for filling an administrative need. That

---

[85] *Laws of New York*, chap. 237, 1816; Miller, *Enterprise of a Free People*, 46–49; Sowers, *Financial History*, 74–75.

[86] Miller, *Enterprise of a Free People*, 61–62. See chapter 4 in this book for an extended discussion of the activities of the Canal Fund Commission.

may well have been the original intent, but the result was quite different. What in fact developed were virtually autonomous agencies that *generated* policy as well as *administered* it. The legislature, in effect, delegated policy-making authority, usually by default rather than by intent, to subordinate institutions, thereby further dividing a vital political function. Such delegations were, of course, common practice among early-nineteenth-century state governments and reflected not only contemporary administrative styles but also prevailing concepts of authority. The practice did not go unchallenged, however. As early as 1826, one New Yorker criticized the delegation of vast powers to the Canal Board as "both dangerous in nature, and without . . . a single other precedent in practice in any other free government."[87] The legality and desirability of such methods, furthermore, came under increasing attack during the 1830s. In 1838, when Governor William L. Marcy proposed to aid New York banks by allowing the Canal Fund Commission to lend them more state stocks, Whigs objected on the grounds that it constituted an improper exercise of legislative power. The plan, according to the Whig opposition, involved a "dangerous delegation of sovereign power" to "subordinates and merely administrative officers."[88] Whether from political considerations or legitimate concern for the welfare of the state, the Whigs succeeded in defeating the Marcy plan. But the incident foreshadowed a far more significant debate over the legality of delegating legislative authority which erupted in the 1840s.

Before concluding this discussion of administrative developments in New York in the early nineteenth century, we must take note of the single most decisive step taken by the state before 1840 toward the development of a modern regulatory structure. In 1829 the legislature passed "An Act to Create a Fund for the Benefit of Creditors of Certain Monied Corporations," thereby establishing the safety-fund banking system. In addition to providing a "safety fund" from bank contributions and guaranteed by the state to insure the redemption of bills issued by insolvent banks, this act created the Banking Commission to investigate and supervise monied corporations in New York. There were to be three commissioners, one of whom was appointed by the governor and senate, the remaining two by the banks themselves. Their term of office was two years, subject to removal by the governor for misconduct or neglect of duty. The commissioners were to visit each safety-fund bank at least once every four months to examine the affairs of the corporation and ensure compliance with the law. They had power to examine

[87] Quoted in Shaw, *Erie Water West*, 242.
[88] Quoted in Miller, *Enterprise of a Free People*, 242–243.

officers under oath and to apply for an injunction against any bank that was financially insolvent or guilty of wrongdoing. Finally, the legislature required that the commissioners prepare annual reports of their activities and the condition of New York's banks. We will consider the commission's regulatory activities, its successes, and its failures more fully in the next chapter. Here, it is enough to note that establishing the commission represented a significant and very early departure from prevailing modes of regulation. It provided, for the first time, regular, periodic, all-round examinations of the banking industry by a board of three commissioners who were knowledgeable if not expert in the business of banking. For all its innovativeness, however, the Bank Commission would become embroiled in the political turmoil over banking policy during the 1830s and would ultimately be abolished in 1843.[89]

The New York experience in the early nineteenth century is a classic illustration of a society seeking to reconcile the need for rational and efficient administration to deal with new responsibilities with the concepts of direct representation and democracy. On the one hand, as the state was called on to perform new and largely unforeseen tasks, it responded by assigning enlarged duties to existing structures and by experimenting with a commission style of administration. The result was a kind of administrative centralization, but a very particular kind. The state's administrative capacity depended on a number of institutions and officials, each with separate jurisdictions, each performing specific functions, and none responsible to any other. The various agencies were effectively insulated from each other by the absence of hierarchical lines of authority. This arrangement was no accident. It reflected American fears of power and authority and was, in fact, in complete harmony with the principle of representation. New Yorkers acted in the revolutionary tradition in seeking to prevent the consolidation of administrative authority by dividing power between several levels and among a number of institutions or agencies at each level. To be sure, this diffusion of power inevitably carried with it a loss of coordination, control, and unity in administration. But in this period at least, the distrust of authority and the desire to implement the principles of representation overshadowed any desire for the rationalization and centralization of authority. It became clear only

---

[89] *Laws of New York*, chap. 94, 1829; Fritz Redlich, *The Molding of American Banking: Men and Ideas*, vol. 2 (New York, 1968), pt. 1, 88–92.

later, and at great expense to the state, that representation was not necessarily compatible with the development of modern administrative structures.[90]

Governments, of course, almost never function exclusively through formal institutions and constitutionally mandated powers. All political systems, whether democratic or totalitarian, depend to one degree or another on informal arrangements for the coordinated, controlled exercise of political authority. It is not surprising that such was the case in New York in the 1820s and 1830s. In practice, the emergence of a well-organized, highly professionalized, statewide political machine provided a measure of cohesion and coordination in an otherwise fragmented legislature and partially compensated for the absence of formal administrative unity in state government. By the 1820s, a totally new conception of political parties had begun to emerge from the maelstrom of New York politics. Rejecting the traditional view that parties were synonymous with factions and therefore subversive of republican government, politicians such as Martin Van Buren developed a positive argument for political parties which not only upheld their inevitability in a free society, but also legitimized partisan competition as a positive benefit. Armed with this justification, Van Buren and the Bucktails seized control of the New York Democratic Party in the early 1820s and created one of the most powerful and successful political machines in the nineteenth century.[91]

---

[90]Both contemporary observers and modern scholars have described administration in the antebellum states in these general terms. Tocqueville, for example, clearly perceived the fragmented nature of American administration and the consequences that followed from the election of administrative officers, their irremovability, and the absence of hierarchy. He concluded that such an arrangement necessitated the extensive use of the judiciary as a "weapon of administration," to "punish disobedience" on the part of otherwise uncontrollable administrative officers (see Tocqueville, *Democracy in America*, 72–84). Alfred de Grazia, a twentieth-century political scientist, relates this type of administrative structure, "when offices are numerous and official responsibility is only to the people" [in this case through the legislature] to "the psychology of direct representation. First, it expresses a belief and a wish that government be as simple and controllable as possible. In the second place, it reduces all administration to politics by making offices of all kinds elective. Third, it expresses a belief that the office is nothing when dissociated from the people, with no specialized concerns of its own, no abilities required to perform it, and no excuse for trappings, insignia, rituals, or secrets of its own. Finally, in essence, it regards government as a transient arrangement, temporarily conducted by representatives chosen almost at random from out of the body of the people" (see De Grazia, *Public and Republic: Political Representation in America* [New York, 1951], 120).

[91]Michael Wallace, "Changing Concepts of Party in the United States: New York, 1815–1828," *American Historical Review*, 74 (1968): 453–491; Robert V. Remini, "The Albany Regency," *New York History*, 29 (October 1958): 341–355; McCormick, *Second American Party System*, 112–124; and Kalman Goldstein, "The Albany Regency" (Ph.D. diss., Columbia University, 1969). For a superb discussion of the origins of the political machine in New York City politics, see Amy Bridges, *A City in the Republic: Antebellum New York and the Origins of Machine Politics* (Cambridge, 1984).

The most prominent members of the Albany Regency, as this network of relationships was dubbed by its political opponents, were Van Buren, William L. Marcy, Benjamin Knower, Samuel A. Talcott, Benjamin F. Butler, Azariah C. Flagg, Silas Wright, Edwin Croswell, and John A. Dix. Above reproach personally and bound together by mutual trust, intense loyalty, and the intimacy of personal and familial association, these men fashioned an efficient and centralized political organization by controlling the legislative caucus, and thus the appointing power, and by emphasizing party discipline. They traded the principal state offices among themselves, determined party policy, selected candidates for elective office, and maintained party discipline by granting or withholding patronage on the basis of political loyalty. Within the legislature, for example, the party caucus, largely under the direction of the Regency, typically controlled the election of speakers and filled state offices that were legislatively appointed. On many issues, particularly those of a clearly partisan nature, inexperienced legislators took their cues from party leaders and party positions.[92] Simultaneously, Regency control of the state offices provided a measure of stability and continuity to administration because the leaders of the Regency held office for long periods of time and were typically replaced by other members of the machine. Azariah C. Flagg, for example, held office for a total of eighteen years between 1826 and 1847 — seven years as secretary of state (1826–1833) and eleven years as comptroller (1833–1839 and 1842–1847). Nor was such tenure atypical. William L. Marcy served as comptroller for six years (1823–1829) before becoming governor. John A. Dix was secretary of state for six years (1833–1838). Abraham Keyser held the position of treasurer for twelve years (1826–1838) and Simeon DeWitt was surveyor general for an equal period of time (1823–1835).[93]

The Regency men, in short, brought to the disparate elements of state government a level of efficiency, continuity, integration and centralization which tends to obscure the contradictions built into formal governmental structures. The extraconstitutional agency of party and political influence served as the glue that prevented the centrifugal forces inherent in the structure of the system from producing complete confusion and disintegration in the face of the rapidly accumulating challenges generated by a modernizing society. It would be a mistake, however, to assume that Regency control was absolute. Far from it. The Albany Regency emerged slowly, over a number of years, as Van Buren and others of its creators sought, as one historian has put it, "to rationalize political life and to create a party capable of harmoniz-

---

[92] Remini, "The Albany Regency," 346–353; Goldstein, "The Albany Regency," 198–199.
[93] Hutchins, *Civil List*, 244–246.

ing the increasingly divergent interests of a growing society."[94] But it was precisely those divergent interests and that growing society which posed the greatest threat to the party discipline and regularity sought by the leaders of the Regency. In an expansive society in which the growth of a region frequently depended on its ability to secure special legislative favors in the form of corporate charters or internal improvement projects, party loyalty often took second place to the requirements of local development. Examples abound during the 1830s of legislators coalescing in support of internal improvements or manufacturing corporations beneficial to their common region, irrespective of party labels. Regency control over party machinery was almost certainly more complete than its influence in the legislative process, but even here challenges to its authority were not uncommon. Independent-minded caucuses, for example, rejected Regency nominations for the speakership of the assembly and for U.S. senator in 1831 and 1832, and throughout the period legislative caucuses were characterized by numerous ballots and considerable wrangling over the choices for appointive offices.[95]

What emerges most clearly from recent analyses of the Albany Regency is that it was most effective at coordinating party policies, less effective when it tried to dictate to those at the local levels of the party structure. Even this degree of control, which was by no means inconsiderable, depended on Democratic dominance at the polls, a relatively stable electoral environment, and minimal consensus at the leadership level on the major issues confronting the state. By 1842, however, the Regency had fallen victim to divisions within the party over internal improvement policy, an increasingly vigorous and successful Whig party, and an inability to maintain a consensus among its leadership on the proper response to the most disruptive economic crisis of the century.[96] The dissolution of the Regency removed the single most powerful force for the integration and centralization of state government.

EVEN WITH the qualifications noted, the Albany Regency contrasted sharply with the loosely organized society and political system of which it was a part. Indeed, the Regency's success, to the extent that it was successful, flowed from its ability to organize political functions in an essentially disconnected

---

[94] Goldstein, "The Albany Regency," 64.

[95] Ibid., 197–199.

[96] Ibid., 197–198; D. S. Alexander, *A Political History of the State of New York* (1906–1923, reprint, 4 vols., Port Washington, N.Y., 1969), 3: 53. The electoral environment of New York politics is succinctly described and analyzed in Lee Benson, Joel H. Silbey, and Phyllis F. Field, "Toward a Theory of Stability and Change in American Voting Patterns: New York State, 1792–1970," in *The History of American Electoral Politics*, ed. Joel H. Silbey, Allan G. Bogue, and William H. Flanigan (Princeton, N.J., 1978), 78–105, especially 83–91.

society and to coordinate the disparate elements of a polity that remained, as late as the 1830s, essentially "premodern." New York's political system was neither very differentiated nor integrated. Although virtually unchallenged as the principal agency of government, the legislature was fundamentally incapable of providing leadership for the society as a whole in this period. Rapid turnover, the inexperience of its members, the lack of functional differentiation, and the debilitating effects of localism hindered the rational consideration of policy alternatives. Policy, as a consequence, took the form of individualized and incremental decisions. This is significant in itself, but it also suggests that New Yorkers had a very poorly developed sense of political community. On balance, in fact, it is unclear whether New York had a single, centralized political authority, a prerequisite for political modernization, or a multiplicity of authorities. The legislature did not make law, except in rare instances; rather it provided an arena for the resolution of highly specialized demands emanating from individuals, groups, and communities.

Although important steps were taken during the 1820s and 1830s toward the development of administrative structures, the rational implementation of policy was similarly handicapped. The closest thing to a bureaucracy in New York in this period was the canal administration, and it was riddled with political favoritism and conflict of interest, hamstrung by a system of divided responsibility, and was not exclusively administrative in any case. Executive functions at the state level were divided among several state officers who existed independent of the governor, were effectively insulated from each other, and whose operations were also highly politicized. The most important administrative innovation in this period was the establishment of the Bank Commission, in many ways a forerunner of the modern regulatory commission, and this would prove short-lived. It was a remarkably disjointed edifice, held together and able to perform in unison only because of the existence of such informal arrangements as the Albany Regency, and that too was beginning to crack by the end of the 1830s.

It was a political system, in short, whose members focused their attention on the locality and went about their private concerns with little regard for a generalized public interest. There was neither inclination nor a structural mechanism for the expression of a general will. "In regard to individuals of all classes," as Horace Greeley put it in 1841, "those political objects are the most important that immediately affect their interests . . . to a Merchant in this city [New York] the acts of the Common Council are matters of more direct interest than the proceedings of the State Legislature, and the latter more so than those of the General Government."[97]

[97] *New York Tribune*, April 21, 1841.

The irony, of course, is that political development and economic development were proceeding in opposite directions. Even as New Yorkers institutionalized the legacies of the Revolution—legislative supremacy, distrust of power and authority, direct representation, and expanded participation—to produce a decentralized political system, economic relationships, as we saw in chapter 2, were becoming more impersonal and market structures increasingly centralized. The functional relevance of such a system of politics in an increasingly market-dominated society would be severely tested after 1837.

[4]

The Political Economy
of Distribution

STRUCTURE, PROCESS, and policy converged most conspicuously, and with the greatest impact for New Yorkers, in the arena of public economic policy. During the first four decades of the nineteenth century, New Yorkers fashioned a distinctive political economy, the most notable feature of which was the commitment to large-scale, pragmatic state intervention to stimulate and direct the course of economic development. There is, of course, nothing new or startling in the observation that government played a major role in the economic development of the state. Historians have long since laid to rest the myth of laissez-faire, at least insofar as it was thought to describe reality in the American states before the Civil War. Although scholarly disagreements, on specifics as well as interpretation, continue to exist, few historians today would dispute the extraordinary range and variety of activities antebellum state governments employed in support of economic growth and development.[1] For present purposes, what is important is not the fact, or even the extent, of governmental involvement in New York's economy, but rather the character and quality of such intervention, the dynamic relationship between policy outputs on the one hand and structure and process on the other, and those aspects of this policy system which would ultimately force New Yorkers to question its continued validity. This chapter seeks to assess the record of New York's involvement in the economy before 1840 from the perspective of political development and in terms of what that record can tell us about the process by which a new political order emerged in the state.

---

[1] See works listed in footnotes 1, 5, and 8 in chapter 1.

NEW YORK entered the nineteenth century predisposed, by tradition and a conscious awareness of self-interest, to take an active part in economic activities. The state had only recently emerged from colonial status in an empire built on the mercantilist assumption that the political system had wide-ranging responsibility for the encouragement and regulation of economic activity for the common good. Throughout its colonial experience, and, indeed, into the Revolutionary and Confederation periods, New York was involved in such activity on a broad scale. Colonial and state governments regulated weights and measures, established price and wage rates, encouraged particular activities such as manufacturing through bounties, and imposed import duties on goods entering the state.[2] There was clear precedent, therefore, for governmental intervention in the economy.

Nothing in the colonial period, however, could have prepared New Yorkers for the extraordinary breadth of state economic activity in the first half of the nineteenth century. For fifty years after 1790, when the state first subscribed to one hundred shares of stock in the New York Manufacturing Society,[3] New York pursued a variety of policies designed, either directly or indirectly, to create favorable conditions for economic growth. Although the only principle governing such intervention appears to have been pragmatic concern for what would work in specific circumstances, for analytic purposes the state's economic activities can be organized around several broad categories. The most obvious example of state intervention in the economy involved the direct distribution of what Harry N. Scheiber has called "public largess" to individual, group, or community supplicants.[4] In the New York case, such largess consisted of bounties, subsidies, grants, stock ownership, and loans. Less direct, but no less significant, the state also distributed a variety of legal privileges and immunities—franchises, corporate privileges, tax exemptions, and exemptions from jury and militia duty—to "deserving" individuals and companies. More dramatically, New York assumed direct responsibility for the construction and operation of the canal system, thereby providing transportation facilities vital to the state's economic development. The state also regulated economic activities—through restrictive clauses in corporate charters, such institutional arrangements as the Bank Commission, inherited mercantilist policies such as compulsory inspection, and informal efforts to manage the economy through such agencies as the Canal Fund Commission. Finally, government profoundly shaped the state's economy by providing a legal and institutional framework conducive to eco-

[2] Miller, *Enterprise of a Free People*, 10.
[3] Lincoln, *Constitutional History of New York*, 2: 91.
[4] Scheiber, "Federalism and the American Economic Order," 88.

nomic growth, private enterprise, and a large role for the private sector in the allocation of resources. Each form of state intervention provides significant clues to the nature of public economic policy in this period, as well as to the relationship between the political and economic systems.

The government's role in the distribution of public largess is most clearly evident in New York's efforts to aid private enterprise through subsidies designed to stimulate production of particular commodities, encourage experimentation with new species, or reward producers for achievements in quality. Within this category, New York resorted to bounties, premiums, and grants to individuals or companies engaged in agriculture, manufacturing, or transportation. In an effort to disseminate knowledge with regard to agricultural improvements, for example, the state gave financial support to such organizations as the Society for the Promotion of the Useful Arts and awarded premiums for raising particular crops or livestock. Some $23,000 was thereby expended between 1809 and 1819 to encourage home production of woolens.[5] After 1819 New York instituted a broad program of premiums and matching funds to go to county agricultural societies that raised money, through voluntary contributions, to be used to reward farmers participating in countywide competition. Under the umbrella of this "Berkshire Plan," the state funneled about $42,000 into the agricultural sector between 1819 and 1825. At the same time, a Board of Agriculture, made up of the presidents of the county societies, received additional funds for distributing seeds and publishing articles of interest to farmers.[6] Aid to agriculture constituted more than half of the state's total support of private enterprise before 1825, when state financial support of county societies was withdrawn, not to be reinstituted until 1841.[7]

Similar subsidies went to struggling industries and to private transportation ventures in the early nineteenth century. The Non-Importation, Embargo, and Non-Intercourse Acts before the War of 1812 necessitated that Americans produce their own finished goods. To stimulate home manufacturing, New York offered premiums for household fabric in 1808 and 1809. Similarly, a law of 1812 encouraged the production of woolen goods, and the New York legislature appropriated $10,000 in 1819 to encourage household manufactures.[8] The state also tried to stimulate the construction of a transportation network by private enterprise in the early years through direct

[5] Miller, *Enterprise of a Free People*, 15–16.

[6] Ibid., 17.

[7] Beatrice G. Reubens, "State Financing of Private Enterprise in Early New York" (Ph.D. diss., Columbia University, 1960), 245, 267–268, 277–278.

[8] Carman, "Beginnings of the Industrial Revolution," 344–345; Fox, *Decline of Aristocracy*, 324n; and Miller, *Enterprise of a Free People*, 14.

grants to transportation companies. In 1792, for example, the legislature granted $25,000 to the Western and Northern navigation companies to aid the building of canals in the Mohawk and Upper Hudson river valleys. In 1798 the legislature included in the corporate charter creating the Niagara Canal Company a gift of state land for a similar purpose.[9] Such grants stopped in the 1820s, however, after a total expenditure of a little over $50,000.[10] The relatively small amount expended for such projects can be attributed to the fact that the state's responsibility for transportation facilities was much clearer than in other areas of the economy and to the growing realization that private enterprise would not be able to undertake projects of the scale required to link different sections of the state. Also, by the late 1820s other means of aiding transportation companies had been discovered, principally by lending the credit of the state rather than by making actual cash outlays.

On balance, direct subsidies were a relatively minor aspect of New York's economic involvement. Although such aid totaled more than a quarter of a million dollars by 1826, this amount represented only a fraction of the $6.5 million that Beatrice Reubens, the leading student of the subject, estimates the state expended for economic aid during the first fifty years of its existence. Reubens also argues that subsidies were used only when loans or investments proved impractical and that, insofar as it was regarded as a means of allocating resources, New York's bounty policy was ineffectual.[11] Still, the willingness of political leaders to engage in such activity at all illustrates the extent to which the mercantilist tradition continued to shape policy into the nineteenth century as the state confronted the new demands of a rapidly developing economy.

New York also experimented with direct state investment in private enterprise. Either by reserving stock rights in corporate charters or through purchases on the market, the state invested in some fifteen banks and the Bank of the United States, reaching a peak investment of $847,950 in 1814. Although there appears to have been some consideration for the developmental impact of such stock subscriptions, particularly with regard to country banks, the principal motive for such investments was related to the state's investment needs and the quasi-public nature of banks. In any case, the state ultimately absorbed a net capital loss of over $10,000. Outside of banking, New York held stock in only five corporations, the significance of which was minimal. In comparison with other states, such as Pennsylvania and Massa-

---

[9] Lincoln, *Constitutional History of New York*, 2: 91.
[10] Reubens, "State Financing," 271.
[11] Ibid., 234, 240.

chusetts, New York's brief flirtation with the mixed corporation proved a not very successful episode.[12]

More significant was the state's loan policy. By five separate acts—1786, 1792, 1808, 1837, and 1840—the New York legislature established state loan offices whose purpose was to lend money to private citizens. These loan funds were appropriated and administered through the counties and required that recipients provide security in the form of land. Like the colonial land banks earlier, the intent of the acts establishing the State Loan Office was clearly to provide a source of credit for farmers who were generally excluded from the credit activities of commercial banks. As a consequence, the legal definition of what was acceptable security purposefully excluded land speculators and nonresident owners, at least until 1837, when ownership became the only requirement. Similarly, the 1808 act excluded nonagricultural areas such as the Southern District (New York, Long Island, and Westchester) from consideration and increased the allotment to western areas. The 1837 Loan Act, which stemmed from the need to invest the state's share of federal surplus revenues, was also directed toward farmers. It is difficult to determine the impact of these loans with any accuracy since the state failed to develop a check on the uses to which the funds were put and since the amounts themselves were small. Still, the loans did add to available credit and appear to have made a contribution to relief efforts in times of distress, particularly in 1837.[13]

Two other loan policies based on landed security deserve mention. The legislature periodically authorized that accumulated surpluses from the several state funds be loaned to citizens. Such acts passed on ten separate occasions between 1797 and 1817. In each instance, the state's investment needs were the primary considerations in making the loans. Although a number of the larger loans under these acts went to prominent politicians such as Martin Van Buren, most borrowers owned modest farms. Between 1817 and 1824, when such loans were at a peak, $250,000 was outstanding. Finally, the state also loaned money to individuals to allow them to purchase land from its 20-million-acre public domain.[14]

In addition, throughout the late eighteenth and early nineteenth centuries, the legislature passed numerous special acts providing loans to individuals or companies. The principal beneficiaries of this policy in the early years were struggling manufacturers. Between 1790 and 1820, for example, the leg-

---

[12] Ibid., 48–129.

[13] Ibid., 132–163; the original amounts of the loans are listed by Reubens as follows: 1786, $375,000; 1792, $500,000; 1808, $450,000; 1837, $5,352,694 (actual amount was only $4,014,520.17); 1840, $49,326; "State Financing," 158.

[14] Ibid., 167–184.

islature authorized 48 loans to manufacturers totaling $273,000.[15] The War of 1812 was clearly the greatest stimulant to such activity with 28 loans amounting to $143,500 authorized in the four years between 1812 and 1816 for the encouragement of cotton, woolen, iron, and steel manufacturing.[16] Most such loans, in fact, appear to have gone to producers of textiles, machinery, and iron, with an avowed intention of encouraging industries that could potentially decrease the state's dependence on imports. Although the repayment rate was dismal and it is difficult to ascertain indirect effects,[17] the loan policy, at the very least, prepared the way for much more active and direct intervention in the economy in the 1830s.

Banks and transportation companies also received loans through special acts of the legislature. There was only one bank loan before 1830, but during the succeeding decade the state lent or deposited canal funds in banks, made loans to banks in 1837 to bolster the state's credit system, and came to the rescue of the Safety Fund banking system when its resources were exhausted in 1842[18]. Transportation companies received more loans in the early years than banks, but their greatest period was also during the 1830s. By 1840 the legislature had granted eighteen loans totaling more than $5 million to such companies. The development of a new technique made the task easier. Throughout the 1830s New York resorted to a policy of lending its credit to private companies.[19] This had the obvious advantage of precluding direct outlays of state funds, which might thereby dangerously diminish the state's surplus, and of avoiding additional taxation. On the other hand, it necessitated the creation of a contingent debt and inexorably linked the fate of New York's financial system to the fluctuations of the business cycle. The extent to which the state was dependent on favorable economic conditions became painfully clear in the Panic of 1837 and the subsequent depression of 1839–1843.

In the meantime, this policy was critically important in underwriting development capital for the construction of a railroad network. As Governor William C. Bouck indicated in his annual message of 1843, aid to railroad companies overwhelmingly dominated in this category. As of that year, nine of eleven incorporated companies that had received over $5 million in such assistance were for the construction of railroads.[20] Harry N. Pierce has esti-

[15] Ibid., 186–188.
[16] Miller, *Enterprise of a Free People*, 14.
[17] Reubens, "State Financing," 188–189, 214–221.
[18] Ibid., 228, 231–233; see below for details of these activities.
[19] Ibid., 224–227.
[20] Charles Z. Lincoln, ed., *Messages from the Governors* (11 vols., Albany, N.Y., 1909), 4: 10.

mated that between 1827 and 1878, the state expended over $1 million in subsidies, mostly through loans of credit, for the construction of its railroads.During the same period, municipalities added almost $37 million. Although a number of railroads ultimately defaulted on their loans, the timeliness of state assistance and its pioneering role in taking the initial risk and in aiding marginal lines far outweighed whatever waste occurred.[21]

IN ADDITION to distributing direct financial assistance to private individuals and groups, the state also had at its disposal a variety of less tangible, but no less significant, benefits with which to stimulate economic growth and development. It could, in effect, distribute legal privileges and immunities to favored entrepreneurs in the same ad hoc, disaggregated manner that it dispensed bounties, subsidies, and loans. On occasion, for example, the state reduced potential financial burdens on manufacturers by offering tax benefits. Thus, in 1817 the legislature exempted producers of woolen, cotton, and linen goods from taxation. This act continued in force until 1823 when a new tax law omitted the exemption clause, though preferential treatment for woolen manufacturers was reaffirmed in 1824. The 1817 law included other privileges and immunities as well. It specifically exempted textile employees from militia and jury duty.[22]

By far the most significant such mechanism, however, centered on the legal advantages associated with the privilege of incorporation. Indeed, it would not be an exaggeration to suggest that the emergence of the corporation in the late eighteenth and early nineteenth centuries profoundly transformed the relationship between the state and the economy. The corporate charter proved to be an extremely useful device through which the legislature could grant special privileges, franchises, or legal advantages to favored individuals or groups. Transportation companies, for example, received charters that included the powers of eminent domain and the right to fix and collect tolls; banks were given specific authority to issue notes. Such charters frequently carried virtual monopoly privileges in certain areas by explicitly prohibiting the issuance of charters to potential competitors. Of course, not all the attributes of the modern corporation were present in the early years. Rather, the legal status of the corporation evolved over a period of several decades through legislative and judicial interpretation. By 1827 the "general powers,

---

[21] Harry N. Pierce, *Railroads of New York: A Study of Government Aid, 1826–1875* (Cambridge, Mass., 1953), 15, 25; see Taylor, *Transportation Revolution*, 93, for a slightly lower estimate of state aid to New York railroads; Beatrice Reubens estimates that New York lost some $7 million because of defaulted loans and interest; Reubens, "State Financing," 227.

[22] Carman, "Beginnings of the Industrial Revolution," 355–356; Fox, *Decline of Aristocracy*, 324.

privileges and liabilities of corporations" included the right of perpetual succession, unless limited by charter; the right to sue and be sued; to have a common seal; to buy, sell, and hold real and personal estate, subject to charter limitations as to amount; to appoint officers and agents; and the right to make bylaws. Corporations were forbidden from exercising any other powers unless authorized by charter. The legislature, furthermore, retained the right to alter, suspend, or repeal any charter. Finally, the principle of limited liability, after the entire capital of the corporation had been paid in, was established.[23]

The process by which the private business corporation emerged and ultimately came to dominate the American economy is an extremely complex subject with profound implications for our understanding of the political economy in antebellum New York. Most corporations were created in the early period by special acts of the legislature, a process that typically began with a petition from the incorporating group setting forth the purpose of the enterprise, the privileges sought, and, invariably, an attempt to justify those privileges by appeal to the public interest. Initially, at least, there was nothing particularly cynical or duplicitous in this attempt to associate the prospective corporation with the public interest. In the late eighteenth and early nineteenth century, the corporation was quintessentially a political institution. Legally a "body politic" and thus dependent on a creative act of the sovereign power for existence, it enjoyed a special, and mutually beneficial, relationship to government. The state came to rely heavily on corporations to provide essential public services, in return for which the corporations were endowed by government with a variety of special privileges, such as exclusive franchises, the right of eminent domain, and, later, limited liability.[24] This special relationship is most clearly evident in the fact that through the early nineteenth century, use of the corporate form was limited primarily to nonbusiness, clearly public-related or noncontroversial activities such as municipalities and benevolent, religious, or educational societies. When business corporations were created in this period, they were clearly and directly

---

[23] *Laws of New York*, 50th Session, 1827, vol. 2; Oscar and Mary Flugg Handlin, "Origins of the American Business Corporation," *The Journal of Economic History*, 5 (May 1945): 1–23.

[24] The standard references for the origins and early development of the corporation in the United States are Davis, *Essays in the Earlier History of American Corporations*; Evans, *Business Incorporation*; Edwin M. Dodd, *American Business Corporations until 1860* (Cambridge, Mass., 1954); James Willard Hurst, *The Legitimacy of the Business Corporation in the Law of the United States, 1780–1970* (Charlottesville, Va., 1970); Handlin and Handlin, "Origins of the American Business Corporation;" and Seavoy, "Origins of the American Business Corporation." Two indispensable contemporary sources are James Kent, *Commentaries on American Laws* (New York, 1826); and James K. Angell and Samuel Ames, *A Treatise on the Law of Private Corporations Aggregate* (Boston, 1832).

related to the public interest. The New York legislature did incorporate a few mining and manufacturing companies as early as the 1790s, but the overwhelming majority of incorporations were in the field of public utilities (principally transportation) and banking. All five of the businesses receiving charters in 1800, for example, were for the construction of turnpikes; nearly 90 percent of all business corporations created between 1800 and 1809 were public utilities.[25]

The public nature of the corporation in the early years contrasted sharply with the essentially private uses to which it was put later in the century. As the state's economy grew and matured, the number of corporate charters increased and the relationship between corporations and the public interest became increasingly more remote. By the 1830s, for example, when 573 businesses were incorporated, the proportion of public utilities to the total had declined to just under 50 percent, with mining and manufacturing constituting the second largest category of incorporations, followed by banking.[26] The proliferation and privatization of the corporation was a product of government's continuing efforts to promote economic enterprise by granting generous corporate privileges, the organizational needs of businesses operating in an ever-widening market, and the desire of entrepreneurs for the advantages of unlimited life, limited liability, and corporate personality before the law. Something of the nature of the dynamic process by which the corporation was redefined, and its impact on the character of state intervention in the economy, can be gleaned from a brief examination of manufacturing and banking during the years 1800 to 1838.

Although two manufacturing companies had been incorporated before 1800, it was not until 1808 that New Yorkers turned to the corporate device as a means of organizing manufacturing ventures on a meaningful scale. As we have seen, deteriorating relations between the United States and Great Britain after 1807 necessitated governmental action to encourage domestic manufacturing. As imports declined because of the international situation, New York legislators sought to stimulate manufacturing by providing direct subsidies to new ventures and, no less significant, by making the advantages of incorporation available to manufacturers. Only one such company was incorporated in 1808, but the following year witnessed the creation of eight manufacturing companies, and fifteen charters were granted in 1810. By 1811 the demand for corporate privileges was so great and the need for native

---

[25] Evans, *Business Incorporation in the United States*, 12, 17, 20.

[26] These figures are based on Evans and my own examination of the session laws of the 1830s.

industry so apparent that the legislature enacted the first general incorporation law for private business in American history.[27]

The General Incorporation Act of 1811 was designed to facilitate the production of textiles, glassware, metals, and paints. It provided that five or more people engaged in the manufacture of these articles could incorporate by simply filing a certificate in the secretary of state's office listing such information as the company's purpose, amount of capitalization, number of shares, names of trustees, and the location. Maximum capitalization was $100,000, and the life of the company was limited to twenty years. Shareholders were liable under this act for the amount of their investment. Legislative acts in 1816, 1819, and 1821 extended the list of products covered so that by 1827 it included chemicals, paints, sugar refining, marble, bricklaying, and breweries. The act continued in existence until it was superseded in 1848.[28]

The 1811 law unquestionably stimulated manufacturing in New York. It made unnecessary the expenditure of time and money normally required to lobby a charter through the legislature and facilitated the accumulation of capital from small investors. Although the $100,000 maximum-capitalization provision may have caused the largest manufacturers to seek special charters, it does not seem to have been strictly enforced—a number of corporations clearly exceeded the limitations. In any case, that only 150 manufacturing companies of a total of 362 incorporated between 1811 and 1848 chose the special charter method suggests that the act was not unduly restrictive.[29]

Although the public interest was an important aspect of the rationale for extending the privilege of incorporation to manufacturing in the early period of growth, manufacturing corporations were essentially private. This accounts for the rapid acceptance of the principle of incorporation and for the early date at which New Yorkers adopted a general law for the creation of manufacturing companies. Banking, however, was an entirely different matter, involving the state's responsibility for providing a stable currency and financial system. It is not surprising that, given the quasi-public nature of

---

[27] Evans, *Business Incorporation in the United States*, 17, 20.

[28] *Laws of New York*, chap. 67, 1811; since this act was one of the first general incorporation laws in the United States, it has received considerable attention over the years. Although not everyone agrees on its significance, it is discussed in Clark, *History of Manufactures in the United States*, 1: 266; Carman, "Beginnings of the Industrial Revolution," 355; W. C. Kessler, "A Statistical Study of the New York General Incorporation Act of 1811," *Journal of Political Economy*, 48, 6 (December 1940): 877–882; Reubens, "State Financing," 199–218; Ronald E. Seavoy, "Laws to Encourage Manufacturing: New York Policy and the 1811 General Incorporation Statute," *Business History Review*, 46 (Spring 1972): 85–95; and Evans, *Business Incorporation in the United States*, 17, 20.

[29] Carman, "Beginnings of the Industrial Revolution," 355; Reubens, "State Financing," 199–201; Kessler, "Statistical Study of the New York General Incorporation Law of 1811," 879.

banks, the privatization of the corporation occurred more slowly in banking than in manufacturing and the entire process occurred in a politically charged atmosphere. Indeed, no other aspect of economic policy in New York was as intimately connected to politics.

Banking in New York ceased to be a common-law right and became a jealously guarded privilege with the passage of an act in 1804 making it illegal to engage in banking unless authorized by law. This meant that a corporate charter, granted by the legislature, was required and that the six banks created before 1804 would enjoy a monopoly. This so-called restraining law was reenacted in 1813 and 1818, thereby continuing the monopoly character of banking, enhancing the desirability of bank charters, and adding fuel to the incessant legislative wrangling over corporate charters. The corruption and logrolling associated with the creation of banks became so sordid, in fact, that on one occasion the governor actually had to prorogue the legislature for a period of two months. The constitutional convention of 1821 attempted to check the worst abuses of the chartering process by requiring the assent of two-thirds of the elected members of the legislature to such bills. In practice, however, this provision did little to curtail the bribery and corruption associated with bank charters, though it later became a major stumbling block to the passage of general incorporation laws.[30]

After 1829, under the Safety Fund System, the marriage of banks and politics reached its apex. The Albany Regency, which dominated the legislature, maintained tight control over the creation of new banks and used the chartering process to solidify its political position. Loco-Foco and hard-money Democrats criticized the state's banking policy as part of their broader attack on banks and monopolies; representatives of capital-short regions of the state correctly charged that the distribution of new charters was determined more by political calculations than by economic reality. In the aftermath of the national bank war, for example, the Regency insured that the expansion of bank capital in the state would be politically advantageous by naming Democrats as commissioners to distribute the stock of new banks.[31]

---

[30]*Laws of New York*, chap. 117, 1804; Bray Hammond, *Banks and Politics in America from the Revolution to the Civil War* (Princeton, N.J., 1957), 572–584; Lincoln, *Constitutional History of New York*, 4: 63–64; Hammond, *History of Political Parties*, 2: 447–452.

[31]Hammond, *Banks and Politics*, 572–584; Fritz Redlich, *Molding of American Banking*, 187–190; Robert E. Chaddock, *The Safety Fund Banking System in New York, 1829–1866* (Washington, D.C., 1910), 369–381; Benson, *Concept of Jacksonian Democracy*, 90–104; Roger Sharp, *The Jacksonians Versus the Banks* (New York, 1970), 316; Hammond, *History of Political Parties*, 2: 447–452; and A. D. Johnson, "The Legislative History of Corporations in the State of New York," *Merchants Magazine and Commercial Review*, 23 (December 1850).

After several unsuccessful attempts to repeal the restraining law, the legislature passed an act in 1837 permitting individuals to receive deposits and make discounts. In the same session, however, it rejected a bill "authorizing associations for the purpose of banking." Two successive attorneys general declared that such a general law was unconstitutional because it was contrary to the two-thirds provision of the 1821 constitution. Constitutional or not, it was clearly contrary to the best interests of the Democratic party and that fact probably carried more weight among legislators. Thus, it was not until 1838, under the prodding of Governor William L. Marcy who, though a Democrat, favored a general law, and after the election of a Whig legislature, that free banking became a reality in New York.[32]

The report of the select committee of the assembly which recommended passage of a general bank law provides a good summation of the forces behind free banking. The existing Safety Fund System, according to Chairman G. W. Patterson, was considered by many a monopoly, with a few persons enjoying privileges that "the great body of the people" could not hope to enjoy. Furthermore, the distribution of banking stock had created "a greater proportion of banking facilities in one section of the state than in others" and had been "a source of general complaint among the inhabitants in the less favored portions." Finally, the flood of petitions to the previous legislature reflected a public sentiment in favor of general banking. "Such a law," Patterson explained, "if properly guarded, would not only do away with the prejudice against the banking system generally, but it would secure such an equal distribution of capital to all portions of the state . . . as would produce universal confidence in the system itself, and greatly promote . . . the commercial and manufacturing operations of the country." All of this could be achieved, moreover, without sacrificing the stability of the currency or the safety of the bill-holder and without violating the two-thirds rule for the creation of corporations.[33]

Under the terms of the Free Banking Act, any number of persons could establish a banking association, with a minimum of $100,000 capitalization, simply by filing a certificate with the secretary of state specifying its name, location, amount of capital stock, names of shareholders, and the date it

---

[32]Hammond, *History of Political Parties*, 2: 464–465; Hammond, *Banks and Politics*, 580–584. The opinion of Attorney General Greene C. Bronson in 1835 on the constitutionality of a general law is in *Senate Document*, no. 4, 1835; that of Samuel Beardsley is in *Assembly Document*, no. 303, 1837.

[33]*Assembly Document*, no. 122, 1838. For a sampling of the public sentiment in favor of general banking, see "Memorial of Sundry Inhabitants of Nunda, in Allegany Co.," in *Assembly Document*, no. 195, 1837, and "Proceedings of a Public Meeting of the Inhabitants of 7 Towns in the Counties of Allegany and Cattaraugus," *Assembly Document*, no. 200, 1837.

would begin operations. Financial responsibility was safeguarded through a security-deposit system and strict regulation of banking operations. The comptroller was authorized to issue specially prepared circulating notes to banks on receipt of an equal amount of public stocks to be held as security for the notes. In addition, the act required that banks report semiannually to the comptroller and maintain a specie reserve of not less than twelve and a half percent of the amount of bills or notes in circulation.[34] Thus, the business of banking was opened to anyone who could meet these conditions. The result, as Bray Hammond has so aptly put it, was that "it might be found somewhat harder to become a banker than a brick-layer, but not much."[35] By 1843, eighty-five associations and individuals had begun operations under the general banking law, and in 1850, 136 such banks were in existence.[36]

This brief summation of the early history of the business corporation tells us a great deal about the character and quality of public economic policy in New York in the early nineteenth century. In the first place, the fact that corporations were originally imbued with a public character is an important clue to the nature of the political system and the policy process. The corporation began as a surrogate instrument for organizing essentially public functions. Not only did the state, through the corporate device, facilitate the accumulation of capital, but it also allowed the development of organizational and managerial skills that the political system could not provide.[37] The Handlins' conclusion with reference to the corporation in Massachusetts was no less true in New York: "It was conceived as an agency of government, endowed with public attributes, exclusive privileges, and power, and designed to serve a social function for the state."[38] Hampered by a lack of funds, poorly developed administrative structures, and a preference for private over governmental action, New York, in effect, resorted to private arrangements to provide transportation facilities and a system of currency and finance. This was a solution completely compatible with the American preference for dispersed, decentralized authority and, given the poor state of administrative development in government, may have been the only solution available. That it involved the delegation of political coercion, in the form of eminent domain, assessments against shareholders, regulation of toll rates, and the issuance of bank notes, did not unduly concern political authorities until the

---

[34] *Laws of New York*, chap. 261, 1838.

[35] Hammond, *Banks and Politics*, 572.

[36] William C. Bouck, "Annual Message to the Legislature, 1843," in Lincoln, *Messages from the Governors*, 4: 35; Sowers, *Financial History of New York State*, 58.

[37] Hurst, *Legitimacy of the Business Corporation*, 23–24.

[38] Handlin and Handlin, "Origins of the American Business Corporation," 22.

demand for similar privileges arose from so many quarters as to make the "public interest" argument untenable.

Second, the special incorporation system, however effective it may have been as a tool for distributing governmental favors, ultimately contained the seeds of its own destruction. Since within certain boundaries the terms of the corporate charter were negotiable and since the legislature had to act on each individual corporation, the process lent itself to lobbying, corruption, and logrolling. A. B. Johnson's mid-century description of the chartering process was probably an accurate portrayal of "lobbying" at its worst:

> To resist the creation of new banks, or to assist in procuring them, came . . . to be a regular mercenary employment, by men, who . . . attended the halls of legislation, to be hired, and were sarcastically called lobby members. They disguised their venality by feigning to possess a reputable interest in the projects they undertook to support; or to be patriotic promoters of the measures for merely an alleged public benefit; or if they were hired to oppose the measures, they feigned to be disinterested exponents of an alleged hostile public sentiment. Some of the persons thus engaged were otherwise respectable; and some were even distinguished as men of station, talent, and wealth.[39]

Special incorporation also encouraged legislative "backscratching": members agreed to vote for other legislators' bills in return for a similar consideration. And corporations were occasionally empowered, by the artful inclusion of some obscure provision, to engage in enterprises totally distinct from the professed purpose of the company. Thus, although the Manhattan Company was incorporated in 1799 ostensibly to provide water for New York City, it actually became a bank.[40]

Apart from its corrupting influence, the special charter system also severely strained the legislature's ability to perform its lawmaking function. The rising volume of business corporations in the 1830s, added to the number of municipal and benevolent charters granted each year, meant that more and more of each legislative session was devoted to corporations. In 1836, for example, more than 46 percent of total legislative output, as reflected in the session laws, involved either a new charter or an amendment of an old one.[41] This, plus the tendency of the system to breed logrolling, persuaded many New Yorkers to view special incorporation as the root cause of political corruption. It should not be surprising, therefore, that by the middle of the 1830s,

[39]Johnson, "Legislative History of Corporations in the State of New York," 611.
[40]Hammond, *Banks and Politics*, 149–151; Davis, *Essays in the Earlier History of American Corporations*, 2: 100–101.
[41]See *Laws of New York*, 1836–1846.

pressure had begun to build for a drastic revision of the state's corporate policy. New Yorkers of all political persuasions lamented the burden that special incorporation placed on the legislative process. Groups such as the Equal Rights party and radical elements of the Democratic party stressed the monopolistic character of corporations and couched their attack on special incorporation in the language of "equal rights." At length these two strains of opposition to existing policy flowed into, and overlapped with, the increasing demands of individuals and groups who had been denied access to the economic advantages of incorporation and the pressure from undeveloped sections of the state for equal participation in New York's phenomenal growth. In the short term such concerns led directly to passage of the Free Banking Act of 1838. By the early 1840s, however, what had begun as an attack on the corporation, or more precisely the special incorporation system, was transformed into something much broader and more significant: a direct challenge to the legitimacy of the political system itself.[42]

The activities described here do not exhaust the economic potential inherent in the state's chartering power. On occasion, New York used the corporate charter to generate development capital by requiring recipients to invest in state stocks issued for canal construction. The Free Banking Act of 1838, for example, facilitated the financing of internal improvements because banks incorporating under its terms had to deposit with the comptroller state bonds equal to the amount of notes to be issued.[43] Earlier, government regulation of mutual savings banks significantly aided the mobilization of capital. In chartering the Bank for Savings in New York City, the largest mutual bank in the country in the antebellum period, the state restricted that institution to investments in "government securities or stock created and issued under and by virtue of any law of the United States, or of this State, and in no other."[44] Since the federal debt was rapidly being retired, the bank had little option but to invest in canal funds. As a result of these investment constraints, according to Alan L. Olmstead, "the Bank for Savings in the City of New York became the most important financier for the internal improve-

---

[42] The best account of the Equal Rights Party is F. Byrdsall, *The History of the Loco-Foco or Equal Rights Party, Its Movements, Conventions and Proceedings With Short Characteristic Sketches of Its Prominent Men* (New York, 1842); see also Hammond, *History of Political Parties*, 2: 489–503; Walter Hugins, *Jacksonian Democracy and the Working Class: A Study of the New York Workingmen's Movement, 1829–1837* (Stanford, Calif., 1960); and Carl N. Degler, "The Loco-Focos: Urban 'Agrarians,'" *Journal of Economic History*, 16 (September 1956): 322–333.

[43] *Laws of New York*, chap. 260, 1838; Harvey H. Segal, "Cycles of Canal Construction," in *Canals and American Economic Development*, ed. Carter Goodrich (New York, 1961), 191.

[44] Alan L. Olmstead, "Investment Constraints and New York City Mutual Savings Bank Financing of Antebellum Development," *Journal of Economic History*, 32 (December 1972): 818.

ment projects of New York state, Ohio, and New York City."[45] It was clearly the largest holder of New York's Erie Canal debt from 1819 to 1833, often accounting for 30 percent of the total stocks issued. Moreover, its impact was even greater because its investments came at a critical moment for Erie Canal financing, before the profitability and safety of canal stocks had been proved. It thus helped to establish the state's credit, which made subsequent borrowing easier.[46] Whether or not New York City mutuals were "development banks" in the modern sense, as Olmstead argues, the state's manipulation of their investment portfolios to its own ends is dramatic evidence of the indirect power and control inherent in the chartering process.

THE MOST visible, the most direct, and certainly the most famous example of state intervention in the economy in the antebellum period was New York's decision to build and operate the Erie Canal at public expense. That decision, apart from its profoundly significant social and economic consequences, constitutes a watershed in the history of New York's involvement in the economy. Before that time, state support of private enterprise outweighed direct state action in the total calculus of economic aid. Between 1785 and 1826 New York expended some $6.5 million in aid of agriculture, banking, manufacturing, and transportation. During the same period, the cost of direct state action, principally in the form of road, bridge, river and harbor improvements, was only slightly more than $600,000. By contrast, while aid to private enterprise rose to $12 million between 1827 and 1846, the state directly constructed transportation facilities costing nearly $50 million.[47] It is clear, therefore, that New Yorkers regarded a piecemeal policy of stock subscriptions, loans, and subsidies as inadequate to the task of constructing the canal network on which the very economic viability of the state depended. Nothing less than direct funding and operation by the state was required. Once that commitment was made, the need for capital and an administrative structure to oversee financing, construction, and operation of the canal system inevitably drew the state deeper and deeper into economic involvement. By 1841, as we saw in chapter 2, New York had constructed more than six hundred miles of canals, with another three hundred miles in progress. In the process, however, the state incurred a debt of $27 million, and the future of the state's improvement policy became the central issue in New York politics.[48]

[45] Ibid., 813.
[46] Ibid., 817, 822.
[47] Reubens, "State Financing," 273–277.
[48] Taylor, *Transportation Revolution*, 79; Goodrich, *Government Promotion*, 57.

Ironically, though there were clear regional differences within the state based on geography and levels of development, intrastate local or sectional rivalries were largely subdued until internal improvements became a major issue.[49] Economic development, through increased communications and improved transportation, had the paradoxical effect initially of aggravating dormant local and sectional identifications. Rather than unifying the state politically, the drive for better roads and canals became the victim of its disunity and exposed the fragility of the political community and the concept of the public interest. Improvement policy until the early 1840s was molded by localism and sectionalism and contributed significantly to demands for structural changes in the political system during the mid-1840s.

Specific illustrations of the impact of what one New Yorker called "that contemptible locality of calculation" abound.[50] From the earliest discussions of the Erie Canal, the interplay of local and sectional interests determined the ultimate form of improvement policy. The canal commissioners realized that they would have to reconcile diverse economic interests if they were to win legislative approval for the canal. Farmers in the Hudson Valley and on Long Island understandably opposed internal improvements because they would open up fertile lands in the West, the products of which would compete with their own in the profitable New York City market. At the same time, New York City businessmen were unlikely to support a vast system of public works involving a heavy increase in taxation. The issue was made even more perplexing by the fact that some easterners purchased real estate in western and central New York with the hope of realizing quick profits with the construction of the canal.[51]

Since the principal opposition to the canal revolved around calculations of the financial burden a particular section would have to bear in relation to prospective benefits to be derived, the legislative solution hinged on a complicated financial plan intended to placate various sectional interests. As finally passed by the legislature, the enabling act established a canal fund to consist of the proceeds from a 12½ percent per bushel tax on salt, part of the auction duties collected in New York City, a tax on steamboat passengers, tolls from the canal (along with grants and donations), and a tax on real estate located within twenty-five miles of the canal.[52] George Tibbets, senator from Rensselaer County and one of the authors of the plan, summed up the thinking behind this solution:

---

[49]Reubens, "State Financing," 290.
[50]Quoted in Fox, *Decline of Aristocracy*, 334.
[51]Miller, *Enterprise of a Free People*, 66–67.
[52]*Laws of New York*, chap. 262, 1817; Sowers, *Financial History of New York*, 62.

It was presumed that the City of New York (notwithstanding her representation opposed the canals) must be more than compensated by them for the loss of the share of the auction duties which she had so long enjoyed; . . . that the West, who were the exclusive consumers of the salt made there, would consent to a heavy tax upon it rather than not have the canals; that some of the towns and counties who were conceded to be benefitted would consent to a small addition to their ordinary taxes; that the state could . . . devote a section of its wild lands for this purpose; that a steamboat tax might right or wrong be imposed.[53]

The key factor was probably the provision for a real estate tax on property along the canal route which, though it was never actually collected, enabled eastern representatives to support the plan.[54] In addition to assuring passage of the canal bill, however, this tax provision reveals something of the social psychology affecting policy formulation. It is significant that there was no serious discussion of a statewide property tax to finance improvements. This resulted partly from a general abhorrence to taxes, but it also reflects a fundamental unwillingness to subordinate local or sectional aspirations to an abstract public interest. The general attitude was that those who benefited from public policies should bear the financial burden and that those who did not benefit directly and tangibly should not be asked to contribute. Indeed, they should be compensated in some way for expenditures made in other areas. In time this economic rationale would be embellished with appeals to equality, justice, and "the equalization of benefit." Whether from economic considerations or a genuine attachment to the principle of egalitarianism, the inability to conceive of a public interest beyond that of the locality prevented the rational allocation of the state's resources.

The pattern of bargaining and compromise established during discussions of the first canal bill reemerged each time an improvement proposal was made between 1825 and 1837. Once the Erie Canal was completed and had proved itself, other sections of the state lobbied for similar projects, thereby precipitating a new round of sectional haggling. When the legislature authorized the Seneca and Cayuga Canal and the Oswego Canal in 1825, for example, the chief opposition came from the southern tier of counties, which stood to gain nothing from the project. To quiet their opposition, a state road was proposed in 1826, to run through the southern counties from Lake Erie to the Hudson River. By this time, however, a new element in the pattern had appeared. Localities that already enjoyed improved transport facilities

[53]Quoted in Miller, *Enterprise of a Free People*, 70.
[54]Ibid.

opposed further state expenditures for such projects in other areas. Consequently, after some months discussing alternative routes for the road, the assembly defeated the proposal by a 50 to 48 margin. All but ten of the negative votes came from representatives residing in counties that bordered either the Erie or the Champlain Canal. Indeed, such was the sectional character of the vote that Jabez Hammond, a member of the road commission and an astute observer, decried the existence of an "Erie Canal party." "Whether federalists or democrats, bucktails or Clintonians, anti-masons or loco-focos," he wrote, "if they were from the counties bordering the Erie Canal, they were always found together on all questions in relation to any considerable expenditure of public money, on all commercial questions, and on all questions affecting the financial concerns of the state."[55]

By the 1830s, however, pressure for extension of the system on the grounds of sectional parity had become irresistible. Completion of the Erie proved the utility and desirability of canals; it also constituted a highly visible reminder to unimproved regions of the economic consequences of better transportation and of their own underdevelopment. Michael Hoffman captured the prevailing sentiment in 1826: "To stop where we are will be a robbery of those who had aided and have not yet been served."[56] Such was the power of the "equalization of benefit" rationale that the legislature authorized construction of the Chenango Canal in 1832 despite a warning from the Canal Commission "that it would not produce an amount of toll . . . equal to the interest on the cost and the expense of its repairs and superintendence or of either of them."[57]

But the Chenango was only the beginning. In 1836 New York embarked on an even more extensive improvements program embracing a massive enlargement of the original Erie and the construction of the Black River and Genessee Valley canals. By this time the configuration of canal policy was complete in all essential respects. Few New Yorkers paused to weigh either the long-range costs or economic impact of canals, and the voices of those who did were muted by the scramble for local projects. Moreover, improvement policy was nonpartisan, at least in the sense that regions seeking state aid united on this issue regardless of party. Indeed, Hammond charged that electors in Chenango and Broome counties literally "put themselves in market" during the election of 1830 and declared "that the party which would

---

[55] Hammond, *History of Political Parties*, 2: 222; see pages 218–225 and 245 for a general discussion of the fate of the state road.

[56] Quoted in Shaw, *Erie Water West*, 306.

[57] Quoted in Sowers, *Financial History of New York*, 65; see also Hammond, *History of Political Parties*, 2: 327–328, 413–414, 424–427 for a discussion of the Chenango Canal.

give them a canal . . . should receive their votes."[58] Similarly, at the Western Canal Convention held in Rochester in 1837, at the height of agitation for a speedy enlargement of the Erie, Seth Hawley told delegates from fourteen counties: "Let the voice go forth from this convention that we will stand by those, and those alone, who will perform this work in the shortest time, and be their backers."[59]

Apparently the voice did go forth because in 1838 the legislature authorized the expenditure of some $8 million, $4 million of which was to be borrowed on the credit of the state.[60] But even this did not silence the outcry. Bypassed districts in western and northern New York continued to demand compensation. The resolutions passed in January 1840 at a meeting in Day are typical:

> Resolved that we ask of the state as a matter of right, and expect as an act of justice, the improvement of the northern and western branches of the Hudson River by canal. As a matter of right we ask it from the fact that nature in her bounties has bestowed on us the requisites for such improvement. And as an act of justice we ask it for the reason that we have heretofore contributed our mite for the construction of similar improvments in other sections of the state, thereby crippling our energies and resources by bringing distant sections in the immediate vicinity of market, and placing us comparatively further in the background.[61]

By this time, however, the consequences of a lack of planning in the state's improvement policy had become manifest. The reconciliation of local and sectional demands had been accomplished by granting something to all, without regard for rational financing based on an assured revenue or a systematic analysis of long-range effects on the total economy. As a result, by 1841 New York had incurred a massive debt and found itself hard pressed, particularly after the Panic of 1837, to meet its financial obligations.

THE FOURTH broad category in our typology of state intervention in the economy is regulation. Throughout the late eighteenth and early nineteenth centuries New York adopted regulatory policies designed either to control business in the public interest or to foster particular economic ends by managing macroeconomic conditions in the state. These policies took several

---

[58] Hammond, *History of Political Parties*, 2: 426n.
[59] Quoted in Shaw, *Erie Water West*, 311.
[60] Ibid., 312.
[61] *Albany Argus*, January 14, 1840; see also January 3, 1840, for a similar meeting at Northville on December 12, 1839.

forms: compulsory inspection of export commodities; restrictive clauses in special incorporation charters; the first cautious attempt to create an independent regulatory commission; and informal management of specific facets of the economy through such tactics as canal-toll manipulation and administration of the Canal Fund as a "development bank." Despite the range of such activities, and a few notable successes, in the final analysis the state was no more able to develop and sustain a rational regulatory policy than to formulate and implement a coordinated policy of resource allocation. The fragmented and underdeveloped political system predetermined the form of such activities and severely limited their effectiveness in a complex and rapidly expanding economy.

One of the earliest, and most traditional, examples of state regulation of economic activities was the policy of compulsory inspection of export commodities. In this instance, government used one of its most potent tools for affecting economic development: the mobilization of legal coercion. Most of the English colonies in the seventeenth and eighteenth centuries had regarded it as a right and a duty for the political embodiment of society to regulate prices, wages, weights, measures, and even the exploitation of economic resources. Such activities were deemed essential to the maintenance of economic prosperity and a well-ordered society. By the same logic, colonial governments also lent their authority to the task of assuring the quality of goods shipped from or through their jurisdictions. Gradually, over a period of years, an elaborate system of compulsory inspection laws evolved. Although concern for the prevention of fraud and the protection of the consumer was clearly a factor, these policies were not primarily consumer-oriented. A more significant goal was to give the products of New York a competitive advantage over those of other colonies in foreign markets.

The compulsory inspection system, and the mercantilist philosophy on which it was based, carried over into statehood. By 1800 laws were on the books requiring the inspection of wheat, flour, meal, bread, dressed meats, staves, headings, timber, board, flaxseed, pot and pearl ashes, butter and lard. Fish, fish oil, hops, and leaf tobacco were added in 1807, 1818, 1819, and 1828. Similarly, laws in 1814, 1828, and 1829 covered distilled spirits, hay, and lime.[62] The justification for such laws, furthermore, remained essentially the same, as evidenced by the following statement by Governor DeWitt Clinton in his message to the assembly in 1825: "It has been suggested to me, by well informed persons, that great improvements may be introduced into our system for the inspection of beef and pork intended for exportation; and that at present, cattle are frequently driven from the banks of the Hudson to Bos-

[62] Miller, *Enterprise of a Free People*, 11n.

ton, for sale, where a higher price can be afforded than at home, in consequence of the superior credit of the Massachusetts inspection, in foreign markets."[63]

Even as Clinton spoke, however, the forces transforming the New York economy were eating away at the commercial and intellectual supports of compulsory inspection. By the 1830s many New Yorkers had come to believe that the system of inspection had outlived its usefulness. What had begun as an attempt to stimulate the commerce of the state had come to be regarded as a restraint on trade rather than a benefit. The growing complexity of both domestic and international commerce, the emergence of free-trade ideas, and discontent with the proliferation of politically appointed inspectors led to appeals, by the end of the 1830s, for the abolition of the inspection laws. After an extended debate and intense lobbying by the New York City Chamber of Commerce, the Free Trade Association of New York City, and leading merchants, the legislature, on April 18, 1843, enacted into law a bill repealing the compulsory aspects of state inspection.[64]

As in virtually all areas of public economic policy, the emergence of the corporation profoundly affected the character and quality of the state's regulatory activities. Indeed, in the first half of the nineteenth century, the corporate charter was the only regulatory device in most industries. We have already noted the potential for promoting economic development inherent in the chartering process and commented on some of the limitations of the special incorporation system. But a continuing theme in New York's corporate policy was the desire to balance the promotional goals implicit in many of the original charter grants with the necessity to guard against improper use of special privileges. Thus, charters generally contained elaborate provisions establishing the corporation's responsibilities in return for the privileges granted it by the state. The legislature established the duration of the company, set maximum and minimum limitations on capitalization, created and regulated the procedure for the election of directors, required newspaper advertisements before application for a charter or modification of an existing one, restricted corporate real-estate holdings and the purpose for which its capital could be used, regulated the payment of dividends and the transfer of stocks, and after 1824, reserved to itself the right to alter, amend, or repeal any charter. More important, the state sought to define the extent of corporate liability for debts. Initially, stockholders in New York were com-

---

[63] Lincoln, *Messages from the Governors*, 3: 99.

[64] *Laws of New York*, chap. 202, 1843; *Assembly Documents*, nos. 22, 69, and 142, 1843; *Senate Documents*, no. 63, 1839; nos. 78, 82, 83, and 87, 1841; Lincoln, *Messages from the Governors*, 4: 45.

pletely liable to the extent of their individual capacities for corporate liabilities. It was not until 1828 that limited liability became a regular feature of corporate charters. The Revised Statutes of that year freed stockholders from responsibility once the full capitalization was paid in. The general incorporation act of 1848, as we shall see later, continued this practice with the stipulation that stockholders were individually liable for debts owed to labor.[65]

The foregoing regulations developed piecemeal over a period of fifty years through almost continous negotiation between the legislature and groups seeking incorporation. Successive legislatures appear to have recognized that the granting of special privileges, legal immunities, and public power to corporations required some form of control. But their reliance on the necessity for each corporation to apply to the legislature for its charter as a control device proved inadequate as the number and variety of industries seeking charters increased. Regulation by self-enforcing corporate charters proved increasingly inadequate in a rapidly modernizing economy. Although the tendency was for certain charter provisions to become standardized, there was no guarantee of industrywide uniformity; nor was there any machinery for continuous monitoring of corporate activities or for the rational accumulation of information on which to base policy. In addition, fragmented legislative structures and the logrolling, lobbying, and corruption that all too often characterized the granting of charters made it extremely difficult, if not impossible, to develop a consistent approach to regulation. The constitutional provision requiring a two-thirds vote on any bill "creating, continuing, altering, or renewing any body politic or corporate"[66] was an early effort to ameliorate the worst abuses of the chartering process, but it was not until general incorporation laws replaced the special charter method that conditions favorable to the emergence of modern regulatory techniques were created.

Although most efforts to regulate business followed this pattern, there was at least one very notable attempt to develop regulatory procedures more effective than reliance on self-enforcing or judicially enforced charter provisions. This refers, of course, to the Bank Commission created by the Safety Fund Banking Act of 1829. As the bill's principal author, Joshua Forman, and the legislative committee that drafted it pointed out, the principle of supervision was not new. Corporate charters typically required reports and inspection, but usually these controls were justified as protection for stocks owned

[65] Charles M. Haar, "Legislative Regulation of New York Industrial Corporations, 1800–1850," *New York History*, 22 (April 1941): 191–207.
[66] Lincoln, *Constitutional History of New York*, 4: 63–64.

by either the state or the federal government. Moreover, bank examinations were normally very limited and were conducted, at the state level, by legislative committees. The establishment of a permanent Bank Commission with personnel specifically chosen to oversee bank operations, therefore, was an important departure in that it created the mechanism for continuous and systematic supervision and regulation of the business of banking.[67]

Under the terms of the Safety Fund Banking Act, to reiterate briefly points made in chapter 3, the commissioners were required to visit each bank at least once every four months to examine its condition and determine its ability to fulfill all obligations. More frequent inspections were required if requested by any three of the member banks. The act also empowered the commissioners to examine bank personnel under oath, and, if evidence of insolvency or violations of the law existed, to obtain an injunction from the Court of Chancery suspending the bank's operations. Finally, the commission was required to report annually to the legislature giving an account of its activities and forwarding abstracts of banking statistics.[68]

The Bank Commission was an imposing structure on paper, but its effectiveness was undermined at the outset by making it, to some extent, a clientele agency. The law prohibited the commissioners from having any connection with a bank; but the banks played a major role in the choice of commissioners, and the commission itself reflected the divisions within the banking community more than any abstract public interest. The governor, with consent of the senate, appointed one commissioner, and the banks themselves were responsible for selecting the remaining two. Banks in the First, Second, and Third senate districts (southern New York) elected delegates to a convention held in New York City. These delegates voted for one commissioner, with each delegate having one vote for every $5,000 capital stock of the bank he represented. The person receiving a majority was elected. This procedure, of course, favored the larger banks. A similar convention was held in Auburn representing banks in the Fourth, Fifth, Sixth, Seventh, and Eighth senate districts.[69]

Sectional representation on the Bank Commission mirrored the tension between country and city banks. New York City banks opposed the entire Safety Fund System on the grounds that by taxing the capital rather than the circulation of member institutions, the system discriminated against sound, conservative city banks in favor of less solvent country banks. Indeed, so strong was their opposition that banks in New York City initially refused to

---

[67] *Laws of New York*, chap. 94, 1829; Redlich, *Molding of American Banking*, 2, pt. 1: 88–92.
[68] *Laws of New York*, chap. 94, 1829.
[69] Ibid.

accept charters under the new law. The method of appointing the bank commissioners, therefore, had an explicit and practical purpose: it was designed to balance the influence of the country and the city banks, with each to provide a check on the other.[70]

The commissioners were tied to the banks in another way as well. Their salaries were paid out of the Safety Fund—in other words, by the banks. This does not in itself imply any improper influence, but some New Yorkers clearly believed the worst. One critic charged that the relationship between the commission and the banks was like that of "cur dogs" assigned to "watch a meat market, and were as easily subsidized by suitable food."[71] Such rhetoric aside, on at least one occasion, the presidents and cashiers of New York banks did petition the legislature to increase the commissioners' salaries, claiming that the commissioners' duties had greatly increased and that "the faithful administration of the law" required a higher remuneration. The legislature responded in 1834 by increasing commissioners' salaries from $1,500 to $2,000, $500 less than the banks requested.[72]

Bankers accepted supervision by a regulatory commission because they quickly perceived the economic advantages that would flow from such regulation and because supporters of the Safety Fund System assured them that the commission would not be effective enough to do any real harm in any case. Inspection would benefit those holding stock in banks by increasing the confidence of the community in bank notes. The banks themselves would be protected from losses for which, under the Safety Fund System, they were accountable. Supporters were also quick to point out that the law granted the power of inspection only to the commission and that the Court of Chancery had the final word on the issuance of an injunction against a bank. In short, there was little danger that banks would suffer excessive injury at the hands of the commission. Ironically, additional reassurance came from critics of the new commission who doubted its effectiveness in preventing fraud or insolvency because it had to rely on the statements of bank officers for information.[73]

With these limited powers, the Bank Commission embarked on a fourteen-year career, which spanned the most turbulent period of New York's banking history. The entire Safety Fund System operated reasonably well

[70]Hammond, *History of Political Parties*, 2: 297–301; Redlich, *Molding of American Banking*, 93–94; Davis Rich Dewey, *State Banking before the Civil War* (Washington, D.C., 1910), 131; and Sowers, *Financial History of New York*, 51–52.

[71]Quoted in John Jay Knox, *A History of Banking in the United States, Revised and Brought up to Date by Bradford Rhodes and Elmer H. Youngman* (New York, 1903), 401.

[72]*Assembly Document*, no. 27, 1834, vol. 1; *Laws of New York*, chap. 7, 1834.

[73]Chaddock, *Safety Fund Banking System*, 264–267.

throughout the 1830s, weathering both the pressure for expansion of bank capital before 1835 and the suspension of specie payments after the Panic of 1837. Indeed, the Bank Commission was a major factor in efforts to slow down the creation of new credit facilities. In 1832, 1833, and 1834 it warned against "the dangers of overissue and too much bank credit." It recommended that existing banks be strengthened rather than new ones created, a policy that it felt would meet demands for more capital while holding note circulation to reasonable limits. The legislature heeded the commission's advice, at least temporarily, and issued no new charters in 1835. It was a brief respite, however, before a torrent of new banks was created in 1836. Even during the panic, New York's banks generally fared better than those of other states. Specie payments were suspended in May 1837, but they were resumed in the spring of 1838, and New York banks did not have to resort to suspension in 1839 as did others in the nation. Until 1841, in fact, the Safety Fund suffered no losses as a result of having to redeem the notes of an insolvent bank.[74]

During this period, moreover, the powers of the Bank Commission were increased slightly. In 1840, for example, the legislature charged it with the responsibility for supervising free banks and increased the number of commissioners from three to four.[75] An 1841 act, furthermore, required all banks to submit an annual report of their affairs to the commissioners by January 20 of each year. Failure to report was grounds for legal proceedings and even dissolution. To assure uniformity of such statements, the commissioners prepared forms and transmitted them to the banks. Required information included the amount of capital stock paid in; value of real estate; shares of stock held by the bank; debts owed to and by the bank; any other claims not recognized as debts; amount of circulating notes, loans, discounts, and specie on hand, as well as projections for July 1; amount of bank losses and dividends; and the amount of real estate mortgages and state stocks.[76]

Given the fervor of partisanship in the 1830s and the close ties between politics and banking, it was perhaps inevitable that the Bank Commission would be politicized. As long as the banks appointed two of the commissioners, partisan wrangling over control of these officers was limited. But in 1837 the legislature gave exclusive control of the appointing power to the governor and senate, thereby removing the banks from the selection process.[77] Although this action helped to insulate the commission from the banks it reg-

---

[74] Ibid., 275–279; Hammond, *Banks and Politics*, 405–408.
[75] *Laws of New York*, chap. 363, 1840.
[76] Ibid., chap. 319, 1841.
[77] Ibid., chap. 74, 1837.

ulated, it also had a less positive effect. By the early 1840s, the appointment of bank commissioners had become embroiled in two equally unsettling controversies: a broad trend toward reduction of executive patronage and the beginnings of the split within the Democratic party, a division that often manifested itself in conflict over control of the patronage.

In 1842 a newly elected Democratic legislature once again tried to restructure the Bank Commission by transferring the appointive power from the governor to the legislature, decreasing the number of commissioners from four to three, and shortening their term of office from two years to one. Governor William H. Seward, a Whig, vetoed the bill. In his veto message, Seward argued that implementation of the laws was an executive, not a legislative, function and that immediate supervision of the banks, through the power of appointing and removing bank commissioners, was not properly within the purview of the lawmaking body. Control of the Bank Commission should not be given to the legislature, he continued, because that body already appointed the chief fiscal officers of the state. "The Bank Commissioners stand between the banks and the fiscal administration," Seward wrote, "conservatives of the rights and interests of the people. . . . The bill under review, proposes to transfer the power of appointing and removing these officers to the same hands which confer the banking privileges and the fiscal trusts, and would thus bring the banks and the Treasury into close conjunction with each other and with the legislature." Legislative appointment, furthermore, would encourage a renewal of the logrolling and corruption associated with banking policy in earlier years.[78]

Governor Seward's veto was sustained in 1842, but proponents of the changes introduced a similar bill the following year. By 1843, however, circumstances had changed. The governorship had passed from Seward to William C. Bouck, a conservative Democrat. The solid Democratic support for legislative appointment registered the previous year, when the Whigs controlled the governorship, now was split to reflect the division within the party between "Conservatives" and "Radicals." Conservatives favored the existing method of appointment, and Radicals sought to transfer that function to the legislature over which they exercised considerable control. The debate, which took up most of March, was bitter and intensely partisan. Midway through the wrangling, however, Radicals shifted tactics and introduced a bill abolishing the Bank Commission and transferring its supervisory powers to the comptroller. (The incumbent comptroller, it is interesting to note, was Azariah C. Flagg, leader of the Radicals and, most observers

---

[78]Lincoln, *Messages from the Governors*, 4: 1000–1008.

believed, the force behind the attempt to shift the appointing power to the legislature.)[79]

Support for such a policy was not difficult to muster. A devastating wave of bank failures between 1840 and 1842 had seriously undermined the Bank Commission's reputation. In a two-year period, eleven banks failed,[80] and though the causes were probably beyond the commission's control, it was inevitable that some of the blame would be attached to that body. Governor Bouck, for example, though attributing the failures to "great abuse in their [the banks] management, and a reckless disregard of moral obligations," still wondered "how it should have happened that a bank could so improperly conduct its affairs as to cause a total loss to the stock holders and leave no assets for the redemption of its bills in circulation, and yet escape the timely observation of the Bank Commissioners." He reluctantly concluded that "the appointment of Commissioners has not answered all the valuable ends which were anticipated from the measure."[81]

Some observers explained the commission's apparent failure in political terms. Millard Fillmore, writing as comptroller several years later, charged that with the 1837 law giving control of appointments to the governor, the commissioners "were brought within the vortex of the great political whirlpool of the State, and that place was sought for and conferred upon partisan aspirants without due regard in all cases to their qualifications to discharge the delicate trust committed to them."[82] A more fundamental problem, however, was that the commission had no way to assure the accuracy of the information it received and could not act in a decisive and timely manner to prevent insolvencies. Banks were known to restrict their loans immediately preceding an inspection and expand them after the visitation had been completed, thereby presenting an inaccurate view of the bank's loans and discounts.[83]

The Bank Commission was acutely aware of its own deficiencies. In its 1843 report to the legislature, the commission complained that it could not prevent the kind of failures that had just occurred. Under existing legislation, it was virtually impossible to force a bank to suspend operations until it had become completely insolvent, which, of course, was like closing the barn door after the horse had fled. The commission could request an injunction against a bank only if that institution had violated a positive law. This left a

---

[79] The debates on this subject may be followed in *Albany Argus*, February 27, 28, March 2, 4, 7, 9, 10, 11, 14, 1843.

[80] Chaddock, *Safety Fund Banking System*, 309.

[81] Lincoln, *Messages from the Governors*, 4: 33–34.

[82] Quoted in Knox, *History of Banking*, 405.

[83] Miller, *Enterprise of a Free People*, 153n.

wide range of undesirable activity by banks beyond the reach of the commission. As the 1843 report noted, a bank's "administration may exhibit the most dangerous improvidence, its discounted debt may be distributed in such large sums to particular individuals or so inadequately secured as to render its collection extremely doubtful, the officers of the Bank may be found to be the principal borrowers, and everything conspire to cause a well-grounded belief that its management are seriously hazarding or impairing its capital." None of this, however, gave the commissioners authority to intervene. The examination system, moreover, was not adequate to the task of obtaining accurate information. Inspections occurred once every four months and were usually conducted by an officer from some other part of the state, who had no direct knowledge of the bank's debts or assets. To remedy these defects, the commission recommended that its powers be increased to allow it to intervene in the affairs of any bank "whose operations, however, conducted, shall in their opinion be adverse to the interests of the stockholders or the safety of the public."[84]

Rather than increase the Bank Commission's powers, however, the legislature chose to abolish it. The assembly committee to which the bill had been referred generally agreed with the commission's assessment of its shortcomings. It had originally been thought that frequent visitations and inspections would prevent public losses from the excessive issuance of bank notes. Practice proved the contrary: "When bank officers are honest, commissioners are unnecessary; when they are dishonest, commissioners are unavailing. They have not been able to prevent fraud, nor to detect them, until detection is useless." The committee recommended, therefore, that the commission be abolished and that Safety Fund banks be authorized to circulate notes received from the comptroller in the same manner as free banks. This would provide greater uniformity of the currency; prevent overissues; protect the bill-holder; and stimulate investment in state stocks (since the Free Banking Act required banks to deposit stocks equal to the amount of circulating notes). In addition, the committee proposed that all Safety Fund bank notes be countersigned and registered in the comptroller's office.[85]

The "Act to Abolish the Bank Commission" passed the legislature with the Radical Democrats and Whigs allied against the Conservative Democrats, who continued to maintain that it was a Radical ploy to curtail the governor's patronage and delegate more power to the comptroller.[86] The final law

---

[84]"Annual Report of the Bank Commissioners, 1843," *Assembly Document*, no. 34, 1843, vol. 2.

[85]*Assembly Document*, no. 154, 1843, vol. 6.

[86]*New York Tribune*, April 20, 1843; Hammond, *History of Political Parties*, 3: 357–359.

was very similar to that reported out of the committee. It required banks to deposit their note plates with the comptroller who thenceforth counter-signed and registered all bank notes. It made quarterly reports to the comp-troller mandatory, and empowered that officer to make banks redeem their circulation whenever he felt their capital had been reduced. In addition, the comptroller could appoint a special agent, with all the powers of a bank commissioner, to examine any bank suspected of improper activity. But the new law did not include the principle of regular inspection, since it was believed that the comptroller's powers over note issues would prevent many of the worst abuses.[87]

During its relatively brief career, the New York Bank Commission achieved some success, but it succumbed in the final analysis to economic and political pressures over which it had little control. From the beginning, its intimate ties with the banking community and too great a reliance on the good faith of the banks had undermined the commission's effectiveness. The principle of regular inspection was a noteworthy innovation in regulatory techniques, but the commission never possessed sufficient authority to pre-vent willful fraud or deception. As the commission itself explained in 1843, it could act only after a law had been broken, and then it was usually too late. From an administrative point of view, moreover, the commission could not develop the independence, continuity, and expertise generally regarded as essential in effective, modern regulatory agencies. Commissioners served two-year terms, and after 1837 they were essentially political appointees. By the early 1840s, furthermore, at a critical moment for New York banks, the commission had become hopelessly entangled in the internecine struggle within the Democratic party. General dissatisfaction with the commission's failure to prevent the bank collapses of 1840–1842 combined with the mach-inations of factional politics, therefore, led to its abolition in 1843. The comptroller assumed responsibility for bank supervision until 1851 when a separate bank department was created.

New York also resorted to regulation to safeguard the state's investments and to promote and manage the overall economic prosperity of the state. A good illustration of the first objective involves railroads. New York handled most aspects of railroad regulation in the traditional manner of relying on the chartering process, at least until the 1850s, when the state experimented briefly with a railroad commission.[88] But the state's policy of promoting rail-road development by lending its credit to such corporations placed it in the

[87] *Laws of New York*, chap. 218, 1843.
[88] Lee Benson, *Merchants, Farmers, and Railroads: Railroad Regulation and New York Politics: 1850–1887* (Cambridge, Mass., 1955), 1–2.

ambiguous position of supporting a transportation system in direct competition with the state-owned canal network. To protect its investment in canals, therefore, New York attempted to regulate railroads to prevent the loss of traffic on the state's waterways. The earliest railroad charters restricted them to carrying passengers. Only gradually and in response to insistent demands from the railroads were such restrictions loosened. The New York Central Railroad made the first significant inroad in 1836, winning the right to carry freight on the condition that it pay the regular canal tolls on such freight. In 1844 the privilege was extended to all railroads. Over the next seven years, the railroads slowly gained ground as the state first decided to enforce the toll regulation only during the period in which canals were navigable and then expanded the list of articles that railroads could carry toll free. In 1851 the state capitulated entirely, abolishing all canal tolls on railroads. From then on New York fought valiantly to protect its canals against an increasingly powerful railroad interest, but ultimately succumbed to the realization that the future of transportation lay with railroads.[89]

The attempt to regulate railroads in the interest of the canals, and the role the canal tolls played in that effort, illustrates the potential power and control inherent in a state-owned transportation system. In the early 1840s New York began manipulating canal tolls in an attempt to stimulate the state's salt manufacturing. Hoping to improve the competitiveness of native producers against foreign and out-of-state manufacturers, the canal board authorized a three-cent per pound rebate on locally produced salt intended for export. The state resorted to direct legislative bounties when the rebate was declared unconstitutional but continued to charge high canal rates on imported salt. Although the effectiveness of this policy may be questioned, it typified the aggressiveness of the state in its search for continued economic prosperity.[90] Indeed, all the canal states tried to manipulate freight rates to superimpose a measure of rationality on their individual economies. Often these separate policies arose from competitive rivalries between states, as was the case when Ohio and New York engaged in a rate war during the 1840s with domination of the salt market as the prize. At other times, however, several states acted in concert against other areas in the constant search for competitive advantage which characterized the American economy in this period. In one short year, for example, New York, Ohio, and Indiana shifted the flow of Indiana's surplus agricultural products away from the Ohio River and in favor of New

---

[89]Sowers, *Financial History of New York State*, 85–90.
[90]Taylor, *Transportation Revolution*, 381.

York by reducing freight rates on grain, meat, and similar farm goods shipped to the New York market.[91]

A more effective source of control over the state's economy than rate manipulation was the administration of the canal revenues by the New York Canal Fund Commission. From very inauspicious beginnings in 1826, when the legislature authorized the commissioners to invest surplus canal revenues in stocks of the United States, New York, or Albany, the canal fund grew in importance until by 1832, according to Nathan Miller, it closely approximated a modern development bank. The process of "diffusing" the revenues throughout the state began when the commissioners realized that they would be unable to make the kinds of investments the legislature recommended or to retire outstanding canal stock. Consequently, they deposited canal revenues in banks in Troy and Albany. Over the next few years, this system of deposits spread to banks near toll-collection points along the canal route. By 1833, seventeen banks held canal funds in amounts ranging from $6,000 to $184,000. In the meantime, the legislature in 1831 approved the policy of making time deposits in banks. This had the dual advantage of assuring a profitable investment for surplus funds and, because the commissioners were required to give banks a sixty-day notice before withdrawal, aided marginal institutions by increasing their reserves, thereby affording additional protection against sudden withdrawals. By 1836 participating banks owed more than $3.6 million in such "loans" to the canal fund.[92]

The policy of depositing and lending canal funds to the state's banks began simply and specifically as a means of resolving the surplus problem. It gradually became clear to the commissioners, however, that the introduction of large sums of state money into the economy through local banks directly affected the prosperity and economic well-being of local communities and the state as a whole. The potential existed for both good and ill. On the one hand, canal-fund deposits increased the credit available to farmers and businessmen and therefore helped to underwrite economic activity. On the other, the stability of the economy could be adversely affected by any sudden or ill-conceived shift in the commissioners' policy with regard to the surplus revenues. It is to the credit of the men who served as commissioners that they were cognizant of the potential impact of their decisions. As the success of the Erie Canal increased the revenues at the commissioners' disposal, the pervasiveness of their influence increased accordingly, and they were com-

---

[91] New York's toll policy can be followed in the annual reports of the Canal Commission. Scheiber's *Ohio Canal Era* is the most sophisticated statement of these activities I have seen, especially 247–263.

[92] Miller, *Enterprise of a Free People*, 115–125.

pelled to weigh every administrative decision against its likely consequence for the state's economy.[93]

On at least three occasions during the 1830s, the commissioners of the canal fund directly and deliberately used their potential control over the economy to cushion the impact of adverse economic circumstances. In the first instance, the commissioners' policy was passive. During the 1834 recession, brought about at least partially by the Bank of the United States' policy of credit constriction, the commissioners drew on canal funds only for unavoidable maintenance and interest payments, thereby permitting banks maximum use of canal-fund deposits during the recession. The purpose of this policy was to relieve the pressure on New York banks occasioned by Nicholas Biddle's policy during the bank war. The decision, combined with the enactment of a loan law in 1834 which, although never implemented, would have allowed the issuance of $2 million in state stocks for loans to banks, appears to have bolstered public confidence in New York's financial institutions and aided economic recovery.[94]

The 1835 fire that destroyed large sections of New York City provided the commissioners with an opportunity to play an even more active role in the state's economy. Despite opposition from sections of the state that stood to lose a part of the surplus funds, the commissioners shifted some of the canal fund's loans and deposits to the city's banks in an attempt to provide additional credit for reconstruction. Under the Relief Act of 1836, which provided loans at 5 percent interest with a guarantee not to call the loans in before July 1837, credit in the city increased by slightly more than $1 million.[95] This is admittedly not a large amount, but it did establish a precedent for the utilization of state funds for disaster relief and constitutes additional evidence of the state's growing recognition of its responsibility for assuring economic prosperity.

The Panic of 1837 occasioned the most energetic effort yet to use the canal fund to manage the economy. Recognizing the importance of bolstering New York's banks against the steady depletion of specie reserves, in April 1837 the canal fund commissioners agreed to lend banks $3,395,000 of canal stocks earmarked for financing construction on the Black River, Genessee Valley, and Chenango canals. The stock was to be divided among eight banks in New York City for subsequent sale to the city's merchants and importers who were indebted to foreigners, thereby substituting, it was hoped, state stocks

---

[93] Ibid., 127–152.
[94] Ibid., 172–173; Reubens, "State Financing," 231.
[95] Miller, *Enterprise of a Free People*, 172–191.

for the drain of specie in the settlement of foreign debts. But the plan came too late, and New York City banks suspended specie payments on May 11.[96]

Having failed to prevent suspension, the commissioners concentrated on maintaining specie payments on the state's obligations and devising a plan to aid banks in the resumption of specie payments at the earliest possible date. With the assistance of leading New York City bankers, the state's interest payments were met and foreign bondholders reassured of the state's good faith. In the meantime, Azariah C. Flagg, the state's comptroller, and Albert Gallatin, former U.S. secretary of the treasury and the leading New York banker, arranged for a loan of more than $2 million of state stocks to seven banks in New York City. An elaborate series of restrictions and conditions assured that the stocks would be used strictly to obtain specie, not for speculative purposes.[97] The following year, in 1838, the banks asked for additional state assistance in preparation for resumption. Once again, Governor Marcy was amenable to the suggestion and proposed to lend more state stocks to the banks. This time, however, Whig opposition in the legislature thwarted his effort to underwrite economic recovery with the credit of the state. Although the bill went down to defeat when the legislature became stalemated between Whigs and Democrats,[98] the incident occasioned one of the most explicit statements of the entire period about the responsibility of the state for assuring economic prosperity. In his special message to the legislature on April 12, 1838, in which he reviewed the financial situation and outlined his plan for aiding the banks, Marcy concluded that it was "the duty of the state to stand forth in its strength, and by the use of its credit, and the sanction of its name to shield its institutions and its citizens from harm."[99]

THE FINAL category of state economic intervention is also the broadest, the most difficult to explicate, and the most susceptible to varying interpretation. Scholars as diverse as J. Willard Hurst, Harry N. Scheiber, and Morton J. Horwitz have amply demonstrated that government profoundly shaped the society and economy of the antebellum states through the provision of a legal order and institutional framework conducive to economic growth and private enterprise. Although disagreement exists on the precise meaning of these developments, with Horwitz, for example, stressing the role of emerging entrepreneurs in shaping the legal order to meet their needs and aspirations, all appear to agree on the basic question of how such a legal order emerged.

[96] Ibid., 197–205.
[97] Ibid., 220–221.
[98] Ibid., 244.
[99] Lincoln, *Messages from the Governors*, 3: 705.

In effect, what Scheiber calls "the legal environment of enterprise"[100] was created through legislative and judicial interpretation of property rights; the evolution of corporate, contract, and commercial law; the establishment of a framework of stability and predictability for market decisions through the enactment and interpretation of criminal, tort, bankruptcy, and stay laws; and last, but not least, the exercise of state police and tax powers. The result was a legal/political system whose primary function was to establish a context for the allocation of resources and the mobilization of scarce capital by private agencies.

The transformation of contract law lay at the heart of this legal order. Before the nineteenth century, the validity of a contractual obligation in English and American law depended ultimately on the justice or fairness of the bargain. Even if the contract clearly represented a "meeting of the minds" of the parties to the agreement and satisfied the principle of "consideration," the court could still invalidate the contract if, in its opinion, the things being exchanged were not of roughly equal value. Implicit in this "substantive theory of contracts" was a belief that contractual obligations were enforceable only to the extent that they were consistent with custom, community mores, and the principle of the "sound price." The purpose of the law was to preserve community values and restrain individual will in an essentially static, premodern society.[101] Among its other characteristics, eighteenth-century contract law, as Horwitz has pointed out, "was essentially antagonistic to the interests of commercial classes. The law did not assure a businessman the express value of his bargain, but at most its specific performance. Courts and juries did not honor business agreements on their face, but scrutinized them for the substantive equality of the exchange."[102]

By the early nineteenth century, a new conception of contract law had begun to appear. Rejecting the traditional common-law emphasis on the equity of contractual agreements, judges increasingly validated contracts on the basis of "the convergence of the wills of the contracting parties."[103] Individual intent, not substantive impact, became the standard of validity. "The formalities of contract formation," as one historian has put it, rather than the bargaining positions of the agreeing parties became the chief concern of nineteenth century courts. In short, with the emergence of the "will theory of contracts," the functional necessities of an expanding market took prece-

[100]Scheiber, "Federalism and the American Economic Order," 96.

[101]Zamil Zainaldin, *Law in Antebellum Society: Legal Change and Economic Expansion* (New York, 1983), 55–58; George Drago, *Law in the New Republic: Private Law and the Public Estate* (New York, 1983), 37–41; Horwitz, *Transformation of American Law*, 160–173.

[102]Horwitz, *Transformation of American Law*, 167.

[103]Ibid., 160.

dence over community standards and values in the legitimation of contractual arrangements between private parties.[104]

Needless to say, contract law in the United States evolved gradually through the accumulation of court decisions in the various states in the late eighteenth and early nineteenth centuries. In New York, the key case was *Seymour v. Delancey*,[105] first heard in the Court of Chancery in 1822 and later reviewed and overturned in the Court for the Correction of Errors in 1824. The case arose out of a contract in 1820 whereby one Thomas Ellison agreed to exchange two farms in Orange County for a one-third interest in two lots in the village of Newburgh. When the agreed-on conveyance of property failed to occur in June 1820, and after Ellison's death in August, the owner of the village lots sued Ellison's heirs (Delancey) for performance of the contract. Reviewing the facts of the case and common-law precedent, Chancellor James Kent refused to order the execution of the contract on the grounds that equity and good conscience rendered the agreement questionable. According to Kent's decision, the exchange was not "fair and just, and reasonable," because, in his judgment, "the village lots were not worth half the value of the country farms." Inadequacy of price alone did not necessarily warrant setting aside the transaction, but in this case, "the inadequacy is so great as to give the character of hardship, unreasonableness and inequality to the contract." A further extenuating circumstance in the case was Ellison's habitual drunkenness, "a matter of public notoriety in the village of Newburgh," which raised doubts about his competence to enter into a binding contract. Kent thus refused to order "a specific performance of so hard and so extravagant a bargain, gained from a habitual drunkard, in the last year of his life, and just before his infirmities had begun to incapacitate him entirely for business."[106]

Kent's decision in *Seymour v. Delancey* was firmly rooted in precedent and true to the social goals expressed in the substantive theory of contracts. But by 1822 new social and economic circumstances demanded a more flexible view of contracts, one oriented less toward the preservation of the status quo and more toward the exploitation of capital and other resources in a dynamic economy.[107] The origins of a market-oriented conception of contract can be detected in the decision of the Court for the Correction of Errors in 1824 to

[104] Drago, *Law in the New Republic*, 41; Zainaldin, *Law in Antebellum Society*, 57–58; Lawrence Friedman, *A History of American Law* (New York, 1973), 244–245; and Hurst, *Law and the Conditions of Freedom*, 11–14.

[105] *Seymour v. Delancey*, 1822, 6 Johnson 222.

[106] Ibid., at 224, 225, 232, 233, and 234.

[107] Zainaldin, *Law in Antebellum Society*, 56–57.

overturn the Chancellor's decision in *Seymour v. Delancey*.[108] A divided court (14 for reversing, 10 for affirming the previous decision) rejected Kent's reasoning in the case and concluded that in the absence of clear evidence of fraud or an inadequacy of price "so flagrant and palpable as to convince a man at first blush that one of the contracting parties had been imposed upon by some false pretense" the contract should be enforced. Ellison, in the words of Senator Sudam, "deliberately and with his eyes open, entered into the contract," "with a full knowledge of all the circumstances," and "after much deliberation." Indeed, that Ellison had previously purchased two-thirds of the village lots over a period of several years not only established his competence to enter into business dealings, but also strongly suggests that he anticipated a profitable return from the property because of the proposed construction of a naval yard at Newburgh.[109] The speculative nature of the exchange, therefore, precluded any consensus on a "just" price for the property. To rule otherwise, according to Sudam, "would lead to very injurious results. Every member of this court must be well aware how much property is held by contract; that purchases are constantly made upon speculation; and that there, most generally, exists an honest difference of opinion in regard to any bargain as to its being a beneficial one or not." Thus, the validity of contracts must be presumed and be enforceable "when all is fair, and the parties deal on equal terms."[110]

The emergence of modern contract law and the expansion of the freedom of contract doctrine had profound implications for early-nineteenth-century political economy in New York and the American states generally. It facilitated the expansion of the market by presuming the legality of transactions between individuals, by providing standardized forms of dealing, and by creating the mechanism through which bargains could be negotiated and consummated among strangers, at a distance, within an impersonal system of exchange. By invoking the compulsive power of the community to enforce valid agreements between private parties, furthermore, contract effectively delegated public authority to private decision-makers. The effect, to borrow James Willard Hurst's famous phrase, was to encourage "the release of individual creative energy," while, at the same time, maximizing the role of the private sector in the allocation of society's resources.[111]

---

[108] *Seymour v. Delancey*, 1824, 3 Cowens, 445.
[109] Ibid., 529–531.
[110] Ibid., 533.
[111] Hurst, *Law and the Conditions of Freedom*, 7, 11–15; James Willard Hurst, *Law and Markets in United States History: Different Modes of Bargaining Among Interests* (Madison, Wis., 1982), 37; Zainaldin, *Law in Antebellum Society*, 57–58; Drago, *Law in the New Republic*, 40–41; and Bernard Schwartz, *The Law in America* (New York, 1974), 20–21, 60–61, 85–86.

The role of the legal and political environment in shaping the course of economic development in New York is further illustrated by the state's policy of delegating the power of eminent domain to the private sector. Under the special incorporation system, as we have seen, the state regularly authorized turnpike and railroad companies to acquire land needed for rights-of-way by exercising the power of eminent domain. The justification, of course, was that turnpikes and railroads were in the public interest and, therefore, that the sovereign power residing in the state to take property for the benefit of the general community could be invoked. Although these contentions did not go unchallenged, an important series of court decisions upheld their validity. In 1823, for example, the Court of Errors, reversing an earlier decision of the supreme court, held that a turnpike, though privately owned, was "a public road or highway, in the popular and ordinary sense of the words. . . . Turnpike roads are, in point of fact, the most public roads or highways known to exist, and, in point of law, they are made entirely for public use, and the community have a deep interest in their construction and preservation." Thus, the court concluded, private property could be taken for their use.[112]

In 1831 the Court of Chancery upheld the delegation of eminent domain to railroads. Although complainants argued that railroads were private property, distinct even from turnpikes because only the company could use its tracks, and could not, therefore, take land under the public-use doctrine, the court ruled that the community derived a public benefit from such roads and that the legislature had the power to appropriate private property, with just compensation, for their construction. *Beekman v. the Saratoga and Schenectady Railroad Company* is also notable for the expansiveness of the court's interpretation of eminent domain. According to Chancellor Walworth, speaking for the court, "the aggregate body of the people in their sovereign capacity . . . have a right to resume the possession of . . . property, in the manner directed by the constitution and laws of the state, whenever the public interest requires it. This right of resumption may be exercised not only where the safety, but also where the interest or even the expediency of the state is concerned." Although the power of eminent domain ultimately resides in the legislature, acting for the people, it could, furthermore, be exercised either directly by agents of the government, through the medium of corporate bodies, or by means of individual enterprise.[113]

The decisions of the various state courts, the statements of public officials, and the growing practice of delegating eminent domain lend support to the

---

[112] *Rogers v. Bradshaw*, 1823, 20 Johnson 735.
[113] *Beekman v. the Saratoga and Schenectady Railroad Company*, 1831, 3 Paige 45.

argument that by the end of the 1830s public utility corporations were regarded as extensions or surrogates of the state. One of the most explicit statements of this view is that of one of the senators involved, as a member of the Court of Errors, in the case of *Bloodgood* v. *The Mohawk and Hudson Railroad* in 1837. The primary consideration of the legislature or courts in determining the public or private use of a railroad, he argued, was the object of the enterprise, not the instrument: "The legislature, who are constituted the judges of the expediency of taking private property for public use, came to the conclusion that the public required the use of a railroad between the cities of Albany and Schenectady. It deemed it inexpedient to construct it at the public expense, and adopted the policy of having a company construct it at its own expense and risk, having the money expended refunded by way of tolls or fares from the individuals who should travel upon it."[114]

Governor William H. Seward affirmed this view three years later. "Such associations had their origins in the necessities of a scanty population," he wrote in 1840, "dispersed over a broad territory, requiring extensive improvement. . . . Their agency has always been employed in constructing works not deemed of sufficient importance to warrant their assumption by the state, and yet of too great magnitude to be constructed by railroads."[115] There were, of course, dissenters. One senator warned in the *Bloodgood* case that this was "a delegation of the power of the sovereignty of the state; not to public officers or to a political corporation, or even to designated individuals, but to a private corporation, to be by that corporation exerted according to its own judgment of its own necessities."[116]

Simultaneously with the development of this rationale for the delegation of the eminent domain power, the courts also specified certain legal restrictions governing such policies. The purpose for which property was taken had to be in the public interest, and it had to be done through due process of law with just compensation for the owner.[117] Government was not authorized to expropriate the property of one citizen and transfer it to another if the public interest was not promoted.[118] Nor could any property be taken for private use.[119] Even with these limitations, however, it still seems remarkable that the state delegated what amounted to an attribute of sovereignty to private corporations. The devolution of this doctrine to the private sector has

[114] *Bloodgood* v. *The Mohawk and Hudson Railroad Company*, 1837, 18 Wendell 9 at 21.

[115] Lincoln, *Messages from the Governors*, 3: 808–809.

[116] *Bloodgood* v. *The Mohawk and Hudson Railroad Company*, 1837, 18 Wendell 9 at 71.

[117] *Beekman* v. *The Saratoga and Schenectady Railroad Company*; *Bloodgood* v. *The Mohawk and Hudson Railroad Company*.

[118] *Varick* v. *Smith*, 1835, 5 Paige 136.

[119] *Taylor* v. *Porter and Ford*, 1843, Hill 140.

been called "the most important single development in early nineteenth century eminent domain law."[120] Certainly few aspects of the legal order were more significant in shaping the configuration of public economic policy in New York in this period.

A final example of the impact of the legal and political environment on economic development concerns the issue of taxation. One of the most potent tools at the disposal of any political system is its ability to mobilize the resources of the society for the achievement of public purposes through compulsory levies on the wealth and property of the community. Conversely, the effectiveness of a political system, and therefore, in an ultimate sense, its legitimacy, depends to some degree on the level of this "extractive" capability. Thus the character of public policy in a given historical context may be profoundly shaped by restraints placed on the taxing power by the political culture, the opposition of powerful propertied interests, or the inability of government to administer and collect taxes efficiently and equitably. Complicating the relationship between taxation and economic policy even further is the fact that taxes can perform a multiplicity of functions in society. In addition to the strictly fiscal function of providing money necessary to carry on the activities of government, taxes also have economic, educational, political, and social functions. As we have seen in this chapter, taxes can be an important stimulant or constraint on economic activity. They can also play an important educational role by encouraging desirable or inhibiting undesirable human behavior. Politically, taxes have been used to define citizenship and suffrage eligibility or, as in the case of the poll tax, to deny certain social groups access to political participation and power. Finally, taxes have social functions. The structure of all tax systems reflects, to one degree or another, social values and goals concerning the distribution of wealth, the desirability of a static versus a dynamic social order, and in capitalistic societies, the role of the public and private sectors in the accumulation of capital.[121]

This consideration of some of the functional implications of taxation helps to make sense of New York's reluctance to resort to its taxing power in pursuit of economic objectives in the antebellum period. Even at the height of economic involvement, the state refused to levy meaningful taxes in support of its economic policies, preferring instead to subsidize economic growth

---

[120] Harry N. Scheiber, "Property Law, Expropriations, and Resource Allocation by Government: The United States, 1789–1910," *Journal of Economic History*, 33 (March 1973): 237.

[121] Rudolf Braun, "Taxation, Sociopolitical Structure, and State-Making: Great Britain and Brandenburg-Prussia," in *The Formation of National States in Western Europe*, ed. Charles Tilly (Princeton, N.J., 1975), 246–248.

through indirect and therefore, one suspects, politically safe methods.[122] Indeed, one of the most striking aspects of the early history of New York State is the infrequency with which it resorted to taxation for any purpose. For most of the first half century of its existence, the state's revenues derived from the sale of public lands; indirect taxes such as auction duties, lotteries, and fees paid to public officials; the return on state investments; and, when caught short, bank loans.[123] New York did raise specified sums of money on a year-by-year basis during the 1770s and 1780s, but the first general property tax was a one-mill assessment levied in 1799, and it survived only three years. In 1801, the last year the tax was collected, the legislature authorized the comptroller to borrow money to meet any legal demands against the state which it could not pay. On occasion, such as in 1808, the comptroller was authorized to borrow money from the banks to make the appropriation voted in the same legislative session. As a result of this system, by 1814 New York was indebted to seven banks for the amount of $1,503,000.[124]

The growth of this state debt, however, necessitated a temporary return to taxation. In 1814 New York levied a two-mill tax which was collected in 1815, 1816, and 1817. In 1818 the legislature reduced the tax to one mill, and it was cut in half again in 1824. Finally, in 1826, the legislature discontinued the tax entirely. With the steady reduction of the tax rate, the amount of money received through taxation declined from a high of $524,934.92 in 1818 to $147,534.17 in 1826. Still, the general property tax brought the state more than $3 million in revenues between 1816 and 1826.[125]

The decision to allow the tax to expire was partially a reflection of the pervasive distaste for direct taxation in American society in this period. But it also had a more specific source. Internal improvement enthusiasts did not wish to see canal construction linked to the necessity for taxation, for fear that it would dampen support for the system of lateral and feeder canals then in the planning stages. Besides, state assistance to the economy had always been predicated on the existence of surplus revenues, not on long-range financial planning based on taxation or even a debt that would require tax-

---

[122] I have been influenced in this interpretation by Horwitz, *Transformation of American Law*, 100–101.

[123] Sowers, *Financial History of New York State*, 114; Miller, *Enterprise of a Free People*, 79–80.

[124] "Annual Report of the Comptroller," *Assembly Document*, no. 5, January 6, 1836; Miller, *Enterprise of a Free People*, 80.

[125] The history of the general property tax before 1826 is outlined in the "Annual Report of the Comptroller" for 1835 and 1836, *Assembly Documents*, no. 5, 1835, 14, and no. 5, 1836, 23; see also Sowers, *Financial History of New York State*, 114–115, and Horace Secrist, "An Economic Analysis of the Constitutional Restrictions Upon Public Indebtedness in the United States," *Bulletin of the University of Wisconsin, Economics and Political Science Series*, vol. 8 (1914–1917), no. 1:. 23–24.

ation.[126] When the Erie Canal was approved in 1817, for example, the legislature pledged proceeds from the auction and salt duties to the repayment of the debt. Even this precaution was abandoned after 1825, however, and the legislature made no provision for repayment of loans contracted for the construction of lateral canals comparable to the financing of the Erie and Champlain. As a result, these financial obligations fell on the General Fund.[127]

Even without this additional burden, the General Fund would have been hard pressed to meet the ordinary expenses of the government in the face of declining and, ultimately, nonexistent tax revenues. It is true that per capital expenditures for government operations actually declined from $.50 in 1800 to $.19 in 1830, but this was caused by an increasing population, not by an actual decrease in the cost of government. More important, during the same period, total per capita expenditures (including debt payments) nearly doubled, from $.53 to $1.02. Predictably, this trend was accompanied by a decline in the share of total per capita expenditures represented by ordinary expenses. In 1800 operating expenses accounted for nearly the entire amount ($.50 of $.53); in 1820 the ratio had dropped to approximately half ($.46 of $.87); and in 1830 it was less than a quarter ($.19 of $1.02).[128]

New York's refusal to commit itself to direct taxation during the 1830s, when state involvement in the economy was at its peak, had enormous consequences for public economic policy. First, the antipathy to direct taxation, the roots of which lay deep in the revolutionary experience and the principles of Jeffersonian democracy, placed severe restraints on what government could in fact do. The lack of a regular, predictable source of revenue inevitably restricted government economic policies to what could be accomplished out of surplus funds and through loans or to projects that could reasonably be expected to become self-supporting. It also made virtually impossible any kind of long-range planning and assured that the state's administration would be understaffed, underpaid, and inadequate to the tasks confronting it. Second, New York's tax policies reflected the intensity of localism and regionalism and the absence of any clearly articulated concept of the public interest or commitment to the notion of a statewide political community. A signifi-

---

[126]Reubens, "State Financing," 278–279, 285–286.

[127]Sowers, *Financial History of New York State*, 65; Secrist, "Restrictions on Public Indebtedness," 24; and Hammond, *History of Political Parties*, 2: 250–251.

[128]Figures compiled from data on state expenditures in Sowers, *Financial History of New York State*, 295–339. No claim is made here that these figures are precise. Given the number of separate funds making up the state's financial system, attempts to arrive at total expenditures in this early period are hazardous at best. Even as approximations, however, they reflect a meaningful trend. See also Paul Studenski and Herman E. Kroos, *Financial History of the United States*, 2nd ed. (New York, 1963), 129n.

cant source of opposition to direct taxation in this period was apprehension on the part of unimproved sections of the state that if internal improvements were made contingent on taxation, public aid for canals and railroads would cease. Equally important, areas that did not expect improvements or that were tangibly injured by better transport facilities in other regions were unwilling to share the burden for such public works through taxation. Finally, whether conscious or not, the state's inability or unwillingness to resort to its taxing power to subsidize economic growth meant that society at large, including its weakest members, would bear the principal burden of economic development, rather than property owners who had the most to gain from economic growth and the most to fear from the redistributional effects of direct taxation.[129] Thus, the failure to base public economic policies on the firm foundation of a systematic and rational tax structure had profound implications for the distribution of wealth in the state, a fact that did not go unnoticed when New York found itself, after 1837, on the verge of financial collapse and confronted by increasing demands for a return to taxation.

THE PATTERN of state intervention in the economy reveals both the strengths and the weaknesses of the political system and political economy that emerged in New York in the first four decades of the nineteenth century. Laissez-faire, it is clear, did not limit the permissible range of governmental activity in the economy. Indeed, one is most impressed with New Yorkers' willingness to have the state assume an active role in the process of economic development and with the variety and range of such policies. But if the state recognized few ideological restraints on its economic activities, it does not follow that a logically consistent philosophy or ideology emerged to legitimate public economic intervention either. Quite the contrary. The most striking characteristic of New York's approach to the problem of economic development, and perhaps its greatest strength, was its pragmatism. Although much of the impetus for the state's activities in the early period was a carryover from mercantilism, the needs of an underdeveloped society and economy were ultimately more important in conditioning the types of economic demands made on the political system. Government's response, in turn, was highly eclectic and nonideological, at least within the broad parameters of a shared commitment among policymakers to capitalistic goals. The state, in short, used the complete range of resources at its disposal to assist in the process of capital accumulation and to remove obstacles from the path of private enterprise. It provided subsidies, legal privileges, social overhead capital, and

---

[129] Horwitz, *Transformation of American Law*, 99–100.

a regulatory and legal system conducive to private enterprise and economic growth, all of which was accomplished within the framework of a political culture profoundly distrustful of power and authority.

It is doubly ironic, therefore, that the pragmatic and expedient approach to state economic intervention, in combination with traditional political structures and processes, should also have been the principal weakness in New York's political economy. Pragmatism and the absence of an explicit ideology legitimizing public economic policies placed an unusually high premium on performance. The legitimacy of the system by which the state's resources were allocated depended on the effectiveness of the system itself. Effectiveness, furthermore, was measured not only by the success or failure of a given economic policy, but also, in the political sense, by the ability of those in authority to maintain minimal levels of support for the process itself. In the context of the existing political culture, this meant that the allocative process had to be perceived as open, equitable, and in harmony with the principles of representative democracy and minimal government.

In neither respect was New York's political system completely successful. With the exception of canal construction and the crude attempts by the Canal Fund Commission to "manage" the economy, economic policy in New York was primarily concerned with removing obstacles from the path of private enterprise. The ideological context or, more accurately, the absence of ideology encouraged government promotional activities, but in the final analysis, the structure of the political system was the most significant determinant of policy. It shaped the types of demands made, the manner in which such demands were resolved, and the effectiveness of policy responses. Ultimately the success or failure of public economic policies depended on the continued compatibility of political methods with the level of economic development. As the economy surged into a period of unprecedented growth and structural transformation, the control and promotional devices at the state's disposal remained essentially unchanged. Thus, despite the range of state economic activities, most policy decisions were made on an ad hoc basis, case by case, and usually in response to supplication from the individuals or groups seeking aid. For the most part, there was neither inclination nor opportunity for systematic policy formation, much less long-range planning. Policy, as suggested in chapter 3, was incremental in nature and consisted of the accumulation of highly individualized decisions usually bearing little relationship to earlier or later decisions. The state's loan policy, for example, seemingly a well-organized and vigorous effort to supply development capital, consisted of a series of unrelated, poorly administered acts dependent on the existence of treasury surpluses for funding.[130] Similarly, the use of corporate charters as instruments of promotion and regulation, particularly under the special incorporation system, precluded the development of a uniform, rationally conceived "policy" or the establishment of consistent, industrywide regulatory procedures. Even canal policy, usually cited as the best example of modern administrative practices in the antebellum states, was fundamentally shaped by local and regional political demands and by a lack of effective planning. Conditioning all aspects of public economic policy, furthermore, was the deep antipathy to direct taxation and the failure to develop a modern, rational tax system.

Further undermining the legitimacy of the system, at least in the long run and among certain groups, was the state's heavy reliance on private enterprise to perform such clearly public functions as providing roads, bridges, and a system of currency and finance. To assist in these tasks, the state granted such legal privileges as eminent domain, limited liability, and special-action franchises to corporations. In doing so, however, it delegated away an important measure of its sovereignty in these areas. Moreover, the identification of transportation and banking corporations with the public interest led to a further fragmentation of decisionmaking. The proliferation of such corporations, each justifying its existence on grounds of public interest, obscured the distinction between public and private spheres of social activity and made the concept of public interest virtually meaningless. Unless one assumes an extremely pluralistic position, government, by relying on the private sector to perform esentially public functions and by universally gratifying private, local, and sectional demands, abdicated ultimate responsibility for making authoritative decisions for the society.

[130]Reubens, "State Financing," 189.

[5]

The Crisis of Distributive Politics

BY THE END of the 1830s, the central dilemma of New York politics was how to satisfy the burgeoning demands created by rapid economic growth, social differentiation, and the expansion of the market while, at the same time, maintaining the legitimacy of the political system. Although the problem was inherent in the state's political culture and in a political economy that had evolved piecemeal over half a century, it was given new urgency by one of the worst commercial crises of the nineteenth century. The Panic of 1837 and the ensuing depression provided a crisis atmosphere within which New Yorkers began to reevaluate the role of government in society and to question some of the basic premises of their system of politics.

State debts and the future of development policy dominated political discussion between 1837 and 1842. But the critical issue, which lay just beneath the surface, transcended specific economic policies. As the failures and contradictions of the state's political economy became apparent, New Yorkers, who had traditionally looked to government for support for economic growth and development, began to view the state as the source of their distress. They began to take stock of the role government had come to play in society and its effectiveness in performing that role. In an even larger sense, New Yorkers were forced to consider the fundamental problem of who decides public questions, how they decide, and what attributes of this decision process legitimate the decisions that are finally made. The politics of distribution, it became increasingly clear, could no longer be counted on to resolve the problems of allocation and legitimation in a rapidly modernizing society and economy. Out of this realization, there eventually emerged new political expectations, new institutional arrangements and distributions of power, a new configuration of public policy, and, ultimately, a political order profoundly different from the system of politics with which the state had entered the nineteenth century.

ENCOURAGED BY the success of the Erie and Champlain canals and the relative ease with which canal revenues were expected to pay off the financial obligations incurred in their construction, New York had embarked on an even more ambitious program of internal improvements after 1825. In the fifteen years between 1825 and 1840, the state authorized construction of nine major canal projects, including the Seneca and Cayuga, the Oswego, the Chenango, the Black River, and the Genesee Valley canals. During this period, New York also granted loans totaling nearly $5 million by 1843 to private companies for the construction of railroads. Rather than resort to taxation, however, the state borrowed to finance these activities, anticipating that revenues from the state-owned transportation system would be sufficient to meet the principal and interest due each year. Consequently, the New York state debt rose to more than $20 million by 1840 and increased to $27 million by 1842.[1] A comparison of the amount of state stock issued during the 1830s with receipts and expenditures of the state treasury during the same years will help place this policy into perspective. From 1835 to 1840, New York issued more than $14 million in stocks. During the same period, state expenditures gradually overtook revenues, until by 1840 the surplus had become a $42,000 deficit.[2] Repayment of the loans did not, however, depend on regular state income; nor was it expected that it should. But any sudden decline in canal revenues, such as that occasioned by the panic and depression, would severely strain an already overburdened treasury, assuming that the state dutifully sought to maintain the annual payments on its obligations.

New York was not alone in this predicament. The internal-improvements enthusiasm in the wake of the Erie's success had generated a similar reliance on credit in other states. As a consequence, the total indebtedness of the American states increased dramatically in the 1830s. It has been estimated, for example, that in 1820 the combined state debt totaled just under $13 million. By 1830 the total had risen to more than $26 million; by 1838 it had reached $170 million; and by 1843 the states had outstanding obligations totaling more than $230 million. It is interesting that the largest increase in this debt came during the five-year period between 1835 and 1839, when the total trebled.[3] The bulk of the debt, moreover, was held by foreign investors.

[1] *Albany Argus*, March 31, 1841; Pierce, *Railroads of New York*, 16.
[2] *Albany Argus*, March 13, 1841, and March 31, 1841.
[3] U.S. Bureau of the Census, *Compendium of the 10th Census, 1880* (Washington, 1883), 526; Reginald C. McGrane, *Foreign Bondholders and American State Debts* (New York, 1935), 6, 35.

According to one estimate, by 1839 British subjects alone accounted for between $110 and $165 million of American stocks.[4] In 1843 Governor Bouck of New York reported that foreign capitalists held three-fourths of the state's debt that would fall due in 1845.[5] The states, of course, had turned to a policy of lending their credit to underwrite investment in a capital-short economy. As Frederick Huth, a London capitalist, put it, American stocks were "palatable to European capitalists" primarily because the states guaranteed them.[6] Thus, any real or perceived erosion of such guarantees would not only result in intensified pressure for repayment, but could potentially dry up the major source of investment capital in the United States.

The Panic of 1837 precipitated just such a crisis.[7] Even as the total amount of state debts increased between 1835 and 1839, public confidence in the ability of the states to repay those loans waned. By the end of 1842 Florida, Mississippi, Arkansas, Indiana, Illinois, Maryland, Michigan, Pennsylvania, and Louisiana had defaulted on payments due. Before the crisis was over, three states (Arkansas, Michigan, and Mississippi) repudiated debts totaling nearly $10 million.[8] In this atmosphere, new state loans could be obtained only at severe discounts. By 1838 New York six-percent stocks sold at below par. A $200,000 advance to the Auburn and Rochester Railroad in 1839, for example, brought only $182,990 in revenues. Similarly, the $3 million loan to the New York and Erie Railroad realized only a little more than $2.5 million.[9] In July 1841 the *Albany Argus* lamented that the state officers, attempting to negotiate a loan of $300,000, were forced to accept an offer of $84¼ for each $100 of state stock. The credit of the state, the *Argus* calculated, had declined more than 32 percent since 1833 when similar state stocks had commanded a premium of more than $17 for each $100 of stock issued.[10] By November 1841 New York five-percent stocks sold for 82 cents on the dollar, and six percents had fallen to 20 percent below par. As the year ended, the state found itself in arrears to contractors, who were compelled to borrow on their own credit to pay their workers, and confronted by investors increasingly reluctant to

---

[4]McGrane, *Foreign Bondholders*, 9.

[5]Lincoln, *Messages from the Governors*, 4: 20.

[6]Quoted in McGrane, *Foreign Bondholders*, 11.

[7]For discussions of the Panic of 1837 and its aftermath, see Reginald C. McGrane, *The Panic of 1837* (Chicago, 1924); North, *Economic Growth of the United States*, 198–203; Peter Temin, *The Jacksonian Economy* (New York, 1969), 113–171; and Samuel Rezneck, "The Social History of An American Depression, 1837–1843," *American Historical Review*, 40 (October 1934–July, 1935): 662–687.

[8]Taylor, *Transportation Revolution*, 375; Carter Goodrich, "The Revulsion Against Internal Improvements," *Journal of Economic History*, 10 (November 1950): 154.

[9]Pierce, *Railroads of New York*, 16.

[10]*Albany Argus*, July 29, 1841.

risk their capital in state stocks. Faced with its inability to obtain permanent loans on favorable terms, and with the possibility of having to suspend its public works, the state resorted to short-term, "temporary" loans, usually for nine to twelve months, to meet current obligations.[11]

The need to restore faith in New York's credit, and that of its similarly distressed sister states, went far beyond the question of financial solvency and the future of specific improvement projects. As the value of state stocks declined, as interest payments went unpaid, and as some states began to consider the alternative of repudiation, European creditors, concerned for the security of their investments, began to question the integrity of Americans and their system of government. Throughout Europe, but particularly in England, which accounted for the majority of foreign investors, the viability of American political institutions became the subject of ridicule and derision. Typical of such sentiments were the comments of a London correspondent of the *American* in September 1842: "There grows up an opinion among the more reflecting, that the original cause of danger is to be found in the too democratic nature of the institutions of your country, which, by throwing all elections in the hands of the multitude, and by making those elections recur perpetually, cause those institutions to be attacked by demagogues, addressing themselves to the passions of the ignorant who form the numerical majority."[12] Opinions such as these struck a sensitive nerve in a society already acutely aware of the peculiar moral demands of republicanism and the fragility, historically, of republican governments.[13] To the economic reasons for finding a solution to the financial problems of the states was thus added a moral one: repudiation would constitute an intolerable stain on republican institutions.

The denigration of American institutions emanating from Europe was part of an orchestrated campaign by British creditors and their American supporters to arouse public awareness of the financial plight of the states. The intended result would be the passage of new tax laws to reduce the debt or the assumption of state debts by the federal government. The Baring Brothers of London, for example, issued a circular in October 1840 calling for a "more comprehensive guaranty than that of individual states" and suggesting

[11]Ibid., November 8, 1841; Hammond, *History of Political Parties*, 3: 268; D. A. Donovan, *The Barnburners: A Study of the Internal Movements in the Political History of New York State and the Resulting Changes in Political Affiliations*, 1830–1852 (New York, 1925), 22–23.

[12]*Albany Argus*, September 24, 1842; McGrane, *Foreign Bondholders*, 40; see also *A Vindication of the Public Faith of New York and Pennsylvania in Reply to the Calumnies of the "Times"* (London, 1840).

[13]For the significance of these themes in early American history, see Bailyn, *Ideological Origins of the American Revolution*, and Gordon S. Wood, *Creation of the American Republic*.

that a "national pledge" be given that the debts would be repaid.[14] The possibility of federal assumption was discussed in the press and debated in Congress between 1839 and 1843, but to no avail. In March 1843 the House of Representatives tabled a proposal of William Cost Johnson to liquidate state indebtedness by distributing $200 million of United States stock among the states, to be backed up by public land sales. The defeat of Johnson's proposal placed the burden of restoring American credit and vindicating American political institutions squarely on each individual state.[15] New York was ultimately to meet that obligation by halting construction on improvement projects and by returning to a policy of direct taxation, but only after four years of intensely partisan debate over the future of the state's development policy.

That debate began in earnest with the triumph of the Whig party in the 1837 legislative elections. The Whig success in capturing control of the assembly ended nearly two decades of Bucktail-Democratic dominance of state politics and signaled the emergence of a united, well-organized opposition under a leadership equal to that of the Albany Regency. The election of William H. Seward to the governorship in 1838 and a Whig state senate in 1839 solidified the Whig party's gains and launched a period of balanced, two-party competition in New York politics. With Whig ascendancy at the polls, New York's development policy took a sharp turn in the direction of expansion.[16]

Under Governor William H. Seward and a Whig-controlled legislature, the state initiated a policy of deliberate deficit spending to finance the Erie Enlargement and completion of the Genesee Valley and Black River canals. The result was a $16 million increase in the state debt during the four years of Whig rule.[17] Such boldness, undertaken in the midst of the century's worst depression, has occasioned comparisons with the New Deal policies of the 1930s and earned for the Whig party a reputation for foresight and modernism. According to Ronald Shaw, for example, "the Whigs were real innovators and saw the important role that government must play in the formation of the 'social overhead capital' which W. W. Rostow today has described as one of the preconditions for the 'take-off' stage of economic growth."[18] Similarly, Lee Benson has argued that "the Whig modernists" visualized an

[14]*Albany Argus*, January 26, 1841.

[15]McGrane, *Foreign Bondholders*, 35.

[16]McCormick, *Second American Party System*, 112–114; Benson, Silbey, and Field, "Toward a Theory of Stability and Change in American Voting Patterns," 84–91.

[17]Donovan, *The Barnburners*, 22–23; Segal, "Canals and Economic Development," 192; David M. Ellis et. al., *A Short History of New York State* (Ithaca, 1957), 217–218.

[18]Shaw, *Erie Water West*, 318–319.

"increasingly dynamic, complex, and industrialized society," and "developed a theory of positive liberalism" to achieve such a future.[19]

The Whig rationale for continuing and expanding the state's public works lends support to such a view. Samuel Ruggles, for example, chairman of the ways and means committee of the assembly and author of its "Report on the Finances and Internal Improvements" in 1838, confidently reported that, based on estimates of future canal revenues made by the canal commissioners, the state could safely borrow up to $40 million and repay it within thirty years, without recourse to taxation.[20] As evidence, Ruggles pointed to the growth of population and wealth in the areas through which the existing canals passed, and even more important, suggested that the increase of canal revenues thus created was inconsequential when compared to the increase that would result from commerce with the West. In explaining the impact of the canal system on trade and commerce, furthermore, Ruggles articulated a surprisingly modern understanding of the role played by transportation in creating regional specialization of economic function: "The consequence then of perfecting these systems of intercommunication will inevitably be a distribution of labour, on a grand scale, through the whole northern part of the continent: the maritime portions engrossing the active pursuits of navigation, commerce, and manufactures, while this central group of agricultural states will become the common granary of the Union, and discharge the important duty of supplying subsistence to all the surrounding communities."[21]

Governor Seward's views, as expressed in his annual messages to the legislature between 1838 and 1842, are further evidence of Whig modernism. In his efforts to combat the increasing demands for a halt to public-works construction and a return to direct taxation, Seward marshaled an array of both practical and theoretical arguments. Analyzing the financial situation in his 1840 message, for example, he warned that any immediate interruption of such public expenditures would exacerbate economic conditions by flooding the state with unemployed laborers. He accompanied this warning, however, with a recommendation that stock issues be limited so that the interest on the total debt would never exceed surplus revenues, even though this would result in a slowdown of construction. Seward also proposed the creation of a Board of Internal Improvements, whose membership would include com-

---

[19]Benson, *Concept of Jacksonian Democracy*, 105–106.

[20]New York (State Legislature), Assembly, Committee on Ways and Means, "Report upon the Finances and Internal Improvements of the State of New York, 1838," (reprinted, New York, 1838), 41–42.

[21]Ibid., 54–55.

petent engineers, to ensure that future policy was not based on faulty estimates, a major cause in his view of New York's embarrassment in 1840.[22]

In addition to such practical considerations, Seward justified the state's
public-works program by appealing to a broader vision of society than that
which had shaped government policies in the past. To critics who evaluated
improvement projects solely on the basis of expected revenues, he replied that
the true test was not "a mere question of dollars and cents"; rather, the benefits included increased land values, the growth of agriculture and manufactures, the enlargement of domestic and foreign trade, improved
transportation and communications, population growth, urbanization, and
"all the consequent advantages of morality, piety, and knowledge."[23] To those
who persistently assumed a local or sectional perspective, he pleaded for
moderation and urged them to put aside regional jealousies by recognizing
"the importance to the whole state of the improvement of each section."[24]
And to assertions that the state had no right to enact policies that would burden future generations with debt, Seward retorted that society possessed an
identity and existence that transcended the present. "Reason and experience,"
he wrote, "teach that every human society has a continuous identity susceptible of indefinite prolongation, and incapable of division. The citizen of
every state feels . . . that although mortal himself, he is part of a community
that may . . . be perpetual."[25] Here, then, was an enlarged view of the public
interest. The greater good of the historical community transcended the
immediate interests of its separate parts.

In any case, according to Seward, the principles on which policy should
be based were already well established. Past legislatures had accepted it as
their duty to assist trade and commerce by providing improved communications and by assuring that each region of the state possessed an outlet to
the commerce of the world. New Yorkers, through their representatives, had
also come to accept the idea that the prosperity and growth of New York
City benefited all sections of the state and that the state's welfare depended
on its capturing the trade of the West. Other principles were revealed in the
way in which past improvement projects had been implemented: wherever
possible, lateral and auxiliary works should be constructed to "equalize the
benefit of internal improvements"; the state should rely on its own resources
for such construction or authorize associations for the purpose; and, since
"taxation for purposes of internal improvements must necessarily be une-

---

[22] Lincoln, *Messages from the Governors*, 3: 795–797.
[23] Ibid., 3: 734.
[24] Ibid., 3: 801.
[25] Ibid., 3: 801–802.

qual," the state should rely principally on revenues from the public works themselves rather than resort to taxation.[26]

Sentiments such as these suggest the beginnings of a modern approach to public policy. Seward was keenly aware of the importance of an explicit concept of the public interest and sought to articulate such a concept in his annual messages. He also appreciated the importance of basing public policy decisions on reliable information—thus his proposal for a centralized Board of Internal Improvement staffed by competent engineers. But Seward refused to make the final leap. New York's financial embarrassment was partly a result, as he himself argued, of discrepancies between expenditures and estimated revenues. Seward's solution was to create a system that would more accurately estimate future revenues, though the difficulty of this process could never be completely eliminated. He rejected the one alternative most likely to assure a rational financial system: taxation. In view of his previous pleas for sacrifices for the good of the whole and his statements that the prosperity of each section contributed to the well-being of the entire state, his rationale for this decision appears strange: that taxation "must necessarily be unequal." Most likely, Seward's timidity on this issue stemmed from his fear of political reprisal for any party so bold as to advocate increased taxes and his fear that predicating improvements on increased taxation would doom the state's public-works program. In any event, Seward provided a modern justification for taxation but proved unwilling, or incapable, of committing the state to such a policy himself.

Ironically, it was the Radical Democrats who ultimately led the state back to a policy of direct taxation, though the rationale for doing so was quite different from the concept of the public interest evolving among leading Whigs. By the early 1840s the Democratic party had split into two distinct groups, identified by their different views on the issue of internal improvements and, more generally, the extent to which they wished to carry the doctrine of the negative state. Conservatives, such as Edwin Croswell, Daniel Dickinson, William C. Bouck, Henry Foster, and Horatio Seymour generally favored continuing the improvement program, though at a pace calculated to minimize the burden on the state's credit. Radicals, on the other hand, led by Azariah C. Flagg, Michael Hoffman, Samuel Young, Arphaxed Loomis, and Silas Wright, opposed any increase of the state debt for internal improvements, favored a general retrenchment in expenditures, and sought to limit the legislature's power to contract debts in the future. A few Dem-

[26]Ibid., 812–813.

ocrats, most notably William Cullen Bryant and Gerrit Smith, even advocated that the state sell its canals.[27]

The key to the Radical Democratic position was its attack on the credit system, which went beyond the immediate problem of repaying the debt and encompassed a vision of society distinctly different from that of future-minded Whigs such as Seward. Typical of Radical arguments were those put forth by Samuel Young in a "Lecture on Civilization" to the Young Men's Association of Saratoga Springs in 1841. According to Young, the corruption, incessant warfare, and moral decline that, in his reading of history, had come to characterize the nations of Europe were directly attributable to the creation of the debt system. The same fate awaited America, he warned, unless the state ceased to ape "the most detestable acts of corrupt ministers and kings." Already, he noted, the states had "attempted to hypothecate the earnings of after times in order to satiate the vulture rapacity of the present; they had endeavored to appropriate the toil of subsequent generations to glut the hungry cravings of this; to eat the bread of unborn children . . . and to bind the limbs of the men of future days with the iron chains of public debt." Recalling Jefferson's warning that one generation cannot bind succeeding ones, Young charged the advocates of public debt with appropriating the inalienable rights of posterity.[28] The *New York Evening Post* echoed these sentiments: "For the legislature to assume to dispose of the credit of the state . . . is to assume the control of the property and credit of every individual citizen, and for any number of years."[29] Implicit in such statements was a sharply limited conception of society as either isolated or immune from time, with each generation competent to determine its own destiny free from the burdens of the past or responsibilities to the future.

But the Radicals worried about more than the credit system's debilitating effects on future generations. The moral implications of debt and avarice for the present were equally significant. Most Democrats could accept, in a general way, the observation of Governor William L. Marcy in 1838 that "looking back to the period immediately preceding the present revulsion . . . it would seem that a strange delusion had spread far and wide, filling the minds of many with extravagant hopes, and leading them on to the wildest adventures. It was scarcely reasonable," he noted, "to expect that this delusion would long continue, or that it could suddenly pass off without producing a

---

[27] Ellis et al., *Short History of New York State*, 217–218; Donovan, *Barnburners*, 19–20, 119; Shaw, *Erie Water West*, 308; see also Benson, *Concept of Jacksonian Democracy*, 228, for a discussion of Democratic principles.

[28] *Albany Argus*, November 30, 1841.

[29] Quoted in *Albany Argus*, February 13, 1841.

disastrous change in our business transactions."[30] But Radicals were much more specific. "We have been making too great haste to get rich," as General Dix of Albany put it in a speech to the assembly in March 1842, "and we have incurred the penalty which has been denounced against the inordinate thirst for gain." The stakes were high because "the too great love of money has, in all countries and in all ages, been the certain forerunner of social and political degradation." The present situation was critical, moreover, because public and private morality were intimately related. If states repudiated their obligations, "how can it be expected that individuals will scrupulously fulfill their contracts?" A weakening of moral rectitude was the logical consequence. Already the signs were present: "Ostentation, ease, luxurious living . . . display." The time had come for a change. "These are not the vices of freedom," Dix warned, "and when we see them springing up in republican soil—when we see the legislature of the country turned away from great public purposes, and running into the channels of private and local speculation—we may be sure that radical errors have stolen in among us."[31] A letter to the *Albany Argus* in January 1842, signed "A Republican of the Old School," made the same point more bluntly: "The prevalence of vice in any shape is intimately connected with the prosperity or adversity of our country."[32]

These two strains of the Radical position—its view of society as existing only in the present and its identification of the credit system with a weakening of the moral base of society—permeated efforts to find a solution to the financial crisis.[33] During 1841 and 1842 these efforts focused on a series of

---

[30] Lincoln, *Messages From the Governors*, 3: 658.

[31] "Speech of General Dix, of Albany, in the Assembly, March 23, [1842] on the Resolutions for an amendment to the constitution in relation to the borrowing of money or the issuing of state stocks," printed in the *Albany Argus*, March 31, 1842.

[32] *Albany Argus*, January 8, 1842.

[33] It should be pointed out that these ideas are related to broader trends in American society in this period. Major L. Wilson, for example, has suggested a dichotomy between Whigs and Democrats, at the national level, based on their differing concepts of time. "Behind the conflict of interest," Wilson writes, ". . . and vitally involved in the accompanying theories of man and society are fundamentally different concepts of time. How free is each individual or each generation to shape his own destiny? To what degree, on the other hand, is the pursuit of happiness collective and cumulative in nature and the state a corporate entity subsisting through time?" According to Wilson, by the 1850s a form of "negative liberalism" had triumphed, with "little of the corporate sense of freemen within a temporal process" surviving. See Major L. Wilson, "The Concept of Time and the Political Dialogue in the United States, 1828–1848," *American Quarterly*, 19 (Winter 1967): 620–621, 643. A major theme of Fred Somkin's *Unquiet Eagle: Memory and Desire in the Idea of American Freedom, 1815–1860* (Ithaca, 1967), on the other hand, is the relationship between prosperity and fears of corruption and vice.

constitutional amendments known collectively as the "People's Resolutions." The object of these proposals was to amend the constitution to require that every law authorizing the creation of a debt or the issuing of stocks creating such a debt be submitted directly to the people for approval before its implementation. First introduced in the legislature on February 3, 1841, by Arphaxed Loomis of Herkimer County, the People's Resolutions came to a vote on May 19 but failed to pass by a tie vote of 53 to 53. They were reintroduced in the 1842 session, but were again defeated, this time by a vote of 49 to 53.[34] The specific legislative history of these resolutions need not detain us here. More important is the debate over the People's Resolutions in the legislature and in the press, for that debate reveals a great deal about New Yorkers' changing attitudes toward the political system.

Two assumptions lay at the heart of the People's Resolutions. First, New York owed its financial difficulties and embarrassment to the abuse of legislative power. Second, the appropriate solution was to limit the legislature's authority to borrow money by allowing "the people" a greater role in such decisions. In language reminiscent of old Republican rhetoric, Arphaxed Loomis, John Dix, and other supporters of the resolutions charged that the legislature, representing local and sectional interests, had made improvement policy and handled debt questions through logrolling and lobbying, at the expense of the broader community's interest. The problem, as Loomis explained, was not one of "corrupt influences being brought to bear directly, but of that influence which, unconsciously perhaps, grows out of a personal or local interest in the success of certain projects."[35] Experience had also shown, according to Loomis, that legislatures in New York, and in other states as well, had often been hasty in their decisions and had shown remarkably poor judgment in such matters as the proper time and circumstances in which to borrow money. Indeed, it was the absence of such a constitutional limitation on borrowing power which had brought New York to "the verge of bankruptcy, discredit and dishonor."[36]

The *Albany Morning Atlas*, the leading Radical newspaper in the state, was even sharper in its criticism of legislative power. "The history of all ages," according to a December 1841 article, "proves the facility with which power runs into abuse, and how it increases with accelerated speed, and continually frees itself from responsibility, in its progress."[37] The representative system,

---

[34] *Albany Argus*, February 4, 1841; January 11, 1842; May 20, 1841; Hammond, *History of Political Parties*, 3: 287–288; Shaw, *Erie Water West*, 326–327; and Donovan, *Barnburners*, 23.
[35] "Speech of Arphaxed Loomis in the Assembly, March 16, 1842," printed in the *Albany Argus*, May 9, 1842.
[36] Ibid.
[37] *Albany Morning Atlas*, December 6, 1841.

as the past several years had proved, was as susceptible to this evil as other forms of government. "The mere representatives of sectional interests in our legislature have exhibited as much of the disgraceful spirit of combination and intrigue as ever characterized the countries of the most profligate monarchy."[38] What was worse, reliance could not be placed on the virtue and public spiritedness of legislators to safeguard against these tendencies:

> The men who are selected for our representatives are generally chosen from a class ever ready to pervert public legislation to private advantage, and most faithfully do they represent the class from which they are selected. Their ambition, their generosity, their sympathy, with their associates; their common interests in the success of local enterprises, their very pride in representing and carrying out what they consider the will of the section they represent all prompt them to become advocates of partial interests, instead of the representatives of the people.[39]

The remedy for these abuses of legislative power was clear. According to the *Atlas*, "the *limitation of power*, in every branch of our government is the only safeguard of liberty. We do not mean a re-adjustment of power between the several departments of state, but its restoration to the people, leaving to the agents of the people only so much as cannot conveniently be exercised by the former."[40]

This emphasis on "the people" as the ultimate repository of political power proved to be the most effective argument in support of the People's Resolutions. They were, in the words of Arphaxed Loomis, "eminently democratic—perfectly in harmony with the spirit of our government and institutions."[41] Since it was the people's interests that would be taxed by debt legislation, the people should be the best judges. Besides, as the *New York Evening Post* put it, the people were free from "partialities to indulge . . . and would not consent to relinquish control of their credit until the subject had undergone a full, luminous, and satisfactory investigation."[42] Although this was admittedly a slower method of legislation, there was no better way to restrain future spending. It was efficient and honest, and would prevent the operation of localism and lobbying tactics. "Among the people at large," the *Atlas* explained, "the arts of the lobby must be inoperative, and the mysteries of log-rolling unknown. The mass can never be so selfish, so subservient, so

[38] Ibid., February 9, 1842.
[39] Ibid., February 4, 1842.
[40] Ibid., February 9, 1842.
[41] *Albany Argus*, May 9, 1842.
[42] Reprinted in *Albany Argus*, February 13, 1841.

time-serving, as those who are sent to represent them. No county can be bribed into silence or into change of opinion by champagne or supper; no Senate district will agree to absent itself from the polls for the sake of bank stock."[43] In addition to preventing abuses of power, furthermore, the People's Resolutions would contribute to the "genius and spirit" of the people by bringing before them for consideration subjects of the greatest importance.[44]

Despite disclaimers to the contrary, the Radical Democratic argument involved nothing less than a direct attack on the representative system. Some, like John Dix, were quite clear on this point. The unrestrained authority of the legislature was the principal cause of the growth of the credit system. Unlike the federal legislature, he argued, which possessed no powers but those expressly granted, the New York legislature exercised all powers not expressly forbidden. Furthermore, though administrative officials were carefully confined by law, the legislative power was virtually unlimited. The only check on the lawmaking body was its representative character. It was this very "representativeness," as we have seen, that had traditionally given the legislature its claim to legitimacy and supremacy. Dix argued, however, that the "direct amenability of the legislature to the people," through annual elections and strict accountability to constituents, "has not proved an effectual safeguard against the abuse of its authority."[45]

This line of attack is intriguing. Given the extraordinary rate of turnover among its members, the legislature appears to have been more responsive to "the people" in the 1830s and 1840s than in any previous era, a fact that would seem to undermine the Radical position. But did the legislature really represent "the people"? Or would it be more accurate to view the legislature as reflecting the political aspirations of local communities, sections, regions, and, specifically, those who were most influential at these levels of the political system? Viewed from this perspective, the Radical critique of the legislature not only becomes more comprehensible, but also takes on a higher significance. It implied that the legislature was not responsive to the *whole* people; that there was an identifiable public interest that should take precedence over local, sectional, or group interests; and that public policy would reflect the will of "the people" more precisely if they played a direct role in policy-making. In the final analysis, this argument struck at the concept of direct representation, which, though theoretically providing for the representation of all interests in society, also led inevitably to the institutionalization of pluralist conflict and a bargaining style of politics.

[43] *Albany Morning Atlas*, December 6, 1841.
[44] *Albany Argus*, January 8, 1842.
[45] Ibid., March 31, 1842.

Opponents of the debt-restriction amendments, recognizing the fundamental nature of the attack on legislative power, charged that their adoption would overthrow the representative power, subvert the principle of constitutionalism, and jeopardize the rights of minorities. The opposition's chief spokesman, John W. Tamblin of Jefferson argued from principles strikingly similar to those of Madison in *Federalist* Number 10. Passage of the People's Resolutions, according to Tamblin, would "throw us back on the crude democracies of antiquity; a form of government, adapted only to the regulation of a tribe or a township." The effect would be to create a government by simple majority, without the restraints that only a "solemn and inveterate veneration of a constitution" could provide. With remarkable insight, Tamblin foresaw the future consequences of such a policy. If the debt-restriction amendments were passed, he argued, it would open the door for an unlimited number of similar amendments. The result would be to undermine constitutional authority: "If we enact laws by the same solemn ceremonies that we do constitutional provisions, shall we not transform the power and glory of the constitution into a perfect image of ordinary laws?" "Putting the law and the constitution on a level," he continued, "is precisely tantamount to having no constitution at all. Its power will be destroyed, and the majority will wield the power of sovereignty without limitation or control and the government will be nothing more nor less than a majority despotism." The submission of debt legislation to popular vote, moreover, far from preventing a system of logrolling, would tend to excite local and sectional feelings and subject the polity to the disruptive influences of faction.[46]

Tamblin's arguments struck to the heart of the issue. The debate over the People's Resolutions focused squarely on the relative merits of representative government versus direct democracy. The *Albany Atlas* also saw the issue in these terms and rushed to defend the democratic principle. Enemies of the People's Resolutions who feared an "unmixed democracy," according to the *Atlas*, "found their opposition on principles hostile to all democracy." Opponents of the amendments believed the people were sufficiently competent and trustworthy to delegate "the whole power of the state" to their representatives, yet were incapable of deciding public issues for themselves. All that was required to satisfy the principle of popular sovereignty, according to this view, was for legislators to seek and obtain the support of the people in an election. The *Atlas*, on the other hand, argued that the whole power of government rested with the people. The legislature "is a mere labor-saving machine,

[46]"Speech of Mr. Tamblin, of Jefferson, on Mr. Loomis's Resolutions in relation to an amendment of the constitution, in Assembly, March 23, 1842," printed in *Albany Argus*, April 18, 1842.

an invention to save time and trouble; but the power of which is with the people, and whose machinery, is under their control." The People's Resolutions, therefore, were "harmless, judicious and in perfect consonance with the theory of our government." Fears that submitting debt legislation to popular vote would excite local and sectional feelings among the people, furthermore, were unjustified: "They misinterpret human nature, who dread tumultuous assemblages of the people and immense and dangerous sectional combinations, as the consequence of this resolution. Avarice and ambition," the *Atlas* continued, "which cause all the tumults and coalitions of party warfare in the present day, will have too wide a field for efficient action, and too little hope to stimulate them to action."[47]

Although the People's Resolutions were ultimately defeated, the amendments were not without significance. They represented an effort to incorporate the principle of direct democracy into the state constitution. At the most fundamental level of political discourse, the Radical Democratic response to the financial crisis directly challenged the representative system. The people, as the *Atlas* put it in a December 1842 article, have found "that the overaction of government has caused the evils under which they are suffering. They have found the chartered monopolies, artificial credit systems, fraudulent paper currencies, the perpetual taxation of public debt, and the whole vile progeny of class legislation are the fruits of unlimited power in their own representatives."[48] Believing that a succession of legislatures had abused the representative principle, the Radical solution was direct democracy, which assumed "the people" were immune from the pressures and excitements that buffeted legislatures. Although attempts to implement this solution in 1842 failed, the issue would reappear later in the movement for constitutional revision. The debt-restriction principle was, in fact, ultimately incorporated into the new constitution adopted in 1846.

THE PEOPLE'S RESOLUTIONS were designed to assure popular control over public economic policy and to prevent a recurrence of the state's financial debacle in the future. Even if the amendments had passed in 1842 and had become part of the constitution, they would have done nothing to alleviate the existing economic situation. It was to meet the immediate necessity of restoring faith in the state's credit, therefore, that the new, predominantly Democratic legislature turned in 1842. Under the leadership of Michael Hoffman, Herkimer County Democrat and chairman of the ways and means committee of the assembly, and Azariah C. Flagg, the state comptroller, the

---

[47]*Albany Morning Atlas*, February 15, 1842.
[48]Ibid., December 31, 1842.

Radical Democrats passed a law suspending further internal-improvement projects and enacting a statewide, general property tax, the first such tax in fifteen years. Neither accomplishment was particularly novel in 1842, since both policies had been advocated by various groups and individuals throughout the 1830s. But each represented a significant departure in public policy and each, in its own way, was a harbinger of the future.

The "Stop and Tax" policy was the culmination of two separate but converging circumstances: the steady deterioration of the state's credit after 1837 and a long-term effort, dating to the 1820s, to establish a rational financial system based on taxation. By 1841, as we have seen, the depression had so devastated public confidence in the credit of American states that New York five- and six-percent stocks sold at twenty to thirty percent below par. The state responded with temporary loans to meet current obligations, but it had become increasingly difficult to negotiate even these short-term loans at reasonable rates of interest. As the situation worsened and normal sources of credit disappeared, the search for a solution to the state's financial crisis emerged as the central issue in New York politics. Whigs, who still controlled the state government in 1841, persisted in the argument that public-works construction could go forward and the state's credit be preserved without resorting to taxation, though they were unclear about specifics and could not deny that the debt had risen to an unprecedented $18 million. Democrats, on the other hand, advocated retrenchment and the levying of a direct tax to retire the state debt and assuage the fears of reluctant investors.[49]

Demands for a return to direct taxation were not new in 1841. Leading Democrats had opposed termination of the tax in 1826 and argued consistently throughout the 1830s against use of the General Fund to meet the annual expenses of the state. William L. Marcy, for example, comptroller and chief financial officer of the state, had opposed the financial system adopted in 1827 and the decision to go ahead with construction of the Chenango Canal on the grounds that it would deplete the General Fund. Samuel Young, then a member of the Canal Commission, also objected, arguing that state investments should be evaluated solely on the basis of whether the state's revenues were thereby increased. Both views, of course, were directly contrary to those held by DeWitt Clinton, who argued that the only criterion should be whether or not such expenditures increased total state wealth.[50]

---

[49] The best modern account of the relationship between internal improvements and state politics in New York in this period is Shaw, *Erie Water West*, especially 303–329, which cover the years 1835–1841. For a sampling of newspaper opinion supporting the Democratic position, see articles from the *Journal of Commerce*, *New York Sun*, and *Daily Advertiser*, reprinted in *Albany Argus*, May 5 and 25, and October 18, 1841.

[50] Hammond, *History of Political Parties*, 2: 250–251, 264–265.

Although the enthusiasm for further internal improvements swept aside the Marcy–Young position in 1827, the opposition to continuing the internal-improvements program without taxation could not be stifled. Each year thereafter the comptroller called for a tax to meet the state's ordinary expenses and to preserve the General Fund.[51] In 1830 and 1831, furthermore, Governor Enos Throop pointed to the gradual diminution of the General Fund and proposed a tax. In the latter year he based his argument, at least partially, on the difficulty of accurately calculating state expenditures and revenues under the existing system.[52] Throop reiterated his warning in 1832 and urged the adoption of some new source of revenue. In response, Senator Alvin Bronson of Oswego introduced a bill providing for a one-mill tax for three years, but the bill went down to defeat, receiving only five affirmative votes. Opponents of the tax bill successfully argued that by the time the General Fund was exhausted, the canal debt would have been paid off and surplus revenues could then be used to meet ordinary expenses.[53] Instead of levying a new tax, the legislature authorized the comptroller to borrow from the Literature and Common School funds.[54]

As the capital of the General Fund continued to decrease during the 1830s, demands for a return to taxation assumed an air of urgency. William L. Marcy, now governor, importuned the legislature to devise a system of finance to support the government in each of his annual messages between 1833 and 1836. In 1833 Marcy added to the obvious financial reasons for taxation a political argument. "When the public funds are not drawn immediately from the people," he wrote, "a proper sense of dependence on the part of those who have the appropriation of them is lost; and a salutary check to improvident and profuse expenditure is removed." Conversely, he continued, "when the motive for the constituent to scrutinize the conduct of the representative is enfeebled, the latter ceases to feel and act under the consciousness of due accountability." The result was to derange the "whole political system."[55] The senate committee on finance argued similarly: "However useful the principle of direct taxation may be in other governments, in ours it appears to be indispensable. A fund drawn from the people by secret and indirect means, in its disposition cannot be safely confided to an agency so numerous and so transitory as our legislature; dividing responsibility so min-

[51]"Annual Report of the Comptroller," *Assembly Document*, no. 5, 1835, 12.

[52]Hammond, *History of Political Parties*, 2: 318; Lincoln, *Messages from the Governors*, 3: 322–23.

[53]Lincoln, *Messages from the Governors*, 3: 371; Hammond, *History of Political Parties*, 2: 411–12; Sowers, *Financial History*, 65.

[54]*Laws of New York*, chap. 196, 1832.

[55]Lincoln, *Messages from the Governors*, 3: 425; see also 3: 439–440 and 503–505.

utely, self-interest, that useful impulse of our natures, working wrong would work its ruin, while a fund drawn from the people by direct taxation, would be protected by the same principle."[56] The committee recommended a one-mill tax, but the legislature again refused to provide new revenues.[57]

In 1835 Comptroller Flagg reported that the General Fund was so near exhaustion that further delay in levying a tax could only lead to a state debt. After reviewing the history of taxation in New York, he reminded the legislature that the comptroller had urged the passage of a tax every year since 1826 and that the General Fund would have long since been consumed except for the policy of borrowing from other funds. The alternative was now either to create a debt or levy a light tax of at least one mill to preserve a sound financial system. Such a tax, he explained, would yield $400,000 annually, a sum at least sufficient to defray current charges on the treasury. Failure to levy a tax would necessitate borrowing for the annual support of the government, a policy that, he predicted, would result in a $1.5 million debt by the end of 1837.[58]

The 1836 Comptroller's Report reiterated these themes. Appealing to "the intelligence and correct business principles of the people of this state," Flagg pleaded with the legislature to levy a direct tax at least sufficient to pay the interest on new loans. "If the object of the expenditure is a proper one," he wrote, "there is no reason to suppose that an intelligent people will disapprove it. . . ."[59] In the face of such warnings from the governor and comptroller, the legislature not only refused to levy a tax, but also voted a $3 million loan to the New York and Erie Railroad and approved construction of the Genesee and Black River canals, without providing for repayment of the loans thereby created.[60] Indeed, the only effort made during this period to replenish the treasury was a constitutional amendment passed in 1835 that restored the salt and auction duties to the General Fund.[61] Thus, the advocates of taxation failed to slow the momentum of the internal-improvements movement, an enthusiasm that reached its peak with the ascendance of the Whigs in 1838 and the subsequent construction boom under Governor William H. Seward.

But Whig control of state government was short-lived. Seward alienated many former supporters by becoming embroiled in a controversy with Vir-

---

[56]*Senate Document*, no. 55, 1833, 9.

[57]Ibid., 11.

[58]*Assembly Document*, no. 5, 1835.

[59]*Assembly Document*, no. 5, 1836, 22.

[60]Hammond, *History of Political Parties*, 2: 457; Secrist, "Economic Analysis of the Constitutional Restrictions upon Public Indebtedness," 25.

[61]Submitted for popular approval by chap. 147, *Laws of New York*, 1835.

ginia over that state's slave code and by proposing special schools for the children of the foreign-born. More important, the Whig policy of deficit spending to enlarge the Erie and to complete the Genesee Valley and Black River canals increased the state debt to $18 million and shook public confidence in the state's financial system. Capitalizing on popular discontent with the party in power, the Democrats recaptured control of the state legislature in the 1841 elections and initiated a new approach to development policy and to the debt question.[62]

When the new legislature convened in January 1842, Whigs sought to quiet criticism of their policies and restore confidence in the state's credit by introducing resolutions in the senate denouncing the doctrine of repudiation and pledging the state's good faith.[63] The Democratic response was swift and devastating. "Can any sane man believe," the *Albany Argus* asked, "that the passage of Mr. Franklin's resolution can recall this credit? No, no . . . its sensitiveness has received a shock from which it can recover only by years of prudence—not by resolutions against repudiation, accompanied by a reckless profligacy in incurring new debts."[64] The credit of the state can and should be preserved, Michael Hoffman roared from the assembly, "but if, seeking popularity for an hour, dreading the influence of this or that locality, we go on, winking there at a railroad and here at an extension, the credit of the state in peril, and itself on the verge of bankruptcy—when calamity comes upon us, and we call upon the mountains to cover us, the earth itself would spurn us."[65] In the senate, Robert Denniston of Orange County ridiculed the intent of the resolutions by comparing them to the assurances of a businessman who, confronted by his creditors, lamely exclaims: "'My credit is good; I am resolved to fulfill my contracts!'"[66]

Hyperbole was replaced by practical policy considerations when the Annual Report of the comptroller appeared on February 15. Azariah Flagg, now returned to the post he had held for six years before the Whig victories in 1837 and 1838, issued a pessimistic appraisal of the state's finances and called for a one-mill tax on real and personal property. The comptroller reported a $454,392.97 deficit in the General Fund, and debt against that

[62]Ellis et al., *Short History of New York State*, 217–218; and Dennis Tilden Lynch, "Party Struggles, 1818–1850," in *The Age of Reform*, vol. 6 of *History of the State of New York*, ed. Alexander C. Flick, 74.

[63]*Albany Argus*, January 10 and 11, 1842.

[64]*Albany Argus*, January 18, 1842.

[65]Quoted in Hammond, *History of Political Parties*, 3: 269–270. For an elaboration of Hoffman's views, see his speech in the assembly on the message from the governor, reprinted in the *Argus*, January 21, 24, 29, 1842.

[66]Denniston speech on "The State Credit, and the State Debts, in the Senate, February 18, 1842," printed in the *Argus*, March 4, 1842.

fund, due in 1842, of $797,829.40. The remedy for this financial situation, according to Flagg, was for the state to resort to its vast resources. He estimated that the assessed value of real and personal property amounted to $650 million; annual revenues of the state, $2.5 million; and annual production of the state (agriculture, manufactures, mines, forestry), $238 million. Sound policy dictated that the state tap these resources. That meant taxation. A one-mill tax, Flagg explained, would bring in $600,000 annually. Further, once the immediate financial embarrassments had been mitigated, a sinking fund should be established to pay the state's yearly obligations down to 1845. Flagg concluded by appealing to the public interest: "At such a time, local interests, and every consideration merely personal, must yield for the time being, to the paramount welfare of the whole."[67]

Traditional Democratic journals such as the *Albany Argus*, the *Albany Atlas*, and the *New York Evening Post* supported Flagg's proposal, but so did many commercial and business papers, particularly in New York City. "A small direct tax, in addition to the other confessed and ample means of the state," according to the *Commercial Advertiser*, "is all that is necessary to an entire restoration of the public credit." Similarly, the *New York Sun*, supposedly a neutral paper, exclaimed that "the Comptroller recommends the mode which we have always urged as the only proper one for every state to adopt in order to free itself from pecuniary embarrassments—that is, Direct Taxation. There is no other effectual remedy.—However bitter the pill, we must swallow it, and the sooner the better."[68] And the *Journal of Commerce* warned that "a people who will not submit to be taxed when the public interests require it, are not fit to be Republicans."[69]

The principal bankers of New York also supported this course of action. When Michael Hoffman, acting for the ways and means committee of the assembly, inquired of bankers whether the state could expect to receive additional loans to aid it in meeting its financial obligations, the response was negative. In a letter to the committee, Albert Gallatin, George Newbold, John J. Palmer, and C. W. Lawrence explained that they felt further loans would be "highly inexpedient and improper." Undoubtedly, the fact that the banks over which these men presided already held nearly $750,000 of state loans and their concern for the declining value of state stocks influenced their reluctance to grant new loans to the state. In any event, they took the opportunity to suggest an alternative method of restoring the state's finances to a safe footing. The remedy proposed was twofold: first, to provide for the

---

[67] *Assembly Document*, no. 61, February 15, 1842; the quotation is from page 15.
[68] Quoted in *Albany Argus*, February 21, 1842.
[69] Ibid., March 16, 1842.

payment of the interest and reduction of the principal of the existing debt; second, to guarantee that no additional debt would be incurred unless provision was made at the same time for its repayment. The initial step was to levy a tax of one mill "on the assessed property of the people of the state."[70]

The financial plan advocated by Flagg and the New York City bankers was the core of the bill reported out of the assembly ways and means committee on March 7, 1842. Titled "An Act to Provide for Paying the Debt and Preserving the Credit of the State," the bill provided for the suspension of all canal work (except that essential to navigation) and for a one-mill tax. The proceeds of the tax were to be divided between restoration of the General Fund and canal work, with all the first-year receipts going to the General Fund, and half thereafter. Although there was substantial opposition to the bill in the assembly, it passed by a 50-to-27 margin on March 19. Nearly all the negative votes came from Whigs.[71] In the senate, the opposition was more formidable, consisting of dissatisfied Democrats as well as Whigs. Daniel Dickinson, a Democrat, proposed a substitute bill that called for a one-percent tax on the capital stock of banks, banking associations, insurance, and trust companies and a continuation of the public works on a smaller scale. When this proposal failed, Conservative Democrats proposed other amendments to preserve public works on which construction had already begun. These, too, were voted down. Finally, on March 28, the tax bill passed the senate unchanged by a vote of 13 to 11.[72]

Passage of the "Stop and Tax" law did not remove development policy as an issue in New York politics. Most Democrats supported the new tax bill, as did New Yorkers living in the vicinity of completed canals.[73] It was also received favorably in New York City, even though, according to the *Journal of Commerce*, "it is well known that the burden will fall heaviest on this city." The *New York Evening Post* commented that "the passage of the tax bill by

---

[70]The letter was appended to the "Report of the Committee on Ways and Means" sent to the assembly on March 7, 1842, and reprinted in the *Albany Argus*, March 8, 1842. The *Argus* pointed out that two, and possibly three, of the signers were Whigs. And Jabez Hammond suggested that Whig bankers supported the finance bill because its effect was to raise the value of state stocks which they held as security for temporary loans; Hammond, *History of Political Parties*, 3: 285n. In an article titled "State Debts and Public Improvements," A. B. Johnson of Utica listed state loans from these banks as follows: Bank of America, George Newbold, president—$175,000; Bank of the State of New York, C. W. Lawrence, president—$22,302.59; National Bank, Albert Gallatin, president—$60,000; *Commercial Advertiser*, March 19, 1842.

[71]New York State, *Assembly Journal*, 65th Session, 528–533; the *Argus*, March 18 and 21, 1842; Hammond, *History of Political Parties*, 3: 278–279; Shaw, *Erie Water West*, 330–333; and Donovan, *Barnburners*, 24.

[72]*Albany Argus*, March 19, 1842; Hammond, *History of Political Parties*, 3: 279–285; Donovan, *Barnburners*, 24–25.

[73]Shaw, *Erie Water West*, 335.

the New York legislature, notwithstanding that it imposes a new burden upon the people, is a most popular measure. It is an act honorable to the virtue of our legislators, and its reception is equally honorable to the good sense of the people."[74]

Whigs, however, as well as communities along the line of uncompleted canals, generally opposed the tax bill. Some charged that it was designed solely to raise the value of stocks owned by capitalists and bankers.[75] But most opponents focused not on the one-mill tax, but on the provision in the law suspending further internal improvements. The *Commercial Advertiser*'s position was typical: "Of that portion of the act imposing the tax, we most cordially approve; but of the other features of the bill, arresting the progress of the public works, we entirely disapprove. The effect," according to the *Advertiser*, "is to saddle the people with the burden of interest upon a debt of $15 millions of dollars, for an indefinite length of time, when the anticipated profits from the works themselves . . . are deferred for a period of unequally indefinite length."[76] Horace Greeley, of the *New York Tribune*, reacted similarly. He charged that the "Loco-Foco policy" of stopping public works, in the midst of a depression, aggravated the economic situation by throwing three or four thousand laborers, most of them immigrants, out of work.[77] In October Greeley clarified his position even further: "If the legislature had deemed even a larger tax necesssary to the *vigorous prosecution* [sic] of those works, we should have sustained its adoption. But to tax merely to raise the price of stocks, or rather, we suspect, to render Internal Improvements unpopular with the people, by charging upon it the necessity for taxation, seems a wanton aggravation of the public burthens at a time of great and general depression, and as such we oppose it."[78]

The debate over the "Stop and Tax" policy dominated New York politics for the remainder of 1842. Governor Seward, whose term in office had not yet expired, mounted an unsuccessful effort to resume internal improvements when the legislature met in special session in August to reapportion congressional districts.[79] In the fall elections, the new taxing policy overshadowed all other local issues.[80] In the end, the Radical position was sustained, though the split within the Democratic party between the "Hunkers," who

[74]Quoted in the *Argus*, April 2, 1842.
[75]Ibid., August 19 and September 28, 1842.
[76]*Commercial Advertiser*, March 29, 1842.
[77]*New York Tribune*, June 21, 1842.
[78]Ibid., October 4, 1842.
[79]Lincoln, *Messages from the Governors*, 3: 1039–1050; *Albany Argus*, August 1, 26, 27, 1842.
[80]For a summary of the Whig position, see "Address of the Whig State Convention," reprinted in the *New York Tribune*, September 15, 1842.

favored continuation of the public works, and the "Barnburners" or Radicals ensured that internal-improvements policy would continue to play a vital role in New York politics.[81]

Despite opposition to the new policy, few could deny that the "Stop and Tax" law dramatically increased the value of state stocks. In the first month alone, the value of New York five-percent issues increased from 76 to 84, and six percents increased from 80 to 88½.[82] By the end of two months, seven percents sold at par; six percents reached par within six months; and five percents sold at face value within fifteen months. The combined effects of reduced expenditures, the direct tax, and the return of A. C. Flagg to the comptrollership restored confidence in the state's financial system and reassured capitalists of the safety of investment in New York state securities.[83]

But what of the long-term effects of the "Stop and Tax" law? To answer that question, we must examine the two distinct facets of the law: retrenchment and taxation. New York would ultimately resume construction on the canals in 1854, but the principle involved in the suspension policy set the pattern for future solutions to the problems generated by modernization. It foreshadowed a much broader withdrawal of the state from economic activities in the 1840s and 1850s.

More significant, the 1842 law established taxation as a permanent feature of state government. Although appealing to an older republican tradition, sponsors of the new tax law initiated the process by which a modern, rational financial system based on the taxation of real and personal property at a uniform rate would be established in New York State. To be sure, the levying of a one-mill tax in 1842 was but the beginning of a gradual development leading to the establishment of a State Board of Equalization in 1859 and an even more fundamental transformation of tax policy after 1880–1882.[84] After 1842 New York imposed the general property tax with regularity and came to rely on it as the principal source of state revenue. By 1860 it provided more than 80 percent of the revenue, as compared with 25 percent in 1820 and nothing in the period 1827–1842, when the state collected no such tax.[85]

---

[81] According to Hammond, the amendments to the "Stop and Tax" law proposed in the senate by Democratic members were "the first public demonstration in our *state legislature* of the difference . . . between that portion of the Democratic party called the Barnburners or radicals, and those that were afterwards called conservatives or Hunkers" (Hammond, *History of Political Parties*, 3: 283).

[82] *Albany Argus*, April 22, 1842.

[83] Hammond, *History of Political Parties*, 3: 285–286; see also Donovan, *Barnburners*, 25, and Shaw, *Erie Water West*, 335.

[84] *Laws of New York*, chap. 312, 1859; Sowers, *Financial History*, 130–132.

[85] Paul Studenski and Herman E. Kroos, *Financial History of the United States*, 2d ed. (New York, 1963), 130.

This increased reliance on taxation to finance state government may be viewed as part of the gradual rationalization of the political system. Given the state's phenomenal growth and enhanced importance in the national economy, it is inconceivable that New York could have long continued with a financial system as lacking in regularity and predictability as that which existed before 1842. If the internal-improvements experience proved anything, it was that long-range policy decisions could no longer be based on estimates of future revenues derived from investment dividends, lotteries, canal tolls, and land sales, all of which were subject to fluctuations beyond the control of the state. As New York's expenditures grew, so did the need for a continuous, dependable income. After 1842 taxation provided that source of revenue.

The increasing importance of taxation was not unique to New York. As noted earlier, many other states, particularly in the Northeast and Midwest, had embarked on extended improvement projects after the success of the Erie, only to confront similar financial difficulties after the Panic of 1837. Like New York, they typically resorted to retrenchment in the 1840s to stave off impending bankruptcy. As they did in so many other areas of social and economic policy, many also followed New York's lead and turned to taxation as the basis for a rational financial system. Indeed, the period from 1796 to the Civil War, according to Richard T. Ely, "witnessed complete establishment of the American system of state and local taxation."[86] Although not the only contributing factor, the debate over state debts and development policy in the states gave that process a powerful impetus.

But the acceptance of taxation was significant for another reason as well. It was a step toward a more explicit definition of political community. Central to the idea of general property taxation is the presumption of a commonality of interest the support of which justifies the use of the coercive power of the state. This attitude, of course, was not totally absent in the early period, but the vehement opposition to taxation for internal improvements suggests that local and regional sentiments were stronger. Moreover, an exalted conception of the public interest did not appear miraculously in 1842 as a result of statewide taxation. Indeed, tax assessment and collection remained a local matter until 1859 when the State Board of Equalization was created to deal with inequitable assessments among the counties. But even with these qualifications, the 1842 tax law stands out as a landmark on the road to a modern conception of the state.

---

[86]Richard T. Ely, *Taxation in American States and Cities* (New York, 1888), 131.

ALTHOUGH INTERESTING and important in their own right, the People's Resolutions and the "Stop and Tax" law were symptomatic of a much broader transformation of politics and governance in New York in response to the emergence of a market economy. Perceptions of the economic crisis between 1837 and 1843 and attempts to minimize its corroding effect on political legitimacy established a pattern of response that shaped the state's political system for decades to come. Central to that response was the belief that the financial crisis was essentially a political problem, both in the practical and theoretical sense. New Yorkers, therefore, sought political remedies. Intense partisan debate, furthermore, shaped the solutions that ultimately emerged. Indeed, partisan differences prevented the emergence of a consensus on the proper response to this "crisis of distributive politics."

Partisan divisions alone, however, do not explain either the nature of the debate over state debts and development policy or its significance. For one thing, the most intense conflict occurred *within* the Democratic party and was partially responsible for a breach within the leadership of that party that would endure throughout the 1840s. Nor was the Whig party united on the issue. Although most Whigs opposed the final form of the "Stop and Tax" law, some Whig bankers clearly favored it. It is equally clear that local and regional interests, when state policy affected them, were more important than partisanship. A liberal–conservative dichotomy also fails to explain the debate. Radical Democrats echoed old republican principles in their rhetoric even as they advocated a form of direct democracy and committed the state to a modern system of direct taxation. Whigs, on the other hand, whom historians have come to see as positive liberals and modernists because of their support for internal improvements and their acceptance of the positive state, rejected taxation as a solution to the state's financial problems even as some of their number, such as Ruggles and Seward, formulated a modern rationale for such a policy.

Viewed broadly, however, from a developmental perspective, certain patterns do emerge. In the first place, New York's political and financial problems were systemic in nature. Undoubtedly, there was a sufficient number of corrupt, selfish, and conniving men to make contemporary arguments that the state's difficulties were caused by corruption and a betrayal of the public interest sound plausible. But there were others, many others, who were not demonstrably less public-spirited or more corrupt than those who elected them. In any case, reliance on such an interpretation to explain New York's predicament fails to account for the similar experiences of many other states in this period. In the final analysis, the problem was less in the hearts of men than in a system of allocation no longer capable of sustaining support for the political system.

It was no accident, furthermore, that the legislature became the target of public discontent. According to tradition and political theory, the legislature was preeminently the embodiment of the popular will. But the ideology of republicanism, in conjunction with deeply rooted fears of power and authority, had created a particular kind of legislature, one characterized by frequent elections, rapid turnover, intense localism, and a profound antipathy to the positive exercise of power. In the context of a rapidly changing society and economy, the legislature proved incapable of rationally allocating the state's resources and governing authoritatively. Failure, in the popular mind, became synonymous with corruption; lack of power to govern was translated into abuse of power.[87]

Confronted with the excesses of a system of politics based on distribution and threatened with financial collapse and further erosion of political support, New Yorkers were forced to choose between the continuation of an activist government, with perhaps a reformed system of politics, and a government of reduced powers and a minimal role in the economy. The solution ultimately adopted was not to change the system of politics, but to reduce pressure on the political system by withdrawing the state from certain types of economic activities—thus the decision in 1842 to halt further public works construction. At the same time, New Yorkers increased the political system's capacity to function effectively in meeting the demands placed on it by creating a more rational financial system based on general property taxation. Finally, with the People's Resolutions, Radical Democrats sought to strengthen the participatory elements of the system by shifting the basis of legitimacy from representation, which had served to legitimate government since the Revolution, to a form of direct democracy. In effect, two competing, but also overlapping, strategies of legitimacy were emerging. One, combining both radical and conservative elements, sought to resolve the tensions and contradictions in the political system by drawing on the radical Revolutionary tradition and advocating further democratization. The second, competing strategy was to reshape the structure of politics and government along more modern lines, emphasizing the values of efficiency, stability, and predictability. The interaction of these two strategies of legitimacy would continue to shape patterns of governance in the state through the middle decades of the century and beyond as New Yorkers struggled to develop a political order consistent with democratic principles, yet functional in a capitalist, market economy.

---

[87] A similar point is made in J. Mills Thornton, III, *Politics and Power in a Slave Society: Alabama, 1800–1860* (Baton Rouge, Louisiana, 1978), 78–79.

[6]

The Constitution of 1846 and the
Democratic Strategy of Legitimacy

THE DEMOCRATIC strategy of legitimacy prefigured by the debate over state debts and development policy in 1841 and 1842 is most clearly evident in the movement to revise the state constitution. This episode, which held center stage in the political arena for more than three years, culminated in the Constitution of 1846. Demands for a new constitution stemmed most immediately from the failure of the "People's Resolutions" and the desire of Radical Democrats to place the "Stop and Tax" policy beyond the reach of subsequent legislatures. But the roots of constitutional reform went deeper. Its origins must ultimately be sought in a system of politics fundamentally incapable of the rational allocation of resources in a modernizing environment and in the inevitable erosion of legitimacy that resulted.

In the broadest sense, constitutional revision was part of the continuing effort to resolve the twin problems of allocation and legitimation. Theoretically, the kinds of pressures that confronted the political system in the 1830s and 1840s might have been expected to stimulate greater efficiency in the processing of demands and, thus, development. But the dictates of a political culture predicated on the dispersal of power proved more important than the desire for efficiency in determining the political response to socioeconomic modernization. Faced with the excesses of a system of politics based on distribution, New Yorkers sought to maintain support for the political system by imposing stringent constitutional restraints on this type of policy and, simultaneously, strengthening citizen attachments to the system by expanding opportunities for participation. Both responses were firmly rooted in the existing political culture and in perfect harmony with traditional understandings of the meaning of democracy. To that extent, therefore, the Constitution of 1846 can be viewed as a stage in the process by which the basis of legitimacy for the political system shifted from representation to a form of direct democracy.

THE CONSTITUTION of 1821 provided the basic framework of politics and government in New York for nearly a quarter of a century. During these years, the legislature proposed and the voters ratified eight amendments to the fundamental law. None of these changes, however, challenged basic constitutional principles, and all were achieved through the normal amendment process. In 1826, for example, New Yorkers adopted two amendments broadening still further the role of the people in the political process. One abolished the tax or militia requirement for suffrage, thereby extending the right to vote to "every [white] male citizen of the age of twenty-one years," provided that he had been a resident of the state for one year and of the county for six months. A second amendment provided for the popular election of justices of the peace. An 1833 amendment gave to the people of New York City the right to elect their mayor, and that privilege was extended to all cities in 1839. On two occasions, in 1833 and 1835, the constitution was amended to alter the mechanics of state financing: in the first instance, the duty on manufactured salt was lowered; in the second, salt duties and auction duties were restored to the General Fund of the state. Finally, in 1845 New Yorkers abolished property qualifications for holding office and established more equitable procedures for the removal of judicial officers.[1]

Despite the obvious significance of some changes, not all New Yorkers were satisfied with piecemeal revisions of the fundamental law. By the end of the 1830s there were increasing demands for a complete overhaul of the existing constitution. A notable example of such discontent was the position taken by the Equal Rights party. Delegates to a state convention meeting in Utica in September 1837 issued an "Address" to the people of New York calling attention to "a multitude of political and social abuses in our state, which cry aloud to you for reform, and to heaven for judgment." The source of these abuses was the growth of an "aristocracy of wealth" which governed society under the "cloak of republicanism." The remedy was to restore the

[1] New York State, *Constitution of 1821*, Amendments 1–8. The best modern account of constitutional revision in the state is Lincoln, *Constitutional History of New York*. Also useful, however, are John H. Dougherty, *Constitutional History of the State of New York*, 2d ed. (New York, 1915); Benjamin F. Butler, "Outline of the Constitutional History of New York, An Anniversary Discourse, Delivered at the Request of the New York Historical Society in the City of New York, November 19, 1849," *Collections of the New York Historical Society*, 2d series, vol. 2 (New York, 1849): 9–75; Alexander, *Political History of New York*; and Hammond, *History of Political Parties*.

constitution to its proper function: "to prevent the officers of government from assuming powers incompatible with the natural rights of men." The constitution, therefore, should be revised to "define the powers and duties of legislators" and guarantee the "rights of the people against legislative usurpation." Of particular concern were legislatively created monopolies and what was termed the "system of artificial credit."

In addition to its "Address," the Utica convention drafted a proposed constitution, which it hoped would stimulate interest in constitutional reform and provide the basis for discussion of the changes to be made. Among the more specific reforms suggested were a requirement that the legislature pass only general and equal laws; that it "not charter or create any corporate or artificial body, nor confer on any individual or company either exclusive advantages or special privileges"; that the legislature not be allowed to borrow or create debts without the specific approval of the people at a general election; and that there should be no restriction on membership in any profession, business, or trade. The proposed constitution also included an elaborate plan for reorganizing the judiciary.[2]

Although many New Yorkers undoubtedly shared these concerns, most were not prepared in 1837 to support the drastic action of calling a constitutional convention. Further contributing to the failure of this early effort at reform was the fact that the Equal Rights party was absorbed into the Democratic party and ceased to exist as an independent force in New York politics after 1837. Loco-Foco principles, however, did not die. The changes proposed in 1837 formed the core of demands for constitutional revision in the1840s—particularly the emphasis on the limitation of legislative power— while former members of the Equal Rights party kept the question alive and provided an organizational base for the constitutional reform movement later. William F. Byrdsall, for example, who was secretary of the Equal Rights party, was also corresponding secretary of the New York Constititional Reform Association in 1843.[3]

The failure of the People's Resolutions in 1841 and 1842 marked the beginning of the successful drive for a state convention to revise the constitution. Frustrated in their attempts to limit the legislature's power to create debts, Radical Democrats had had to settle for the "Stop and Tax" law which halted further public-works construction and levied a modest direct-property tax. But this policy, though successful in restoring a measure of stability and con-

---

[2] "The Address and Draft of a Proposed Constitution; Submitted to the People of the State of New York, by a Convention of Friends of Constitutional Reform, held at Utica, September, 1837" (New York, 1837). See also Byrdsall, *History of the Loco-Foco or Equal Rights Party.*
[3] *Albany Argus,* August 22, 1843.

fidence in the state's financial system, lacked permanency. As early as the fall of 1841, leading Radicals such as Samuel Young, Michael Hoffman, and Azariah Flagg had expressed doubts concerning the wisdom of relying on a legislative solution to the debt problem and had begun to consider ways to place the "Stop and Tax" policy beyond the reach of future legislatures. Those earlier doubts about the permanency of legislative action were rekindled by Governor Seward's unsuccessful effort to repeal the tax law in the special session of 1842. There were also fears that the new conservative Democratic governor, William C. Bouck, would ally himself with internal improvement interests in an effort to circumvent the 1842 act. Consequently, by 1843 Radicals had accepted the necessity for constitutional revision, either by amendment, or failing that, a full-scale constitutional convention made up of delegates chosen by the people.[4]

Early in 1843 advocates of constitutional revision adopted a two-pronged strategy that would continue to characterize their efforts for the next three years. The issue was kept constantly before the legislature; at the same time, reformers conducted a well-organized public-relations campaign designed to sway public sentiment in favor of a constitutional convention. In February the issue was introduced into the legislature by Herkimer County Democrats proposing a debt-restriction amendment similar to the People's Resolutions. According to the "Herkimer Memorial," the legislature should not have the power to create debts except with the express approval of the people. State debts, it was argued, were different from every other type of legislative action. They could be created to buy political support, reward political followers, gratify particular interests, or bribe particular localities. Once created, furthermore, debts imposed a moral obligation on the present and future citizens of the state which too often led inevitably to the imposition of new taxes. The remedy was to restrict the power of the legislature to create new debts in excess of $1 million without the clear approval of a majority of the voters of the state at a general election.[5]

The Herkimer Memorial was referred to a select committee of the assembly which reported its findings to the full house on April 1. After reviewing the growth of the state debt, the increased taxation this had necessitated, and

---

[4] Hammond, *History of Political Parties*, 3: 269, 286–287; Lincoln, *Messages from the Governors*, 3: 1039–1050. Although fears of collusion were probably unjustified, Governor Bouck did recommend in his annual message that unfinished canals be completed "with strict reference to the financial condition of the State." See Bouck's 1843 message in Lincoln, *Messages from the Governors*, 4: 17–18.

[5] "Memorial of a Convention of Democratic Delegates, held at Herkimer in the County of Herkimer, on the 18th February, 1843, asking for an amendment to the Constitution, relative to the creation of a State debt, etc.," *Assembly Document*, no. 90, February 1843.

the inadequacy of existing constitutional safeguards against imprudent legislative appropriations, William McMurray reported that a majority of the committee favored adoption of the proposed changes.[6] More interesting, because it struck to the very heart of the issue, was the minority report submitted by Wells Brooks. According to Brooks, the proposed amendments involved nothing less than "the great principle of whether *the* [sic] laws for the creation of debt, should *or should not* [sic] be submitted to the people." Implicit in this question was the very nature of the state's form of government. Was it in fact, as the founders had intended, to be a representative government, or a direct democracy in which the people of New York legislated for themselves "in one common gathering"? Adoption of the proposed amendments, he continued, would lead to "an entire abrogation of representative power, and the substitution of anarchy and confusion for that order and efficiency which prevails under a representative or republican form of government." In any event, the charge that past legislatures had abused their powers by creating debts for internal improvements was exaggerated. The great advantages to the state of the system of internal improvements more than outweighed any errors of judgment that may have been made. Besides, the legislature had given the people what they wanted. "The measures, adopted, by which the state has become heavily indebted, whether wise or unwise, were the *measures* [sic] of the people themselves, enacted through their representatives. The judgment of the representative was a true index to that of the people. The voice of the one was but the echo of the other."[7]

Despite the favorable majority report, the 1843 legislature took no further action on the Herkimer Memorial. Thus, with the close of the legislative session, emphasis shifted to the public-relations campaign for a state convention. In county Democratic conventions, mass meetings, and the press, reformers reiterated their demand for constitutional revision. They also organized, by joining together in a loosely coordinated, statewide network of associations favoring constitutional reform. By mid-summer this was formalized with the creation of the State Association for Constitutional Reform, with Michael Hoffman as its president. The executive committee of the association included Charles S. Benton of Herkimer, Henry W. Strong of Rensselaer, Hugh T. Brooks of Wyoming, Henry R. Seldon of Monroe, R. H. Williams of Yates, Hiram McCollum of New York, Lorenzo Sherwood of Madison, George W. Clinton of Erie, and Henry O'Reilly of Albany.

[6]"Report of the majority of the select committee on the Herkimer Memorial," *Assembly Document*, no. 152, April 1, 1843.
[7]"Report of the minority of the select committee on the Herkimer Memorial," *Assembly Document*, no. 153, April 1, 1843.

One of the first acts of the committee was to issue a circular in July prescribing the tactics to be used in generating proconvention sentiment. As elaborated in an open letter from the committee in October, these tactics were to include publishing of the *Democratic Reformer*, a journal to be issued semimonthly from Albany to reprint speeches, essays, and resolutions relating to constitutional reform; discussing the issue in town and county Democratic conventions; questioning senate and assembly candidates about their position on reform; and creating a network of reform associations, with corresponding committees, throughout the state. In response to this appeal, associations for constitutional reform began to appear in various parts of the state. It is not surprising that one of the first to be created was in Herkimer County. On July 24, 1843, reform-minded inhabitants of Herkimer, mostly Democrats, organized, with Humphrey G. Root as chairman and J. L. Hamilton as secretary, and adopted a "Declaration of Principles."[8]

The centerpiece of this organizational strategy, however, was New York City. As early as July 4, the executive committee of the state association had announced plans for a series of meetings to be held in New York in early August to publicize the need for a constitutional convention. On July 18 New York City's Association for Constitutional Reform was organized with Abraham D. Wilson as president, Hiram McCollum and John Windt as vice presidents, J. S. Schultz as treasurer, William F. Byrdsall as corresponding secretary, and Edward Smith as recording secretary. A committee of arrangements, consisting of John Commerford, Elisha P. Hurlburt, J. Bogert, D. D. Smith, and J. W. Brown, was appointed for the mass meeting now scheduled for August 15. At a subsequent meeting of the association on July 17, invitations were extended to prominent advocates of constitutional reform throughout the state to attend and address the August 15 meeting. Among those invited were C. C. Cambreleng, Michael Hoffman, Arphaxed Loomis, Gerrit Smith, Lorenzo Sherwood, Albert H. Tracy, Henry W. Strong, Silas Wright, Azariah C. Flagg, Henry O'Reilly, and George P. Barker. Most, as it turned out, were unable to attend, sending letters expressing their support for the movement instead. Nevertheless, a "mass convention" was held at the Broadway Tabernacle in the afternoon and evening of August 15. Those at the meeting, presided over by Mayor Robert H. Morris, heard speeches from

[8] *Albany Argus*, October 22 and 23, 1843; "History of Constitutional Reform in the United States," *The United States Magazine and Democratic Review*, 18 (June 1846): 405; and *The Albany Democratic Reformer, Embodying Documents Concerning Governmental Reformation in the State of New York* (Albany, N.Y., 1844), 1–8.

Morris, Lorenzo Sherwood, Theodore Sedgwick, and others, and adopted nine resolutions outlining the objectives of the association.[9]

The New York City convention was but the largest of several such gatherings around the state which kept the issue of constitutional revision before the people during the waning months of 1843. On November 21, reformers met in Albany to pass resolutions, hear Michael Hoffman deliver a two-hour speech advocating reform, and organize a reform association for the County of Albany. Before the end of the year, similar meetings were held in Newburgh, Poughkeepsie, and some of the smaller towns and communities of the state, and constitutional reform associations began to appear modeled after those created in New York City and Albany.[10] Simultaneously with these developments, essays and editorials debating the issue of constitutional reform began to appear with increasing frequency in the New York press. And in December the first of a series of articles written by John Bigelow, New York City attorney and advocate of reform, was published in *The United States Magazine and Democratic Review*.[11] Thus, by the end of 1843, the mechanisms were in place for a full-scale debate over the necessity for constitutional revision.

Radical or Barnburner Democrats formed the core of the movement. And although their initial interest centered on the debt-restriction amendment, they soon widened their demands to include more general restraints on the legislature, the reorganization of the judiciary, and the election of state officers. Speaking principally through the *Albany Atlas* and *New York Evening Post*, Radicals such as Michael Hoffman, Elisha P. Hurlbut, Samuel Young, and Arphaxed Loomis kept up a constant agitation for a convention to bring about constitutional change. Hoffman's views were typical of the Radical position. In a letter to the corresponding secretary of the New York constitutional-reform association in August 1843, he charged that the unrestrained delegation of power under the existing constitution had allowed the creation of artificial wealth and huge state debts; had lent millions to fraudulent and bankrupt companies (such as the New York and Erie Railroad); had created banking systems without personal responsibility on the part of

[9]*New York Tribune*, August 11, 1843; *Albany Argus*, August 22, 1843; *The Albany Democratic Reformer*, 5–21.

[10]*Albany Argus*, November 24, 1843; Hammond, *History of Political Parties*, 3: 387–388; and *The Albany Democratic Reformer*, 27.

[11]"Constitutional Reform," *The United States Magazine and Democratic Review*, 13 (December 1843): 463–576; other articles in the series are "History of Constitutional Reform in the United States," 18 (June 1846): 403–420; "The New York Constitutional Convention," 19 (November 1846): 339–348; "Constitutional Governments," 20 (March 1847): 195–204. Although none of the articles was signed, there is no doubt that Bigelow wrote them. See Margaret Clapp, *Forgotten First Citizen: John Bigelow* (Boston, 1947).

the bankers; had filled the statute books with charters and special privileges; had multiplied the number of state officers; had endowed the legislature with the highest judicial authority; and had rendered the law "deformed, dark, doubtful and uncertain." To remedy these abuses, Hoffman argued, constitutional reform must include financial retrenchment and the creation of a revenue system to repay the public debt; limitation of the legislature's power to create debts along the lines of the People's Resolutions; preservation of the Common School, Literature, and Deposit Funds; individual liability of bankers and bank corporations; prohibition of special legislation; election of most public officials; and separation of the judicial from the legislative power.[12]

In a December article of the *Democratic Review*, John Bigelow reiterated Hoffman's objections to the existing constitution and added a few of his own. The union of judicial and legislative functions in the Court for the Correction of Errors, he argued, made the constitution unduly susceptible to "political prejudices and partisan interests" and placed the senate in the ludicrous position of passing on the constitutionality of laws that it had participated in enacting. Furthermore, the relatively short tenure of most members of the court prevented "that stability and comprehensiveness in their decisions which the dignity and influence of the court demand." Bigelow also proposed that the state be made liable to suit by its creditors, as a matter of right and as a way to eliminate the mass of private bills passed at each legislative session. Other objections included the unrestrained delegation of eminent domain, the delay and expense of litigation, the growth of patronage, and the centralization of state power at the expense of counties and towns.[13]

Conservative Democrats, whose chief spokesman was Edwin Croswell, editor of the *Albany Argus*, generally agreed with Radicals on the need for some form of debt-restriction amendment, but opposed a constitutional convention. An amendment requiring that any new debt be approved by popular vote, according to the *Argus*, "could scarcely fail to prevent a return to the Whig policy of extravagance and debt. It is desired, if not demanded by a large body of democratic taxpayers. . . . It is due to them and to the magnitude of the subject, that such a proposed amendment be submitted to the people, for their ratification or rejection." But a convention, bred in a "spirit of demogoguism—a desire to overturn and remodel, for the sake of overturning—a desire of political and personal capital, from the belief that popularity will follow in the wake of a forward advocacy of sweeping changes through a convention in the organic law," was neither required nor demanded

[12]*Albany Argus*, August 22, 1843.
[13]"Constitutional Reform," 569–570.

by the people. Only four or five of the fifty-seven counties, according to Croswell, had called for a convention.[14] And despite constitutional reform meetings in various cities, there was no evidence that these reflected a popular movement. "When the people manifest literally no feeling on a given subject, and any movement in relation to it . . . is the result of labored effort and the extraordinary appeals of a few persons in one or two cities, it is scarcely to be regarded as an emanation from the popular voice."[15] Besides, as the *Catskill Democrat* pointed out, "there is a way, pointed out by the constitution itself, in which it may be modified, and the delay thrown around any material alteration, while it does not prevent its modification whenever necessary, yet tends to preserve it from being swept away in moments of popular excitement."[16]

Constitutional revision had also infected segments of the Whig party by the end of 1843. Their principal spokesman was Horace Greeley, editor of the *New York Tribune*, who in November proclaimed his support for reform and advocated a convention to accomplish that purpose. Specifically, Greeley favored biennial elections and legislative sessions; judicial reorganization; diminution of executive power and patronage; single-member legislative districts; abolition of all qualifications for black voters; some form of voter registration; and repeal of restrictions on clerical officeholding.[17] There were substantial differences between Greeley's reforms and those advocated by Radical Democrats. Financial retrenchment and individual liability for corporations received little support in Whig journals. Very few Democrats, on the other hand, favored unlimited black suffrage. But there were also significant areas of agreement, the most important of which for the future of constitutional reform was the acceptance of the necessity for a convention. Indeed, the *Tribune* seemed willing to forgo restrictions on any convention that might be called: "We are willing to carry the convention first, then let the Delegates, as elected and instructed by the People, make such reforms as they shall deem requisite and proper."[18]

Clearly, support for constitutional reform transcended established party lines. But the particular configuration of party politics in New York at this time favored constitutional revision. With the breach between the Barnburner and Hunker wings of the Democratic party widening each day, the Whigs seized every opportunity to drive a wedge between them, for their own party advantage. Thus, the Whigs, who held the balance of power

---

[14]*Albany Argus*, October 31, 1843.
[15]Ibid., November 24, 1843.
[16]Ibid., November 30, 1843.
[17]*New York Tribune*, November 15, 1843.
[18]Ibid., November 20, 1843.

within the legislature, sided first with one and then the other faction, depending on the issue and the likelihood of its perpetuating dissention among their opponents. On the question of a constitutional convention, the Whigs supported the Radical position and Whig assistance proved crucial in 1844 and 1845.[19]

A major obstacle to the cause of comprehensive reform was the fact that the Constitution of 1821 made no provision for amendment by a convention. According to the existing constitution, amendments had to pass two successive legislatures, first by a *majority* of the elected members of both houses, and then, in the following year, by *two-thirds* of the elected members of both houses. Only then could proposed amendments be submitted to the people at a general election. If a majority of the electorate approved, the amendments became part of the constitution.[20] Thus, as long as the possibility of constitutional revision through amendment procedures remained open, the chances for a convention were dim. As Jabez Hammond pointed out, convening a constituent assembly to alter the constitution was so revolutionary that to justify it, supporters had to prove that the changes advocated were "absolutely indispensable and necessary" and that they could not be achieved through the regular process.[21]

Conservative Democrats seized on this flaw in the reformers' position to try to deflect the momentum that was clearly building in favor of a convention. With the support of Governor Bouck, amendments were introduced into the 1844 legislature to (1) incorporate the essence of the "Stop and Tax" policy into the constitution; (2) restrict the power of the legislature to contract debts or lend the credit of the state without popular approval; (3) abolish property qualifications for officeholding; (4) safeguard judicial officers from removal by the legislature without cause; (5) increase the size of the Court of Chancery by adding three associate chancellors; and (6) enlarge the supreme court by adding two justices.[22] As the legislature debated these proposals during February and March 1844, Radicals kept up their pressure, through public meetings and petitions to the legislature, for a law submitting the question of a convention directly to the people.[23] In the end, however, their efforts failed, and the proposed amendments passed with the required

---

[19] Donovan, *Barnburners*, 44.

[20] *Constitution of 1821*, Article 8, Section 1.

[21] Hammond, *History of Political Parties*, 3: 423–424.

[22] Lincoln, *Messages from the Governors*, 4: 52–60; Hammond, *History of Political Parties*, 3: 539; and "History of Constitutional Reform," 405. See also *Senate Documents*, nos. 11, 13, 15, 16, 17, 22, 29, 36, and 90, 1844, and *Assembly Documents*, nos. 150 and 178, 1844.

[23] *New York Tribune*, February 5 and 10, 1844; *Albany Argus*, March 15, 1844; and Lincoln, *Constitutional History of New York*, 2: 102.

majority.[24] According to contemporary observers, a major factor in their success was the fear of party disharmony on the eve of the 1844 presidential and gubernatorial elections.[25]

For the amendments to be incorporated into the constitution, they still had to be approved by a two-thirds majority of the 1845 legislature and submitted to the voters for popular ratification. The newly elected Democratic governor, Silas Wright, threw his support behind constitutional change through the amendment process in his annual message to the legislature:

> Our present constitution has remained the fundamental law for nearly a quarter of a century, several amendments having been in that time adopted, in conformity with the provisions of that instrument for its own amendment. Hitherto that provision has satisfied the public mind, and led to the amendments demanded by the popular feeling and judgment. I consider it extremely desirable that this should continue to be found practically true, and that such a degree of harmony shall at all times prevail between the popular will and the legislative action, in reference to further proposed amendments, as shall supersede demands for constitutional change in any other form.[26]

Despite the governor's plea, however, the demand for a convention could not be silenced. Outside the legislature, constitutional reformers laid plans to "concentrate and systematize efforts for a most thorough agitation of the subjects of constitutional and legal reform." Some advocated that a state convention of reformers be held in Syracuse, Utica, or Auburn to promote constitutional change; others proposed a series of senate-district conventions for the same purpose.[27] A citizens meeting at Aurelius in Cayuga County recommended the organization of town and county associations to promote constitutional revision.[28] An additional impetus to the convention movement was the appearance of the Antirent party. As noted in chapter 2, after Stephen Van Rensselaer's death in 1839, tenants in the Hudson Valley rose up in protest against the leasehold system of land tenure and began to demand the right to purchase their land outright. By 1844 Antirenters were resorting to violence and terror in their campaign against the landlords. They also became a potent political force in the state. Antirent associations

---

[24] *Albany Argus*, March 20, 1844; Lincoln, *Constitutional History of New York*, 2: 71–72.

[25] Both Whig and Democratic papers commented on the impact of the upcoming elections on the issue of constitutional reform. See *New York Tribune*, February 5, 1844; and samplings of the Democratic press quoted in *Albany Argus*, March 21, April 26, 27, 1844.

[26] Lincoln, *Messages from the Governors*, 4: 108.

[27] *New York Tribune*, January 14, 1845.

[28] *Albany Argus*, February 7, 1845; *New York Tribune*, February 10, 1845.

appeared in eleven southeastern counties and resolved to support candidates for office who favored land reform. In the November 1844 election, seven counties sent Antirent assemblymen to Albany to seek the abolition of the leasehold system of land tenure, through a constitutional convention if necessary.[29]

When the amendments came before the assembly for the required second passage, therefore, they faced a formidable coalition of Barnburners, Whigs, and Antirenters. Central to this coalition were the Whigs, under the able leadership of John Young. The first step in procuring passage of a convention bill was to defeat the pending amendments, whose passage would, of course, made a convention unnecessary. Young and the Whigs joined with the Barnburners to defeat all but two of the amendments.[30] Then the Whigs and Barnburners united to pass a bill introduced by William C. Crain of Herkimer County to call a convention. Although conservative Democrats offered several amendments to the bill designed either to defeat it outright or to severely limit the activities of the convention, the bill finally passed on May 13, 1845. The final vote was 83 to 33 in the assembly and 18 to 14 in the senate, with every negative vote being that of a Hunker Democrat.[31]

According to the convention bill, a referendum was to be held at the annual election in November 1845. If a majority of the electorate favored a convention, 128 delegates were to be chosen at a special election in April 1846, with the convention to meet the following June. The people of New York would be given the opportunity to accept or reject the work of the convention at a general election in November.[32]

In the 1845 referendum, the electorate approved the calling of a convention by a vote of 213,257 to 33,860. The following April delegates were chosen in a special election, with the Democrats receiving a majority, and the convention met in Albany on June 1, 1846, to begin its work. After more than four months of mostly nonpartisan deliberation, on October 9 the convention adopted a new constitution with only six dissenting votes. Less than a month later, on November 3, the people of New York approved the new document by a vote of 221,528 to 92,436, while at the same time rejecting, by

---

[29] Cheyney, "The Anti-Rent Movement and the Constitution of 1846," 283–321; Ellis, *Landlords and Farmers*, 225–283; Christman, *Tin Horns and Calico*.

[30] The two amendments that passed were those abolishing property qualifications for holding office and safeguarding judicial officers from removal by the legislature without cause; both were subsequently approved by the voters and incorporated into the constitution; see Thorpe, *Constitutions*, 5: 2653.

[31] Hammond, *History of Political Parties*, 3: 535, 544, 554; Donovan, *Barnburners*, 68–69; Alexander, *Political History of the State of New York*, 2: 97–100.

[32] *Laws of New York*, chap. 270, 1845.

an overwhelming margin, a separately submitted provision that would have granted equal suffrage to free blacks.[33]

Several conclusions seem warranted by this brief examination of the movement for a constitutional convention. First, constitutional reform did not emerge spontaneously from an aroused citizenry. Rather, the issue was kept alive by highly committed individuals and groups who, though often disagreeing on specific goals, were united in the belief that comprehensive reform of the fundamental law held the best hope for a durable solution to their particular grievances. This is not to suggest the absence of broad popular support for constitutional revision. On the contrary, the margins of victory in those elections that might be regarded as referenda on the question were consistently and impressively large. As is often the case in the twentieth century, however, constitutional reform does not appear to have aroused the enthusiasm or stimulated the levels of participation one often finds in the more partisanly oriented elections of this period. Thus, although New Yorkers approved the calling of a convention by a margin of 179,397, the 213,257 yes votes in the 1845 election represented only about 40 percent of the eligible voters. The combined vote on the issue, furthermore, was substantially below the 487,283 votes cast in the gubernatorial election the previous year and well below the 334,632 votes cast in the 1845 senatorial elections. A similar pattern of participation characterized the April 1846 special election to select delegates to the convention, when only about 250,000 New Yorkers bothered to vote, less than one half of the potential electorate. Even the 313,964 total vote on final approval of the new document was small by contemporary standards.[34]

It is tempting to conclude from these figures that most New Yorkers were indifferent to the subject of constitutional reform. But low voter participation is not necessarily a reflection of citizen apathy. Rather, it may simply mean that New Yorkers were not particularly divided on the necessity for fundamental change. The fact of the matter is that dissatisfaction with the existing system of politics was widespread. Through organization and agitation, reformers effectively appealed to this popular discontent and channeled it into the effort to reshape the political system through constitutional revision.

Second, the constitutional revision movement does not lend itself to a straight party analysis. Elements of both major parties, as well as other polit-

[33]Ibid.; Thorpe, *Constitutions*, 5: 2692; "Constitutional Reform in the United States," 407; Dougherty, *Constitutional History of New York*, 159–161; and Alexander, *Political History of the State of New York*, 2: 103. On the issue of Black suffrage in New York, see Phyllis Field, *The Politics of Race in New York: The Struggle For Black Suffrage in the Civil War Era* (Ithaca, 1982).
[34]*Albany Argus*, July 8, November 24, 1846; Thorpe, *Constitutions*, 5: 2692.

ical groups such as the Antirenters, eventually joined together to demand changes in the state's constitution. There were major differences of emphasis, to be sure, but there was also substantial agreement on the necessity for judicial reorganization, a limitation on legislative power, the reduction of executive patronage, and the substitution of general for special laws.

This is not to say that party considerations played no role in the debate. Obviously they did. For one thing, the issue of constitutional revision further divided the Radical and Hunker wings of the Democratic party, a division the Whigs were quick to exploit. Throughout the debate, furthermore, all factions sought to protect the vested interests of the party as institution. Democrats and Whigs alike were acutely aware that any tampering with the fundamental rules of the political game opened up the possibility of one party achieving a partisan advantage over its opponents. The *Albany Argus*, for example, charged that "a convention is an experiment extremely hazardous to the democratic interests, and to the public well-being to which the democratic ascendancy has contributed. . . . It is greatly desired and urged by the Whigs as a party measure, from which they hope to reap a party advantage." Other Democratic journals favored a convention but were reluctant to join hands with the Whigs to accomplish that purpose.[35] The *New York Tribune*, on the other hand, pleaded for a nonpartisan convention but warned Whigs to be vigilant in preserving their interests on such questions as single-member districts, executive privilege, and any changes in suffrage laws.[36] Whigs, of course, being out of power at the time, had nothing to lose by a convention; conservative Democrats feared that a convention would jeopardize their control of the state. Jabez Hammond explained the latter's position this way: "We have now the whole judiciary; and the appointing power, both executive and legislative, is now in our hands and likely to remain so. We, therefore, can, by no possibility, gain any thing, but may lose much."[37]

Thus, despite a great deal of rhetoric and posturing by party leaders, the role of parties in this debate was essentially negative: though support for constitutional revision transcended party lines, vested party interests proved to be a major obstacle to the calling of a convention. It would be extremely shortsighted, therefore, to attribute passage of the Constitution of 1846 solely to the machinations of political parties. To do so would be to seriously misjudge the significance of the critique of the existing constitution and to trivialize the long-range implications of constitutional change for the political system.

[35] *Albany Argus*, April 28, 1845.
[36] *New York Tribune*, November 8, 1845; April 7, 1846.
[37] Hammond, *History of Political Parties*, 3: 535–536.

THE CONSTITUTIONAL revision movement was ultimately rooted in a systemic crisis. By the 1840s an increasing number of New Yorkers, representing diverse political persuasions, had begun to question the existing system of politics and, implicitly, its ability to resolve the problems of allocation and legitimation in a rapidly expanding society and economy. The array of criticisms, proposals, and counterproposals at times appeared bewildering; there nevertheless existed a core of concerns that transcended partisanship and that reflected structural and ideological factors inherent in the nature of the political system. Those concerns are ultimately traceable to eroding support for the legislature and, by extension, for the representative system of government itself. They produced a constitution that radically altered the political expectations of New Yorkers by limiting legislative authority, redistributing power within the government, making the entire system more directly responsive to the people, and generally redefining the role of government in society.

The single most important change was a dramatic reduction of legislative power. For more than half a century, the legislature had enjoyed virtually unchallenged dominance in the political system. By the mid-1840s, however, many New Yorkers had come to believe that the result of unrestricted representative government was corruption; special interest domination of the legislative process; legislative agendas overwhelmed by the annual flood of special, local, and private bills; and huge state debts, arising principally from the logrolling of ill-conceived and untimely internal-improvement projects. The politics of distribution, in short, had run amok. The remedy was to drastically curtail distributive outputs while, at the same time, imposing tough new standards of legislative procedure and bringing the legislature more directly under popular control.

No aspect of public policy was more controversial than the state finances, and none received greater attention in the new constitution. The desire to limit the legislature's power to create debts had, of course, been one of the principal reasons for calling a convention. Moreover, preceding legislatures had expended vast amounts of time and energy debating whether or not to continue the state's policy of promoting internal improvements and how best to retire the existing state debt. Article 7 of the constitution attempted to resolve both problems. The canal debt was to be paid by the creation of a sinking fund out of the canal revenues. The sum of $1.3 million was to be set aside, after expenses and repairs on the canals, each year until 1855 for liquidation of the principal and interest; after 1855 the figure was to be $1.7 million. A similar fund was to be created for repayment of the General Fund debt, with $350,000 pledged to that purpose until such time as the canal debt was paid; then the amount would increase to $1.5 million. Only after these sums had been supplied, and an additional $200,000 set aside for the state's yearly expenses, could the legislature apply any remaining canal revenues to enlargement of the Erie Canal or completion of the Genesee Valley and Black River canals.

The constitution also anticipated future financial contingencies. If state revenues proved inadequate to defray necessary governmental expenses, for example, the legislature was authorized to dip into surplus canal revenues for an additional $150,000 per year, provided that the two sinking funds remained inviolate. Furthermore, if either or both sinking funds proved inadequate to satisfy public creditors, the legislature was required to levy taxes to increase those funds to the appropriate level.[38] Thus, by specifically outlining a financial system of repayment of the state's debts and making further expenditures for internal improvements contingent on the successful operation of that system, the constitution severely circumscribed the legislature's discretion in financial matters.

In an effort to prevent a recurrence of past financial debacles, the convention wrote into the new constitution precise guidelines for handling future state appropriations and the creation of new debts. Henceforth, no money could be paid out of the treasury without a specific appropriation by the legislature, and such appropriations were not to exceed two years in duration.[39] The legislature was also expressly forbidden from lending the state's credit to any individual, association, or corporation.[40] And, just as the convention prescribed the manner in which old debts were to be repaid, so too the circumstances under which new debts could be incurred were spelled out. The state could meet "casual deficits or failures in revenues" by borrowing, so long as the debt at no time exceeded $1 million. In addition, the legislature could contract debts to "repel invasion, suppress insurrection, or defend the state in war." But no other debt could be incurred unless it was authorized by law, limited to a single objective, included provision for a direct annual tax sufficient to pay interest as it came due and to retire the principal within eighteen years, and was approved at a general election.[41]

These financial provisions reflected a decade of frustration and the depths to which confidence in the legislature had sunk. Not only did the constitutional convention, in effect, assume "legislative" powers in the most controversial area of public policy, it virtually removed that issue from the

[38] *Constitution of 1846*, Article 7, Sections 1–5. For the debates in the convention, see S. Croswell and R. Sutton, *Debates and Proceedings in the New York Convention for the Revision of the Constitution* (Albany, N.Y., 1846).

[39] Article 7, Section 8.

[40] Article 7, Section 9.

[41] Article 7, Sections 10–12.

legislature's domain for the future. On the one hand, certain types of economic activity (such as lending the state's credit) were strictly forbidden; on the other, final approval for any new debts beyond the minimal $1 million for "casual" expenses was vested directly in the people. At the same time, the constitution struck at the practice of logrolling by requiring that all such debt bills be limited to a single object and that popular approval be achieved in a general election when no other law, bill, or amendment was being considered.[42] Clearly, New Yorkers blamed the legislature for the overexpansion of improvement projects during the 1830s and the fiscal problems that followed.

Next to state finances, no aspect of public policy had been so frequently and vociferously criticized as New York's corporate policy. Charges of "special privilege" and "monopoly" had been part of political rhetoric since the first business corporation was created by special charter. Early in the century, concern over the political influence and logrolling that seemed so much a part of the process of creating corporations led to the inclusion of a provision in the 1821 constitution requiring that all special incorporation charters be passed by a two-thirds majority of the legislature.[43] In the context of the rapidly expanding economy of the 1820s and 1830s, however, this provision had little impact on the proliferation of special charters. Thus, by the mid-1840s, demands for the prohibition of special incorporation had merged with the larger constitutional-revision movement. Delegates at the constitutional convention discussed the issue of corporate policy at length, adopting in the end a compromise position requiring that most corporations be created by general law, the only exceptions being municipalities and "cases where in the judgment of the legislature, the objects of the corporation cannot be attained under general laws."[44] The door was thus left open for a continuation of special incorporation, but the principle of general incorporation was given constitutional sanctity, and successive legislatures after 1846 worked to implement that principle.[45]

Although the convention treated banks separately from other corporations, new constitutional provisions relating to their incorporation affirmed the principle of general laws. The legislature was forbidden to pass "any act granting any special charter for banking purposes."[46] The effect of this provision was to legitimize the Free Banking Act of 1838 and to lay to rest the

---

[42] Ibid.

[43] *Constitution of 1821*, Article 7, Section 9.

[44] *Constitution of 1846*, Article 8, Section 1.

[45] See Seavoy, "Origins of the American Business Corporation," 189–205. The consequences of this provision will be examined in detail in a later chapter.

[46] Article 8, Section 1.

controversy over its constitutionality which had raged in the courts. The legislature was also barred from passing laws that sanctioned the suspension of specie payments, and bank stockholders were made "individually responsible to the amount of their respective share or shares of stock" for debts of the corporation, a provision amounting to a form of "double liability."[47] Thus, by carefully prescribing the liability of bank stockholders in the text of the constitution, the convention effectively superseded the legislature in this sensitive area of public policy. At the same time, however, the new constitution left it to the discretion of the legislature to determine the extent of personal liablity in other corporations, thereby, in practice, reaffirming the limited liability provided in the Revised Statutes of 1828.[48]

The problem of special legislation was not restricted to corporations. By the 1840s New Yorkers had come to realize that the sheer volume of private and special laws clogged legislative operations and hindered the rational formulation and administration of public policy. One critic complained, "It is almost impossible to secure the thorough discussion and passage of any law of a strictly general nature. Special laws occupy four-fifths of each volume of the laws which have been published in this state for several years past." The legislature, he continued, is occupied incessantly from the commencement to the close of its annual session in the passage of special acts, and finally rises year after year with a calendar of three or four hundred bills . . . not disposed of from the want of time."[49]

In addition to the proscription against special incorporation, therefore, the convention sought to reform legislative procedures to curtail logrolling and thus reduce the volume of special legislation. According to the new constitution, a majority of members of both houses would be required in the future to pass a bill. All private or local bills, furthermore, were to be limited to one subject.[50] More important, the legislature was authorized to delegate additional powers of a purely local or administrative character to county boards of supervisors, thereby reducing the number of such matters to be dealt with at the state level.[51] Although much needed and long overdue, these procedural and jurisdictional changes failed to completely resolve the problem of special legislation. They did nothing, for example, to decrease the

---

[47] Article 8, Section 7; Seavoy, "Origins of the American Business Corporation," 199–203; Hammond, *Banks and Politics in America*, 559n.

[48] Article 8, Section 2; Haar, "Legislative Regulation of New York Industrial Corporations," 196.

[49] "The New York Constitutional Convention," 343.

[50] Article 3, Sections 15 and 16.

[51] Article 3, Section 17; such a law was passed in 1849 (*Laws of New York*, chap. 194). This act and other developments in the growth of county boards of supervisors will be discussed in a later chapter.

number of claims against the state processed each year, claims that might well have been handled by the courts if the constitution had made the state liable to suit as some advocates of constitutional reform had suggested.[52] Indeed, it was not until 1874 that New York, through amendment, forbade the passage of private or local bills in a wide range of policy areas.[53]

A final area of public policy specifically affected by the Constitution of 1846 related to the old mercantilist laws ensuring the quality of goods through state inspection. "All offices for the weighing, gauging, measuring, culling or inspecting any merchandise, produce, manufacture, or commodity, whatever," according to the constitution, "are hereby abolished, and no such office shall hereafter be created by law."[54] The effect of this provision was more symbolic than practical, because compulsory inspection had ended three years earlier.[55] It was included primarily in response to demands for a reduction of state patronage. Still, it symbolized the change in political expectations wrought by the constitution. Active participation of the state in economic affairs was no longer regarded as a legitimate function of government. Indeed, a common characteristic of all the constitutional articles directly affecting policy was that each, in one way or another, diminished the role of government. In the process, the political system itself was redefined. The active, intimate, palpable connection between the political system and the socioeconomic environment gave way to a passive, supervisory, formalized system whose chief function was to provide a stable and predictable arena for the resolution of social and economic issues. The goal of such an arrangement was to give "utmost latitude" to individual action and industry, "leaving to custom and the convenience of those interested, to establish laws for their own guidance and regulation, in matters of trade, commerce, and

[52] This was one of the defects of the constitution pointed out by John Bigelow, "The New York Constitutional Convention," 343.

[53] Article 3, Section 18, added to the constitution by amendment in November 1874. The legislature was forbidden to pass private laws or local bills changing the names of persons; laying out, opening, altering, working or discontinuing roads, highways or alleys, or draining swamps or other low lands; locating or changing county seats; providing for changes of venue in civil or criminal cases; incorporating villages; providing for election of members of boards of supervisors; selecting, drawing, summoning or impaneling grand or petit jurors; regulating the rate of interest on money; the opening or conducting of elections or designating places of voting; creating, increasing or decreasing fees; granting to any corporation, association, or individual the right to lay down railroad tracks; granting to any private corporation, association or individual any exclusive privilege, immunity or franchise whatever; and providing for bridges.

[54] Article 5, Section 8.

[55] *Laws of New York*, chap. 202, 1843.

manufacture, compatible with equal rights of the community."[56] This principle, of course, lay at the heart of the Free Trade and Equal Rights movements, general incorporation, the philosophy of laissez-faire, and the liberal state.

In addition to losing power and influence as a result of this general redefinition of governmental functions, the legislature's character and its role in the political system were drastically altered in other ways as well. Whereas under the Constitution of 1821 the legislature (by joint ballot) appointed the principal state officers and the senate had concurrent power with the governor to appoint many lesser officials such as judges, the new constitution completely eliminated the legislature's appointive power by making virtually all administrative and judicial officials elective.[57] The legislature was also authorized to delegate such matters as highway administration, collection of taxes, and other strictly local functions to county boards of supervisors, thereby enlarging the authority of those agencies to handle local matters and reducing the range of administrative tasks falling within the purview of the state legislature.[58] Finally, the Court for the Correction of Errors was abolished and replaced with a Court of Appeals, thereby differentiating judicial and legislative power and preventing the legislature from ruling on the constitutionality of its own actions.[59]

The new constitution also altered the basis of representation in several significant ways. It reduced senatorial terms from four to two years, with all senators elected simultaneously, and created 32 senatorial and 128 assembly districts, each to elect one legislator.[60] The rationale for creating single-member districts was to increase the "representativeness" of the legislature. "The nearer the representative may be brought to his constituents," John Bigelow had written, "the greater will be his accountability, the more likely is he to be competent and disposed to represent them adequately and honestly, and the less chances are there for corrupt or perverse influences to

[56]"Report of the Select Committee in Relation to the Inspection laws," *Assembly Document*, no. 142, 1843, vol. 6.

[57]Articles 8, 9.

[58]Article 8, Section 17.

[59]Article 6, Sections 2 and 25. Critics of this fusion of legislative and judicial power frequently pointed to the General Banking Law of 1838 as an example of the senate, acting in its judicial capacity, upholding the constitutionality of a legislative action. This law had been passed by a simple majority of both houses despite the constitutional provision requiring that corporations be created by a two-thirds vote. When appealed from lower courts, the constitutionality of the law was upheld by the Court for the Correction of Errors. See John Bigelow's discussion of this issue in "Constitutional Reform," 569.

[60]Article 3, Sections, 2, 3, and 5.

operate upon the primary assemblies, in which the qualification and character of their representatives are determined."[61]

This was a classic justification for direct representation. But the triumph of this principle was made possible by underlying political and social realities. Much of the pressure for the establishment of single-member districts came from Whigs who felt that the general ticket unfairly discriminated against the minority party whose strength often lay in isolated pockets and was, therefore, absorbed and rendered meaningless by the nature of the system.[62] This argument in turn reflected a vastly more significant trend: the growing diversity of interests in the New York political system as a result of social differentiation, especially the divergence of country and city. As Horace Greeley put it in February 1846:

> There is no good reason whatever—not even that of convenience—for making the city of Albany dependent for her own especial Assemblymen on the rural portion of the county—so with Troy and Rensselaer Co.—Rochester and Monroe—Buffalo and Erie, etc., etc. Very often different portions of the Senate District, and even of the County, have diverse interests (real or fancied) which prevent even members of the same party acting in harmony. The very genius of Representation requires that the districts be as small as practicable and the selection of the member thus brought as directly as may be home to the constituency.[63]

Establishing single-member districts was thus a logical attempt to harmonize the idea of direct representation with the realities of social development. The necessity for this kind of change had been built into the political system from the beginning. It was part and parcel of the idea of dynamic representation, with periodic reapportionments based on the census. But the adoption of single-member districts also had consequences for the larger process of political development. For one thing, it meant even greater decentralization of the political system because counties were now broken up into smaller units for representational purposes. It also signaled a shift from political units to population as the basis for representation. To be sure, this transformation was by no means complete in 1846. The county was not entirely removed as a unit of representation since members of the assembly were apportioned among the counties, with local boards of supervisors being given the responsibility for dividing each county into assembly districts.[64] Still, it may have

[61] "History of Constitutional Reform in the United States," 408.
[62] *New York Tribune*, May 23, 1845.
[63] Ibid., February 23, 1846.
[64] Article 3, Section 5.

been the beginning of a process by which local attachments were undercut in preparation for a later mobilization of political identification with a broader political community. In the short term, however, it served to weaken even further the idea of any statewide public interest in New York. Finally, the shift to single-member districts may have contributed to the extraordinarily high rates of legislative turnover at mid-century. The evidence is unclear since the trend toward high turnover had been under way since the 1820s, but it is worth noting that the average number of first-term assemblymen reached 82.7 percent in the 1850s, after the change in the mode of electing legislators.[65] At the very least, it can be said that single-member districts did nothing to stabilize membership in the New York legislature.

The executive branch of government fared no better than the legislature at the hands of constitutional reformers. The relative power of the legislature and governor was not really in contention in 1846 as it had been in 1777 and 1821. Rather, reformers sought to diffuse the power of state government generally. Thus, far from benefiting from the antilegislative spirit of the convention, the governor's power was also diminished by the new constitution, albeit less dramatically than that of the more popular branch of government.

The chief complaint against the executive related to the distribution of patronage or, as it was often labeled, "executive influence." A frequent contributor to the *Albany Argus* wrote, "If to one man, or to a few men, be confided the choice of all or a large proportion of the subordinate officers of a government, the inevitable tendency of this is to promote subserviency and monopolize influence." Besides, such an arrangement inevitably "degenerates into a system of mere favoritism" because no executive could possibly judge of the qualifications of all his appointees.[66] The *Argus* agreed: "The genius of our government demands the greatest possible reduction of executive influence. It regards with jealousy the concentration of power in individual hands, where it may serve as a lure to make its possessor . . . the subject which the selfish or unprincipled strive to mislead or control."[67] Almost all who sought constitutional revision expressed similar sentiments. Indeed, few

---

[65] The nature of this trend is evident in the figure for the average number of first-termers by decade: 1820–29, 64.2%; 1830–39, 69.1; 1840–49, 78.6; 1850–59, 82.7. That this decade represented the peak is clear because the number of first-termers dropped below 80 percent in only one year in the 1850s (1857); the figure declined to 57.4 percent in 1865 and 55.0 percent in 1870. Figures were compiled from Franklin B. Hough, comp., *The New York Civil List*, (Albany, N.Y., 1860); and S. C. Hutchins, comp., *Civil List . . . of New York, 1869* (Albany, N.Y., 1869).

[66] "Western New York," *Albany Argus*, April 7, 1846.

[67] *Albany Argus*, March 17, 1846.

goals united the various groups involved in the constitutional reform movement as closely as the reduction of executive patronage.[68]

At the heart of this issue was the fear of centralization and the belief that "democracies are designed to be diffusive in their tendencies." The remedy, therefore, followed logically: divide the lawmaking and administrative power as far as possible, by transferring appointive powers "from the capital to the several counties, to be exercised either directly by the people, or through the agency of the boards of supervisors.[69] This was the solution adopted by the convention. All state officers were henceforth to be chosen at a general election; provision for the election of local administrative and judicial officials was to be made by the legislature on application of boards of supervisors.[70] The effect of these changes was to reduce the governor's power by removing the most effective means of maintaining party discipline on the one hand and the only means the governor had of exercising control and direction over the administration on the other. This was exactly the intent of reformers.

The authority of state officers was similarly reduced, and for basically the same reasons. Before 1846 the secretary of state, comptroller, treasurer, and attorney general were neither technically nor practically under the control of the governor. Each enjoyed an autonomous existence and independent power base by virtue of his being selected by the legislature. Such had been the accretion of power and influence to some of these officers, most notably the comptroller, that by the 1840s there were demands for a complete reorganization of the state departments to redistribute and balance their respective powers.[71] But the chief complaint, and the only one acted on at this time, had to do with the mode of selection. Theoretically, state officers were responsible to the legislature. In practice, critics charged, the reverse was true. "The length of time for which they are appointed," according to the *Argus*, "their habits of association and their position as political leaders, have rendered them more influential than the constantly changing body by which they are selected." Moreover, the existing method of appointment favored the localities in the immediate vicinity of the capital at the expense of more remote areas. "The election of state officers by the people," it was hoped, "will render the State Departments and the legislature more independent in their respective spheres of action; will check the inducements to intrigue and

---

[68]See, for example, the *New York Tribune*, March 4, 1846, and "History of Constitutional Reform in the United States," 412–413.

[69]*Albany Argus*, March 17, 1846.

[70]Articles 4 and 5; Article 6, Sections 15, 16, 17, and 18.

[71]See the series of articles signed "Western New York" published in the *Albany Argus*, May 22, June 4 and 9, 1846, and the *Argus*'s discussion of this issue March 25, 27, 28, 1846. This subject will be considered in greater detail in a later chapter on administrative developments.

interference; will result in a fair distribution of public officers throughout the State, and will impose reasonable periods for the tenures of their stations."[72] With these considerations in mind, the convention provided for the popular election of the secretary of state, comptroller, treasurer, attorney general, and state engineer. In addition, the new constitution reduced their terms of office from three to two years.[73]

The judicial branch was no more immune to criticism than the legislative and executive branches of government. Indeed, the desire for judicial reorganization and legal reform had been a major stimulant to the constitutional revision movement from the beginning. Lawyers and laymen alike complained of the inefficiency, delays, and expense of justice under the New York system. John Bigelow, for example, a New York City attorney, charged that as of June 1846 the supreme court, chancery, and Court of Errors were from two to four years in arrears in hearing cases and that such a state of affairs constituted a denial of justice.[74] Critics also deplored the fusion of legislative and judicial functions in the Court of Errors and the distinction between law and equity jurisdiction in the courts. Simultaneously, there was a determined effort to revise and simplify the rules of practice in the courts and to replace the "formless waste" of the common law, statutes, constitutions, commentaries, and reports that made up the "law" in New York with a code. Although numerous proposals for judicial change were discussed in the years preceding the convention, most critics accepted the general goals expressed by Bigelow as a minimum: a simplified system of procedure and an increase of justices adequate "to all the business, term by term, which shall arise within its jurisdiction."[75]

The convention responded to such concerns by completely reorganizing the state's judicial system. The new constitution created a court of appeals, with final appellate jurisdiction, to be made up of eight judges, four of whom were to be elected at large for eight-year terms and four chosen from among the justices of the supreme court having the shortest time to serve. It established a new supreme court with general jurisdiction in law and equity, to be composed of thirty-two justices elected from eight judicial districts for eight-year terms. There was also to be a system of county courts, with civil

---

[72]*Albany Argus*, March 25, 1846.
[73]Article 5.
[74]"History of Constitutional Reform in the United States," 413.
[75]"Letters From Honorable Michael Hoffman . . . on Judicial and Legal Reform," in Thomas P. Kettell, ed., *Constitutional Reform, in a Series of Articles Contributed to the Democratic Review* (New York, 1846), 58–70; "Constitutional Reform," 569–570; "History of Constitutional Reform in the United States," 413–419. For typical proposals for judicial reform, see *New York Tribune*, March 30, 1844; August 13, 1845; January 14, 1846; and February 23, 1846.

jurisdiction, the judges of which were to be elected for four-year terms. In addition, the legislature was instructed "at its first session after the adoption of this constitution" to appoint three commissioners to revise and simplify the rules and practice of the New York courts. Finally, in an effort to curtail the volume of litigation, the constitution authorized the creation of Tribunals of Conciliation, with no coercive power, to mediate between the parties of a controversy.[76]

THE CONSTITUTIONAL CONVENTION of 1846 is one of those pivotal events in American political history the deciphering of which promises to yield fresh insights into the dynamics of political development and governance in the nineteenth-century states. Marvin Meyers recognized as much when he chose to close his seminal study *The Jacksonian Persuasion* with an extended commentary on the constitutional debates and concluded that the convention represented "an epilogue to Jacksonian democracy." Meyers shrewdly, and correctly, observed that the differences between Democrats and Whigs became significantly narrower in the quarter century between 1821 and 1846, as the former grudgingly accepted the new economic order, including the corporation, and the latter came to terms with the reality of political democracy.[77]

Our review of the constitutional revision movement lends support to Meyers's interpretation of the partisan significance of the convention and underscores the importance of placing that event in the larger context of social and political forces transforming New York society. As suggested at the beginning of this chapter, demands for a new constitution were deeply rooted in contradictions in the political system itself. In the context of a rapidly changing society and economy that made new and qualitatively different demands on government, the politics of distribution became increasingly dysfunctional. As rising state debts, the growth of special-interest legislation, and charges of corruption and inefficiency in state government revealed the limits of a system of allocation based on distribution, the legitimacy of the political system began to be eroded. New Yorkers across the political spectrum began to question the efficacy of the representative system of government and to demand constitutional changes designed to democratize the political regime and return power to the people.

The central thrust of the new constitution was to restrict the scope of representative government, expand the opportunities for popular participation,

---

[76]Article 6; Dougherty, *Constitutional History*, 170–171; Butler, "Outline of the Constitutional History of New York," 66.

[77]Meyers, *Jacksonian Persuasion*, 253–275; the quote is from page 267.

and transfer important political authority to "the people" directly. It sharply curtailed the legislature's power in economic policy areas by forbidding it to contract new debts except under carefully prescribed conditions and with popular approval; by prescribing in detail the manner in which the existing debt was to be paid; by requiring specific appropriations of limited duration; by forbidding it to lend the state's credit; and by requiring the passage of general incorporation laws. In addition, the convention sought to reduce the annual outpouring of special legislation by imposing strict procedural guidelines designed to control logrolling and by delegating many duties previously performed by the legislature to county boards of supervisors. Thus, constitutional reformers placed vast areas of economic policy beyond the reach of legislative discretion and generally redefined the parameters of public authority by establishing specific, unambiguous limits on the functions of government and its role in society.

In addition to curtailing legislative authority, the Constitution of 1846 continued a trend begun earlier in the century toward increasing citizen participation in government. This is evident in provisions reducing the executive appointing power and requiring that most local officials be either elected or appointed by local governmental agencies. Similarly, state administrative officers and judges were to be elected rather than appointed after 1846. Single-member legislative districts replaced the general-ticket system, thereby increasing the representation of local patches of opinion. Finally, senatorial terms and those of the principal state officers were shortened. These changes contributed to the overall decentralization of the political system, making it more responsive to voters.

By far the most extraordinary development, however, was the tendency to involve "the people" directly and actively in the process of government. Inclusion of detailed provisions in the new constitution enjoining specific legislative actions gave the constitution the character of a legal code or super statute. Even then, the work of the convention had to be approved by the people in what amounted to a constitutional referendum. In the future, moreover, such referenda were to be a regularized part of government. The process of amending the constitution was liberalized and, more important, the people of New York were to be given the opportunity to express themselves on the issue of holding a constitutional convention at a general election every twenty years. But the most explicit manifestation of the desire to shift authority from the legislature to the people was the tendency to delegate ultimate decision-making power in important policy areas to the electorate. The convention, for example, chose to bypass the legislature on the explosive issue of granting the suffrage to free blacks, preferring instead to submit that question directly to the people. The new constitution also gave the people the final say in financial matters, requiring popular approval of any new debts in excess of $1 million. In short, the people were becoming a kind of "fourth branch of government."[78]

The democratizing tendencies of the Constitution of 1846 are beyond dispute. But what about its impact on the broader process of political development? Here the evidence is more ambivalent. Certainly, constitutional changes encouraged higher levels of participation in the political system, and such is usually considered a prerequisite of development. Less clear, however, is whether or not the system's capacity to manage the problems of a modernizing society was similarly enhanced. New procedural regulations on legislative behavior, the mandating of general incorporation laws, the delegation of many essentially local matters to local boards of supervisors, and the reorganization of the judicial system suggest a desire to increase the efficiency of the political system.

But there were contrary tendencies as well. By limiting legislative discretion, prohibiting certain types of economic activity altogether, and generally reducing the quantity and character of political demands, the constitution effectively eliminated a major impetus to development. As the range of permissible governmental activity was drawn more tightly, the necessity for rationalized political structures and processes became less compelling. Thus, the government's ability to affect the nature and direction of change was diminished, and its role became that of passive overseer rather than active participant. At the same time, decentralization and the popular election of administrative officials undermined the structural integration of the system, further inhibiting the process of political development.

In the final analysis, the Constitution of 1846 mirrored the tension between two competing strategies of legitimacy, both of which had their origins in the rejection of representative government. One sought to check the erosion of political support by democratizing the system even further; the other, less clearly articulated strategy emphasized the need for efficiency and rationality in policy-making and administration. It is not surprising that given the American political culture, New Yorkers opted in favor of a form of direct democracy. The fact that this response may have in some ways impeded the modernization of the political system was less important than the fact that it was consistent with traditional American principles. Given the political heritage of the Revolution and the popular commitment to democratic ideals,

---

[78]For the notion of "the people" as a "fourth branch of government," I am indebted to Abernethy, *Constitutional Limitations on the Legislature*, 16.

the choice was inevitable. The irony, however, is inescapable. In the face of rapid social and economic modernization, the price of maintaining the legitimacy of the political system was emasculation of government. Indeed, Americans have yet to reconcile the need for sufficient power to govern with the equally strong necessity for democratic controls.

[7]

The Administrative
Strategy of Legitimacy

EVEN AS New Yorkers restructured their political system along more democratic lines through constitutional revision, the nature of governance in the state was being transformed by other, less dramatic forces as well. Here too the impetus for change was ultimately the need to resolve the problems of allocation and legitimation in a rapidly changing society. But whereas the central thrust of the constitutional reform movement was to restrict the authority of government and institutionalize a form of direct democracy, this second and competing strategy of legitimacy involved the emergence of administration and the legitimation of policy processes through the establishment of uniform, politically neutral norms for formulating and implementating policy.

The emergence in recent years of the "organizational synthesis" of American history has tended to relegate the first half of the nineteenth century to a kind of prebureaucratic age characterized by the absence of significant progress in the development of modern, rational administration.[1] Although the general utility of such a conceptualization has been convincingly demonstrated, the New York experience reveals elements of continuity between the earlier and later periods. During the three decades between 1830 and 1860, New Yorkers struggled to develop an administrative capability to deal with the increasingly complex problems created by rapid social and economic change. Inevitably, the state's efforts to meet the accelerating demands of a modernizing society were shaped by traditional fears of centralized power,

---

[1] See, for example, Louis Galambos, "The Emerging Organizational Synthesis in Modern American History," *Business History Review*, 44 (Autumn 1970): 279–290.

the impact of social mobilization in the form of increased electoral participation, democratic pressure for elective officials at all levels of administration, and the fluctuations of inter- and intra-party conflicts. It is not
surprising that given this context, the record of achievement was modest.
Still, such early efforts cannot be ignored; they were significant forerunners
of later bureaucratic developments.

More important, the beginnings of administration are to be found not
only in the appearance of bureaucratic structures per se, but also in the
increasing tendency to administer or adjudicate social conflicts and policy
issues previously handled politically.[2] This tendency is strikingly evident in
at least two major developments in the pre-Civil War decades: the separation
of law and politics consequent on the rise of legal formalism and the emergence of incorporation by administrative procedure. This chapter traces
administrative developments and the resurgence of judicial power in the three
decades before the Civil War. Chapter 8 will explore the political significance
of the emergence of the principle of general incorporation from a similar
perspective. Only then will it be possible to elucidate the essential features
of the new political order emerging in New York at mid-century.

ONE OF THE most important administrative developments in the two decades
before the Civil War was the movement to divest the legislature of its essentially local duties. As noted earlier, the doctrine of legislative supremacy and
the relatively undifferentiated character of the political system in the early
nineteenth century had combined to make the legislature, in a very real
sense, the chief instrument of administration. Legislative influence extended
into the most remote village, and no issue—from tax collection to the regulation of dogs to the private claims of individuals—was too trivial for its
attention. Inevitably, this fusion of legislative and administrative functions
overloaded the legislative agenda with special acts of a purely local or administrative nature, thereby hindering both the formulation and implementation
of public policy and, at the same time, inhibiting the development of more
rational policy procedures.

Constitutional reformers had addressed this problem as part of their
broader attack on legislative power in the 1840s. Indeed, many procedural
and substantive changes wrought by the Constitution of 1846 had the effect,
either directly or indirectly, of reducing the administrative functions of the

---

[2] Two recent studies of bureaucracy and institutional development in the nineteenth cen-
tury which have influenced my thinking on this subject are William E. Nelson, *The Roots of
American Bureaucracy, 1830–1900* (Cambridge, Mass., 1982), and Skowronek, *Building a New
American State*.

legislature. Such was an inevitable byproduct of broad constitutional limitations of legislative power as well as specific prohibitions against aiding private enterprise, lending the state's credit, and creating debts. More directly, the curtailment of the legislative appointing power removed one of the principal mechanisms by which the legislature had traditionally penetrated the administrative process. No less significant, the constitutional mandate requiring the passage of general incorporation laws held the potential for stripping the legislature of one of its most time-consuming and consequential administrative roles. Finally, the Constitution of 1846 specifically authorized the legislature to delegate greater responsibility to local governmental bodies, thereby significantly reducing the legislature's role in local administration.

The delegation of such authority led directly to reinvigoration of local governmental institutions, particularly county boards of supervisors. From the Revolution to 1838, county boards of supervisors had slowly but steadily grown in power, as the legislature periodically granted new authority to one or more county boards by special acts and on occasion enacted limited general laws applicable to all counties. Such grants typically included the power to erect courthouses and jails; to annually examine all accounts against the county, apportion tax assessments among the towns, and appoint a clerk and county treasurer; to raise money for the construction of public buildings when required by the legislature; to pay the fees of district attorneys; to certify the accounts of loan officers; to award bounties for wolves; and to raise money for the encouragement of agriculture.[3]

In 1827 the legislature enlarged the duties of county boards relative to the assessment of taxes; distribution of school money; and the construction of highways, bridges, and ferries.[4] Over the course of the next decade, furthermore, special legislative acts delegated specific powers to particular county boards on about 350 occasions.[5] Finally, in 1838, the legislature enacted a general law "to enlarge the powers of boards of supervisors." It authorized supervisors to levy and collect such taxes as might be required to construct and maintain bridges, courthouses, jails, clerks' offices, and roads. In addition, the law empowered county boards to appoint special commissioners to lay out public highways, provided that the roads applied for were important and that the authority already granted to highway commissioners "cannot or will not be exercised to accomplish the laying out of such roads."[6]

---

[3] *Laws of New York; 1774–1775*, chap. 65, 1788; chap. 14, 1807; chap. 283, 1818; chap. 36, 1819; chap. 26, 1822; chap. 256, 1822.
[4] *Laws of New York*, 50th Session, 1827, vol. 2: 223–230.
[5] William C. Morey, *The Government of New York: Its History and Administration* (New York, 1902), 100n.
[6] *Laws of New York*, chap. 314, 1838.

Despite this gradual enlargement of the powers of county boards over local affairs, the question of local legislation became a major issue in the constitutional revision movement during the 1840s. Reformers seized on the mass of local and private laws passed by each legislature as a favorite target, pointing to the practical and theoretical absurdities of existing practice. Some focused on such inconsistencies as the fact that the 1838 general law was immediately followed in the session laws by "An Act Imposing a Tax on Dogs in the County of Putnam."[7] Others took the high ground of political and constitutional theory. Writing in 1843, for example, John Bigelow objected that the Constitution of 1821 had "seriously and unnecessarily diminished the legislative power of the counties and towns. . . . Our government is based upon the doctrine that every town [or county] knows its own wants and their remedies better than they are known by any other town."[8] Pursuing this theme in an 1846 article, Bigelow referred to counties as "small republics" within the state and declared that "the due moral influence of government can only be preserved where the states attend to the duties which are *necessarily* [sic] theirs, the countiès to theirs, the towns to theirs."[9]

Similar sentiments appeared in the *Albany Argus* on the eve of the constitutional convention. All local legislation, according to one correspondent, "should be removed from the capital, and placed in the hands of those immediately interested. It can be exercised by local tribunals more economically and more understandingly." The reasons given for this move were the amount of time and effort expended by the legislature on such "purely sectional objects"; the inability of the central government to ascertain the facts of a local problem sufficiently to assure due consideration; and the stimulus such action would give to legislative attention to "the great and general interests of our state . . . if they can be rescued from the mass of local and private bills which over-ride and bury them." Most important, however, such delegations of power would tend to break up centralization, divide the lawmaking power, and remove any improper influences on local matters resulting from mistaken opinions about the capital.[10] These arguments were even more persuasive when joined to the general attack on the centralization of the appointing power. The most frequently suggested remedy for the swollen patronage of the executive was to transfer that function to the counties. It was assumed, of course, that local communities would be better judges of the fitness of public officials.[11]

[7] Ibid., chap. 315, 1838.
[8] "Constitutional Reform," 570.
[9] "History of Constitutional Reform in the United States," 412.
[10] *Albany Argus*, March 17, 1846.
[11] Ibid.

Members of the constitutional convention were apparently persuaded by such arguments. The Constitution of 1846, as noted earlier, specifically authorized the legislature to delegate additional powers to local authorities.[12] In response to this constitutional mandate, a bill to vest legislative powers in county boards of supervisors was introduced in the 1847 legislative session.[13] Not until two years later, however, was such a law passed by both houses of the legislature. Governor Hamilton Fish, among others, supported passage of the bill, arguing that "a majority of the members of the legislature can have but little personal knowledge of the merits of most of the local questions upon which they are called to act. A transfer of the power over these questions . . . would bring the local legislation more nearly home to those directly interested in its results."[14]

The 1849 general law "to vest in the board of supervisors, certain legislative powers" is interesting both for what it did and as an illustration of the kinds of local matters that previously consumed a large proportion of each legislature's attention. It empowered county boards to create new towns, divide existing ones, or change their boundaries; to purchase real estate needed for county buildings or for support of the poor; to determine the site of public buildings; to sell or lease any real estate owned by the county; to change the location of any county building (not to exceed one mile); to levy and collect up to five thousand dollars annually for the above purposes; to borrow money for the use of the county; to authorize towns to borrow up to four thousand dollars per year; to abolish or revise the distinction between town and county poor; to extend the time for tax collections; to pass laws for the destruction of wild animals, regulation of game, and taxation of dogs; and to require periodic reports, under oath, from county officers.

Some New Yorkers expressed fear that the county boards would become too powerful under the new law, especially in those counties where the apportionment of representation on county boards was suspect. To assuage such concerns, procedural safeguards were included in the law with regard to several of the more sensitive powers. Thus, a majority of all elected members was required to exercise any of the powers listed in the act. But a two-thirds vote was required to divide or create a town, to change the site of county buildings within one mile, to abolish the distinction between town and county poor, and to regulate the destruction of wild animals. Finally,

[12] *Constitution of 1846*, Article 3, Section 17.
[13] *Albany Argus*, February 24, 1847.
[14] Lincoln, *Messages from the Governors*, 4: 434.

only by a two-thirds majority of two succeeding annual meetings could a board move the site of any county building beyond one mile.[15]

Contemporary New Yorkers tended to view this delegation of powers to the localities in terms of its impact on specific institutions at the state and local levels of government. As Governor Fish put it, the law would effectively "elevate the office of supervisor" and "leave to the State Legislature a larger portion of its time for the consideration of subjects of more general bearing."[16] The delegation of authority to local government would reduce the volume of local matters that regularly jammed legislative proceedings and provided the fodder for the bartering of votes and the logrolling of legislation so characteristic of this period. As one observer noted, such circumstances had made a farce of the legislative process:

> It is desirable that members of a representative body should take an interest in most of the subjects which come before them, and vote understandingly. What interest can a member from the city of New York take in a bill to regulate the killing of game or catching of fish in the county of Cattaraugus, or a bill to authorize a tax for building a court-house in the county of Chemung, or to designate the place for holding the next town meeting in the town of Bullville. These bills generally passed as a matter of course . . . or perhaps it forms an instrument for logrolling in relation to some bill of great public importance, some charter, or private claim. In a board of supervisors, every person would feel a personal responsibility for every vote he should give on these questions, and they would be decided more on their merits; or, if there was bargaining for votes, the interests of the whole state would not be made to turn on a local matter.[17]

In the final analysis, however, the significance of this delegation of power to counties transcends the obvious need to reform legislative procedure. From a developmental perspective, such grants of responsibility were part of the process by which political structures became functionally differentiated. The legislature, in effect, parceled out to local political authorities those duties no longer regarded as legitimate concerns of the central government. In doing so, it had to define, for the first time, really, exactly what constituted a strictly "local" matter. At the same time, by implication, the legislature designated what was properly within the jurisdiction of the state government. Thus, in

[15] *Laws of New York*, chap. 194, 1849; see *Albany Argus*, April 14, 1849, for a discussion of the principal objections to the law.

[16] Lincoln, *Messages from the Governors*, 4: 434.

[17] "Commercial Legislation in New York," *Merchant's Magazine and Commercial Review*, 21 (July 1849): 51.

the broadest sense, the growth of local government in the mid-nineteenth century may be viewed as another step toward a more explicit, formal definition of political community.

THE BEGINNINGS of a modern administrative approach to decision making was also manifested in the creation of new, functionally specific state agencies and departments in the two decades before the Civil War. Chapter 3 described the process by which the principal state officers—comptroller, secretary of state, treasurer, surveyor general, and attorney general—gradually accumulated power in the half century after the Revolution as the state confronted new challenges generated by social and economic development. In the mid-1840s this fusion of administrative functions, and particularly the growing power of the comptroller, came under increasing attack from several sources. On the one hand, New Yorkers began to reassess the role and power of their chief administrative officials as part of the much broader attempt to bring public officials under democratic control through popular election. Simultaneously, the authority of state officers became a major point of contention in a power struggle between opposing factions of the Democratic party. These two circumstances, in turn, converged with a growing realization on the part of many New Yorkers that such policy areas as banking, insurance, and education were of such complexity and importance to the state to warrant separate and nonpolitical consideration. Out of this amalgam, there emerged in the 1850s new state departments devoted exclusively to the administration of bank, school, and insurance policy.

The growing power of state officers first began to be challenged in the early 1840s, as New Yorkers engaged in a general reevaluation of the institutions of government and prepared to write a new constitution. That attack is especially interesting because of its source. Most Radical Democrats and others favoring constitutional revision focused on legal reform and a reduction of legislative power. To the extent that they were concerned with state administration, it was part of an overall desire to see patronage reduced and the state officers elected. The reason for this attitude is clear: all the state officers were Radicals and, though advocates of constitutional change, they did not wish such a revision to diminish their power and position within the government.[18] The "Hunker" or Conservative wing of the Democratic party, however, jealous of the power exercised by its opponents and bitter over its defeat on the convention question, launched a major campaign in the *Albany Argus* to reorganize and curtail the influence of the state departments. Their assault

---

[18] Hammond, *History of Political Parties*, 3: 524.

dovetailed perfectly with the broader trend toward popularly elected officials, the reduction of executive patronage, and the general decentralization of state government. As events turned out, the constitutional convention did not see fit to redistribute power among the state officers, but the arguments raised by critics foreshadowed subsequent administrative developments.

Critics of the state officers joined with constitutional reformers in demanding that they be popularly elected. The chief defect of the existing mode of appointment, according to the *Argus*, was that the state officers powerfully influenced legislative deliberations. Because of their longer terms of office and their status as political leaders, the argument ran, they were able to control the relatively inexperienced and constantly changing body of legislators. Such had indeed been the case, Conservatives suspected, in the selection of a speaker in 1845. Popular election would make the legislature and state departments completely independent. "We think the Executive, the State Departments, the Legislature, and the Judiciary," the *Argus* editorialized, "should be distinct and independent branches of government; all serving as checks upon each other, and all alike responsible to the community for whose benefit they are created." Another advantage of popularly electing administrative officials was the effect it would have in distributing such offices throughout the state. Whereas a very few senatorial districts in the immediate vicinity of the capital had monopolized these positions in the past, nominating conventions would naturally try to apportion them more equitably among the various sections of the state.[19]

A more telling criticism of the state departments, and one Radicals did not readily accede to, concerned accumulation of power. Here the principal target was the comptroller. "He is the one-man of the government," a correspondent of the *Argus* charged in June 1846; "he is not simply an officer, but a bundle of officers. There is hardly a branch of administration of which he is not a prominent member; so prominent, in some cases, that the affairs of that branch cannot be conducted without his actual presence. He is the chief of finances, the superintendent of banks, and the virtual quorum of the Commissioners of the Canal Fund." Legally the canal office was separate from the comptroller, the same writer explained in a later letter, but his influence was paramount because of his residence at the capital, his control of finances, and his connection with the other branches of the canal service.[20]

Accepting this critique, the *Argus* made reorganization of the state departments and curtailment of the comptroller's power prominent features of its

---

[19] *Albany Argus*, March 25, 1846. Similar views were expressed by "Western New York" in the *Argus* on May 20 and 22, 1846.

[20] Ibid., June 4 and 9, 1846.

proposed constitutional changes. "The amount of business transacted in the legislative halls each year," it stated flatly, "is less in importance and pecuniary amount than that which is transacted in the Comptroller's office." He controlled twenty-two funds, making the finances of the state "a great mystery," and was the center of New York's banking system. In addition, the comptroller was authorized to make loans and create legally binding debts without any action of the legislature. It was remarkable, according to the *Argus*, that so little attention had been paid to the comptroller's power in this last area, given the depth of concern over the legislature's debt-creating powers.[21]

The conclusion seemed inescapable. A succession of comptrollers had aggrandized power and elevated the office to a position of preeminence in the state government. The solution was equally clear. The power of the comptroller's office should be reduced and the duties of the state departments equalized. Specifically, the *Argus* suggested that the banking department be transferred to the treasurer's office and that the canal department be attached to that of the surveyor general. An annual appropriations bill, moreover, should be substituted for the comptroller's power to create debts.[22] Other critics argued in favor of increasing the number of departments. The comptroller's office, it was pointed out, could easily be divided into its natural components: the financial, canal, and banking departments, and a tax department. Such a "subdivision of labors would tend to simplicity and clearness" in state finances, and certainly the canal and bank departments had grown sufficiently to warrant independent existences.[23]

The constitutional convention stopped short of reorganizing the state departments, but it did provide for the popular election of the administrative officers and reduced their terms from three to two years. The new constitution also forbade the payment of any money from the treasury without specific authorization by the legislature, thereby curtailing the comptroller's power over finances.[24] Although the impact of this last change is unclear, popular election of officers had a dramatic effect. The longevity of administrative officers dropped sharply after 1846. Until at least the 1870s, the dominant pattern was for the state officers to serve only one term.[25]

The question of administrative reorganization did not disappear with ratification of the new constitution. Indeed, within a decade after the convention, most of the proposals discussed in the mid-1840s had been implemented

---

[21] Ibid., March 27 and 28, 1846.
[22] Ibid.
[23] Ibid., June 4 and 9, 1846.
[24] *Constitution of 1846*, Article 7, Section 8; Article 5.
[25] *Civil List and Forms of Government of the Colony and State of New York . . . Arranged in Constitutional Periods* (Albany, 1874), 372–375.

in one form or another. In 1848, for example, the comptroller's role in canal administration, though not entirely eliminated, was sharply reduced by the creation of an auditor of the canal department. This officer replaced the chief clerk of the department[26] and was empowered to perform all the duties of the clerk *and* the comptroller (except the role of commissioner of the canal fund). In effect, the auditor became the chief financial officer of the canals, charged with the disbursement of funds and the collection of tolls. He served a three-year term and it is surprising that, given earlier demands for popularly elected administrative officials, he was appointed by the governor with consent of the senate.[27]

In 1851 the legislature transferred responsibility for New York's banking system from the comptroller to a separate bank department. An earlier attempt to relocate this responsibility in the treasurer's office had failed.[28] By mid-century, however, both the governor, Washington Hunt, and the incumbent comptroller, Philo C. Fuller, supported the creation of an independent administrative structure. In his annual message to the legislature, Hunt called attention to the "growing importance of the Bank Department" and the "already overburthened" comptroller's office.[29] Fuller, who had been comptroller for less than two months and was destined to serve only one year, followed the governor's lead, recommending that the legislature "relieve the Comptroller from this portion of his official labors" because "it is physically impossible for that officer to give to the bank department the personal care and supervision which should be exercised in the discharge of so responsible a trust." In support of such a move, he pointed to the expansion of the comptroller's duties with the growth of the state in wealth and population; the time taken up in performing the disparate functions of that office and the necessity for a full-time custodian of the millions of dollars of security and large sums entrusted to the bank department; and the larger political principle that discouraged "an excessive accumulation of powers in the hands of a single officer. Each prominent and distinct branch of the public administration," he explained, "should constitute an independent office, especially where the details are too complicated and multifarious as to require constant supervision."[30]

---

[26]The canal department was organized in 1841 to consolidate in one location all canal-related business performed by the commissioners of the canal fund, the canal board, and the comptroller (*Laws of New York*, chap. 218, 1841).

[27]S. C. Hutchins, comp., *Civil List . . . of New York* (Albany, 1869), 407.

[28]*Albany Argus*, September 21, 1847.

[29]Lincoln, *Messages from the Governors*, 4: 563–564.

[30]Annual Report of the Comptroller, 1849/50, *Assembly Document*, no. 9, 1851, vol. 1.

The legislature responded by creating a "separate and distinct department" charged with the execution of all laws relating to both safety fund and free banking associations. It was headed by a superintendent appointed by the governor and senate for a three-year term. His duties included all those relating to banks which had previously been performed by the comptroller. He was prohibited from having any interest in any bank, but his salary, those of his clerks, and all expenses of the department were paid by the banks. In addition, banks were required to report quarterly to the bank department, and the superintendent was required to submit an annual report to the legislature.[31] In 1857 the superintendent's responsibilities were extended to include savings banks.[32]

Fuller also recommended in his report that the powers over foreign and domestic insurance companies granted to the comptroller by the general insurance law of 1849 be transferred to the new bank department.[33] In this instance, the legislature chose not to follow the comptroller's advice. Instead, an 1851 law required that all life-insurance companies deposit a security fund with the comptroller to guarantee their solvency. In addition, he was given broad discretionary powers over the insurance industry similar to those affecting banks. Thus, the comptroller's role relative to insurance companies during the 1850s closely followed the pattern established in banking policy between 1843 and 1851.[34] In 1857, however, after a number of bankruptcies in the insurance business, a senate committee recommended that the comptroller's regulatory powers in this area be transferred to the bank department.[35] Two years later the legislature created a separate insurance department with general supervisory powers over insurance companies and all the duties previously delegated to the comptroller. As with the bank department, the insurance department was headed by a superintendent, appointed by the governor and senate for a three-year term, who was required to report annually to the legislature.[36]

The power of the secretary of state was also reduced in the 1850s by transferring certain of his responsibilities to specially created agencies. In 1851, for example, the legislature created a superintendent of weights and measures, thereby relieving the secretary of state of those duties.[37] More significant,

---

[31] *Laws of New York*, chap. 164, 1851.

[32] Hutchins, *Civil List*, 408.

[33] Annual Report of the Comptroller, 1849/50, *Assembly Document*, no. 9, 1851, vol. 1.

[34] *Laws of New York*, chap. 95, 1851; Seavoy, "Origins of the American Business Corporation," 245–250.

[35] *Senate Document*, no. 94, 1857, vol. 3.

[36] *Laws of New York*, chap. 366, 1859; Hutchins, *Civil List*, 409.

[37] *Civil List and Forms of Government*, 1874, 394.

however, was the decision to detach the superintendent of common schools from the secretary of state's office. Such a move had been suggested on several occasions in the past. In 1835, for example, an assembly committee had proposed the creation of a separate "Department of Public Instruction" to be headed by a "Secretary of Public Instruction." No action was taken.[38] In his annual message to the legislature in 1839, Governor William H. Seward recommended the creation of a department of education to be made up of a superintendent appointed by the legislature and a board composed of delegates from subordinate county boards. The objective, according to Seward, was to "alleviate the partisanship and patronage politics involved in the present system of common school inspection."[39]

Despite such efforts, however, the secretary of state continued to exercise the duties of superintendent until 1854. The debate over free schools in the late 1840s and the passage of the Free School Act in 1851, more than any other single event, stimulated a desire for more efficient, nonpartisan administration of the school system. Several secretaries of state advocated a separation, as did the incumbent governor and the state association of teachers. Governor Horatio Seymour argued for a separate department on the grounds that it would "give more prominence to the subject [education]," "elevate it in public estimation," and "harmonize our system of instruction."[40] The senate committee on literature, to which the governor's recommendation was referred, reported in favor of a "distinct and efficient organization" headed by a state superintendent elected by joint ballot of the legislature. "The public interest demands an immediate and effective organization of this department," according to the committee, "independently of all political bias, and free from the agitation and excitement inevitably consequent upon a popular canvass at the polls." Besides, the union of the secretary of state and the superintendent of schools was "an anomaly which finds no precedence or countenance in our government."[41]

With the support of Governor Seymour and the secretary of state, therefore, the legislature created the Office of State Superintendent of Public Instruction in 1854. The superintendent, appointed by joint ballot of the legislature for three years, was charged with the general supervision of New York's public schools. His principal duties involved apportionment of state funds, visitation, interpretation of school laws for local officials, manage-

[38]Samuel S. Randall, *The Common School System of the State of New York* . . . (Troy, N.Y.), 39.
[39]Lincoln, *Messages from the Governors*, 3: 743–744.
[40]Ibid., 4: 716.
[41]*Senate Document*, no. 39, 1854.

ment of teachers' institutes, and collection and distribution of information relative to the state's school system.[42]

The creation of the banking and insurance departments and the office of state superintendent is clear evidence that New York was moving, albeit cautiously, in the direction of administrative specialization by the decade of the 1850s. Ironically, however, this development was not simply the result of a conscious effort to rationalize political authority, but also of a desire to check the accumulation of power by the state officers. Demands for administrative reorganization in the 1840s were rooted in two seemingly contradictory impulses. Certainly the diminished capacity of the political system to govern in a rapidly modernizing society generated proposals to rationalize decision making processes in the interest of greater efficiency. But the specific partisan context also contributed to administrative developments. New Yorkers, clinging to an inherited distrust of power, were uneasy with the expanded roles of the state's administrative officers. Engaged as they were in the mid-1840s with restructuring the political system to reduce the legislature's authority and increase popular participation in government, they readily accepted the notion that the power of the state officers should also be reduced. Partisan politics provided the catalyst. Conservative Democrats sought to curtail the influence of the state officers because the officers were controlled by the Barnburner faction of the party. Such was the extent of that control, indeed, that no action was taken to redistribute administrative duties until after the Barnburners left office. By 1850, however, there was a growing realization that the state's responsibilities vis-à-vis banks, insurance, and education had grown to the point where independent administrative structures were not only feasible, but essential. This realization, combined with a desire to remove partisan politics from the administrative process, culminated in the first halting steps toward the development of functionally differentiated administrative structures in New York state government.[43]

OF ALL THE administrative problems confronting New York between 1830 and 1860, none was more troublesome than that of regulation. Initially, regulation was a legislative function and was usually effected through the instru-

---

[42]Hutchins, *Civil List*, 411; Lawrence A. Cremin, *The American Common School: An Historic Conception* (New York, 1951), 176; Thomas E. Finegan, *Free Schools: A Documentary History of the Free School Movement in New York State* (Albany, 1921), 486.

[43]William E. Nelson has similarly located the origins of bureaucracy in the nineteenth century in the desire to break up concentrated power rather than in the desire to rationalize and centralize authority structures. See *Roots of American Bureaucracy*, 5.

ment of special incorporation laws. Once enacted, however, such charters were self-enforcing since the legislature had no capacity for continuous oversight. As the need for regulation of corporations, banks, railroads, and other economic activities grew, the state attempted to devise some system of permanent supervision. As we have seen, the legislature frequently delegated this function to existing administrative offices, thereby increasing their powers and leading ultimately to the creation of separate departments in the 1850s. But New York also experimented with independent regulatory commissions, administrative structures that have a decidedly modern ring to them. The state resorted to the commission solution to the problem of regulation on two occasions between 1830 and 1860. We have already discussed the successes and failures of the Bank Commission and its ultimate demise in 1843. The second attempt at a commission style of regulation occurred in the 1850s when New York was confronted with the need for uniform regulation of the state's rapidly expanding railroad system.

In 1855, following the precedent of several New England states,[44] the New York legislature created a Board of Railroad Commissioners. Until that time, railroad regulation had followed the general pattern established in the early years of banking policy, with principal reliance on the potential for regulation implicit in the chartering process. As long as the legislature passed each charter, it theoretically possessed the power to assure that railroads operated in the public interest. Regulation by self-enforcing statutes, however, could be only as effective as the railroads themselves wished, and by the 1840s some New Yorkers were already complaining about rate structures, poor service, monopolistic tendencies, and corrupt management. But apart from early efforts to regulate railroads to protect the state's canal investment and a requirement in 1842 that railroads report periodically to the legislature, there was little in the way of comprehensive regulation of New York's railroads until 1850.[45]

With passage of the general incorporation act of 1850, New York took a major step toward formulation of a generalized regulatory policy. The next chapter will say more about this important piece of legislation. For present purposes, it is enough to note that the practical effect of the new law was to open the railroad industry to free competition and to delegate away the state's control over the eminent-domain power. But the railroads paid a price for these advantages. The law established limits on rates, restricted profits, cre-

---

[44]Rhode Island seems to have created the first railroad commission in 1839. New Hampshire followed in 1844; Connecticut, in 1853. See Thomas C. Cochran, "The Social Impact of the Railroad," in *The Railroad and the Space Program*, ed. Bruce Mazlish, 175. See also Cochran, *Business in American Life* (New York, 1972), 121.

[45]Benson, *Merchants, Farmers, and Railroads*, 1–6.

ated a reporting system, and imposed safety standards. Railroads were forbidden from charging passenger fares in excess of three cents per mile. Dividends, however, could not exceed 10 percent of capital actually expended, and the legislature reserved the right to alter or reduce rates and fares to maintain this profit margin. Railroads were also required to report annually to the state engineer and surveyor on their condition and operations. Finally, the law laid down a series of safety regulations, including a requirement that passenger cars be attached at the end of trains; that all locomotive engines be equipped with either a bell or steam whistle to be sounded at all road crossings; that crossings be marked by signboards; that fences be built along rights-of-way; and that engineers and conductors abstain from alcoholic beverages while operating trains.[46]

Despite such provisions, however, the 1850 law stopped short of the one requirement for effective regulation: machinery for permanent enforcement. Thus, even though the principle of regulation was established, in practice enforcement still depended on individual suits in the courts. This flaw was immediately apparent. Railroads completely ignored the 10-percent profit restriction, and either did not report at all or did so improperly.[47] In 1852, for example, thirty-three railroads failed to report and only twenty-seven abided by the law. Although in subsequent years the majority of corporations did report, a sizable minority failed to do so in 1853 (seventeen), 1854 (twenty-one), and 1855 (ten). Successive state engineers complained to the legislature about the railroads' failure to comply and their own lack of authority to enforce the law. William J. McAlpine and John T. Clark went even further and recommended the creation of a board with broad powers to require full reports.[48]

The idea of a state railroad commission received support from other sources as well. In 1852 Governor Washington Hunt called attention to the rising number of railroad accidents: "A large proportion of these calamities might have been avoided by due care in the construction, management, and service of the roads and their moving equipment. The obligation of the State Government to extend its protection to the lives of railroad passengers is imperative, and rests on high moral grounds." Hunt went on to recommend that the legislature pass "such laws as may, on mature consideration seem most proper and efficient for preventing the recurrence of these lamentable disasters."[49] Hunt's successor, Myron H. Clark, sought legislation to prevent

[46]*Laws of New York*, chap. 140, 1850.
[47]Benson, *Merchants, Farmers, and Railroads*, 5.
[48]*Senate Document*, no. 96, 1856, vol. 2.
[49]Lincoln, *Messages from the Governors*, 4: 612–613.

dubious financial practices on the part of railroads, particularly the floating of mortgage bonds in excess of the amount of capital paid in to the corporation.[50] These specific complaints occurred in the context of general public distrust of railroads and stockholders' frustration at the fraud, stockjobbing, and mismanagement of railroad officials.[51]

In an effort to put some teeth into railroad regulation, the legislature created a board of railroad commissioners in 1855. The commission was made up of the state engineer and surveyor, one person selected by the stock and bond holders of the railroads, and one person appointed by the governor and senate. Its formal powers were extensive, including the right to examine company records, question officers under oath, investigate charges of mismanagement, and inquire into the causes of accidents. Railroads were required to make annual reports, but the commission could only refer violations of the law to the attorney general, not enforce such infractions themselves. One power, however, was especially important: no railroad could open until it had been inspected and certified by the board.[52]

Armed with this authority, the railroad commission seemed poised to bring effective supervison to the railroad industry. In its first annual report to the legislature, the commission pressed for more-accurate reports, recommended a standard bookkeeping system for railroads, and proposed that all lines adopt a uniform operating code in the interest of public safety. In addition, it suggested a pro-rata system for long- and short-haul rates, to protect intrastate lines and to safeguard canal revenues.[53]

Despite this promising start, the board of railroad commissioners was destined for a brief existence. In the very next session of the legislature, in 1856, a bill was introduced in the assembly to repeal the act creating the commission. It is surprising that it was supported by the state engineer and surveyor, who argued, in a memorial to the legislature, that his duties were already too arduous and too important to allow him to faithfully perform his responsibilities as president of the board. Besides, although he was the most important member of the commission, he was constantly in a minority and should not, therefore, be held legally responsible for the actions of the board. His presence, the memorial continued, merely gave prestige to proceedings otherwise dominated by the railroad member, who represented his constituents, and the state member, who was likely to be a party favorite and thus

---

[50] Ibid., 4: 805.

[51] Benson, *Merchants, Farmers, and Railroads*, 7.

[52] *Laws of New York*, chap. 526, 1855.

[53] Annual Report of the New York Railroad Commission, 1856, in *Assembly Document*, no. 12, 1856. Seavoy, "Origins of the American Business Corporation," 235–236; Benson, *Merchants, Farmers, and Railroads*, 7.

unfit for the job. As a consequence, neither the interests of the people nor those of the railroads were served. The best policy of the state, he argued, was to rely on the vested interest of the railroads in safety, competent operatives, economy, and regularity.[54]

The bill was referred to the assembly committee on railroads, which prepared a lengthy report urging repeal on grounds similar to those suggested by the engineer. First, the committee argued, members of the board would always be inferior to railroad managers because of the differences in salary and the fact that management of railroads required men of talent and special education. Directors, furthermore, would be inclined out of self-interest to find the best men possible. Thus, the public would be best served by the "enlightened avarice" of the directors. Second, the method of appointment created a divided board, with each member representing his particular constituency. Third, it resulted in an unnecessary increase in public officials and expense, evils that should be avoided in a republic. Fourth, the railroad interest was so powerful that it would probably find a way to control the commission in any case. Fifth, the extraordinary powers of the board violated due process of law. Finally, the board of railroad commissioners established an "unnecessary inquisition into the business of the citizen."[55]

The committee summed up its position with one of the most explicit statements in the entire period of the supposed advantages of a free, competitive system:

> The best safety to the public, and the most efficient and careful management of roads, will be attained by leaving the undivided power with the railroad company, and imposing upon them a rigorous and individual responsibility. The cupidity natural to all men, will ensure that all railroad managers will seek to commend themselves to favor, by a management which shall excel the rivals in all the elements which are attractive to the public. The rivalry of *interest* [sic] and the rivalry of *pride*, stimulates them to the adoption of the best and most thorough system, and to the exercise of the keenest vigilance.[56]

Following the committee's recommendation, the assembly approved the bill.

The senate committee on railroads held a different view and opposed repeal, arguing that it was the "imperative duty of the Legislature" to supervise corporations once charters were granted. The commission had been created for that purpose and had been highly successful, providing a great

---

[54]"Memorial of the State Engineer to the Legislature for Repeal of the Board of Railroad Commissioners," *Assembly Document*, no. 123, 1856, vol. 4.

[55]*Assembly Document*, no. 123, 1856, vol. 4.

[56]Ibid., 13.

amount of well-organized information. The only ones complaining about the commission, the committee charged, were the railroads with substandard conditions. Every sound company recognized the benefits deriving from the commission. The only petition for repeal, furthermore, came from the state engineer; no railroad had asked to be relieved from the expense (commission expenses were assessed on the railroads) or urged abolition of the commission. The committee report was apparently persuasive. The senate refused to join the assembly in repealing the act establishing the board.[57]

The bill was reintroduced in the 1857 legislative session. This time, supported by a majority of the commissioners as well as by the senate committee on railroads, it passed easily after less than a week's discussion. At the time, the abrupt change of heart on the part of the commissioners and the senate committee appeared strange. Twenty years later, during the Hepburn Committee investigations of the late 1870s, it was learned that the railroads, acting through Dean Richmond of the New York Central, had bribed the commissioners to recommend repeal. Thus, New York's board of railroad commissioners was abolished, after less than two years, as a result of a corrupt bargain.[58]

It is virtually impossible to evaluate the commission's effectiveness, given the short time it existed and the circumstances of its abolition. That it held considerable potential seems evident from the fact that railroads opposed it and were instrumental in its destruction. The railroad commission, moreover, differed markedly from the bank commission in one important respect, which may account for its more limited success. The former was designed to regulate the railroads in the public interest. The bank commission, on the other hand, had a dual function. Although professing its concern for the public, it also operated as an internal regulatory mechanism within the banking community, protecting banks from adverse economic conditions resulting from the mismanagement of other banks. Railroads did not yet possess such a commonality of interest, though a similar attitude among railroad leaders in later years may have contributed to the movement for federal regulation.

There is a final consideration. Many of the arguments of the state engineer and assembly committee in 1856 recommending abolition have a surprisingly plausible ring to them. Viewed in the context of what historians now know about politics and business in the 1850s, the suggestion that railroad managers would necessarily be superior to those selected to regulate them is not so outrageous. It was generally believed then, and has been

---

[57] *Senate Document*, no. 96, 1856, vol. 2.
[58] Benson, *Merchants, Farmers, and Railroads*, 8–9.

assumed by most scholars since, that the most talented men went into business rather than politics. Indeed, the 1850s witnessed the emergence of "business executives," who, as one historian put it, "were as much a new species in nineteenth century culture as the technological innovations they organized and managed."[59] If this was true in a general sense, it was especially applicable to railroad leaders, who, more than any other group, were responsible for the development of modern administration with "a systematized, bureaucratic management."[60] Thus, we shall never know whether, given the chance, New York's board of railroad commissioners could have developed the administrative ability to regulate the most innovative industry in the economy. We do know, however, that New York's railroads successfully resisted such regulation until 1882, when a new railroad commission was created.

ACCOMPANYING THESE early efforts to develop administrative modes of decision making was an equally decisive resurgence of judicial power vis-à-vis the more popular branches of government. As Morton Horwitz and others have demonstrated, the role and function of the judiciary grew steadily in the eighty years after the Revolution. Rejecting the eighteenth-century view of the law as, in Horwitz's words, "an eternal set of principles expressed in custom and derived from natural law,"[61] nineteenth-century jurists adopted an instrumentalist conception that saw law as malleable, facilitative, and essentially political in character. Throughout the first half of the nineteenth century, but particularly after 1820, judges came to play an increasingly significant role in the making of public economic policy. Through the interpretation of common-law doctrines governing property rights, contracts, torts, and commercial regulations, judges effectively destroyed the anticommercial, antidevelopment ethos of the eighteenth-century legal system and facilitated the creation of a legal framework conducive to growth, innovation, free enterprise, private property, and the expansion of the market economy. Thus, judicial decision making became a crucial component of the public policy system. As this occurred, the role of policy-making institutions of a more overtly political character, such as the legislature, contracted accordingly.[62]

Overlapping with this transformation of private law and similarly contributing to the growth of judicial power was another major development,

---

[59] James C. Malin, *The Contriving Brain and the Skillful Hand in the United States: Something about History and Philosophy of History* (Ann Arbor, Mich., 1955), 220–221.

[60] Alfred D. Chandler and Stephen Salsbury, "The Railroads: Innovators in Modern Business Administration," in *The Railroad and the Space Program*, ed. Bruce Mazlish, 128.

[61] Horwitz, *Transformation of American Law*, 30.

[62] Ibid., 253–256.

namely, the separation of law and politics consequent on the adoption of a formalistic style of judicial reasoning in the arena of public law. In brief, by the 1840s and 1850s lawyers and jurists increasingly argued in favor of a politically neutral, objective legal system, one that distinguished law from policy making, emphasized procedural rather than substantive ends, and, not coincidentally, froze in place the whole body of legal doctrine that had emerged as the underpinning of the market system. The precise origins of this development are deeply embedded in the evolution of jurisprudence, the rise to power of an autonomous legal profession, the abortive codification movement, and the need of commercial and entrepreneurial elites, once their own interests had been solidified, for stability and predictability in the legal environment. Whatever its roots, legal formalism was antilegislative and antipolitical in spirit. Its emergence brought with it new assertions of judicial power and increasing reliance on adjudication for the resolution of social and economic issues.[63]

One measure of the extent of this legal transformation in New York was the increasing frequency with which the judiciary claimed the right to review the constitutionality of legislation. The roots of the principle of judicial review lay in the eighteenth century. As early as the 1780s, New York state courts had begun to challenge the idea of legislative supremacy and the omnipotence of statute law. In the celebrated case of *Rutgers* v. *Waddington*, for example, it was argued that the courts were duty bound to test legislation against the standards of the law of nations, equity, and written constitutions. For reasons already noted, however, this early trend toward judicial review failed to resolve the issue of the relative power of the legislature and the judiciary. Indeed, as the leading scholar of judicial review in New York has noted, no legislative act was so much as challenged in a New York court until 1802, and it was more than a generation after the *Rutgers* v. *Waddington* decision before any statute was declared void by a state court. During the entire period that the state was governed under the Constitution of 1777, only five statutes were declared void by the courts of a total of eleven cases argued on constitutional grounds.[64] After the adoption of the Constitution of 1821, the number of cases argued on such grounds increased, though the courts remained reluctant to invalidate disputed statutes for several more decades. Thus, some sixteen cases were heard between 1822 and 1830, with only one law being overturned. During the decade of the 1830s, fourteen such cases

---

[63] Ibid., 256–266. See Nelson, *Roots of American Bureaucracy*, 133–148, for a discussion of the relationship between the emergence of legal formalism and the creation of bureaucratic authority structures in the late nineteenth century.

[64] Edward S. Corwin, "The Extension of Judicial Review in New York, 1783–1905," *Michigan Law Review*, 15 (February 1917): 283.

reached the courts, but only four were invalidated as being unconstitutional.[65]

Beginning in the 1840s, reliance on the doctrine of judicial review expanded dramatically and steadily into the next century. The decade that witnessed a constitutional reform movement characterized chiefly by its antilegislative spirit also saw the number of cases argued in New York courts on constitutional grounds grow to a total of 58, with 18 resulting in decisions adverse to the statute in question. During the next ten year period, from 1851 to 1860, the courts heard 127 cases involving judicial review of legislation and overturned 34 laws. This trend, furthermore, continued unabated after the Civil War. The comparable figures for the 1860s are 128 and 39; for the 1870s, 251 and 45; for the 1880s, 263 and 49; and for the 1890s, 334 and 99.[66]

This remarkable growth of judicial review over the course of the nineteenth century had several causes. The most obvious was that the extension of judicial power paralleled exactly the growing distrust of the legislature. As New Yorkers became increasingly dissatisfied with the performance of their representatives, successive constitutions included more and more specific limitations on legislative power, both of a substantive and procedural nature. As the number of such restrictions grew, the courts were called on more frequently to consider the constitutionality of legislation. This is especially evident in the large number of judicial review cases involving constitutional prohibitions of private, local, or special legislation.[67] The emergence of judicial review was also intimately tied to the development of the legal doctrines of vested rights and due process. By 1860, and even more dramatically after the Civil War, the courts used the power to review statutes to protect vested property rights against detrimental legislative acts. Indeed, according to Corwin, "the heart and soul of constitutional limitations in New York . . . has been the doctrine of Vested Rights."[68] Finally, the extension of judicial review must also be seen as a logical consequence of the rise of legal formalism. The move away from an instrumentalist conception of law as policy toward the view of law as fixed doctrine, scientifically or morally determined, provided a powerful intellectual support for the increasing propensity of judges to challenge the will of popularly elected legislators.[69]

In the final analysis, the revitalization of judicial power in the middle decades of the nineteenth century was part of a larger process by which law and

[65] Ibid., 285.
[66] Ibid.
[67] Ibid., 286–291.
[68] Ibid., 304; see also 292–299.
[69] Horwitz, *Transformation of American Law*, 259; Nelson, *Roots of American Bureaucracy*, 148–150.

politics became differentiated. Earlier signs of this tendency have already been noted in our discussion of constitutional changes. The Constitution of 1846, for example, stripped the legislature of many of its essentially judicial duties, most notably by abolishing the Court for the Correction of Errors, which had fused legislative and judicial functions, and replacing it with an independent court of appeals with final appellate jurisdiction in the state. Thus the extension of the doctrine of judicial review was the capstone of the drive to establish judicial independence. Taken together, these developments helped shape the emergent political order by establishing judicially monitored parameters of legislative power and by creating a counterweight to the democratizing tendencies of the constitutional reform movement.[70]

THIS CHAPTER has argued that the democratic response to the crisis of distributive politics in the middle decades of the nineteenth century was accompanied by the emergence of administrative and judicial modes of decision making. It would be inaccurate to suggest that state government in the 1840s and 1850s became "bureaucratic" in the twentieth-century meaning of that term, but significant change did occur in the structure of government which pointed in that direction. For one thing, by mid-century we can begin to detect a trend toward the differentiation of governmental institutions. As noted in chapter 3, one principal characteristic of state government in the early part of the century was the extent to which legislative, administrative, and judicial functions were fused. Complicating government even further was the tendency of the state to deal with new problems by adding responsibilities to existing agencies and departments. The result was an overlapping of roles and confusion of functions among institutions that had originally been created to deal with eighteenth-century problems, not those of a rapidly modernizing society.

During the two decades before the Civil War, however, governmental tasks and roles became increasingly separated. Multifunctional institutions began to be replaced with more specialized structures designed to handle particular types or areas of policy. Thus, the legislature was stripped of most of its administrative and judicial functions; power over local matters was delegated to subordinate units of government, thereby necessitating a more precise definition of the respective roles of state and local government; and, in the 1850s New York took the first step toward administrative specialization with the

---

[70]For a particularly incisive discussion of the antidemocratic tendencies of the doctrine of judicial review, see William E. Nelson, "Changing Conceptions of Judicial Review: The Evolution of Constitutional Theory in the States, 1790–1860," *University of Pennsylvania Law Review*, 120 (1972): 1166–1185.

creation of the bank department, insurance department, and the office of state superintendent. Even the unsuccessful attempt to resolve the problem of railroad regulation by creating an independent regulatory commission reveals the underlying tendency toward an administrative style of governance.

The increasing complexity and specialization of government paralleled, and was a function of, the emergence of a more complex and differentiated society in New York. But if there was a certain inevitability in the direction of social development, such was decidedly not the case in the political system. Government, as it interacted with and sought to influence this socio-economic environment, did indeed become more structurally differentiated. But, as our discussion of specific changes indicates, the evolution of governmental structures was a product of the interplay of ideology, politics, and necessity. As New Yorkers strove to develop institutions that were functional in an increasingly modern society and economy, they had to do so within the framework of deeply embedded fears of centralized power, the dictates of democratic ideology, and partisan maneuvering. The appearance of functionally differentiated administrative structures, usually a sign of political modernization, stemmed from a desire to *curtail* the power of the state officers and to *divide* authority, not to rationalize and integrate it. The result was a more complex and differentiated political regime, but one that was still lacking in hierarchical authority structures or integration on a vertical axis. Symptomatic of this trend was the fate of the principal state officers. After more than half a century of virtually continuous growth, the power and influence of these administrative officers was sharply curtailed by the creation of separate agencies or departments to perform many of their former functions, by making them popularly elected, and by shortening their terms of office from three to two years. Whatever impact these changes had in terms of increasing popular control over administration, from a developmental perspective they resulted in greater decentralization. Even the supposed advantages of democratization must be qualified, since the heads of the new banking and insurance departments and the office of the state superintendent were to be appointed rather than directly elected.

What all this suggests is that the rise of administration in New York before the Civil War was accompanied not by the concentration and centralization of power that we traditionally associate with bureaucratization, but by the diffusion of authority among an increasing number of specialized decision-making institutions. Similar consequences flowed from the rise of judicial power. As the courts asserted their independence from the legislature, adopted a new style of reasoning based on formal and objective standards, and expanded their power to review legislation, the judicial system became still another center of decision making. What was even more decisive, these developments were symptomatic of the erosion of politics as the principal method of conflict resolution in the political system. Major policy issues were effectively depoliticized, law and politics became differentiated, and uniform, objective, politically neutral norms for the formulation and implementation of policy were established. In short, the emergence of administration and adjudication began to replace the traditional politics of distribution with more rational, stable, and predictable mechanisms of allocation and legitimation. Such mechanisms were imminently functional in an increasingly impersonal and interdependent market. They also, consciously or not, circumscribed the power of popular majorities even as New York was outwardly adopting an ideology of direct democracy.

[8]

The Political Implications of
General Incorporation Laws

No ISSUE more clearly reveals the character of the emergent political order than the changing relationship between government and the corporation. During the middle decades of the century, New Yorkers repudiated the special incorporation system, in theory if not always in practice, and began enacting general laws establishing simple administrative procedures, equally accessible to all, for the conferring of corporate status. It was a momentous development. The passage of general laws effectively depoliticized the corporation. It ceased to be the focus of political debate (as it had been for most of the preceding quarter of a century), lost its political or quasi-public character, and became essentially private.

Much has been written about the evolution of the corporation and its significance in the early-nineteenth-century states. Historians have commonly, and correctly, emphasized the importance of the corporate device in the process of economic development and the centrality of anticorporation sentiment in the political rhetoric of the day. They have also explored the origins of the general incorporation movement, typically interpreting that development in terms of the equal rights and antimonopoly sentiment of the 1830s, the increasing desire of many Americans to regulate corporate activities, or the demands of emerging entrepreneurial groups for easier access to the advantages of incorporation. These are important themes in the history of the corporation and should be explored even more systematically than they have been thus far.

But there is another dimension to the story which has not been sufficiently appreciated, one which links the emergence of the private business corporation to the concerns of this book. The corporation, it may be recalled, began its phenomenal growth in the late eighteenth and early nineteenth centuries as a political institution enjoying a special and mutually advantageous relationship to the state. The government of New York, its own ability to act inhibited by a shortage of money and the absence of an administrative infrastructure, often relied on corporations to provide roads, bridges, banks, railroads, and other essential public services. The corporation, in turn, benefited from special privileges bestowed on it by government. The result was a highly functional partnership in the context of the developing society of the early nineteenth century.[1] Indeed, corporations played a major role in the expanding economy of this period by providing organizational and managerial skills that the political system was incapable of providing.[2] It follows that the transformation of the corporation from a public to a private institution had profound implications for the political system.

Shifting the focus of analysis from the corporation to the political system itself raises a number of significant questions. Precisely how was the intimate connection between the state and the corporation severed? Under what circumstances and with what consequences was the distinction finally made between the public sphere and the private sector? What was the impact of the emergence of the private business corporation on the willingness and capacity of the state government to play an active role in society? Was it coincidental that this process corresponded in time with the decline of government's role in the economy? Or is there a sense in which we can say that private institutions, especially corporations, displaced government as the legitimate agency for the performance of such functions? Finally, to what extent was the evolution of the corporation a reflection of the more fundamental transformation of state government in the middle of the nineteenth century? All forms of special, local, and private acts were being replaced by general legislation in this period. At the same time, the state began to withdraw from active participation in economic decisions, the role of the legislature declined sharply, and the relative power of the judicial and administrative components of government rose.

This chapter attempts to answer these questions by examining New York's corporate policy between 1800 and 1860. The structure of the inquiry is as follows: first, an overview of the development of the corporation in these

[1]See chapter 4. The standard references for the origins and early development of the corporation in the United States are Davis, *Essays in the Earlier History of American Corporations*; Evans, *Business Incorporation*; Dodd, *American Business Corporations*; Hurst, *Legitimacy of the Business Corporation*; Handlin and Handlin, "Origins of the American Business Corporation"; and Seavoy, "Origins of the American Business Corporation." See also Kent, *Commentaries on American Laws*, and Angell and Ames, *Treatise on the Law of Private Corporations*.

[2]Hurst, *Legitimacy of the Business Corporation*, 23–24.

years with emphasis on the gradual standardization of charter provisions and the appearance of general incorporation laws; second, a consideration of two specific, post-1846 cases—general manufacturing and public-utility corporations—each of which illustrates a significant theme in the transition to general incorporation. The familiar themes associated with the emergence of the business corporation (the development of limited liability, the corporation's status before the law, and regulation of its internal organization), though important in themselves, are relevant here only insofar as they relate to the larger question. The objective, in short, is to probe the implications of general incorporation for the process of political development. Viewed in this way, the movement for general incorporation laws can most appropriately be seen as part of the process by which New Yorkers sought to resolve the problem of allocation and legitimation in a society in which the politics of distribution had gone awry. From the perspective of the political system, the emergence of incorporation by administrative procedure was further evidence of the erosion of politics, the rise of administration, and the diffusion of political authority.

THE HISTORY of corporations in New York before 1860 can be divided into two periods separated by the decade of the 1830s. The first period was characterized by a tremendous expansion of the number and variety of corporations and, at the same time, a gradual standardization of charter provisions within the context of a special incorporation system. In the 1830s, however, the rising tide of antimonopoly feeling—often expressed as part of a broader criticism of special legislation and demands for equal rights—converged with a desire among newly created entrepreneurial groups for greater access to the corporate form. The principal target of both of these ideological and social currents was New York's banking policy. With passage of the Free Banking Act of 1838, a new era in the state's corporate policy began, an era marked by increasing demands for and enactment of general incorporation statutes.

The growth and diversification of the corporation in the early period has been treated adequately in previous chapters. To reiterate, the corporation had become so important and its use extended to such a variety of activities that in one year, 1836, nearly 50 percent of total legislative output, as reflected in the session laws, involved either a new charter or amendment of an old one. The percentage subsequently declined, but it still stood at more than a quarter of total output ten years later, on the eve of the Constitutional Convention of 1846.[3]

---

[3] These figures are based on Evans, *Business Incorporation*, and my own examination of the session laws of the 1830s and 1840s.

Coinciding with this proliferation of corporate charters were two other significant trends: experimentation with general incorporation laws in clearly noncontroversial policy areas and standardization of many structural and substantive provisions included in special charters. The first general law in New York was enacted in 1784 and allowed the trustees of religious congregations to become a "body politic and corporate." Justification for the act was based on the constitutional guarantee of freedom of religion and separation of church and state. The law prescribed the manner in which congregations could elect from three to nine trustees who would become a corporation on certification of their election to the county clerk. Their powers included legal status with the right to sue and be sued; the right to buy, sell, or hold estate; to have and use a common seal; to make laws and regulations for internal management; power to appoint officers; and uninterrupted succession. In addition, the act regulated such internal activities as terms of trustees, procedures for filling vacancies, and determination of ministers' salaries. It also required an accounting of all estate owned by the congregation once every three years, to the chancellor or a judge of the Court of Common Pleas in the county, on penalty of dissolution.[4]

Between 1784 and 1800 New York passed four additional general incorporation statutes, all loosely patterned after the first. In setting up the state's loan program in 1786, for example, county loan officers were incorporated to facilitate their handling of property, a policy that was continued in a 1792 statute.[5] In 1787 the legislature empowered the Regents of the University of New York, itself a corporation, to create colleges and academies. Under the terms of this act, which amounted to a delegation of the chartering power, organizers of colleges were required to apply in writing to the regents, describing the location, the plan, the source and amount of funds, and a list of the first trustees. If the regents approved and if the project was carried through to completion, the regents could declare the college a corporation. The procedure for academies was basically the same.[6] A 1796 law provided for the creation of library companies. A minimum of twenty people and forty pounds were required for incorporation, and library companies were prohibited from owning property valued at more than $500 at any one time, exclusive of books and annual payments of the corporation, and from engaging in any business not pertaining to a library.[7]

---

[4] *Laws of New York*, chap. 18, 1784.
[5] Ibid., chap. 40, 1786; Chapter 25, 1792.
[6] Ibid., chap. 82, 1787.
[7] Ibid., chap. 43, 1796.

The first general incorporation laws in the nineteenth century followed the pattern established in these early years. They were confined to religious associations or to the implementation of public functions. Thus in 1806 the legislature provided for the incorporation of county medical societies as part of a broader effort to regulate the medical profession and standardize the training of doctors.[8] Similarly, in 1808 individual county loan officers were combined to form county loan commissions with corporate powers.[9] And in 1811 a general law was enacted for the incorporation of Bible societies.[10]

The year 1811 was one of the most significant dates in the history of New York's corporate policy. Reacting to the decline of imports brought about by the international situation and the embargo and nonintercourse policies of the federal government, the state embarked on a deliberate program to encourage domestic manufacturing. As part of that effort, the legislature passed a general incorporation act designed to stimulate the manufacture of textile, glassware, metal, and paint products. The 1811 law, the provisions of which were described earlier, was important not only because of the boost it gave to manufacturing, but also because it was the first law providing for the general incorporation of private business enterprises. To be sure, it was justified on the ground of public necessity in a time of international crisis. But manufacturing was hardly in the same quasi-public category as banking or transportation. Indeed, manufacturing corporations could be created by general laws precisely because they were essentially private. They did not seem to need the strict oversight required in the case of transportation companies, for example, which possessed eminent domain and toll-collecting powers.[11]

Despite its significance as a departure from previous policy, the 1811 manufacturing act remained an anomaly for the next quarter century. No similar statute appeared in New York until the vastly more important Free Banking Act of 1838. During this period, however, the extension of the general incorporation principle to nonbusiness organizations continued. Laws were passed relating to school-district trustees and township common-school commissioners; Bible and common-prayer-book societies; and Lancaster and Bell schools.[12]

[8] Ibid., chap. 138, 1806; Seavoy, "Origins of the American Business Corporation," 29–36.

[9] *Laws of New York*, chap. 215, 1808; Seavoy, "Origins of the American Business Corporation," 28–29.

[10] *Laws of New York*, chap. 190, 1811.

[11] Ibid., chap. 67, 1811; Seavoy, "Laws to Encourage Manufacturing, 85–95; Reubens, "State Financing of Private Enterprise," 199–201.

[12] *Laws of New York*, chap. 252, 1815; chap. 114, 1817; chap. 61, 1821.

One reason that general incorporation made so little progress in these years was because many features of the corporate charter became standardized within the context of the special incorporation system. The first half century of the state's existence was one of experimentation and confusion resulting from the novelty of the business corporation and the absence of clear precedent. As of 1800, for example, no body of law dealt specifically with business corporations, and both legislatures and courts operated on the basis of rules that had developed to deal with municipal, philanthropic, or religious corporations.[13] Gradually, however, some consistency was achieved, as a result of increased experience in writing charters and the realization that some categories of economic enterprise required uniform regulation. Thus an 1807 statute, though not a general incorporation law because the legislature still had to approve each charter, fixed the general principles on which turnpike companies could be organized.[14] The Safety Fund Banking Act of 1829 fell into this category as well.[15]

Then, in 1827 the legislature, in effect, codified corporate policy. The Revised Statutes of that year included three titles regulating turnpike and monied corporations and establishing the "general powers, privileges, and liabilities of corporations." Those general powers included perpetual succession, unless limited by charter; the right to sue and be sued; to have a common seal; to buy, sell, and hold real and personal estate, subject to charter limitations as to amount; to appoint officers and agents; and to make bylaws for the corporation, not inconsistent with existing laws of the state. Corporations were to possess no powers except those listed and any that might be authorized by charter, and no corporation was to have any banking power unless expressly incorporated for that purpose. The legislature retained the right to alter, suspend, or repeal any corporate charter. And the Revised Statutes replaced the confusion over stockholder liability which had existed before 1827 with a provision granting limited liability after the entire capital of the corporation had been paid in. Until that time, each stockholder was liable for the unpaid portion of each share.[16]

---

[13] Hurst, *Legitimacy of the Business Corporation*, 7, 9.

[14] *Laws of New York*, chap. 38, 1807; Seavoy, "Origins of the American Business Corporation," 45–47.

[15] *Laws of New York*, chap. 94, 1829.

[16] Ibid., 50th Session, 1827, vol. 2. Before 1827, the extent of stockholder liability appears to have varied with the whims of legislators. Stockholders of some of the earliest corporations (such as the Hamilton Manufacturing Society, created in 1797) were completely liable. Double liability—where the stockholder was liable for an amount equal to his investment—was established in the 1811 Manufacturing Act and was the most common provision until 1825. Some manufacturing corporations created in 1825 possessed unlimited liability, but double lia-

In addition to these general provisions, the Revised Statutes dealt specifically with two classes of corporations: turnpikes and banks. The law prescribed the method of incorporating turnpike companies, the procedures for choosing directors, and their powers. It established elaborate specifications for the actual construction of such roads and detailed the process by which land could be taken through eminent-domain proceedings. Finally, the act regulated the collection of tolls. Banks or "monied" corporations were also regulated, to protect the rights of creditors and stockholders and to prevent insolvency. In addition to spelling out specific restrictions on the activities of banks, the law required that they submit an annual statement to the comptroller containing the amount of capital stock paid in; the value of real estate; shares of stock held by the corporation; debts owed to the corporation; debts; amount of circulating notes or bills, loans and discounts, and specie on hand; and losses and dividends of the corporation since the last statement.[17]

As long as the legislature continued to vote on each individual charter, however, the potential remained for special privileges and all the chicanery associated with the chartering process. The major consequences of these general regulatory acts, therefore, were shorter and simpler charters, since subsequent charters typically contained a provision stating that the corporation was subject to the privileges and restrictions of the Revised Statutes. But the regulations did little to assuage the major criticisms of corporate policy: that the privilege was distributed inequitably and therefore fostered monopoly, and that the volume of corporate charters enacted by the legislature unnecessarily clogged the lawmaking process and bred corruption and logrolling.

The 1830s, therefore, were a turning point. By the middle of the decade pressure was exerted from several sources for a drastic revision of the state's corporate policy. The spectacular increase in the volume of corporations and the stress it placed on the legislative process was a major impetus to demands for general laws. The appearance of a vocal minority party founded on anti-monopoly and equal-rights sentiment, furthermore, gave such demands their sense of urgency and emotional fervor. Added to the appeals of the Equal Rights party, finally, were the demands of emerging entrepreneurial groups and underdeveloped sections of the state for greater access to the corporate form. In the mid-1830s this challenge to existing policy focused on the issue

---

bility seems to have returned in 1826. *Laws of New York*, chap. 68, 1797; chap. 67, 1811. See also Haar, "Legislative Regulation of New York Industrial Corporations," 194–197; and Shaw Livermore, "Unlimited Liability in Early American Corporations," *Journal of Political Economy* (October 1935): 684–685.

[17]*Laws of New York*, 50th Session, 1827, vol. 2.

of banks and culminated, as we saw in chapter 4, in passage of the Free Banking Act of 1838.[18]

The Free Banking Act was one of the most important pieces of state legislation in the first half of the nineteenth century. It became a model for state banking and general incorporation laws and was the prototype for the National Banking Act of 1863.[19] Within the context of New York's corporate policy, it signified the beginning of a new era and was a tremendous stimulant to the movement for general laws. Its importance went beyond this, however, because it also represented a new type of legislation. There was a qualitative difference between a special act incorporating a single bank and a law that prescribed uniform rules for an entire class of economic activity. The perception of banking in such taxonomical terms was in itself a significant social and political development with potentially profound consequences for policy determination. This and subsequent general laws, furthermore, reflected a transformation in the legislature's role. In passing the Free Banking Act, the legislature established general policy guidelines and delegated the authority for implementation to administrative officials. This contrasted sharply with the fragmentation of policy decisions and the fusion of legislative and administrative functions so characteristic of the policy process under the special-incorporation system.

The impact of the Free Banking Act on the general incorporation movement was at first muted by the controversy surrounding its constitutionality. It had failed to remove what many regarded as the chief obstacle to general statutes: the constitutional provision requiring that all corporations be created by a two-thirds vote of all members of both houses. The legislature circumvented this barrier by calling the banks created under the new law associations rather than corporations. This legal fiction was immediately challenged in the courts in 1839, setting off a judicial battle that was to rage inconclusively until the Court for the Correction of Errors upheld the constitutionality of free banking in *Gifford v. Livingston* in December 1845.[20]

---

[18] See Byrdsall, *History of the Loco-Foco or Equal Rights Party*; see also Hammond, *History of Political Parties*, 2: 489–503; Walter Hugins, *Jacksonian Democracy and the Working Class: A Study of the New York Workingmen's Movement, 1829–1837* (Stanford, 1960); and Carl N. Degler, "The Loco-Focos: Urban 'Agrarians,'" *Journal of Economic History*, 16 (September 1956): 322–333.

[19] Michigan passed a Free Banking Act in 1837, but it was modeled after the act introduced and defeated in New York that same year (Hammond, *Banks and Politics in America*, 573).

[20] This court battle, fascinating in itself, can be followed in *Thomas v. Dakin*, 1839, 22 Wendell 9–112; *Warner v. Beers* and *Bolander v. Stevens*, 1840, 23 Wendell 103–189; *Delafield v. Kinney*, 1840, 24 Wendell 347; *The People v. The Assessors of Watertown*, 1841, 1 Hill 616; *The People v. Purdy*, 1841, 2 Hill 37; *Willoughby v. Comstock*, 1842, 3 Hill 389; *The People v. the Supervisors of Niagara*, 1842, 4 Hill 20; *The Matter of the Bank of Danville*, 1844, 7 Hill 504; *Debow v. The People*, 1845, 1 Denio 13; and *Gifford v. Livingston*, 1845, 2 Denio 380. An extended dis-

In the six-year interval, however, free banks operated in a state of legal ambiguity, and the entire question of whether general incorporation laws could be reconciled with the constitution remained open to interpretation. The prevailing opinion was they could not. A general law would not allow consideration of each charter separately and would preclude passage by the requisite majority, even if the general act itself had received a two-thirds majority. This line of argument led the judiciary committee of the assembly to reject a bill in 1844 proposing to extend the provisions of the 1811 act to the mining, smelting, or manufacturing of iron, lead, zinc, or copper. The constitutional provision was designed, according to the committee, to assure that no corporations were created unless they were clearly in the public good. The bill under consideration would abrogate that check and fill the statute books with incorporations for insurance and banking companies, railroads or turnpikes, and even charitable associations.[21] Thus the two-thirds rule remained a formidable roadblock to general incorporation until the 1846 constitutional convention.

By the mid-1840s, however, the demand for general laws had merged with the increasing agitation for revision of the state's constitution. Throughout the constitutional reform literature—whether emanating from Barnburner Democrats, Antirenters, or Whigs—the same theme appears: general laws would relieve the legislature of a time-consuming burden, abolish special privileges, purify government, and assure justice and equality before the law. Everyone agreed, according to the *New York Tribune*, that laws should be "general and not special in their character." "For years the business of incorporating companies to construct this or that public work or pursue some branch of business," the *Tribune* continued, "has engrossed a good share of the time of our successive legislatures. Why should this continue? Nobody desires it—all know it to be wrong. Yet the old mischief drags on."[22]

The most powerful argument for general laws emanated from those who saw the issue in philosophical rather than strictly practical terms. Elisha P. Hurlbut's views on the subject are illustrative. Hurlbut, a New York City attorney and activist in the constitutional revision movement, published a series of lectures in 1845 titled *Essays on Human Rights and Their Political Guaranties*. Special laws and privileges, he said, were inimical to human equality, whose protection was government's only proper function. "A Just

cussion of the judicial history of the Free Banking Act is in Hammond, *Banks and Politics in America*, 585–592; and in Seavoy, "Origins of the American Business Corporation," 169–188.

[21] *Assembly Document*, no. 162, 1844, vol. 6. In 1838 the judiciary committee had declared that a bill to extend the 1811 act to cover silk producing and mining companies *was* constitutional; see *Assembly Document*, no. 277, 1838, vol. 5.

[22] *New York Tribune*, January 20, 1846.

government," he continued, "will confer no special privileges; its powers will be exerted only in the vindiction and defence of human rights. Privilege conferred upon one man implies a derogation from the rights of others; and the office of government is protection only." Laws, therefore, should be "general in their scope and application, equal and impartial to all." They should create no "factitious greatness, confer no partial privileges, and deny no natural rights."

Such was not the case in New York. The "evils of partial legislation" were readily apparent in monopolies, exclusive privileges, private claims against the state, lobbying, and "crafty men" who "beseige the legislative power" for private gain. Yet the remedy was simple enough—enact general laws. General legislation would purify government. It would annihilate "the lobby, or third house, that embodiment of selfishness and gross corruption. The halls of legislation would be cleansed, and the representatives of the people would breathe a purer and freer atmosphere. All 'logrolling' . . . would cease." General legislation, furthermore, would encourage the election of more capable representatives. "A man of very limited capacity," according to Hurlbut, "may present and carry forward a law promotive of local or partial interest; but just and enlightened legislation requires the highest endowments of talent and virtue. The legislator properly represents the State, the whole people, nay, humanity itself." Finally, the preservation of the republic itself depended on general legislation. "A republic cannot endure without it. Public virtue will perish in the halls of special legislation."[23]

Delegates to the 1846 constitutional convention overwhelmingly favored general incorporation, though they soon discovered that it was one thing to accept the principle of equal rights and the positive benefits of general laws and quite another to reduce those principles to practice.[24] The overriding theme running through the convention debates on this issue was the practicality and desirability of establishing rules uniformly applicable to all classes of corporations. When the issue of stockholder liability was discussed, for example, some delegates attempted to exempt insurance companies from proportional liability on the grounds that their losses resulted from accident or calamity rather than mismanagement and that they should not be penalized for an "act of God." There was a similar effort to exempt public-utility franchises because their capital investment was large and because of the expense involved in acquiring rights-of-way.[25] Whether as a result of the force

<hr>

[23] E. P. Hurlbut, *Essays on Human Rights and Their Political Guaranties, with a Preface and Notes by George Combe* (Edinburgh, 1847), 11–15.

[24] *New York Tribune*, January 20, 1846.

[25] Lincoln, *Constitutional History of New York*, 2: 193; Croswell and Sutton, *Debates and Proceedings in the New York State Convention*, 746–748.

of such arguments or the lobbying power of the interests they benefited, the issue proved so intractable that the convention reversed itself. After having decided early in the proceedings to fix corporate liability in the constitution, it voted at the end to leave the whole matter to the legislature.[26] In practice, this meant that limited liability, as prescribed in the Revised Statutes, remained in force.

A more troublesome problem concerned the propriety of delegating eminent-domain powers by general law. Several members pointed to the fact that the state often delegated the right of eminent domain to public-utility corporations and suggested that the public interest would be better served by legislative scrutiny in individual cases. Anticipating arguments against general incorporation laws that would be crucial in legislative deliberations during the next five years, they argued that the delegation of eminent domain, a public prerogative, to private corporations constituted an unwarranted abdication of the sovereign power. Apparently the argument was effective. Although the convention had earlier adopted an absolute prohibition against special incorporation laws, in its final form the provision was tempered by excepting "cases where in the judgment of the Legislature, the objects of the corporation cannot be attained under general laws."[27] Thus, the door was left open for a continuation of special incorporation even after general laws had been written.

Although the convention stopped short of an absolute prohibition of special incorporation, it did give constitutional sanctity to the principle of general laws. This was in itself a significant accomplishment. Indeed, one measure of the constitution's importance to New York's corporate policy is the fact that the legislature, in implementing the new document, enacted more than thirty general incorporation statutes between 1846 and 1857.

THE TRANSITION to general incorporation was not an easy one. The legislature confronted difficult and complex issues in trying to chart a narrow path between the extremes of hostility toward corporations on the one hand and an equally powerful impulse for the expansion of corporations as agencies of economic development on the other. The task of successive legislatures was to balance the promotive and regulative aspects of general incorporation laws, to preserve the beneficial features of the corporation without sacrificing the public welfare. Complicating the problem, moreover, was the fact that not only the corporation but also the political system itself was undergoing

---

[26] Lincoln, *Constitutional History*, 2: 193.

[27] Croswell and Sutton, *Debates and Proceedings*, 737; *Constitution of 1846*, Article 8, Section 1; Lincoln, *Constitutional History of New York*, 2, 192.

transformation. Establishing general policy guidelines for the creation of corporations and delegating their implementation to administrative officials was profoundly different from what had passed for policy making during the decades before the constitution. The challenge was formidable, requiring a consensus on such tough issues as stockholder liability and the degree of public control over the exercise of eminent domain by franchise corporations and the development of at least a rudimentary conception of the public interest. It is not possible to examine here the legislative history of all the general incorporation laws enacted during this period. However, the debates over a general manufacturing law in 1847 and 1848 and a general railroad law in 1848 and 1850 were critical and will serve to illustrate the difficulties encountered in fulfilling the spirit of the new constitution.

A general manufacturing bill was introduced in the 1847 legislative session, but it failed to pass because the senate and assembly were unable to agree on the extent to which shareholders should be held liable for corporate debts. The senate version of the bill provided for full liability until all capital had been paid in. The assembly, however, regarded full personal liability as too restrictive and therefore likely to retard the growth of manufacturing. Efforts by two separate conference committees to effect a compromise between the two houses were unsuccessful, and the session ended without a general manufacturing bill.[28]

The issue dividing the two branches of the legislature was not the advisability of passing a general law, but rather how restrictive such a law should be. As a senate committee reported in 1847, manufacturing was essential to prosperity and should be encouraged. The growth of manufacturing would provide employment and capital for laborers and markets for farmers. The issue was to determine the best way to encourage such activity. Should it be done by creating monopolies and granting exclusive privileges, or should competition be left to regulate itself? A majority of the committee was committed to a general law, but the liability provision in the bill reported out reflected their belief that the purpose of such a law should be "to protect individuals and community against the dangers and abuses of bodies corporate."[29] Arrayed in favor of a liberal law were the governor, business generally and manufacturing interests in particular, and the cities and towns of western New York, which were desperately striving for economic development. The hard-core opposition to limited liability was Democratic; however, the issue in any given area was more likely to turn on economic than on partisan considerations.

[28] Seavoy, "Origins of the American Business Corporation," 208–209.
[29] *Senate Document*, no. 53, 1847, vol. 2.

Governor John Young, a Whig, was a vigorous advocate of general manufacturing. "Wise and enlightened legislation in this regard," he proclaimed in his annual message in 1847, "will secure the investment of capital in manufacturing corporations, here, as in New England, and with like success." In 1848 he took an even broader view, arguing that the growth of industry which would result from a liberal policy would provide a permanent and stable market for the state's agricultural goods. He also assured the legislature that the safeguards written in the assembly bill were more than adequate to counterbalance the privileges of limited liability. The objective of the state's policy, he concluded, "should not be to provide for large dividends, upon the capital to be invested. We should look primarily to the encouragement of industry. But this object can only be attained under laws that will invite the investment of capital."[30]

Young articulated the sentiments of many New Yorkers. Manufacturing interests energetically pushed the bill to encourage the influx of capital from outside. New England capitalists, they argued, had already mapped the best water-power sites in New York for the construction of mills and factories. As the *Journal of Commerce* put it, "The advantages accruing to the landowners, producers, laborers, and taxpayers of this state from the accession of capital to be employed among our people . . . is too striking to need comment."[31] Other editors agreed. "We have not a doubt, wrote Horace Greeley of the *New York Tribune*, "that fifty millions of capital will be called into beneficient activity and 100,000 persons find satisfactory employment under the provisions of a General Manufacturing law."[32] A correspondent of the *Albany Argus* similarly urged immediate passage of the assembly bill: "Capital is waiting. . . . Labor and enterprise are waiting, and have already waited too long. Our unrivalled natural means and resources for such undertakings . . . are also waiting those movements and combinations for their development and employment."[33]

The most vocal agitation for the general-manufacturing law came from western New York. Public meetings were held in Rochester, Oswego, and Albany in September and October 1847 in support of the bill. According to the resolutions of the Rochester meeting: "The General Bill here alluded to is free from all monopolistic features or special privileges. It opens the door alike to the mechanic with his hundreds and the capitalist with his thousands. . . . We believe that this State has advantages and facilities for manu-

---

[30]Lincoln, *Messages from the Governors*, 4: 379, 399–404.
[31]Reprinted in *Albany Argus*, May 4, 1847.
[32]*New York Tribune*, May 4, 1847.
[33]*Albany Argus*, April 28, 1847.

facturing surpassing any State in the Union. With enlightened and liberal legislation, the manufacturing interest would soon be augmented, thereby increasing the demand for agricultural productions, and largely swelling the amount of our commerce."[34]

The desire to encourage small investors was a persistent theme. At the Oswego meeting, for example, the more restrictive senate bill was denounced on the grounds that it would "utterly defeat the purpose of such corporations—would deter capitalists and persons of limited means from embarking in enterprise necessarily hazardous—would drive capital from the state" and would "give a monopoly of such enterprises to individuals of great wealth."[35] By contrast, the liberal assembly bill, according to speakers at Albany, "looked to the interests of the State, by blending the interests of capital and labor. While it properly protected Capital, it rendered Capital subservient to labor. . . . It secured to the Operative the reward of his labor under every conceivable contingency." Its passage "would invite the investment of capital, and operate most beneficially upon every locality in the State."[36]

Confronted with these pressures, the legislature passed a liberal version of the General Manufacturing Act in February 1848. Stockholders were liable to the amount of their shares until the full amount of capital was paid in. But the creditor was protected by a requirement that one half of the capital had to be paid within one year, and the remainder within two years of organization. The corporation, furthermore, was required to publish an annual report in the nearest newspaper stating the amount of capital, the proportion actually paid in, and the amount of existing debts. A similar provision penalized trustees if they paid dividends when the company was insolvent or if such payments diminished the amount of capital stock. The trustees were also liable if the company's indebtedness exceeded the capital stock, and, finally, stockholders were personally liable for the wages of employees.[37] Thus, although the general law included a limited-liability provision, there were substantial safeguards against fraud or reckless management and protection for labor. In effect, a balance had been achieved between privilege and regulation. By 1855, 685 corporations had organized under its provisions, 180 more than the total of all manufacturing corporations created before 1846.[38]

[34]Ibid., September 10, 1847; Blake McKelvey, *Rochester: The Water-Power City, 1812–1854* (Cambridge, 1945), 233.

[35]*Albany Argus*, October 4, 1847.

[36]Ibid., October 9, 1847.

[37]*Laws of New York*, chap. 40, 1848; Seavoy, "Origins of the American Business Corporation," 210–211.

[38]Seavoy, "Origins of the American Business Corporation," 212.

An issue even more difficult to resolve than that of limited liability involved the delegation of eminent domain to public-utility corporations. Under the special-incorporation system, as we have already seen, turnpike and railroad companies had been authorized to acquire land needed for rights-of-way by exercising the power of eminent domain. Such activities, the justification ran, were in the public interest and therefore the sovereign power residing in the state to condemn property for the benefit of the general community could be invoked. As long as the legislature passed each corporate charter separately, it retained ultimate authority to determine whether or not a proposed project was in the public interest. Many New Yorkers feared, however, that this check on the delegation of eminent domain would be removed under a general incorporation law. Although this problem had been discussed in the constitutional convention, it became a major issue when the legislature turned to the task of writing general plankroad, turnpike, and railroad laws in 1847 and 1848.

The problem first arose in connection with the general plankroad and turnpike law when opponents charged that the delegation of eminent domain would remove that power from the legislature and result in the creation of "petty despotisms." The legislature, they argued, had no power to create a sovereignty within itself—an *imperium in imperio*. Since there was no provision in the bill for determining public use, corporations should be compelled to return to the legislature for that decision.[39]

As finally passed, the law did delegate eminent domain, but to local political authorities rather than to the corporations themselves. Each plankroad or turnpike had to be approved by the board of supervisors of the county in which it was to be built. If the supervisors determined that construction of the road on the proposed route promoted the public interest, they were required to appoint three disinterested commissioners to lay out the route. The supervisors' authorization empowered the company to take needed real estate, but the amount of compensation was to be established by a jury.[40]

The general railroad law proved more difficult. A senate committee concluded in 1847 that railroad corporations should be exempt from the constitutional prohibition against special acts because of the difficulty of transferring the right of eminent domain. If a general law delegated such power to corporations without requiring legislative assent, according to the committee report, it would produce a "general scramble" among railroads for the most favorable locations, and "in the controversy individual rights, the

---

[39]See the legislative debate on this subject reported in the *Albany Argus*, March 18, 19, 23, 24, 25, and 29, 1847.

[40]*Laws of New York*, chap. 210, 1847.

rights of private property must necessarily be grossly violated. By such a law, the sacred right of eminent domain would be virtually parcelled out to an indefinite number of self-created, and perhaps irresponsible corporations."

When supporters of a general law proposed several devices to remedy this difficulty, the committee answered each in turn. To the suggestion that a special tribunal be established to determine the public utility of each railroad, it replied that although the legislature could grant eminent domain, it did not have the power to create an agency for that purpose. As the constitutional agent of the people, the legislature was the sole judge in such matters. A second suggestion was to allow corporations, after a survey had been made and stock subscriptions completed, to apply to the legislature for the right of eminent domain. The committee correctly answered that such would defeat the purpose of a general law. Besides, what capitalist would care to risk his investment with no prior certainty that legislative approval would be given? The conclusion the committee reached, therefore, was that the nature of the powers required by railroad corporations precluded their creation by general law. The legislature should continue to grant special charters rather than give up its check on the right of eminent domain.[41]

The impact of the senate committee report was devastating. Although an assembly committee in 1848 upheld the legislature's power to enact a general incorporation law and suggested that the question of public utility be left to the supreme court, it was not as persuasive as its predecessor.[42] Thus, the 1848 general railroad law adhered to the principle that the legislature could not delegate eminent domain. Although providing for the organization of corporations by administrative procedure, it required such companies to petition the legislature, stating the origin and destination of the railroad and its probable route, to determine whether the road was of sufficient public utility to justify an exercise of eminent domain.[43] In short, a special act of the legislature was still necessary for the creation of a railroad corporation. Nor was this declaration of public use a mere formality. The legislature approved six such applications in 1848 and six in 1849, but it rejected the plan for a railroad from Syracuse to Rochester.[44]

By 1850 pressure had mounted for a genuine general law. Governor Hamilton Fish prodded the legislature into rewriting the railroad law along the

---

[41]*Senate Document*, no. 64, 1847, vol. 2.

[42]*Assembly Document*, no. 105, 1848, vol. 3; see also "Report of the Minority Committee on Railroads," *Senate Document*, no. 34, 1848, vol. 2.

[43]*Laws of New York*, chap. 140, 1848.

[44]A. C. Flagg, "Internal Improvements . . . in New York," *Merchants' Magazine and Commercial Review*, 25 (October 1851): 421–422; "Railroad Legislation of New York in 1849," *Merchants' Magazine and Commercial Review*, 21 (July-December 1849): 163–181.

lines of the 1847 plankroad and turnpike act. Although any delegation of the "sovereign prerogative" to private associations should be done with great caution, Fish explained in his annual message, there was no reason why the public utility of railroads could not be decided by the local authorities, as was the case with turnpikes and plankroads. Such a system would satisfy the constitutional prohibition of special incorporations, "would take from these corporations every ingredient of exclusive privilege, and would relieve the legislature from the weight and burden of a large amount of duty entailed upon it under the present system."[45]

The legislature heeded the governor's advice and passed a new railroad law in 1850. Most of the provisions were similar to the 1848 act, but it increased the required capital stock to $10,000 per mile and liberalized the liability provision. More important, the legislature was no longer required to determine public utility. If a railroad company was unable to purchase needed land, it could petition the supreme court to appoint commissioners of appraisal. After notification of all concerned and an opportunity to hear objections, the court was authorized to appoint five disinterested commissioners to ascertain the compensation to be made to landowners. Railroads were thus given considerable power to determine routes with reasonable assurance that the land could be acquired. Although procedural safeguards protected private property from unjust seizure, the burden of proof was on the landowner.[46] The 1850 railroad law, therefore, did delegate the power of eminent domain to corporations. And the legislature's authority to delegate this power was upheld by the New York Court of Appeals in 1853.[47]

THE SUCCESSFUL passage of a liberal manufacturing law and the resolution of the eminent-domain issue removed the two most significant stumbling blocks to general incorporation. Consequently, general laws covering a wide range of economic and noneconomic activities followed. By 1850 there were laws relating to rural cemeteries; plankroad and turnpike companies; villages; telegraph companies; bridge companies; benevolent, charitable, scientific, and missionary societies; and insurance companies.[48] During the fifties the legislature passed general laws for the incorporation of building, mutual loan, and accumulating-fund associations; ocean steamship companies; agricultural and

---

[45] Lincoln, *Messages from the Governors*, 4: 496.

[46] *Laws of New York*, chap. 140, 1850.

[47] *The Buffalo and New York City Railroad Company against Brainard and Others*, 1853, 9 New York 100.

[48] *Laws of New York*, chap. 133, 1847; chap. 210, 1847; chap. 426, 1847; chap. 40, 1848; chap. 265, 1848; chap. 259, 1848; chap. 319, 1848; and chap. 308, 1849.

horticultural societies; life and health insurance companies; libraries; building-erection companies; fire insurance companies; stage companies in New York City; river and lake navigation companies; navigation companies on Lake George; associations for improving the breed of horses; and mutual fire-insurance companies in townships.[49]

Although some classes of corporations created in this period required unique privileges or restrictions, provisions relating to the method of organization, general powers to be exercised, and liability for debts were similar.[50] Incorporation was to be by administrative procedure. Any number of persons, usually above a specified minimum, could organize a corporation simply by meeting the prescribed terms of the relevant law and filing a certificate with either the county clerk or secretary of state (in some cases both). Usually, some form of prior public notice in a newspaper was required, and in the case of turnpikes and railroads this included publication of the proposed route.

Minimum and maximum capitalization requirements were common features of these laws, with the preconditions for public-franchise corporations generally more stringent. Plankroads and turnpikes, for example, could not incorporate until stock equal to at least $500 per mile of road had been subscribed and at least five percent actually paid in.[51] Under the 1848 railroad law, moreover, $1,000 per mile had to be subscribed and 10 percent paid in. The 1850 railroad act retained this provision and further required a minimum capitalization of $10,000 per mile.[52] Insurance companies had to be capitalized at $150,000 in New York and King's counties and $50,000 in all other counties under the 1849 act, but the 1853 law required $100,000 for life and $25,000 for health insurance.[53] Ocean steamship companies required a minimum of $50,000 but not more than $2 million in capital stock, and companies navigating the rivers and lakes were restricted to a figure between $10,000 and $1 million.[54] Finally, building-erection companies needed at least $10,000 to begin operations.[55]

The general powers to be exercised by corporations created under these laws were those established in the Revised Statutes of 1827. Public-franchise

---

[49]Ibid., chap. 122, 1851; chap. 228, 1852; chap. 339, 1853; chap. 425, 1855; chap. 463, 1853; chap. 395, 1853; chap. 117, 1853; chap. 466, 1853; chap. 135, 1853; chap. 142, 1854; chap. 232, 1854; chap. 3, 1854; chap. 269, 1854; chap. 739, 1857.

[50]For a fuller discussion of these laws, see Seavoy, "Origins of the American Business Corporation," 206–262.

[51]*Laws of New York*, chap. 210, 1847.

[52]Ibid., chap. 140, 1848; chap. 140, 1850.

[53]Ibid., chap. 308, 1849; chap. 464, 1853.

[54]Ibid., chap. 228, 1852; chap. 232, 1854.

[55]Ibid., chap. 117, 1853.

companies, however, because of their peculiar character, were granted special powers. Telegraph companies, for example, were authorized to use the right-of-way along public roads and highways.[56] Plankroad, turnpike, and railroad corporations, moreover, could acquire property needed for rights-of-way through eminent-domain proceedings, though the legislature carefully prescribed the procedure and safeguarded the rights of the property owner.[57] And insurance companies were allowed to reinsure their risks and invest their capital or accumulated funds in bonds, mortgages, or public stocks.[58]

Most of the general laws passed after 1846 provided for double liability until all the capital stock was paid in, after which stockholders enjoyed the full benefits of limited liability. There were some exceptions, however. The plankroad and turnpike act, passed in 1847 before the issue had been resolved, called for strict double liability. That provision also applied to building, mutual loan, and accumulating-fund associations.[59] Shareholders in telegraph companies were liable for up to 25 percent of the amount of their stock.[60] The first railroad law included the standard provision, but the 1850 act liberalized it so that stockholders were liable for only the unpaid portion of their stock.[61] A mechanics lien was almost always included making the stockholders completely liable for the wages of the company's employees; directors and trustees were often liable in cases of fraud, mismanagement, or failure to comply with restrictive clauses of the enabling act.

The advantages of limited liability were counterbalanced by careful regulation of internal organization and the corporation's activities. The method of choosing trustees or directors, the appointment of officers and their powers, voting procedures, and the terms under which real or personal property could be bought, sold, or held were typically prescribed by law. Construction specifications and operating procedures of public-franchise corporations were also regulated. In addition, most general acts required some form of periodic reporting system whereby the corporation furnished previously determined information to a state officer—such as secretary of state, comptroller, or state engineer—who forwarded that data to the legislature. In some instances, a state official was given investigative and regulatory powers over

[56] Ibid., chap. 265, 1848.
[57] Ibid., chap. 210, 1847; chap. 140, 1848 and 1850.
[58] Ibid., chap. 308, 1849; chap. 463, 1853.
[59] Ibid., chap. 210, 1847; chap. 122, 1851.
[60] Ibid., chap. 265, 1848.
[61] Ibid., chap. 140, 1848 and 1850.

a class of corporations. The comptroller, for example, possessed authority to supervise the insurance industry.[62]

Taken together, and compared with the state's corporate policy in the first quarter of the century, these general laws profoundly altered the character of public economic policy in New York. To be sure, the transformation was not yet complete. There were still those in New York willing to take advantage of the constitutional loophole by petitioning the legislature for special charters. Despite vetoes of special charters by governors Hamilton Fish in 1850 and Washington Hunt in 1851 and 1852, for example, more than four hundred special charters were passed in 1854 and 1855, during the administration of Horatio Seymour. A measure of restraint was finally reestablished by Myron Clark in 1857.[63] The fact that the legislature continued to grant special charters does not detract from the overall importance of the general laws passed in this period. In vetoing a special incorporation act in 1851, Washington Hunt explained the purpose of the constitutional provision against special incorporation. "It was intended not only to relieve the Legislature from the Numerous applications for special charters, which experience had shown to be unfavorable to the progress of necessary legislation on subjects of general concern," he wrote, "but also to insure a liberal and uniform policy, which should place all of our citizens on a footing of equality in regard to the exercise of corporate privileges."[64] New York took a significant step toward accomplishing these goals in the decade 1847–1857.

NEW YORK's corporate policy to the 1850s can be viewed from two perspectives: that of the corporation and that of the political system itself. For the corporation it was a period of growth and definition. From a device used infrequently and principally for public purposes, it evolved into an essentially private instrument of economic organization. With the passage of general laws, the corporation's ties to the state were effectively severed. Furthermore, to the extent that general laws made it possible for virtually anyone to exercise corporate powers, provided they could meet the legal prerequisites, the corporation lost its stigma of monopoly and attained a degree of legitimacy unthinkable under the special-incorporation system. The price for that newly found legitimacy was a greater measure of regulation. If cor-

---

[62] Seavoy, "Origins of the American Business Corporation," 206–262, contains a good discussion of these general provisions. For the comptroller's authority vis-à-vis insurance companies, see *Laws of New York*, chap. 463, 1853.

[63] Lincoln, *Messages from the Governors*, 4: 513–531, 574–593, 633–635; Seavoy, "Origins of the American Business Corporation," 208–209.

[64] Lincoln, *Messages from the Governors*, 4: 574–575.

porations enjoyed some form of limited liability or possessed the power of eminent domain on the one hand, their capitalization, internal organization, and mode of operation were strictly regulated on the other.

The political implications of the transition to general incorporation are more difficult to assess. Historians are not accustomed to dealing with the political ramifications of corporate policy except in the narrow sense of its being a partisan issue. There has also been a tendency among historians to emphasize the regulatory aspects of general incorporation laws at the expense of other themes. It cannot be denied that more stringent regulation came in response to actual abuses, was very real in its impact, and was strict enough to encourage many entrepreneurs to continue to seek special charters from the state legislature; however, demands for the expansion of the corporation to stimulate growth and development were as important in New York as demands for regulation. The General Manufacturing Act of 1811, for example, grew out of the desire to stimulate manufacturing. The Free Banking Act of 1838 reflected an eagerness for more banking capital, free from political control, as much as a desire to regulate banks. Moreover, the final form of the 1848 manufacturing law was significantly shaped by the wish to encourage investment in manufactures. Even the plankroad, turnpike, and railroad laws were written in such a way as to give maximum freedom to private enterprise, subject only to procedural safeguards for the rights of private property.

This suggests that we need to consider the entire phenomenon of general incorporation from a broader perspective, one that gives adequate attention to the needs of the business community in the rapidly expanding economy of the early nineteenth century and that, at the same time, recognizes that the debate over general laws was symptomatic of a society struggling to resolve the continuing problem of allocation and legitimation. In this light, the transition to general incorporation can quite plausibly be viewed as part of the broader process by which the legal and political systems were "rationalized" in response to the expansion of commerce and the growth of industry. Historically, the commercial and entrepreneurial classes have sought a legal environment conducive to the orderly conduct and expansion of economic activity. Usually such an environment has meant a preference for stability, predictability, and universally applicable rules of behavior.[65] It is striking that the general incorporation movement created precisely these conditions. Whatever else they may have done, general laws established a

[65]See, for example, Max Rheinstein, ed., *Max Weber on Law in Economy and Society* (Cambridge, Mass., 1966), and Richard E. Ellis, *The Jeffersonian Crisis: Courts and Politics in the Young Republic* (New York, 1974), 256–257.

greater measure of rationality in the granting of corporate charters than had existed under the special-incorporation system. Whereas in the early period policy was fragmented, piecemeal, and based on ad hoc or individualized decisions, after the 1840s the trend was toward generalized policy based on universally applied rules. By establishing objective norms uniformly applicable to entire classes of economic activity, moreover, the substantive content of corporate charters was formalized. The impact of public policy was no longer on individual firms, but rather on all corporations engaged in a similar enterprise. The potential for uncertainty, arbitrariness, and political influence in corporate policy was therefore minimized. In practical terms, and over the long haul, this meant that although corporations were regulated as never before and the possibility of acquiring special privileges was sharply reduced, there was at least reasonable assurance that all corporations within one industry would enjoy the same privileges and endure the same restrictions. It also meant that the entire corporate system was legitimated, at least insofar as the distribution of corporate charters and regulation of corporate activities were perceived as equitable and free of political bias.

The transition to general incorporation takes on even greater significance when we consider its impact on the process of political development. For one thing, the shift from the special-incorporation system to incorporation by administrative procedure involved a reorientation of power among the branches of government. Indeed, a major objective was to remove the legislature from the chartering process in an effort to curb the corruption, logrolling, and legislative congestion so often associated with that process. In contrast to the earlier period when the legislature not only made corporate policy each time it granted a charter but also administered that policy, the legislature's responsibility was now limited to establishing general policy guidelines in a single creative act. The routine implementation of those rules was delegated to state administrative or local officials, who were also given substantial powers to oversee corporate activities. The comptroller, for example, possessed investigative and regulatory powers, under certain circumstances, over the banking and insurance industries. And county boards of supervisors played a major role in administering the power of eminent domain, as in the case of plankroads and turnpikes. The passage of general laws also enhanced the power of the courts. Some statutes, for example, delegated specific powers to a particular court, as in the case of the Railroad Act of 1850, which authorized the supreme court to appoint commissioners of appraisers in the event a railroad company could not obtain required land privately. In the long run, moreover, the twin goals of political neutrality and uniformity in the administration of corporate policy meant that the judiciary would ultimately replace the legislature as the principal interpreters of corporate law.

More important than this shift of power among the branches of government was a corresponding decline of political authority generally. As we have seen, from the seventeenth century through the early decades of the nineteenth century, New Yorkers, like other Americans, had been compelled by the exigencies of weak government to rely on private arrangements for the accomplishment of many of the functions normally encumbent on government. As a result, the public and private sectors merged to the point where, as Michael Kammen put it, "the two were virtually conflated."[66] By the early nineteenth century, the principal mechanism by which the public and private spheres were linked was the corporation. In an economy experiencing rapid growth and structural transformation, the corporation proved an ideal surrogate for weak and underfinanced state governments under increasing pressure to provide the social overhead capital (particularly in the areas of transportation and finance) for economic development. New York and most other states delegated substantial sovereignty to corporations to enable them to perform this function.

In the 1830s, however, New York responded to widespread dissatisfaction with this marriage of the state and corporation by routinizing the process by which corporations could be created, establishing general regulatory guidelines, and effectively depoliticizing the corporation. In the process, a crucial distinction emerged between the procedural and substantive aspects of corporate policy. Under the special-charter system, the incorporation of a *specific* group for a *specific* enterprise (bank, turnpike, or railroad, for example) with *specific* rights and obligations was a creative act of social or economic policy-making, even if it did not originate with the legislature. A corporation could not be divorced from the purpose for which it was chartered, and the public interest, at least theoretically, was the justification for its creation. Incorporation by administrative procedure, on the other hand, though ensuring greater rationality and predictability in the granting of charters and legitimating the corporation as an economic institution, further eroded the authority of the state. It is revealing that at no time during the debate over corporate policy was there a sustained effort to have the state assume direct responsibility for such functions as building railroads and turnpikes or providing a banking system, though in retrospect this was clearly one alternative. The state had assumed that role in education and some welfare-related

---

[66]Michael Kammen, "A Different 'Fable of the Bees': The Problem of Public and Private Sectors in Colonial America," in *The American Revolution: A Heritage of Change*, ed. John Parker and Carol Urness (Minneapolis, Minn., 1975), 53–68.

areas by 1850. Instead, the state's role was reduced to that of establishing general guidelines for the creation of private institutions, which would then make allocative decisions for the society through private arrangements.

In the final analysis, the establishment of general objective norms—rational, predictable, stable, formal, and universally applicable—weakened rather than strengthened political control over substantive policy decisions. With the dissociation of the state and the corporation, the latter lost its quasi-public status and the former was deprived of a unique instrument of public activity, without the development of any alternative political structure through which to control the direction of economic development. General incorporation laws established the rules of the game and defined minimal standards for participation. Where, when, and for what stakes the game was to be played, however, were left to the private sector.

[9]

Conclusion: Toward a
Liberal Order of Politics

THE THREE DECADES before the Civil War witnessed the birth of a new political order in New York State. Struggling to make sense of a society in flux and to develop mechanisms to control and shape that society, New Yorkers reevaluated traditional concepts of politics, subjected long-standing assumptions about the role of government to scrutiny, and questioned the legitimacy and utility of time-honored institutions. The result was the emergence of a new configuration of politics and governance, one characterized by broadened participation, the growth of administration and adjudication, and a general diffusion of authority among competing public and private centers of decision making. In the most general sense, the roots of this emergent political order can be traced to the interaction of society, economy, and politics in a context of rapid change. More specifically, new patterns of governance were the product of New Yorkers' response to the problems of allocation and legitimation brought on by modernization and the expansion of the market.

New York's social order underwent a massive transformation in the first half of the nineteenth century. Population growth, urbanization, the commercialization of agriculture, the revolutions in transportation and communications, the expansion and integration of the market, and the growth of manufacturing shattered traditional patterns of social and economic behavior and forged new ones. In the economic sphere, specialized enterprises in commerce, finance, transportation, and manufacturing replaced the general or all-purpose merchant capitalists who had dominated the economy at the beginning of the century. Specialization increased the number and variety of enterprises, enlarged the volume and scale of transactions, and eroded traditional mechanisms of coordination and control. Impersonal market mechanisms became increasingly significant in the regulation of commercial activities. New economic institutions such as banks, corporations, and insurance companies emerged to manage the efficient flow of goods and services through the expanding wilderness of market transactions. This increasing division of labor in the economy was accompanied by an equally significant transformation in the texture of social life. The spread of market relationships, the individualization of political roles, the proliferation of voluntary associations, the intrusion of urban values, and the increasing scale of social interaction restructured society along more functional, cosmopolitan, and pluralistic lines.

Political development initially took a different course. As social and economic relationships became more complex, differentiated, and centralized, the political system continued on a path set by the Revolution and reinforced by the democratic impulse after 1820. Revolutionary concepts of politics merged with traditional political structures to produce a political system that was fundamentally incapable of the rational formulation and administration of policy for a broad public. The central institution in that political system was the legislature, the one agency of government which most exemplified the commitment to republican ideals. Consistent with those principles, the legislature in the early nineteenth century was remarkably sensitive to its constituencies. Direct representation, annual elections for the assembly, yearly sessions, and direct access to the lawmaking process through petitions and memorials blurred the boundaries between the legislature and the society at large. Taking into account localism and the expansion of participation brought about by the liberalization of the suffrage, it is arguable that the legislative system in the middle decades of the century more closely approximated the republican ideal of government than at any other period of American history.

Ironically, the very responsiveness of that system contributed to its inability to govern authoritatively in the increasingly fragmented, mobile, and individualistic society that emerged after 1815. Because of its own lack of internal structures, a fusion of nonlegislative functions, rapid turnover of members, intense localism, and the pervasive distrust of power, the legislature was unable to lead the society as a whole. Rather than a representative forum for the creation of general policy, the legislature can best be described as an arena for the processing of highly fragmentary and particularized policy demands from private, local, and sectional interests. Bargaining and logrolling were the distinctive modes of decision making, and policy outcomes were disaggregative in character.

This is not to argue that the political system was too representative. Indeed, it is still unclear whether the legislature actually represented the people or simply those who were most influential in local communities. Rather, what I am suggesting is that the structures of representation became less and less congruent with the realities of the social order. Political principles conceived to deal with the problems of power and liberty in the relatively undifferentiated society of the eighteenth century created patterns of representation and governance which became increasingly disfunctional as the social context within which those principles had emerged was transformed.

It is not surprising that in a society embued with republican ideals, deep fears of power, and a strong antipathy to executive authority, the implementation of policy decisions was similarly handicapped. Administration in the modern sense was virtually unknown, except perhaps in the management of the canals. Governmental structures were neither very differentiated nor integrated. The administrative function was divided among the state officers and a series of specially created boards and commissions, all of which had developed in piecemeal fashion in response to specific needs, were virtually independent of the governor, and were insulated from each other. In the absence of a central authority to integrate and coordinate their activities, functions and roles inevitably overlapped and became confused. It was a political system, in short, that remained essentially premodern as late as the 1830s: decentralized, undifferentiated, unintegrated, localistic, and particularistic.

The interaction of a rapidly modernizing socioeconomic system with a political culture inherited from the Revolution and predicated on the dispersal of power produced in New York a distinctive political economy. One of the most urgent tasks confronting the state in the initial stages of economic growth and development was the removal of physical, geographical, attitudinal, and political barriers to the extension of the market. Despite its "boundlessness,"[1] or perhaps because of it, the New York political system was well suited to that task. Responding to the needs of the underdeveloped society and economy in the early nineteenth century, the state subsidized enterprise, regulated economic activity, and fashioned a legal order conducive to private enterprise and economic growth. It was a highly pragmatic and, given a political culture profoundly distrustful of power and authority, a very effective response. With little regard for ideology, other than a diffuse commitment to capitalism, New Yorkers mobilized the complete range of state

---

[1]This characterization of early-nineteenth-century New York society as "boundless" is taken from Higham, *From Boundlessness to Consolidation*.

resources to remove obstacles from the path of private enterprise and to clear the way for the creation of a market economy.

Apart from the sheer range and variety of state economic activities, the most distinctive feature of this political economy was the distributive character of public economic policies. With the exception of certain aspects of canal policy, state aid to the economy lacked any systematic direction. A fragmented and localistic political system dictated that policy decisions be made on an ad hoc basis, case by case, and typically in response to supplication from the individuals or groups seeking aid. Government was not so much making "policy," if by that word we imply some sort of conscious plan or rational course of action, as it was universally gratifying private, local, and sectional demands. Further diluting public authority was the state's tendency to relinquish its responsibility for resource allocation to the private sector by delegating the power of eminent domain and other legal privileges to private individuals and corporations who undertook to perform what were essentially public functions. In the final analysis, New York's political economy was a classic example of a state, to borrow Wallace Farnham's phrase, "subsidizing without governing."[2]

By the middle of the 1830s, New Yorkers confronted what can only be termed a crisis of distributive politics. At the heart of that crisis was a classic dilemma of developing societies: how to balance the twin objectives of allocation and legitimation. Distributive allocations had served the needs of society in the early stages of development precisely because it was possible to satisfy all, or at least most, demands without having to choose among competing private, local, and sectional claims against the resources of the state. Ironically, however, the success of this essentially pragmatic and nonideological policy system gave birth to the very stresses that threatened the viability of the political economy of distribution by the 1840s. The increasing complexity of society, the proliferation of interests owing to the division of labor and social differentiation, expanded political participation, and the spread of market relationships overwhelmed the capacity of the existing system of politics to deal rationally and authoritatively with the social and economic issues of the day. It became increasingly difficult to make allocative decisions without straining the resources of the state to the breaking point or alienating important social or geographical interests. Put simply, distributive outputs had gotten completely out of control. Given the nature of the political system, this may have been inevitable. In any case, distributive allocations could no longer sustain support for that system because of the growing number of

[2]Wallace D. Farnham, "The Weakened Spring of Government: A Study in Nineteenth Century American History," *American Historical Review*, 63 (April 1963), 680.

people who felt that their particular demands were not being met, perceptions of inefficiency and corruption in state government, and fears that the allocative process was no longer equitable and consistent with republican values.

From an even broader perspective, the politics of distribution were no longer functional in the emerging market society and economy. Positive state action had been used to remove barriers to the extension of the market, but once the market mechanism was set in motion, its own need for rationality and reasonable expectation became the operative principle. At some point public authority, which had been so crucial to the creation of the market, became the chief hindrance to the smooth operation of that system. Irrational policy processes, a traditional political system oriented toward the locality, and public debts that strained the entire society and threatened taxation were inconsistent with such market values as stability, uniformity, and predictability. In short, the dictates of a rapidly developing market system were beginning to transform society and politics.[3]

The Panic of 1837 and the ensuing depression highlighted and brought to the surface these fundamental contradictions in the state's political economy. Between 1837 and 1843, as New Yorkers debated the issues of state debts and the future of development policy, they also began to reassess fundamental principles of politics. What, for example, should the role of government be? How should allocative decisions for the society be determined? And what principles or mechanisms of politics best served to legitimate those decisions? Although there was little consensus on the answer to these questions among different political groups, there was a general recognition that the politics of distribution could no longer resolve the problems of allocation and legitimation. Out of this realization, and during the course of debates over the People's Resolutions and the "Stop and Tax" law, two broad strategies of legitimacy emerged. One was based on traditional democratic theory and sought to make government more responsive to the people by limiting the power of the legislature and instituting a form of direct democracy. The second strategy, which overlapped with the first, was based more on administrative values. The goal was to manage the tensions and contradictions in the political system by reducing the volume and kinds of demands made on government; by restructuring political processes along more rational, stable and predictable lines; and, more generally, by replacing politics with administrative modes of decision making.

[3]For particularly insightful discussions of the impact of the market on society and politics, see Polanyi, *The Great Transformation*, and Hurst, *Law and the Conditions of Freedom*.

The interaction and accommodation of these two responses to the crisis of distributive politics profoundly shaped patterns of governance in the middle decades of the century. The democratic strategy permeated efforts to revise the state's constitution between 1843 and 1846. Frustrated by the excesses of a system of politics based on distribution, rapidly accumulating public debts, and the corruption and inefficiency of legislative politics, New Yorkers across the political spectrum lost faith in representative institutions and demanded more direct popular participation in decision making. Delegates to the constitutional convention of 1846 responded by curtailing distributive outputs, restricting legislative authority, and broadening the basis of participation in the political system. Constitutional prohibitions of certain types of economic activity redefined government's economic role from that of active participant to passive overseer. At the same time, the extension of the elective principle to administrative and judicial officers, shortened terms of office, single-member districts, and a general decentralization of governmental structures increased the opportunities for participation and strengthened citizen attachments to the system. Nor was this the extent of democratization. Under the new constitution, authority that had previously resided in the legislature was transferred to the people. In a sense, the constitution itself, with its codelike provisions and its elaborate arrangements for constitutional referenda, reflected the new desire to involve the people directly in the governmental process. In some areas of policy, furthermore, such as financial matters, final decision-making authority was formally delegated to the electorate.

But democratization alone cannot explain the configuration of political change in the 1840s and 1850s. The political system also experienced the beginnings of a second transformation during these years, which, in the long run, was as profound as the shift to direct democracy. Although less clear-cut than the process of democratization, this transformation is discernible in the displacement of power from the legislature to other agencies and forces in the society; the reinvigoration of local government; the creation of new, functionally specific state agencies and departments; experimentation with independent regulatory agencies; and the revitalization of judicial power. The origins and specific histories of these developments were various, but they were ultimately elements of a common process: the displacement of politics and the emergence of administration and adjudication as mechanisms of conflict resolution and legitimation.

This transformation of politics was complex and at times ambiguous. For one thing, the democratic and administrative strategies of legitimacy overlapped and, at critical moments, drew strength from one another. Thus, the equal-rights component of democratic rhetoric lent crucial ideological support for the concept of formal legal equality without which the administrative ethic could not have existed. Similarly, the extension of the elective principle to administrative and judicial officials helped to legitimate the enlarged role of those elements of government in the decision-making process. There were also elements of irony in the story. One might reasonably expect, following Max Weber's concept of bureaucratization, that an explicit ideology stressing the virtues of rationalization and centralization would accompany the appearance of bureaucratic traits.[4] Although some New Yorkers did seek greater efficiency in government, the first halting steps toward the creation of modern administrative structures in New York grew out of the desire to curtail power and divide authority, rather than to rationalize and integrate it.

The creative tension between the democratic and administrative strategies of legitimacy and the consequences of that tension for the political system are well illustrated by the evolution of corporate policy. Indeed, no other issue so clearly represented the point at which government and politics intersected with society and economy. By 1860 New York had adopted the principle of incorporation by administrative procedure rather than by special legislative act. This had the effect of democratizing the process by which corporate charters were granted and making the legal advantages of corporate status more broadly accessible. But the emergence of general incorporation also helped to legitimate the corporate system. The removal of the legislature from the chartering process contributed to the depoliticization and privatization of the corporation. With the adoption of general, objective norms applicable to entire classes of economic activity rather than to individual firms, the conferral of corporate status was routinized and the judiciary was elevated to the role of principal interpreter of corporate law and behavior. Democratic critics of the corporation could accept this arrangement because it embodied the principles of equal rights and equality before the law. Entrepreneurs and potential incorporators could accept general laws precisely because they removed the process of incorporation from the realm of politics—with its instability, unpredictability, and sensitivity to popular whim— to the more stable and predictable realm of administration. In effect, a bargain was struck between government and economic interests and between individuals and groups within particular industries wherein the terms of enterprise were rationalized and potential incorporators agreed to accept what Daryl Baskin has called "the known disadvantage,"[5] rather than risk the

---

[4] Max Weber, "Bureaucracy," in *From Max Weber: Essays in Sociology*, ed. H. H. Gerth and C. Wright Mills (New York, 1958), 196–244.

[5] Baskin, *American Pluralist Democracy*, 96.

uncertainties of political decision-making in a popularly based political system.

But all parties paid a price for this rationalization and legitimation of corporation policy. Economic interests were compelled to accept a greater degree of regulation in return for the benefits of stability and predictability. The state, on the other hand, had to accept a less direct role in the establishment of economic priorities. In writing a general incorporation law, the state was essentially creating what Murray Edelman has called "a space in which to act." According to Edelman, "to formulate a law is essentially a job of constructing a setting in the sense of background assumptions and limits that will persist over time and influence the quality of political acts *but not their content or direction*" [emphasis added].⁶ Although he was referring to all general laws, Edelman's distinction between "the quality of political acts" and their "content or direction" goes to the heart of the transformation of corporate policy in this period. In effect, the legitimacy of the corporation, so integral a part of the emergent market economy, was won by divesting it of its public character and function and by emphasizing procedural fairness over the substantive content of corporate policy.

The political significance of the transformation of the corporation from a public to a private institution has not been sufficiently appreciated. Yet it is possible to view the evolution of the corporation as a reflection, in microcosm, of the more fundamental changes occurring in New York's political regime. No other issue posed the problems of allocation and legitimation so persistently and so starkly. Similarly, no other policy issue reveals the underlying tendencies of the political system with such clarity.

Having analyzed the process of political change in some detail, it may be useful at this point to try to distill from that process some of the characteristic features of the emergent political order. The task is fraught with difficulties and interpretive dangers. For one thing, the absence of any systematic discussion of the principles of politics on the order, say, of *The Federalist Papers*, forces us to infer those principles from the structures and processes of the system itself. An additional analytical burden flows from the incremental nature of political change. With the exception of the Constitution of 1846, the political system was transformed piecemeal over several decades in response to specific economic and political circumstances. Furthermore, the process of emergence was by no means complete. The role of government continued to evolve in response to the post–Civil War transformation of economy and society. The trend toward direct democracy, so dramatically evident in the Constitutional Convention of 1846, was even more manifest

⁶Murray Edelman, *The Symbolic Uses of Politics* (Urbana, Ill., 1967), 103.

in efforts to reform the constitutional environment later in the century. Similarly, the administrative impulse, whose beginnings we can detect before 1860, decisively reshaped the political system and the conduct of politics in the late nineteenth and early twentieth centuries.

Despite such difficulties, the broad outlines of a new pattern of governance were clearly visible by 1860. One is struck first by the impression that the middle decades of the century constituted a transition period between two distinct regimes, each of which is identified by a distinctive form of policy. As noted earlier, distributive policies, easily disaggregated and dispensed unit by unit in isolation from one another, were the characteristic political outcome in the early decades of the century. The quintessential such policy was the special corporate charter. Distributive policies were uniquely functional in the developing society of the early nineteenth century, where individuals and narrow, often local, interests competed with one another for largess and favors in a relatively open and unbounded legislative environment. The result was a bargaining style of politics and governance whose legitimacy depended on confidence in its representativeness and, to no small extent, satisfaction with the payoff.

General incorporation laws were the prototypes of the new emphasis on regulation toward which the state was moving after mid-century. Regulatory policies, by definition incapable of infinite disaggregation, reflected conflicts among larger, more organized social and economic interests. The emergence of such interests was a product of the reordering of society along group and associational lines as a result of modernization. The existence of broad, abstract categories or classes of economic activity made universal, impersonal rules feasible and desirable, both from the point of view of a political system striving to legitimate its policy processes and from that of newly emergent entrepreneurial groups demanding rational administrative procedures to advance their economic interests.

Of course, the transition from a distributive to a regulatory policy regime was neither sudden nor clean-cut. The two obviously overlapped, with residues of the former continuing to shape the formulation of policy until the twentieth century. Indeed, Richard L. McCormick has identified distributive policies as a distinctive characteristic of what he calls the party period in American political history extending to the early 1900s.[7] Even so, the process of transition had clearly begun by mid-century, the product of New Yorkers' responses to specific economic and political challenges generated by modernization and the expansion of the market.

---

[7] McCormick, "The Party Period and Public Policy," 279–298.

As striking as this policy transition was the new, enlarged role of "the people" in the processes of government. Nor was it simply the expansion of the suffrage which gave the system its popular character. The emergence of mass-based political parties along with legal and constitutional changes reducing the terms of office, expanding the list of elective positions, and enlarging the responsibilities of local officials brought government into closer contact with the electorate. More significant, "the people," by writing statutory law into the constitution and by legislating on such important matters as state finances through constitutional referenda, assumed lawmaking functions previously performed by representatives. This unprecedented policy-making role suggests that by mid-century "the people" had become, in a sense, an active "fourth branch" of the government.

The expansion of popular influence in government came at the expense of the legislature. We need not reiterate here the litany of functions stripped from the legislature through constitutional provision and statutory law. Suffice to say, from the peak of the legislature's influence in 1777 to the middle of the nineteenth century, the story of legislative development is one of steady decline. To be sure, the legislature neither disappeared from the scene nor ceased to play a central role in public policy-making. But the nature of that role was profoundly different. Its authority no longer reached into every nook and cranny of the political system. Nor did it enjoy the aura of legitimacy which had once made it synonymous with government. The parceling out of legislative functions and the care with which legislative discretion was circumscribed are a measure of the revulsion against representative government and the emergence of a form of direct democracy as the basis of political legitimacy.

Other changes in the political system also narrowed the scope of legislative competence. Responding to the pressure of an increasingly complex and differentiated social order, New Yorkers developed more elaborate and effective administrative structures. Existing institutions became more differentiated; new state agencies appeared to regulate new social and economic activities; and local governments acquired a greater role in the political system as part of a broader trend toward decentralization. Although understandable, and perhaps inevitable, in the context of rapid modernization, these changes nevertheless occurred at the expense of the most popular branch of government. So too did the more general tendency, best exemplified in general incorporation laws, to define problems in administrative terms to be resolved through the application of impersonal rules. The growth of administration reflected the drive for rationality and the growing demand for equality of rights consequent on the emergence of a more pluralistic society and economy. Together with the increasing autonomy of the judiciary, this tendency signified the beginnings of a shift from political to administrative and adjudicative solutions to social problems and conflicts.

A less obvious, but no less significant, characteristic of the new political regime was a fundamental tendency toward the differentiation of the political and economic components of society. This process was readily apparent in the transformation of the corporation and in constitutional restrictions against various kinds of governmental intervention in the economy. But the character and significance of that differentiation went far beyond simply the withdrawal of government from economic activity or debates over the relative merits of laissez-faire. It was a function, at one level, of the emerging distinction between public and private, and, at another level, of the increasingly pluralistic nature of the maturing market economy and society. As Theodore Lowi has pointed out in his brilliant analysis of the emergence of interest-group liberalism, one of the consequences of pluralism is the discontinuity between that which is socioeconomic and that which is political. "Politics in the pluralist model," according to Lowi, "ceases to be an epiphenomenon of socioeconomic life. Politics becomes autonomous as the number of autonomous and competing social units multiplies."[8] A corollary of this principle, as Lowi again reminds us, is that "in a pluralist society there is also a discontinuity between politics and government."[9] The entire thrust of political change in New York in the middle decades of the nineteenth century, it seems, was toward just such a more restricted definition of the public and political elements of society.

Thus understood, the differentiation of the political and economic spheres may be viewed as symptomatic of the growth of multiple centers of decision making. In the political regime of the early nineteenth century, whatever its shortcomings, responsibility for stimulating and managing the course of economic development was presumed to lie with the state government in general, and the legislature in particular. By mid-century, such was no longer the case. The legislature now shared such responsibility with administrative and judicial officials at the state level, local governmental bodies, the electorate, and, most extraordinary of all, private entities such as the newly legitimated business corporation. In short, governmental authority was not simply declining because of constitutionally mandated prohibitions; it was being diffused among a multiplicity of public and private decision makers.

This diffusion of public authority at precisely the moment when political participation was expanding goes to the heart of the emerging political order. On the one hand, it becomes increasingly difficult to conceive of the state as

[8] Lowi, *End of Liberalism*, 45.
[9] Ibid., 48.

a unitary instrument for the implementation of a public interest. On the other, it suggests that for all the democratizing tendencies of the preceding three decades, and they *were* real, there were nevertheless limits to the people's role in substantive policy making. The legislature in the third quarter of the century was but a shadow of what it had been earlier. A whole range of issues, mostly economic, had been either depoliticized or privatized. At the same time, the rise of administration and adjudication, almost by definition, imposed limits on the power of popular majorities. Together, these developments drained political participation of much of its substantive meaning. The people, acting through democratic procedures, constituted one of a growing number of decision-making authorities. But they were by no means the only source of allocative decisions for the society; nor, for that matter, were they necessarily the most relevant ones. Decades of political development, in the context of rapid socioeconomic change and the expansion of the market, had produced in New York a liberal order of politics in which groups competed with one another within the framework of a legal order and political system whose very legitimacy depended on its ability to divorce procedure from substance. Ultimately, the system rested on a delicate balance of democratic and administrative values. The rhetoric of democracy remained to legitimate political relationships, and on extraordinary occasions the people could inject themselves directly into the policy-making process. Administrative values, however, increasingly shaped the day-to-day workings of government.

This pattern of political change may have been inevitable given a political culture and constitutional order so deeply imbued with antipower and antigovernment biases. Still, it is remarkable that during a period of such intense modernization, no sustained argument on behalf of the positive exercise of democratic power appeared. What did emerge was a form of democracy uniquely functional in a market economy, one which was exclusively political and procedural, with vast areas of social and economic life safely beyond the reach of democratic power.

Selected Bibliography

PRIMARY MATERIALS

Government Publications

New York (State). *Annual Reports of the Commissioners of Emigration of the State of New York . . . 1847 to 1860.* New York, 1861.

———. Audit and Control Department. *Annual Report,* 1854.

———. *Census,* 1855.

———. *Constitution of the State of New York Adopted in 1846, with a Comparative Arrangement of the Constitutional Provisions of Other States.* Prepared Under the Direction of a Committee of the New York Constitutional Convention of 1867. By Franklin B. Hough. Albany: Weed, Parsons, 1867.

———. *Debates and Proceedings in the New York State Convention, For the Revision of the Constitution.* By S. Croswell and R. Sutton. Albany: *Albany Argus,* 1846.

———. *Documents of the Assembly of the State of New York,* 1830–1860.

———. *Documents of the Convention of the State of New York, 1846.* Albany: Carol & Cook, Printers, 1846.

———. *Documents of the Senate of the State of New York,* 1830–1860.

———. *General Index to the Documents of New York, 1777–1857.* Prepared by T. S. Gillett. Albany, 1860.

———. *General Index to the Documents of the State of New York, From 1777 to 1865, Inclusive.* Prepared by Ornon Archer. Albany: Weed, Parsons, Printers, 1866.

———. *General Index to the Laws, 1777–1896.* 6 vols. Albany, 1866–1897.

———. Insurance Department. *First Annual Report of the Superintendent of the Insurance Department.* Albany: Charles Van Benthuysen, Printer, 1860.

———. *Journal of the Assembly,* 1830–1860.

———. *Journal of the Convention of the State of New York, begun and Held at the Capitol in the City of Albany, on the First Day of June, 1846.* Albany: Carroll & Cook, Printers, 1846.

[259]

———. *Journal of the Senate, 1830–1860.*

———. *Laws of the State of New York, 1776–1860.*

———. *Messages from the Governors, Comprising Executive Communications to the Legislature and Other Papers Relating to Legislation from the Organization of the First Colonial Assembly in 1683 to and Including the Year 1906, with Notes,* ed. Charles Z. Lincoln. 11 vols. Albany: J. B. Lyon, State Printers, 1909.

———. *Red Book.* Albany: Croswell, Van Benthuysen, & Burt, 1838.

———. "Report upon the Finances and Internal Improvements of the State of New York, 1838." New York: John S. Taylor, 1838.

———. *Report of the Debates and Proceedings of the Convention of the State of New York, 1846.* By William G. Bishop and W. H. Attree. Albany: *Evening Atlas,* 1846.

Reports of Cases Argued and Determined in the Court of Chancery of the State of New York. By Samuel M. Hopkins. New York: Oliver Halsted, 1827.

Reports of Cases Argued and Determined in the Court of Chancery of the State of New York. By Alonzo C. Paige. New York: Banks & Brothers, 1863.

Reports of Cases Argued and Determined in the Supreme Court and in the Court for the Correction of Errors of the State of New York. By Hiram Denio. New York: Banks & Brothers, 1883.

Reports of Cases Argued and Determined in the Supreme Court of Judicature and in the Court for the Trial of Impeachments and the Corrections of Errors, of the State of New York. By William Johnson. 3d ed. New York: Banks & Brothers, 1883.

Reports of Cases Argued and Determined in the Supreme Court of Judicature and in the Court for the Trial of Impeachments and the Correction of Errors of the State of New York. By John L. Wendell. 2d ed. New York: Banks & Brothers, 1883.

Reports of Cases Argued and Determined in the Supreme Court of the State of New York. By Nicholas Hill. New York: Banks & Brothers, 1883.

Reports of Cases Argued in the Court of Chancery of New York. By William Johnson. Albany: D. F. Backus, 1816–1824.

Thorpe, Francis N., comp. *The Federal and State Constitutions, Colonial Charters, and Other Organic Laws of the States, Territories, and Colonies.* 7 vols. Washington, D.C.: U.S. Government Printing Office, 1909.

U.S. Bureau of the Census. *Abstract of the 7th Census, 1850.* Washington, D.C.: Robert Armstrong, Printer, 1853.

———. *Compendium of the 10th Census, 1880.* Washington, D.C.: Government Printing Office, 1883.

U.S. Congress. *Annals of the Congress of the United States, 1789–1824.* 42 vols. Washington, D.C.: 1834–56.

Newspapers

Albany Argus
Albany Morning Atlas
Commercial Advertiser
New York Tribune

Additional Primary Materials

Address and Draft of a Proposed Constitution, Submitted to the People of the State of New York, By a Convention of Friends of Constitutional Reform, Held at Utica, September, 1837. New York: published by the Convention, 1837.

Bibliography

The Albany Democratic Reformer, Embodying Documents Concerning Governmental Reformation in the State of New York. Albany: C. Van Benthuysen, 1844.

Angell, Joseph K., and Samuel Ames. *A Treatise on the Law of Private Corporations Aggregate*. Boston: Hilliard, Gray, Little, & Wilkins, 1832.

Butler, Benjamin F. "Outline of the Constitutional History of New York, an Anniversary Discourse, Delivered at the Request of the New York Historical Society, in the City of New York, November 19, 1847." *Collections of the New York Historical Society*, 2d ser., vol. 2 (1849), 9–75.

Byrdsall, F. *The History of the Loco-Foco or Equal Rights Party, Its Movements, Conventions, and Proceedings with Short Characteristic Sketches of Its Prominent Men*. New York: Clement & Packard, 1842.

Chevalier, Michael. *Society, Manners, and Politics in the United States*, ed. John W. Ward. Garden City, N.Y.: Doubleday, 1961.

"Constitutional Governments," *The United States Magazine and Democratic Review*, 20 (March 1847): 195–204.

"Constitutional Reform," *The United States Magazine and Democratic Review*, 13 (December 1843): 563–576.

DeBow, J. D. B. *Statistical View of the United States . . . Being a Compendium of the Seventh Census*. Reprint. New York: Gordon & Breach, 1970.

Disturnell, J. *Gazetteer of the State of New York*. Albany: J. Disturnell, 1842.

Finegan, Thomas E. *Free Schools: A Documentary History of the Free School Movement in New York State*. Albany: The University of the State of New York, 1921.

Flagg, A. C. "Internal Improvements . . . in New York." *Merchants' Magazine and Commercial Review*, 25 (October 1851): 421–422.

Gordon, Thomas F. *Gazetteer of the State of New York*. Philadelphia: T. K. & P. G. Collins, Printers, 1836.

"History of Constitutional Reform in the United States," *United States Magazine and Democratic Review*, 18 (June 1846): 403–420.

Holly, O. L., ed. *The New York State Register*. New York: J. Disturnell, 1843.

Hone, Philip. *The Diary of Philip Hone, 1828–1851*, ed. Allan Nevins. New York: Dodd, Mead, 1936.

Hough, Franklin B., comp. *The New York Civil List, Containing the Names and Origin of the Civil Divisions, and the Names and Dates of Election or Appointment of the Principal State and County Officers, from the Revolution to the Present Time*. Albany: Weed, Parsons, 1860.

Hurlbut, E. P. *Essays on Human Rights and Their Political Guarantees, with a Preface and Notes by George Combe*. Edinburgh: MacLachlan, Stewart, & Co., 1847.

Hutchins, S. C., comp. *Civil List . . . of New York*. Albany: Weed, Parsons, 1855.

———. *Civil List . . . of New York, 1869*. Albany, 1869.

———. *Civil List and Forms of Government of the Colony and State of New York . . . Arranged in Constitutional Periods*. Albany, 1874.

Johnson, A. B. "The Legislative History of Corporations in the State of New York," *Merchants' Magazine and Commercial Review*, 23 (December 1850): 610–614.

Kent, James. *Commentaries on American Laws*. 4 vols. New York: O. Halsted, 1826–1830.

Kettell, Thomas P., ed. *Constitutional Reform, in a Series of Articles Contributed to the Democratic Review, upon Constitutional Government*. New York: Thomas P. Kettell, 1846.

"The New York Constitutional Convention," *United States Magazine and Democratic Review*, 19 (November 1846): 339–348.

Pitkin, Timothy. *A Statistical View of the Commerce of the United States of America.* Reprint. New York: Johnson Reprint Corp., 1967.

"Railroad Legislation of New York in 1849," *Merchants' Magazine and Commercial Review*, 21 (July–December 1849): 163–181.

Seward, William H. *The Works of William H. Seward*, ed. George E. Baker. 3 vols. New York: C. A. Alvord, Printer, 1853.

Spafford, Horatio Gates. *A Gazeteer of the State of New York.* Albany: Packard & Van Benthuysen, 1824.

A Statement of the Arts and Manufactures of the United States of America, for the Year 1810: Digested and Prepared by Tench Coxe. Philadelphia: A. Cornman, 1814.

Street, Alfred B. *The Council of Revision of the State of New York.* Albany: William Gould, 1859.

Strong, George Templeton. *The Diary of George Templeton Strong, 1835–1875*, ed. Allan Nevins and Milton Halsey Thomas. 3 vols. New York: Macmillan, 1953.

Tocqueville, Alexis de. *Democracy in America*, ed. J. P. Mayer. New York: Doubleday, 1966.

A Vindication of the Public Faith of New York and Pennsylvania, in Reply to the Calumnies of the 'Times' To Which Is Appended a Report, Made to the Senate of New York in Relation to the Debt, Revenue, and Financial Policy of the State. London: J. Miller, 1840.

Whig Almanac and United States Register, 1838–1850, ed. Horace Greeley. New York: Dearborn, 1838–1850.

Williams, Edwin, comp. *The New York Annual Register, 1833.* New York: Peter Hill, 1833.

SECONDARY MATERIALS

Books

Abernathy, Byron R. *Constitutional Limitations on the Legislature.* The University of Kansas Publications, Governmental Research Series, no. 20, Lawrence, Kans.: 1959.

Aitken, Hugh G. J., ed. *The State and Economic Growth.* New York: Social Science Research Council, 1959.

Albion, Robert G. *The Rise of New York Port, 1815–1860.* New York: Charles Scribner's Sons, 1939.

Alexander, D. S. *A Political History of the State of New York.* 3 vols. Reprint. Port Washington, N.Y.: I. J. Friedman, 1969.

Alexander, Margaret C. *The Development of the Powers of the State Executive, with Special Reference to the State of New York.* Northampton, Mass.: Department of History of Smith College, 1917.

Almond, Gabriel A., and G. Bingham Powell, Jr. *Comparative Politics: A Developmental Approach.* Boston: Little, Brown, 1966.

Almond, Gabriel, and Sidney Verba. *The Civic Culture: Political Attitudes and Democracy in Five Nations.* Princeton, N.J.: Princeton University Press, 1963.

Apter, David. *The Politics of Modernization.* Chicago: University of Chicago Press, 1965.

———. *Some Conceptual Approaches to the Study of Modernization.* Englewood Cliffs, N.J.: Prentice-Hall, 1968.

Arieli, Yehoshua. *Individualism and Nationalism in American Ideology*. Cambridge, Mass.: Harvard University Press, 1964.

Bailyn, Bernard. *The Ideological Origins of the American Revolution*. Cambridge, Mass.: The Belknap Press of Harvard University Press, 1967.

———. *The Origins of American Politics*. New York: Vintage Books, 1970.

Baker, Jean H. *Affairs of Party: The Political Culture of Northern Democrats in the Mid-Nineteenth Century*. Ithaca: Cornell University Press, 1983.

Baskin, Darryl. *American Pluralist Democracy: A Critique*. New York: Van Nostrand Reinhold, 1971.

Benson, Lee. *The Concept of Jacksonian Democracy: New York as a Test Case*. New York: Atheneum, 1967.

———. *Merchants, Farmers and Railroads; Railroad Regulation and New York Politics, 1850–1887*. Cambridge, Mass.: Harvard University Press, 1955.

Berthoff, Rowland. *An Unsettled People: Social Order and Disorder in American History*. New York: Harper & Row, 1971.

Bidwell, Percy W., and John I. Falconer. *History of Agriculture in the Northern United States, 1620–1860*. Washington, D.C.: The Carnegie Institution of Washington, 1925.

Billington, Ray Allen. *The Protestant Crusade, 1800–1860: A Study of the Origins of American Nativism*. Chicago: Quadrangle Books, 1964.

Black, C. E. *The Dynamics of Modernization: A Study in Comparative History*. New York: Harper Colophon Books, 1966.

Blumin, Stuart M. *The Urban Threshold: Growth and Change in a Nineteenth Century American Community*. Chicago: University of Chicago Press, 1976.

Breuer, Ernest Henry. *Constitutional Developments in New York, 1777–1958: A Bibliography of Conventions and Constitutions with Selected References for Constitutional Research*. Albany: University of the State of New York, State Education Department, 1958.

Bridges, Amy. *A City in the Republic: Antebellum New York and the Origins of Machine Politics*. Cambridge: Cambridge University Press, 1984.

Brown, Richard D. *Modernization: The Transformation of American Life, 1600–1865*. New York: Hill & Wang, 1976.

Bruchey, Stuart. *The Roots of American Economic Growth, 1607–1861: An Essay in Social Causation*. New York: Harper & Row, 1968.

Burnham, Walter Dean. *Critical Elections and the Mainsprings of American Politics*. New York: W. W. Norton, 1970.

Chaddock, Robert E. *The Safety Fund Banking System in New York, 1829–1866*. National Monetary Commission. Washington, D.C.: U.S. Government Printing Office, 1910.

Chambers, William Nesbit. *Political Parties in a New Nation: The American Experience 1776–1809*. New York: Oxford University Press, 1963.

Chambers, William Nesbit, and Walter Dean Burnham, ed. *The American Party Systems: Stages of Political Development*. New York: Oxford University Press, 1967.

Chandler, Alfred D., Jr. *The Visible Hand: The Managerial Revolution in American Business*. Cambridge, Mass.: Harvard University Press, 1977.

Chester, Alden, ed. *Legal and Judicial History of New York*. 3 vols. New York: National Americana Society, 1911.

Christman, Henry. *Tin Horns and Calico: A Decisive Episode in the Emergence of Democracy*. New York: H. Holt, 1945.

Clapp, Margaret. *Forgotten First Citizen: John Bigelow*. Boston: Little, Brown, 1947.

Clark, Victor S. *History of Manufactures in the United States*. 3 vols. New York: published for the Carnegie Institution of Washington by McGraw-Hill, 1929.

Cochran, Thomas C. *Business in American Life: A History*. New York: McGraw-Hill, 1972.

Cole, Arthur H. *The American Wool Manufactures*. 2 vols. Reprint. New York: Harper & Row, 1969.

Cott, Nancy F. *The Bonds of Womanhood: "Woman's Sphere" in New England, 1780–1835*. New Haven, Conn.: Yale University Press, 1977.

Cremin, Lawrence A. *The American Common School: An Historic Conception*. New York: Columbia University Press, 1951.

Crenson, Matthew A. *The Federal Machine: Beginnings of Bureaucracy in Jacksonian America*. Baltimore, Md.: The Johns Hopkins University Press, 1975.

Cross, Whitney R. *The Burned-Over District: The Social and Intellectual History of Enthusiastic Religion in Western New York, 1800–1850*. New York: Harper & Row, 1965 (originally pub. 1950).

Danhof, Clarence. *Change in Agriculture: The Northern United States, 1820–1870*. Cambridge, Mass.: Harvard University Press, 1969.

Davis, Joseph S. *Essays in the Earlier History of American Corporations*. 2 vols. Cambridge, Mass.: Harvard University Press, 1917.

Davis, David Brion. *Homicide in American Fiction, 1798–1860*. Ithaca: Cornell University Press, 1957.

Davis, Lance and Douglas C. North. *Institutional Change and American Economic Growth*. London: Cambridge University Press, 1971.

Dealey, James Q. *Growth of American State Constitutions from 1776 to the End of the Year 1914*. New York: Ginn, 1915.

De Grazia, Alfred. *Public and Republic: Political Representation in America*. New York: Alfred A. Knopf, 1951.

Dewey, Davis Rich. *Financial History of the United States*. 12th ed. New York: Longmans, Green, 1934.

———. *State Banking before the Civil War*. National Monetary Commission. Washington, D.C.: U.S. Government Printing Office, 1910.

Dodd, Edwin M. *American Business Corporations until 1860*. Cambridge, Mass.: Harvard University Press, 1954.

Dodd, Walter F. *The Revision and Amendment of State Constitutions*. New York: Da Capo Press, 1970.

Donald, David. *Lincoln Reconsidered: Essays on the Civil War Era*. 2d ed. New York: Vintage Books, 1961.

Donovan, Herbert D. A. *The Barnburners: A Study of the Internal Movements in the Political History of New York State and the Resulting Changes in Political Affiliation, 1830–1852*. New York: New York University Press, 1926.

Dougherty, John H. *Constitutional History of the State of New York*. 2d ed. New York: Neale, 1915.

Drago, George. *Law in the New Republic: Private Law and the Public Estate*. New York: Alfred A. Knopf, 1983.

Draper, Andrew Sloan. *Origin and Development of the Common School System of the State of New York*. Syracuse: C. W. Bardeen, 1903.

Durrenberger, Joseph A. *Turnpikes: A Study of the Toll Road Movement in the Middle Atlantic States and Maryland.* Reprint. CusCob, Conn.: John E. Edwards, 1968.

Easton, David. *A Systems Analysis of Political Life.* New York: Wiley, 1965.

Edelman, Murray. *The Symbolic Uses of Politics.* Urbana: University of Illinois Press, 1967.

Eisenstadt, S. N. *Modernization: Protest and Change.* Englewood Cliffs, N.J.: Prentice-Hall, 1966.

Elazar, Daniel. *The American Partnership: Intergovernmental Cooperation in the Nineteenth Century United States.* Chicago: University of Chicago Press, 1962.

Elkins, Stanley. *Slavery: A Problem in American Institutional and Intellectual Life.* Chicago: University of Chicago Press, 1968.

Ellis, David Maldwyn. *Landlords and Farmers in the Hudson-Mohawk Region, 1790–1850.* Ithaca: Cornell University Press, 1946.

Ellis, David M., James A. Frost, Harold C. Syrett, and Harry J. Carman. *A Short History of New York State.* Ithaca: Cornell University Press, 1957.

Ellis, Richard E. *The Jeffersonian Crisis: Courts and Politics in the Young Republic.* New York: W. W. Norton, 1974.

Ely, Richard T. *Taxation in American States and Cities.* New York: Thomas Y. Crowell, 1888.

Ernst, Robert. *Immigrant Life in New York City, 1825–1863.* Port Washington, N.Y.: Ira J. Friedman, 1949.

Evans, G. H., Jr. *Business Incorporations in the United States, 1800–1943.* New York: National Bureau of Economic and Business Research, 1948.

Evans, Peter B., Dietrich Rueschemeyer, and Theda Skocpol, eds. *Bringing the State Back In.* Cambridge: Cambridge University Press, 1985.

Farnam, Henry. *Chapters in the History of Social Legislation in the United States to 1860.* Washington, D.C.: Carnegie Institution of Washington, 1938.

Field, Phyllis. *The Politics of Race in New York: The Struggle for Black Suffrage in the Civil War Era.* Ithaca: Cornell University Press, 1982.

Finegan, Thomas E., ed. *Free Schools: A Documentary History of the Free School Movement in New York State.* Albany: University of the State of New York, 1921.

Fishlow, Albert. *American Railroads and the Transformation of the Antebellum Economy.* Cambridge, Mass.: Harvard University Press, 1965.

Flick, Alexander C., ed. *History of the State of New York.* 10 vols. New York: Columbia University Press, 1933–37.

Fogel, Robert W. *Railroads and American Economic Growth: Essays in Econometric History.* Baltimore, Md.: The Johns Hopkins University Press, 1964.

Formisano, Ronald P. *The Birth of Mass Political Parties: Michigan, 1827–1861.* Princeton, N.J.: Princeton University Press, 1971.

——. *The Transformation of Political Culture: Massachusetts Parties, 1790s–1840s.* New York: Oxford University Press, 1983.

Fox, Dixon Ryan. *The Decline of Aristocracy in the Politics of New York.* New York: Columbia University Press, 1919.

Freyer, Tony Allen. *Forums of Order: The Federal Courts and Business in American History.* Greenwich, Conn.: JAI Press, 1979.

Friedman, Lawrence. *Contract Law in America: A Social and Economic Case Study.* Madison: University of Wisconsin Press, 1965.

——. *A History of American Law.* New York: Simon & Schuster, 1973.

Frisch, Michael H. *Town Into City: Springfield, Massachusetts and the Meaning of Community, 1840–1880*. Cambridge, Mass.: Harvard University Press, 1972.

Garraty, John A. *Silas Wright*. New York: Columbia University Press, 1949.

Gerth, H. H., and C. Wright Mills, ed. *From Max Weber: Essays in Sociology*. New York: Oxford University Press, 1970.

Goodrich, Carter, ed. *Canals and American Economic Development*. New York: Columbia University Press, 1961.

———. *Government Promotion of Canals and Railroads, 1800–1890*. New York: Columbia University Press, 1960.

Green, Fletcher M. *Constitutional Development in the South Atlantic States, 1776–1860: A Study in the Evolution of Democracy*. Chapel Hill: University of North Carolina Press, 1930.

Grew, Raymond, ed. *Crises of Political Development in Europe and the United States*. Princeton, N.J.: Princeton University Press, 1978.

Hammond, Bray. *Banks and Politics in America From the Revolution to the Civil War*. Princeton, N.J.: Princeton University Press, 1957.

Hammond, Jabez D. *The History of Political Parties in the State of New York*. 3 vols. Syracuse: Hall, Mills, 1852.

Handlin, Oscar, and Mary Flugg Handlin. *Commonwealth; A Study of the Role of Government in the American Economy: Massachusetts, 1776–1861*. Rev. ed. Cambridge, Mass.: The Belknap Press of Harvard University Press, 1969.

———. *The Dimensions of Liberty*. Cambridge, Mass.: Harvard University Press, 1961.

Harlow, Ralph V. *The History of Legislative Methods in the Period Before 1825*. New Haven, Conn.: Yale University Press, 1915.

Hartz, Louis. *Economic Policy and Democratic Thought: Pennsylvania, 1776–1860*. Cambridge, Mass.: Harvard University Press, 1948.

Haskell, Thomas L. *The Emergence of Professional Social Science: The American Social Science Association and the Nineteenth Century Crisis of Authority*. Urbana: University of Illinois Press, 1977.

Hasse, Adelaide, ed. *Index of Economic Material in Documents of the States of the United States: New York, 1789–1904*. New York: Carnegie Institution of Washington, 1907.

Heath, Milton S. *Constructive Liberalism: The Role of the State in Economic Development in Georgia to 1860*. Cambridge, Mass.: Harvard University Press, 1954.

Hedrick, Ulysses Prentiss. *A History of Agriculture in the State of New York*. Reprint. New York: Hill & Wang, 1966.

Hepburn, A. Barton. *Artificial Waterways and Commercial Development: With a History of the Erie Canal*. New York: Macmillan, 1909.

Hidy, Ralph W. *The House of Baring in American Trade and Finance, 1763–1861*. Cambridge, Mass.: Harvard University Press, 1949.

Higham, John. *From Boundlessness to Consolidation: The Transformation of American Culture, 1848–1860*. Ann Arbor, Mich.: William L. Clements Library, 1969.

Horwitz, Morton J. *The Transformation of American Law, 1780–1860*. Cambridge, Mass.: Harvard University Press, 1977.

Hugins, Walter. *Jacksonian Democracy and the Working Class: A Study of the New York Workingmen's Movement, 1829–1837*. Stanford, Calif.: Stanford University Press, 1960.

Huntington, Samuel P. *Political Order in Changing Societies*. New Haven, Conn.: Yale University Press, 1968.

Bibliography

Hurst, James Willard. *The Growth of American Law: The Law Makers*. Boston: Little, Brown, 1950.

——. *Law and the Conditions of Freedom in the Nineteenth Century United States*. Madison: University of Wisconsin Press, 1956.

——. *Law and Economic Growth: The Legal History of the Lumber Industry in Wisconsin, 1836–1915*. Cambridge, Mass.: Harvard University Press, 1964.

——. *Law and Markets in United States History: Different Modes of Bargaining among Interests*. Madison: University of Wisconsin Press, 1982.

——. *Law and the Social Process in United States History*. Ann Arbor: University of Michigan Press, 1960.

——. *The Legitimacy of the Business Corporation in the Law of the United States, 1780–1970*. Charlottesville: University of Virginia Press, 1970.

Jenkins, J. S. *History of Political Parties in the State of New York*. Auburn, N.Y.: Alden & Markham, 1846.

Jenks, Leland. *The Migration of British Capital to 1875*. New York: A. A. Knopf, 1927.

Johnson, Paul. *A Shopkeeper's Millennium: Society and Revivals in Rochester, New York, 1815–1837*. New York: Hill & Wang, 1978.

Kammen, Michael. *People of Paradox: An Inquiry Concerning the Origins of American Civilization*. New York: Alfred A. Knopf, 1972.

Kariel, Henry S. *The Decline of American Pluralism*. Stanford, Calif.: Stanford University Press, 1961.

Kass, Alvin. *Politics in New York State, 1800–1830*. New York: Syracuse University Press, 1965.

Kirkland, Edward C. *History of American Economic Life*. 4th ed. New York: Appleton-Century-Crofts, 1969.

——. *Men, Cities, and Transportation*. 2 vols. Cambridge, Mass.: Harvard University Press, 1948.

Knights, Peter. *The Plain People of Boston, 1830–1860: A Study in City Growth*. New York: Oxford University Press, 1971.

Knox, John Jay. *A History of Banking in the United States. Revised and Brought Up to Date by Bradford Rhodes and Elmer H. Youngman*. New York: B. Rhodes & Co., 1903.

Lincoln, Charles Z. *Constitutional History of New York*. 5 vols. Rochester, N.Y.: Lawyers Cooperative, 1906.

Lively, Jack. *Democracy*. New York: G. P. Putnam's Sons, 1977.

Lowi, Theodore. *The End of Liberalism: Ideology, Policy and the Crisis of Public Authority*. New York: W. W. Norton, 1969.

McConnell, Grant. *Private Power and American Democracy*. New York: Vintage Books, 1966.

McCormick, Richard L. *The Party Period and Public Policy: American Politics From the Age of Jackson to the Progressive Era*. New York: Oxford University Press, 1986.

McCormick, Richard P. *The Second American Party System: Party Formation in the Jacksonian Era*. Chapel Hill: University of North Carolina Press, 1966.

McFaul, John Michael. *The Politics of Jacksonian Finance*. Ithaca: Cornell University Press, 1972.

McGill, Caroline E. et al. *History of Transportation in the United States Before 1860*, ed. Balthasar H. Meyer. Washington, D.C.: Carnegie Institution of Washington, 1917.

McGrane, R. C. *Foreign Bondholders and American State Debts*. New York: Macmillan, 1935.

——. *The Panic of 1837*. Chicago: University of Chicago, 1924.

Bibliography

McKelvey, Blake. *Rochester: The Water Power City, 1812–1854*. Cambridge, Mass.: Harvard University Press, 1945.

McNall, Neil Adams. *An Agricultural History of the Genesee Valley, 1790–1860*. Philadelphia: University of Pennsylvania Press, 1952.

McPherson, C. B. *The Life and Times of Liberal Democracy*. New York: Oxford University Press, 1977.

Malin, James C. *The Contriving Brain and the Skillful Hand in the United States: Something about History and Philosophy of History*. Ann Arbor: University of Michigan Press, 1955.

Mandelbaum, Seymour J. *Boss Tweed's New York*. New York: J. Wiley, 1965.

Mason, Bernard. *The Road to Independence: The Revolutionary Movement in New York, 1773–1777*. Lexington: University of Kentucky Press, 1966.

Meyers, Marvin. *The Jacksonian Persuasion: Politics and Belief*. Stanford, Calif.: Stanford University Press, 1957.

Miller, Douglas T. *The Birth of Modern America, 1820–1850*. New York: Western, 1970.

———. *Jacksonian Aristocracy: Class and Democracy in New York, 1830–1860*. New York: Oxford University Press, 1967.

Miller, Nathan. *The Enterprise of a Free People: Aspects of Economic Development of New York During the Canal Period, 1792–1838*. Ithaca: Cornell University Press, 1962.

Miller, Roberta Balstad. *City and Hinterland: A Case Study of Urban and Regional Development*. Westport, Conn.: Greenwood Press, 1979.

Mitchell, Stewart. *Horatio Seymour of New York*. Cambridge, Mass.: Harvard University Press, 1938.

Morey, William C. *The Government of New York: Its History and Administration*. New York: Macmillan, 1902.

Myers, Margaret. *Origins and Development of the New York Money Market*. New York: Columbia University Press, 1931.

Nash, Gerald D. *State Government and Economic Development: A History of Administrative Policies in California, 1849–1933*. Berkeley: University of California Press, 1964.

Nelson, William E. *The Roots of American Bureaucracy, 1830–1900*. Cambridge, Mass.: Harvard University Press, 1982.

North, Douglas C. *The Economic Growth of the United States, 1790–1860*. New York: W. W. Norton, 1966.

Orren, Karen, and Stephen Skowronek. *Studies in American Political Development: An Annual*. New Haven, Conn.: Yale University Press, 1986.

Pateman, Carole. *Participation and Democratic Theory*. New York: Cambridge University Press, 1970.

Pessen, Edward. *Jacksonian America: Society, Personality, and Politics*. Homewood, Ill.: Dorsey Press, 1978.

———. *Riches, Class, and Power before the Civil War*. Lexington, Mass.: D. C. Heath, 1973.

Pierce, Harry H. *Railroads of New York: A Study of Government Aid, 1826–1875*. Cambridge, Mass.: Harvard University Press, 1953.

Polanyi, Karl. *The Great Transformation: The Political and Economic Origins of Our Time*. Boston: Beacon Press, 1944.

Porter, Glenn, and Harold C. Livesay. *Merchants and Manufacturers: Studies in the Changing Structure of Nineteenth-Century Marketing*. Baltimore, Md.: The Johns Hopkins University Press, 1971.

Pred, Allan R. *Urban Growth and the Circulation of Information: The United States System of Cities, 1790–1840.* Cambridge, Mass.: MIT Press, 1973.

Primm, James N. *Economic Policy in the Development of a Western State: Missouri, 1820–1860.* Cambridge, Mass.: Harvard University Press, 1954.

Pye, Lucian. *Aspects of Political Development: An Analytical Study.* Boston: Little, Brown, 1966.

Randall, Samuel S. *The Common School System of the State of New York . . . .* Troy, N.Y.: Johnson & Davis, Printers, 1851.

Redlich, Fritz. *The Molding of American Banking: Men and Ideas.* New York: Hafner, part 1, 1947; part 2, 1951.

Richards, Leonard. *"Gentlemen of Property and Standing": Anti-Abolition Mobs in Jacksonian America.* New York: Oxford University Press, 1970.

Roberts, J. A. *A Century in the Comptroller's Office.* Albany, N.Y.: J. B. Lyon, Printer, 1897.

Rossiter, Clinton. *The American Quest, 1790–1860: An Emerging Nation in Search of Identity, Unity, and Modernity.* New York: Harcourt Brace Jovanovich, 1971.

———, ed. *The Federalist Papers.* New York: The New American Library, 1961.

Rostow, W. W., ed. *The Economics of Take-Off into Sustained Growth.* New York: St. Martin's Press, 1963.

Ryan, Mary P. *The Cradle of the Middle Class: The Family in Oneida County, New York, 1790–1865.* Cambridge: Cambridge University Press, 1981.

Schattschneider, E. E. *The Semisovereign People: A Realist's View of Democracy in America.* New York: Holt, Rinehart & Winston, 1960.

Scheiber, Harry N. *Ohio Canal Era: A Case Study of Government and the Economy, 1820–1861.* Athens: Ohio University Press, 1969.

Schlesinger, Arthur M., Jr. *The Age of Jackson.* Boston: Little, Brown, 1946.

Schneider, David M. *The History of Public Welfare in New York State, 1609–1866.* Chicago: University of Chicago Press, 1938.

Schudson, Michael. *Discovering the News: A Social History of American Newspapers.* New York: Basic Books, 1978.

Schwartz, Bernard. *The Law in America.* New York: McGraw-Hill, 1974.

Scott, William A. *The Repudiation of State Debts.* New York: Greenwood Press, 1969.

Secrist, Horace. *An Economic Analysis of the Constitutional Restrictions upon Public Indebtedness in the United States.* Economics and Political Science Series. Madison: Bulletin of the University of Wisconsin, 1914–1917.

Sharp, James Roger. *The Jacksonians versus the Banks: Politics in the States after the Panic of 1837.* New York: Columbia University Press, 1970.

Shaw, Ronald. *Erie Water West.* Lexington: University of Kentucky Press, 1966.

Skowronek, Stephen. *Building a New American State: The Expansion of National Administrative Capacities, 1877–1920.* Cambridge: Cambridge University Press, 1982.

Smith, Walter B., and A. H. Cole. *Fluctuations in American Business, 1790–1860.* Cambridge, Mass.: Harvard University Press, 1935.

Somkin, Fred. *Unquiet Eagle: Memory and Desire in the Idea of American Freedom, 1815–1860.* Ithaca: Cornell University Press, 1967.

Sowers, Donald C. *The Financial History of New York State from 1789 to 1912.* New York: Columbia University Press, 1914.

Stevens, Frank W. *The Beginnings of the New York Central, 1826–1853.* New York: G. P. Putnam's Sons, 1926.

Studenski, Paul, and Herman E. Kroos. *Financial History of the United States*. 2d ed. New York: McGraw-Hill, 1963.

Taylor, George R. *The Transportation Revolution, 1815–1860*. New York: Harper & Row, 1951.

Temin, Peter. *The Jacksonian Economy*. New York: W. W. Norton, 1969.

Thornton, J. Mills III. *Politics and Power in a Slave Society: Alabama, 1800–1860*. Baton Rouge: Louisiana State University Press, 1978.

Thorpe, Francis N. *A Constitutional History of the American People, 1776–1850*. 2 vols. New York: Harper & Brothers, 1898.

Tilly, Charles, ed. *The Formation of National States in Western Europe*. Princeton, N.J.: Princeton University Press, 1975.

Trescott, Paul B. *Financing American Enterprise: The Story of Commercial Banking*. New York: Harper & Row, 1963.

U.S. Bureau of the Census. *Historical Statistics of the United States, Colonial Times to 1957*. Washington, D.C.: U.S. Government Printing Office, 1960.

————. *The Statistical History of the United States from Colonial Times to the Present*. New York: Basic Books, 1976.

Van Deusen, Glyndon G. *Horace Greeley: Nineteenth Century Crusader*. Philadelphia: University of Pennsylvania Press, 1964.

————. *Thurlow Weed: Wizard of the Lobby*. Boston: Little, Brown, 1947.

Watson, Harry L. *Jacksonian Politics and Community Conflict: The Emergence of the Second American Party System in Cumberland County, North Carolina*. Baton Rouge: Louisiana State University Press, 1981.

Weber, Adna F. *The Growth of Industry in New York*. Albany: New York State Department of Labor, 1904.

Weber, Max. *Max Weber on Law in Economy and Society*, ed. Max Rheinstein. Cambridge, Mass.: Harvard University Press, 1954.

Weiner, Myron, ed. *Modernization: The Dynamics of Growth*. New York: Basic Books, 1966.

Welter, Rush. *Popular Education and Democratic Thought in America*. New York: Columbia University Press, 1962.

White, Philip L. *Beekmantown, New York: Forest Frontier to Farm Community*. Austin: University of Texas Press, 1979.

Whitford, Noble. *History of the Canal System of the State of New York*. 2 vols. Albany, N.Y.: Brandow Printing, 1906.

Wiebe, Robert H. *The Search for Order, 1877–1920*. New York: Hill & Wang, 1967.

————. *The Segmented Society: An Introduction to the Meaning of America*. New York: Oxford University Press, 1975.

Wilentz, Sean. *Chants Democratic: New York City and the Rise of the American Working Class, 1788–1850*. New York: Oxford University Press, 1984.

Williamson, Chilton. *American Suffrage from Property to Democracy, 1760–1860*. Princeton, N.J.: Princeton University Press, 1960.

Wolfe, Alan. *The Limits of Legitimacy: Political Contradictions of Contemporary Capitalism*. New York: Free Press, 1977.

Wood, Gordon. *The Creation of the American Republic, 1776–1787*. Chapel Hill: published for the Institute of Early American History and Culture by the University of North Carolina Press, 1969.

Bibliography

Young, James Sterling. *The Washington Community, 1800–1828*. New York: Harcourt Brace & World, 1966.

Zainaldin, Zamil. *Law in Antebellum Society: Legal Change and Economic Expansion*. New York: Alfred A. Knopf, 1983.

Zuckerman, Michael. *Peaceable Kingdoms: New England Towns in the Eighteenth Century*. New York: Vintage Books, 1972.

Articles

Anderson, Richard T. "Voluntary Associations in History." *American Anthropologist*, 73 (1971): 209–222.

Barkan, Elliot R. "The Emergence of a Whig Persuasion: Conservatism, Democratism, and the New York State Whigs." *New York History*, 52 (October 1971): 367–395.

Benson, Lee, Joel H. Silbey, and Phyllis F. Field. "Toward a Theory of Stability and Change in American Voting Patterns: New York State, 1792–1970." In *The History of American Electoral Politics*, ed. Joel H. Silbey, Allan G. Bogue, and William H. Flanigan. Princeton, N.J.: Princeton University Press, 1978.

Berkhofer, Robert F., Jr. "The Organizational Interpretation of American History: A New Synthesis." *Prospects*, 4 (1979): 611–629.

Bogue, Allan G., Jerome M. Clubb, and William H. Flanigan. "The New Political History." *American Behavioral Scientist*, 21 (November/December 1977): 201–220.

Braun, Rudolf. "Taxation, Sociopolitical Structure, and State-Making: Great Britain and Brandenburg-Prussia." In *The Formation of National States in Western Europe*, ed. Charles Tilly. Princeton, N.J.: Princeton University Press, 1975.

Brown, Richard D. "The Emergence of Voluntary Associations in Massachusetts, 1760–1830." *Journal of Voluntary Action Research*, 2 (1973): 64–73.

———. "The Ideal of the Written Constitution: A Political Legacy of the Revolution." In *Legacies of the American Revolution*, ed. Larry R. Gerlach. Logan: Utah State University Press, 1978.

———. "Modernization and the Modern Personality in Early America, 1600–1865: A Sketch of a Synthesis." *Journal of Interdisciplinary History*, 2 (Winter 1972): 201–228.

Callendar, Guy S. "Early Transportation and Banking Enterprises of the States in Relation to the Growth of Corporations." *Quarterly Journal of Economics*, 17 (1902): 111–162.

Carman, Harry J. "The Rise of the Factory System." In *The Age of Reform*, vol. 6 of *History of the State of New York*, ed. Alexander C. Flick. 10 vols. New York: Columbia University Press, 1934.

Chandler, Alfred D., and Stephen Salsbury. "The Railroads: Innovators in Modern Business Administration." In *The Railroad and the Space Program: An Exploration in Historical Analogy*, ed. Bruce Mazlish. Cambridge, Mass.: The MIT Press, 1965.

Cheyney, E. P. "The Anti-Rent Movement and the Constitution of 1846." In *The Age of Reform*, vol. 6 of *History of the State of New York*, ed. Alexander C. Flick. 10 vols. New York: Columbia University Press, 1933–1937.

Clark, Christopher. "Household Economy, Market Exchange and the Rise of Capitalism in the Connecticut Valley, 1800–1850." *Journal of Social History*, 13 (Winter 1979): 169–189.

Cochran, Thomas C. "The Social Impact of the Railroad." In *The Railroad and the Space Program: An Exploration in Historical Analogy*, ed. Bruce Mazlish. Cambridge, Mass.: The MIT Press, 1965.

Corwin, Edward S. "The Progress of Constitutional Theory between the Declaration of Independence and the Meeting of the Philadelphia Convention." *American Historical Review*, 30 (1925): 511–536.

Cranmer, Jerome H. "Canal Investment in 1815–1860." In *Trends in the American Economy in the Nineteenth Century*, ed. William N. Parker. Princeton, N.J.: Princeton University Press, 1960.

Crouthamel, James L. "The Newspaper Revolution in New York, 1830–1860." *New York History*, 45 (April 1964): 91–113.

Davis, David Brion. "Some Ideological Functions of Prejudice in Antebellum America." *American Quarterly*, 15 (1963): 115–125.

———. "Some Themes of Counter-subversion: An Analysis of Anti-Masonic, Anti-Catholic, and Anti-Mormon Literature." *Mississippi Valley Historical Review*, 47 (1960): 205–224.

Davis, Lance and J. Legler. "The Government in the American Economy, 1815–1902: A Quantitative Study." *Journal of Economic History*, 26 (December 1966): 514–552.

Degler, Carl N. "The Loco-Focos: Urban 'Agrarians.'" *Journal of Economic History*, 16 (September 1956): 322–333.

Deutsch, Karl. "Social Mobilization and Political Development." *American Political Science Review*, 55 (September 1961): 493–514.

Dodd, Edwin M. "The Evolution of Limited Liability in American Industry." *Harvard Law Review*, 61 (September 1948): 1351–1379.

Ellis, David Maldwyn. "Rise of the Empire State, 1790–1820." *New York History*, 56 (January 1975): 5–27.

———. "The Yankee Invasion of New York, 1783–1850." *New York History*, 32 (January 1951): 3–17.

Farnham, Wallace D. "The Weakened Spring of Government: A Study in Nineteenth Century American History." *American Historical Review*, 68 (April 1963): 662–680.

Flick, Hugh M. "The Council of Appointment in New York State: The First Attempt to Regulate Political Patronage, 1777–1822." *New York History*, 15 (1934): 253–280.

Formisano, Ronald P. "Deferential-Participant Politics: The Early Republic's Political Culture, 1789–1840." *American Political Science Review*, 68 (1974): 473–487.

Galambos, Louis. "The Emerging Organizational Synthesis in Modern American History." *Business History Review*, 44 (Autumn 1970): 279–290.

Gallman, Robert E. "Commodity Output, 1839–1899." In *Trends in the American Economy in the Nineteenth Century*, ed. William N. Parker. Princeton, N.J.: Princeton University Press, 1960.

Gitterman, J. M. "The Council of Appointment in New York." *Political Science Quarterly*, 7 (1892): 80–115.

Glazer, Walter. "Participation and Power: Voluntary Associations and the Functional Organization of Cincinnati in 1840." *Historical Methods Newsletter*, 5, no. 4 (September 1972): 151–168.

Goodrich, Carter. "American Development Policy: The Case of Internal Improvements." *Journal of Economic History*, 16 (1956): 449–460.

———. "Internal Improvements Reconsidered." *Journal of Economic History*, 30 (June 1970): 289–311.

———. "Local Planning of Internal Improvements." *Political Science Quarterly*, 66 (September 1951): 411–445.

———. "Public Spirit and American Improvements." *Proceedings of the American Philosophical Society*, 92 (1948): 305–309.

———. "Recent Contributions to Economic History, the United States 1789–1860." *Journal of Economic History*, 19 (March 1959): 25–35.

Greene, Jack P. "The Role of the Lower House of Assembly in Eighteenth Century Politics." *Journal of Southern History*, 27 (November 1961): 415–474.

Grew, Raymond. "Modernization and Its Discontents." *American Behavioral Scientist*, 21 (November/December 1977): 289–312.

Gunn, L. Ray. "The Political Implications of General Incorporation Laws in New York to 1860." *Mid-America*, 59 (October 1977): 171–191.

Haar, Charles. "Legislative Regulation of New York Industrial Corporations, 1800–1850." *New York History*, 22 (April 1941): 191–207.

Hall, Van Beck. "A Fond Farewell to Henry Adams: Ideas on Relating Political History to Social Change during the Early National Period." In *The Human Dimensions of Nation-Making: Essays on Colonial and Revolutionary America*, ed. James Kirby Martin. Madison: University of Wisconsin Press, 1976.

Handlin, Oscar, and Mary Flugg Handlin. "The Origins of the American Business Corporation." *Journal of Economic History*, 5 (May 1945): 1–23.

Heath, Milton. "Public Railroad Construction and the Development of Private Enterprise in the South Before 1861." *Journal of Economic History*, Supplement 10 (1950): 40–53.

Hofferbert, Richard I. "The Relation Between Public Policy and Some Structural and Environmental Variables in the American States." *American Political Science Review*, 60 (March 1966): 73–82.

———. "State and Community Policy Studies: A Review of Comparative Input-Output Analyses." *Political Science Annual*, 3 (1972): 3–72.

Hofstadter, Richard. "William Leggett, Spokesman of Jacksonian Democracy." *Political Science Quarterly*, 58 (December 1943): 581–594.

Holmes, Oliver Wendell. "The Turnpike Era." In *Conquering the Wilderness*, vol. 5 of *History of the State of New York*, ed. Alexander C. Flick. 10 vols. New York: Columbia University Press, 1933–1937.

Horwitz, Morton J. "The Emergence of an Instrumental Conception of American Law, 1780–1820." In *Law in American History*, vol. 5 of *Perspectives in American History*, ed. Donald Fleming and Bernard Bailyn. Cambridge, Mass.: Charles Warren Center for Studies in American History, 1971.

Huntington, Samuel P. "The Change to Change: Modernization, Development, and Politics." *Comparative Politics*, 3 (April 1971): 283–322.

Hyneman, Charles S. "Tenure and Turnover of Legislative Personnel." *Annals of the American Academy of Political and Social Sciences*, 195 (1938): 21–32.

Kammen, Michael. "A Different 'Fable of the Bees': The Problem of Public and Private Sectors in Colonial America." In *The American Revolution: A Heritage of Change*, ed. John Parker and Carol Urness. Minneapolis: Associates of the James Ford Bell Library, 1975.

Kessler, W. C. "A Statistical Study of the New York General Incorporation Act of 1811." *Journal of Political Economy*, 48 (December 1940): 877–882.

Kutolowski, Kathleen Smith. "The Janus Face of New York's Local Parties: Genesee County, 1821–1827." *New York History*, 59 (April 1978): 145–172.

Leuchtenburg, William E. "The Pertinence of Political History: Reflections on the Significance of the State in America." *Journal of American History*, 73 (December 1986): 585–600.

Lively, Robert. "The American System: A Review Article." *The Business History Review*, 29 (March 1955): 81–96.

Livermore, Shaw. "Unlimited Liability in Early American Corporations." *Journal of Political Economy*, 43 (October 1935): 674–687.

Lockridge, Kenneth. "Social Change and the Meaning of the American Revoluton." *Journal of Social History*, 6 (Summer 1973): 403–439.

Lowi, Theodore. "American Business, Public Policy, Case-Studies, and Political Theories." *World Politics*, 16 (July 1964): 677–715.

Lynch, Dennis Tilden. "Party Struggles, 1818–1850." In *The Age of Reform*, vol. 6 of *The History of the State of New York*, ed. Alexander C. Flick. 10 vols. New York: Columbia University Press, 1934.

McCormick, Richard L. "The Party Period and Public Policy: An Exploratory Hypothesis." *The Journal of American History*, 66 (September 1979): 279–298.

McCormick, Richard P. "New Perspectives on Jacksonian Politics." *American Historical Review*, 65 (1960): 288–301.

———. "Political Development and the Second Party System." In *American Party Systems: Stages of Political Development*, ed. William Nesbit Chambers and Walter Dean Burnham. New York: Oxford University Press, 1967.

Marshall, Lynn. "The Strange Stillbirth of the Whig Party." *American Historical Review*, 72 (January 1967): 445–468.

Matthews, Donald G. "The Second Great Awakening as an Organizing Process, 1780–1830." *American Quarterly*, 21 (Spring 1969):23–43.

Miller, Douglas T. "Immigration and Social Stratification in Pre-Civil War New York." *New York History*, 49 (April 1968): 157–168.

Miller, William. "A Note on the History of Business Corporations in Pennsylvania, 1800–1860." *Quarterly Journal of Economics*, 55 (1940/41): 150–160.

Nelson, William E. "Changing Conceptions of Judicial Review: The Evolution of Constitutional Theory in the States, 1790–1860." *University of Pennsylvania Law Review*, 120 (1972): 1166–1185.

Niemi, Albert W., Jr. "A Further Look at Interregional Canals and Economic Specialization: 1820–1840." *Explorations in Economic History*, 7 (Summer 1970): 499–520.

North, Douglas. "The State of Economic History." *American Economic Review*, 40 (1965): 86–91.

Olmstead, Alan L. "Investment Constraints and New York City Mutual Savings Bank Financing of Antebellum Development." *Journal of Economic History*, 32 (December 1972): 811–840.

Olson, Mancur, Jr. "Rapid Economic Growth as a Destabilizing Force." *Journal of Economic History*, 23 (December 1963): 529–552.

Pessen, Edward. "The Egalitarian Myth and the American Social Reality: Wealth, Mobility, and Equality in the 'Era of the Common Man.'" *American Historical Review*, 76 (October 1971): 986–1034.

Polsby, Nelson. "The Institutionalization of the House of Representatives." *The American Political Science Review*, 62 (March 1968): 144–168.

Bibliography

———. "Legislatures." In *Governmental Institutions and Processes*. In vol. 5 of *Handbook of Political Science*, ed. Fred I. Greenstein and Nelson W. Polsby. Reading, Mass.: Addison-Wesley, 1975.

Potter, J. "The Growth of Population in America, 1700–1860." In *Population in History: Essays in Historical Demography*, ed. D. V. Glass and D. E. C. Eversley. London: Edward Arnold, 1965.

Ransom, Roger. "A Closer Look at Canals and Western Manufacturing in the Canal Era." *Explorations in Economic History*, 8 (Summer 1971): 501–508.

Remini, Robert V. "The Albany Regency." *New York History*, 39 (October 1958): 341–355.

Rezneck, Samuel. "The Rise and Early Development of Industrial Consciousness in the United States, 1760–1830." *Journal of Economic and Business History*, 5 (August 1932): 784–811.

———. "The Social History of An American Depression, 1837–1843." *American Historical Review*, 40 (October 1934–July 1935): 662–687.

Rosenthal, Alan. "Turnover in State Legislatures." *American Journal of Political Science*, 18 (August 1974): 609–616.

Salisbury, Robert. "The Analysis of Public Policy: A Search for Theories and Roles." In *Political Science and Public Policy*, ed. Austin Ranney. Chicago: University of Chicago Press, 1968.

Scheiber, Harry N. "At the Borderland of Law and Economic History: The Contributions of Willard Hurst." *American Historical Review*, 75 (February 1970): 744–756.

———. "Federalism and the American Economic Order." *Law and Society Review*, 10 (Fall 1975): 57–100.

———. "Government and the Economy: Studies of the 'Commonwealth' Policy in Nineteenth Century America." *Journal of Interdisciplinary History*, 3 (September 1972): 135–151.

———. "The Road to Munn: Eminent Domain and the Concept of Public Purpose in the State Courts." In *Law in American History*, vol. 5 of *Perspectives in American History*, ed. Donald Fleming and Bernard Bailyn. Cambridge, Mass.: Charles Warren Center for Studies in American History, 1971.

Seavoy, Ronald E. "Laws to Encourage Manufacturing: New York Policy and the 1811 General Incorporation Statute." *Business History Review*, 47 (Spring 1972): 85–95.

Segal, Harvey H. "Canals and Economic Development." In *Canals and American Economic Development*, ed. Carter Goodrich. New York: Columbia University Press, 1961.

Skocpol, Theda. "Bringing the State Back In." In *Bringing the State Back In*, ed. Peter B. Evans, Dietrich Rueschemeyer, and Theda Skocpol. Cambridge: Cambridge University Press, 1985.

Spengler, Joseph. "Laissez-Faire and Intervention: A Potential Source of Historical Error." *Journal of Political Economy*, 57, no. 5 (October 1949): 438–441.

Taylor, George R. "American Urban Growth Preceding the Railway Age." *Journal of Economic History*, 27 (September 1967): 309–339.

———. "The National Economy Before and After the Civil War Era." In *Economic Change in the Civil War Era*, ed. David T. Gilchrist and W. David Lewis. Greenwich, Del.: Eleutherian Mills-Hagley, 1965.

Thernstrom, Stephen and Peter Knights. "Men in Motion: Some Data and Speculations About Urban Population Mobility in Nineteenth Century America." In *Anonymous Americans: Explorations in Nineteenth Century Social History*, ed. Tamara Hareven. Englewood Cliffs, N.J.: Prentice-Hall, 1971.

Tipps, Dean. "Modernization Theory and the Comparative Study of Societies: A Critical Perspective." *Comparative Studies in Society and History*, 15 (March 1973): 199–226.

Trimble, William. "Diverging Tendencies in New York: Democracy in the Period of the Loco-Focos." *American Historical Review*, 24 (April 1919): 396–421.

———. "The Social Philosophy of the Loco-Foco Democracy." *American Journal of Sociology*, 26 (May 1921): 705–715.

Wahlke, John C. "Policy Demands and System Support: The Role of the Represented." *British Journal of Political Science*, 1 (July 1971): 271–290.

Wallace, Michael. "Changing Concepts of Party in the United States: New York, 1815–1828." *American Historical Review*, 74 (December 1968): 453–491.

Wilson, Major L. "The Concept of Time and the Political Dialogue in the United States, 1828–1848." *American Quarterly*, 19 (Winter 1967): 619–644.

Unpublished Manuscripts

Ehrlich, Richard L. "The Development of Manufacturing in Selected Counties in the Erie Canal Corridor, 1815–1860." Ph.D. dissertation, State University of New York, 1972.

Goldstein, Kalman. "The Albany Regency." Ph.D. dissertation, Columbia University, 1969.

McGee, Patricia E. "Issues and Factions: New York State Politics from the Panic of 1837 to the Election of 1848." Ph.D. dissertation, St. John's University, 1970.

Parkinson, George P. "Antebellum State Constitution-Making: Retention, Circumvention, Revision." Ph.D. dissertation, University of Wisconsin, 1972.

Reubens, Beatrice G. "State Financing of Private Enterprise in Early New York." Ph.D. dissertation, Columbia University, 1960.

Seavoy, Ronald E. "The Origins of the American Business Corporation, 1784–1855: New York, The National Model." Ph.D. dissertation, University of Michigan, 1969.

Segal, Harvey H. "Canal Cycles: 1834–1851; Public Construction Experience in New York, Pennsylvania, and Ohio." Ph.D. dissertation, Columbia University, 1956.

Index

Library of Congress Cataloging-in-Publication Data

Gunn, L. Ray.
  The decline of authority.

  Bibliography: p.
  Includes index.
  1. New York (State)—Economic policy. 2. New York (State)—Politics and
government—1775–1865. I. Title.
HC107.N7G86 1988   338.9747   87-47954
ISBN 0-8014-2101-2 (alk. paper)